MENTAL ILLNESS AND AMERICAN SOCIETY,
1875-1940

GERALD N. GROB

Mental Illness and American Society, 1875-1940

PRINCETON UNIVERSITY PRESS

For my father and the memory of my mother

CONTENTS

TABLES

MUCH OF THE historical literature about American social policy reflects contemporary issues and concerns. This is especially true of works that discuss the ways in which American society dealt with the problem of mental illness in the past. Thus many scholars have uncritically accepted the allegation that mental hospital care was a disaster, and they have therefore attempted to shed light on the origins of institutional failure.

In general, the historical literature dealing with the care and treatment of the mentally ill falls into two broad categories. The first—the traditional or liberal—was developed by scholars who celebrated mental hospitals and other antebellum institutions as proof of human progress, humanitarianism, and progressive sentiment. Albert Deutsch's classic *The Mentally Ill in America* (1937) accepted at face value the optimistic claims of psychiatrists and their definitions of mental disease. Conceding that institutional care of the mentally ill was far from successful, Deutsch placed responsibility for past failures upon American society for not providing sufficient material resources. Even in 1948, when he wrote a devastating exposé of public mental hospitals (*The Shame of the States*), he did not despair or conclude that institutional care and treatment was predestined to fail. On the contrary, he upheld the *theory* of institutional practice and urged his fellow citizens to band together "to participate in the common drive toward improved mental hygiene facilities," and to insist that government at all levels provide appropriate funding.

The second (or revisionist) interpretation emerged in its most mature form in the 1960s. Influenced by the critics of orthodox psychiatry, contemporary Marxist theory, and the sociological concept of the total institution, revisionist scholars insisted that mental hospitals were inherently repressive. In their eyes mental illness was not an objective description of a disease within the conventional meaning of the term; it was rather an abstraction designed to rationalize the confinement of individuals who manifested disruptive and aberrant behavior. Mental hospitals, such scholars argued, were established for one of two reasons: either the generalized fear of social disorder, or because of the rise of market capitalism and its concommitant demand for greater productivity. The primary function of mental hospitals, according to this approach, was to confine social deviants and/or unproductive persons. Despite differences in approach and methodology, such scholars as Michel Foucault, David J. Rothman, Andrew Scull, Richard T. Fox, Michael B. Katz, and Christopher Lasch all have one element in common: a critical if not hostile view of psychiatry and mental hospitals.

Curiously enough, there were striking differences between the traditionalist and revisionist approaches. Both began with the assumption that many institutions failed to achieve their purposes. Whereas traditionalists viewed this failure as transitory, revisionists saw it as an inevitable consequence of institutional solutions.

Although yielding rich insights and employing certain kinds of primary source materials hitherto ignored, the traditionalist/revisionist approach had several undesirable side-effects. The use of a presentist framework and the resort to social science models assumed that past problems and policies were not fundamentally dissimilar from present-day ones. The result was a form of scholarship that was essentially ahistorical; the dynamic of change was missing, and there was a tendency to describe the past in monolithic terms. In recent years, for example, some historians have dealt with institutions in terms of their common characteristics and inferred generalizations about the nature of the society that created them. Such an approach, however, avoided certain key questions. Was it appropriate to classify within a single category various kinds of institutions as though there were few significant dissimilarities among them? Were the experiences of patient populations in mental hospitals similar or comparable? Did levels and sources of support, geographical location, and different legal, administrative, and intellectual environments and other phenomena give rise to mental hospitals that were neither as unchanging or monolithic as these scholars assumed?

On another level, much of the scholarship pertaining to the mentally ill rested on a narrow empirical base. Only in recent years have historians begun to plumb the rich and varied collections of printed and unprinted materials on the subject that have survived. In fact, many of the familiar generalizations common to the historiography of the mentally ill still reflect the absence of comprehensive research. Too often generalizations lack a body of supporting data. In the future it is more than likely that many widely held interpretations will be undermined by new data.

In writing this book I have attempted to avoid the pitfall of overgeneralizing without the support of accompanying evidence. The perennial problem of the practicing historian is to place events within some sort of framework of meaning, and, at the same time, to account for the complex and often contradictory nature of human behavior. I have yet to be persuaded that human experience can be explained easily or that all phenomena are necessarily linked within a single comprehensive system.

Because complexity rather than simplicity is characteristic of historical development, a brief discussion of some of the major conclusions of this book is in order at this point. First, mental hospitals—despite their very real shortcomings and failures—did provide *minimum* levels of care for individuals unable to survive by themselves. Moreover, the development of these institutions was shaped not only by psychiatrists and other external professional and social groups, but also by the nature and behavior of their patients and the interactions between patients and staff. Second, by the end of the nineteenth century American psychiatry faced a severe internal crisis. Conceived as a managerial and administrative specialty, its members found themselves moving increasingly away from the mainstream of medicine, which underwent a sharp change of direction toward the end of the century. In seeking to integrate their specialty with scientific medicine, psychiatrists were unaware that their efforts would lead them to modify their commitment to institutional care. More and more they focused on disease rather than on individuals, and therapy rather than care. At the same time they extended their specialty into the community, creating a mental hygiene movement, developing new roles for themselves, and formulating an ideology of professionalism that justified their demands for autonomy insofar as the care and treatment of mental illness was concerned. Third, at precisely the same time that psychiatrists were modifying their commitment to institutional practice, the nature of the patient population changed drastically. Before 1890 the patient population of mental hospitals included a large proportion of acute cases institutionalized for less than twelve months. Between 1890 and 1940, on the other hand, aged persons and individuals suffering from somatic disorders with accompanying behavioral symptoms began to constitute the bulk of hospital patients. These patients tended to remain institutionalized until they died.

By 1923, for example, 54 percent of patients in mental hospitals had been there five years or more; only 17.4 percent had been institutionalized for less than twelve months. For the chronic mentally ill specific treatment was nonexistent; most required comprehensive care. Ironically, as the need for care was magnified, the psychiatric legitimation of this function grew thinner. Fourth, public policy decisions at both the state and local level greatly affected patients, psychiatrists, and mental hospitals. Levels and sources of funding as well as differing structural and administrative systems also played a role in shaping the ways in which the mentally ill would be treated. Yet public policy often reflected professional and political concerns rather than patient needs. Finally, and perhaps most important, the central issue was not access to therapy or therapeutic effectiveness, but rather decent and humane *care* of patients whose physical and mental conditions precluded the possibility that they could care for themselves.

I would be less than honest if I did not speak of some personal views which undoubtedly influence my understanding of the past. I have never been especially impressed by the modern belief that human beings can mold and control their world in predetermined and predictable ways. This is not to argue that we are totally powerless to control our destiny. It is only to insist both upon our fallibility and our inability to predict all the consequences of what we do. Nor do I think that human behavior can be reduced to a set of quasi-deterministic laws or generalizations, or that solutions are available for all problems. Tragedy is a recurring theme in human affairs, and defines perhaps the very parameters of our existence. I have tried, therefore, to deal sympathetically with our predecessors who grappled—so often unsuccessfully, as we still do ourselves—with their own distinct problems. If nothing else, I hope that my work can help to refocus the debate about the care of the mentally ill by a clearer and more accurate understanding of the past.

No book, of course, is the result of the labor of one individual, and mine is surely no exception. I have drawn upon the work of many other scholars. If I have disagreed with them, it has been only after lengthy and serious thought. A number of very good friends—George A. Billias, David Mechanic, Jacques M. Quen, James Reed, and Barbara G. Rosenkrantz—have taken time from their own busy schedules to read successive drafts and to offer me the benefits of their insights; this book would have been much the worse had it not been for their penetrating and insightful comments. I would also like to express my deep appreciation for the assistance provided by Richard H. Kohn, Jonathan Lurie, John C. Burnham, Richard L. McCormick, Kathleen Jones, and Paul E. G. Clemens.

All scholars benefit from the arduous but indispensable work of the many librarians and archivists who collect and organize materials without which history could not be written. A complete list of such individuals and institutions would be impossible, for my research has carried me to libraries throughout the United States. I am also deeply indebted to the Public Health Service, National Library of Medicine (HHR), which supported my work with a generous research grant (No. 2306) without in any way infringing upon my freedom. A fellowship from the American Council of Learned Societies made possible a leave of absence from teaching to gather data during the early stages of this project. Another fellowship from the John Simon Guggenheim Memorial Foundation and an invitation from the Rockefeller Foundation's Bellagio Study and Conference Center, Lake Como, Italy, gave me time to write. Finally, I have incurred a debt to my family that cannot be repaid; they created an atmosphere characterized by patience, understanding, and love.

GERALD N. GROB

Rutgers University
New Brunswick, New Jersey
September, 1982

ABBREVIATIONS USED IN TEXT

AAPSW   American Association of Psychiatric Social Workers

AMA   American Medical Association

AMSAII Association of Medical Superintendents of American Institutions for the Insane (1844-1892)

AMPA   American Medico-Psychological Association (1892-1921)

APA   American Psychiatric Association (1921-   )

ANA   American Neurological Association

NCCC   National Conference of Charities and Correction

NCMH   National Committee for Mental Hygiene

PHS   Public Health Service

MENTAL ILLNESS AND AMERICAN SOCIETY,
1875-1940

DURING THE FIRST HALF of the nineteenth century Americans created an elaborate institutional network to provide care and treatment for the mentally ill.* After 1800 numerous changes in American society undermined traditional ways of caring for poor and dependent persons. During the colonial and early national period, the family and community had accepted responsibility for such individuals. But rapid population growth, urbanization, immigration, and high rates of geographical mobility changed this tradition. Americans increasingly resorted to quasi-public or public institutions for the care of the insane.** The mental hospital, along with the almshouse, poor farm, and house of refuge, became the institutional solution by which American society fulfilled its obligations toward dependent persons incapable of surviving by themselves. Mental hospitals, according to their defenders, benefited the community, the family, and the individual by offering treatment or furnishing custodial care for the chronic insane. In providing for the mentally ill and other dependent groups, the state met its ethical and moral responsibilities, and, at the same time, contributed to the general welfare by limiting, if not eliminating, the spread of disease and dependency.[1]

In their early years, mental hospitals enjoyed a certain measure of success and public acceptance. The first generation of superintendents in the 1830s and 1840s invariably imparted to their institutions a sense of optimism which, coupled with a relatively small patient population, presumably helped patients either to improve or recover. The founding of mental hospitals, a distinguished psychiatrist observed in 1852, "the spread of their reports,

---

* I have dealt with this subject in *Mental Institutions in America: Social Policy to 1875* (New York, 1973), which is in effect the predecessor to this book.

** No doubt some readers will be offended by the constant use of the terms "insane" and "insanity" as contrasted with "mentally ill" and "mental illness." Although the former two have acquired an odious reputation, they were perfectly good terms in the past. Nor was "insanity" a legal term. Between 1844 and 1921 the *American Journal of Psychiatry* was published under the title *American Journal of Insanity*. My usage, therefore, is a historical one and has no derogatory intent. Indeed, it is entirely probable that the word "mental illness" will in the future be looked down upon with the same hostility as "insanity" is at present.

the extension of the knowledge of their character, power, and usefulness, by the means of the patients that they protect and cure, have created, and continue to create, more and more interest in the subject of insanity, and more confidence in its curability. Consequently, more and more persons and families, who . . . formerly kept their insane friends and relations at home . . . now believe that they can be restored, or improved, or, at least made more comfortable in these public institutions."[2]

By 1880 the dreams of early American psychiatric activists such as Horace Mann and Dorothea L. Dix seemingly had been realized. At that time there were almost 140 public and private mental hospitals caring for nearly 41,000 patients.[3] The overwhelming majority of patients were in public institutions, a graphic demonstration of the moral and financial commitment of Americans to the mentally ill. Virtually every state and territory had at least one mental hospital, and many had established several in order to provide equal access for all. That the number of mentally ill patients exceeded available facilities was not an occasion for despair; it was seen rather as an indication of the work that remained to be done.

This impressive institutional facade, however, concealed many problems and unresolved issues. During the second half of the nineteenth century the structure and functions of mental hospitals had undergone a gradual transformation. At the time of their founding, mental hospitals were presumed to be providing restorative therapy (although the first generation of superintendents accepted without hesitation responsibility for caring for the chronic insane). But from the very beginnings hospitals retained large numbers of individuals who failed to show any improvement. The retention of chronic cases, in turn, restricted the efforts to offer therapy to the remaining patients. In their early days mental hospitals had also been designed for small numbers of patients in order to encourage close relationships considered necessary for sound treatment. Hospitals, however, grew in size either because states placed higher ceilings on the number of patients or did not take steps to build new facilities. In theory all patients were to receive the same quality of care; in practice class, race, and ethnicity promoted a different quality of care for different patients. The functions of superintendents were supposed to be defined in medical terms; they became, in fact, hospital administrators deeply immersed in managerial problems.

Between the 1880s and the outbreak of World War II, the foundation was laid for a profound change toward and perceptions of mental hospitals. Prior to that time mental institutions were looked upon favorably as the best means of coping with the problems of mental illness. After that time, however, the reputation and public image of mental hospitals declined precipitously. Ironically, this development occurred at the same time that the patient population was mounting. By the middle of the twentieth century, mental hospitals were widely regarded as the institutional remnants of an earlier social order—outdated institutions that disregarded the rights of sick and dependent persons by isolating and subjecting them to cruel abuse. The result was a renewed interest in other alternatives to institutional care, or—to use modern terminology—toward a policy of "deinstitutionalization." The rejection of the idea of mental hospital care proved to be a development of the utmost social significance. It affected not only the nearly 450,000 patients in public mental hospitals in 1940 but families, psychiatrists and other mental health professionals, legislators, public officials, and the general public.

The purpose of this study, simply put, is to describe and analyze the experiences of American society in seeking to deal effectively with mental illness as both a social and medical problem. In so doing I will describe the complex interrelationships that existed between patients, psychiatrists, institutions, and government. A secondary purpose is to gain a better understanding of the process of change that led to a reversal of the attitudes toward mental hospitals from one of support to one of antipathy.

My narrative cannot be reduced to any single all-encompassing thesis. No particular group had either the authority or autonomy to determine the direction of events, if only because the responses of other interested groups limited the ability to shape policy. The final outcome resulted from the idiosyncratic actions of all involved parties. The most important but least recognized group that affected changes were the institutionalized patients themselves; their presence helped more than any other factor to mold the nature of hospitals. The composition of the patient population, moreover, underwent a basic change during these decades. After 1900 the proportion of aged senile persons residing in hospitals increased sharply, thus altering the functions of an institution that had been designed for quite different purposes.

Equally significant was the change in the specialty of psychiatry, which originally had been conceived and grown to maturity within a hospital setting. But by the beginning of the twentieth century, the intimate relationship between physicians treating the mentally ill and mental hospitals had begun to disintegrate. This development helped to prepare the way for the emergence of new career patterns for psychiatrists and to alter the nature of the specialty itself. Mental institutions, as a result, were left in a more vulnerable position, if only because the legitimacy that they had acquired because of their links with the medical profession was partially undermined.

Nor were patients and psychiatrists the sole determinants of change. Both existed within a particular social setting and political culture. The decentralized nature of the American political system and the division of responsibility between local communities and states had an enduring impact upon both patients and hospitals. Changes in the sources and levels of funding, for example, had a subtle but significant influence upon mental hospitals in different communities, states, and regions.

Few individuals and groups were completely aware of the part they were playing in the evolution of public policy toward the mentally ill. All were persuaded that they were right in their analyses and prescription for change. But intent and outcome were often far removed from each other; the ability to control events, affect changes, and shape behavior was limited in scope. Indeed, the success of the critics of institutional care between the 1950s and 1970s left an equally troubling legacy. During these years thousands of patients were discharged from hospitals and returned to communities that were unwilling and unprepared to accept them. History in a sense had repeated itself; in many instances the treatment of the mentally ill in modern America was similar to the one depicted by Dorothea L. Dix in her famous petitions in the 1840s and 1850s demanding the establishment of public mental hospitals. By the beginning of the 1980s Americans were forced to confront the results of the policy of deinstitutionalization.

The rejection of the idea of institutional care for the mentally ill that occurred after World War II did not develop suddenly or precipitously; its foundations were laid between 1880 and 1940. In order to understand the circumstances that led to this profound reversal in attitudes and practices, it is first necessary to describe the status of mental institutions, psychiatry, and public policy toward the mentally ill in the closing decades of the nineteenth century.

CHAPTER ONE

The Mental Hospital

BY THE 1870s mental hospitals had assumed the form that they would retain in succeeding decades. Their outwardly simple organizational structure, however, concealed a complex and turbulent reality. Although superintendents spoke and wrote as though their personal decisions relating to governance, care, and treatment were decisive, the character of hospitals more often than not was shaped by patient behavior and the nature of staff-patient relationships. To a considerable extent, psychiatrists and supporting staff reacted and adjusted to the actions of their wards. The internal environment of hospitals was therefore marked by a precarious balance between the psychiatric goal of maintaining order and stability, on the one hand, and patient behavior that was often arbitrary, unsettling, and unpredictable, on the other.

That the control of psychiatrists over mental hospitals was less than complete was only partially recognized. Many groups having direct or peripheral responsibility for the mentally ill—psychiatrists, neurologists, public officials, social workers, lawyers, and the informed public—had only a partial understanding of the issues. Their knowledge about mental disease, composition of the mentally ill population, and care and treatment was often filtered through preconceived perceptions and assumptions. Consequently, the debates and conflicts among these groups over policy were not always relevant to the needs of institutionalized mentally ill persons.

Relatively few superintendents of mental hospitals in the late nineteenth century were able to bridge the gap between psychiatric theory and institutional reality. Legally they possessed authority, which enabled them to issue orders within certain prescribed limits. But, like others in comparable positions, superintendents found that there was a fundamental distinction between authority to issue directives and power to ensure their implementation. To establish institutional goals was relatively simple; to control events with any degree of precision was far more difficult, if not impossible. This is not to insist that the destiny of individuals was determined by inexorable or impersonal forces. It is only to say that the choices of individuals and groups were often transformed by considerations that were never perceived to be relevant. This was particularly true of mental hospitals, which reflected all of the contingencies and ambiguities characteristic of human institutions and human behavior. Before we deal with the events and conflicts that shaped the development of mental hospitals from about 1875 to World War II, however, it is first necessary to sketch their character and organization as they existed toward the end of the nineteenth century.

I

According to the census of 1880 there were 91,997 insane persons out of a total American population of 50,000,000. Thirty years earlier the comparable statistics were 15,610 out of 21,000,000, suggesting to some contemporaries that the rate of insanity had more than doubled. Out of the total number of insane persons in 1880, nearly 52 percent were female, 71 percent native born, 93 percent white, and 7 percent black. About 9,300 were kept in almshouses. Of the remainder, half were cared for in mental hospitals and the other half in their own homes. The hospital population was composed of an equal number of males and females; 62 percent were native born and about 96 percent white. In the 74,184 cases in which the form of the disease was listed, the census showed the following breakdown: 38 percent were suffering from mania, 19 percent from melancholia, 2 percent each from monomania and paresis, 28 percent from dementia, 1 percent from dipsomania, and about 9 percent were epileptics. The average age of the mentally ill population, institutionalized or at home, was 43.5. But more than 17 percent of them were 60 years of age or older. Unmarried persons constituted 54 percent of the institutionalized population; 37 percent were married; 9 percent widowed; and less than 1 percent were divorced.[1]

These aggregate statistics, even granting gross inaccuracies arising from shortcomings in census procedures, revealed relatively little about the lives and experiences of the mentally ill. Confinement in any kind of institution was often a deeply emotional experience for an individual as well as a social process, and affected human relationships between family members. Aggregate data, unfortunately, sheds little light on the human dimensions of the problem.

Generally speaking, confinement during the nineteenth century was neither a simple nor an automatic process. Individuals who eventually ended up in asylums usually manifested some form of extreme behavior, including violent, suicidal, and occasionally homicidal acts, hallucinations, excitement, agitation, delusions, and deep depression. Alcoholism was itself not a sufficient cause for commitment. Nineteenth-century psychiatric nosology suggested that institutionalization involved extreme rather than marginal behavioral symptoms.[2]

The diagnosis of insanity often did not involve the community. Nor were most commitments begun by law enforcement personnel. Proceedings were usually initiated by members of the immediate family. Confronted with behavior that threatened the integrity of the family or situations with which they could not cope, relatives began the process of institutionalization as a last resort and with a vague understanding that it was the lesser of two evils. "I reluctantly enclose application filled out for admission of my mother," wrote a respected bank employee to the superintendent of the Wisconsin Hospital for the Insane in 1875.

> Of late she has grown materially worse, so that we deem it unsafe for the female portion of the family to be left alone with her during the day and especially unsafe for the little 2 year old that is obliged to remain continually there, as she has stated several times of late that she or the children must be sacrificed. Should she destroy another us [sic] could never forgive ourselves if the state has a place provided for their comfort and possible need.[3]

Other families were reluctant to accept discharged patients for fear that the conditions that led originally to their commitment would be repeated.

Nineteenth-century psychiatrists were aware of the crucial role of the family. Their annual reports were often written with an eye to assuring anxious relatives that their loved ones would receive kind and humane care as well as good medical treatment. Whether or not families believed what they were told, they resorted to institutionalization as a means of resolving internal crises. In 1846 and 1847, 75 percent of all commitments to the Utica State Lunatic Asylum were begun by the family and only 20.6 percent by public authorities; four decades later, the respective percentages were 57.9 and 38.6. An analysis of commitment proceedings in San Francisco in the early twentieth century demonstrated that 57 percent were begun by relatives, 21 percent by physicians, and only 8 percent by the police. Books written by patients—many of which reflected hostility toward their hospital experiences—also revealed that institutionalization invariably was instituted by the family.[4]

For many families mental illness raised severe economic problems. The afflicted individual was usually unable to work, and the family was obliged to provide continuous care. Mental illness as a result was intimately related to the problem of dependency. The care of the aged insane was a case in point. Most of them were suffering from some form of senility. Some had no families, or else families lacked either the means or the will to care for them. In any case, responsibility for the aged insane was usually divided between local almshouses and mental hospitals. Both of these institutions served in part as old age homes in the late nineteenth century. In 1880 and 1890, for example, the insane constituted nearly a quarter of the total almshouse population. No data is available for the age distribution of all of the mentally ill, but of the almshouse population as a whole 33 percent in 1880 and 40 percent a decade later were 60 years or older. In Massachusetts, where some data are available, more than 60 percent of the insane in almshouses in 1893 were 50 years or older—a statistic which indicates that almshouses provided care for a substantial number of aged insane persons. Similarly, many hospitals cared for significant numbers of elderly patients. Between 1851 and 1898 nearly 10 percent of California's institutionalized insane was 60 years or older; the figures elsewhere ranged from a low of 1.7 percent in Arizona in 1900 to a high in Massachusetts of 12.1 percent between 1880 and 1886.[5]

To commit an individual was seemingly a complex process. In 1892 five states empowered justices of the peace to commit mentally ill persons to hospitals; eighteen granted this authority to judges; five required a lay jury trial; and three others stipulated that at least one member of the jury had to be a physician. Three states utilized a court-appointed commission, and two an asylum board; nine others required merely a medical certificate. Where the power to commit rested with a court, provision was usually made for a medical examination by a physician whose findings were viewed as advisory. In a few states, however, medical findings were binding, and the court simply recorded the decision.[6]

Despite the complexity of the system, the overwhelming majority of families did not find commitment a difficult undertaking or one that involved lawyers and protracted conflict. Where a prominent person was involved, a particular episode might receive national publicity. But such cases were relatively infrequent. On a different level, the legal and psychiatric professions fought bitterly over commitment procedures. This struggle usually involved varying theoretical assumptions about the nature of individual responsibility, human behavior, and mental illness. Although laws tended to become more specific toward the end of the century, they posed no serious obstacle to commitment. Given a family seeking institutionalization for one of its members, or an individual with severe behavioral symptoms but without a family, legal procedures were administered in a loose and informal manner. The problem of commitment was for the most part perceived in human rather than strictly legal terms.

II

Once committed, the individual was admitted to the nearest public mental hospital. But this did not mean that the experiences of patients were similar; hospitals varied in size, organization, and quality of care and treatment. In 1883 the average number of patients in 83 local and state hospitals and one federal institution (excluding private and newly established institutions) was 544. The range, however, was significant; 9 of the largest hospitals had an average population of 1,254, and the 9 smallest about 139. Institutional size depended partly on public policy within political jurisdictions. California and New York City had only 2 hospitals each; Georgia and Indiana 1; all contained more than 1,000 patients. States with a developed hospital system dating back to the mid-nineteenth century, including Illinois, Kentucky, Massachusetts, New York (excluding the Willard Asylum, which originally was intended for chronic cases), Ohio, and Wisconsin, tended more toward the mean.[7]

The typical state hospital of the nineteenth century was constructed according to the "Kirkbride Plan," which had the official endorsement of the Association of Medical Superintendents of American Institutions for the Insane (AMSAII). A center building housed the kitchen, store rooms, reception areas, business and medical offices, chapel, library, and living quarters for the medical officers. Extending laterally on both sides were the patient wings, one for males and the other for females. If additional accommodations were required, a similar structure could be built, either joining existing wings at right angles or else lapping on at the other end and extending on a parallel line. Each wing in turn contained separate wards for the different types of patients. Such a structure in many ways reflected prevailing psychiatric ideology: separation of patients from the community; creation of a new therapeutic environment; the importance of classifying patients; the dominant and controlling role of the psychiatrist-superintendent; and reassurance to the family and community that patients would be cared for in a secure moral and medical environment that would promote their comfort, happiness, and even recovery.[8]

The State Lunatic Asylum at Utica, New York, was in many respects a typical institution. In 1884 it had slightly over 600 patients, 2 percent of whom slept on the floor because the total population exceeded the bed capacity. The wings housing males and females were divided into three departments (each one corresponding to a floor). The departments, in turn, were divided into twelve wards, each intended for a different class of patients. The female department, for example, had two convalescent wards (one for mild cases of melancholia), two for quiet patients (including one for chronic cases), one for demented persons, one for melancholics, one for a mixed group; the remainder were for noisy and disturbed individuals. The men's wing was organized in a comparable manner: one convalescent ward; five for quiet patients (including two for chronic cases); one for suicidal persons; and the remainder for demented, disturbed, or filthy patients. The wards varied in size. They contained as few as 15 patients and as many as 43, the average being about 27. Male wards had slightly more attendants present than female wards (8.4 as compared with 7.9), and disturbed wards for both sexes had more attendants than quiet wards.[9]

The elaborate system of wards had two goals: to retain in the same ward those who were least likely to injure others and those most likely to help each other. Proper classification, therefore, became the first step. Equally crucial was appropriate care and treatment of patients. Generally speaking, nineteenth-century treatment in mental hospitals tended to be eclectic and nonspecific. Given the absence of empirical data that might relate etiology, symptomatology, and physiology, superintendents followed older and more traditional medical practices. Like their colleagues in private practice, they accepted the view that all parts of the body were interdependent, and that health and disease resulted from the interaction of individuals with their environment. The aim of treatment, then, was to restore the normal balance, which would in turn contribute to the alleviation or cure of mental disease. "The theory of localization of brain function," observed Edward C. Mann in a textbook published in 1883, "does not throw as much light as we could wish, or lead to much practical benefit in the treatment of cerebral diseases. In treating such diseases we must look upon the brain as a whole, and our medicines must be calculated to act upon it through the general system." Therapy included a balanced diet that would rebuild the digestive tract and nervous system, a healthful environment, exercise, fresh air, sunlight, as well as the use of tonics and cathartics. There was also a decided receptivity toward novel and experimental therapies. Thyroid extract began to be used in the mid-1890s, along with the administration of electricity. If impaired physiological processes and mental diseases were related, then psychiatrists felt that they could not afford to ignore general advances in the medical sciences relating to the former.[10]

The holistic view which typified the specialty unified care and treatment. Indeed, even the concept of "management"—a word that appeared regularly in nineteenth-century psychiatric literature—was imbued with medical overtones. The physician, by manipulating the environment and patient, could overcome the past associations that had led to the disease and create an atmosphere in which the natural restorative elements could reassert themselves. For this reason, employment of patients, religious observances, and appropriate amusements were also considered crucial elements in the therapeutic regimen.

Although medical treatments for psychiatric and nonpsychiatric patients were similar, hospital physicians were particularly attracted to drugs that tended to calm noisy and troublesome patients. Behavior of such patients hampered their own recovery as well as that of others. Consequently, various sedatives and hypnotics were regularly employed. Hyoscyamin, opium, morphine, various bromide derivatives, chloral hydrate, paraldehyde, sulphonal, calomel, and digitalis were among the most commonly prescribed drugs. The use of such drugs was by no means unique to mental hospitals; opium and its derivatives were used in all medical practice.

Within mental hospitals reliance on sedatives and hypnotics varied considerably. A report to the Massachusetts legislature in 1875 noted that medication constituted "a very important agency in the cure of the insane," even though other means had assumed relatively greater significance in more recent times. The committee, however, was struck by the wide variations in the use of drugs in Massachusetts hospitals. Some institutions spent two to three times as much for drugs as others; one or two expended five to six times the state average. Such variations were characteristic of the country as a whole, suggesting that in some hospitals the use of drugs became an end in itself. The administration of drugs was determined exclusively by the medical staff without any external restraints. Oftentimes the goal was to quiet unruly patients in order to facilitate the efficient management of a complex social institution. Faced with managerial problems that were related to disruptive behavior of patients, a substantial number of hospital superintendents turned to medication as a palliative. In 1881 Dr. H. B. Wilbur noted that the use of mechanical restraint and "chemical restraint" were directly related; the more mechanical restraints were employed, the greater reliance there was on sedatives and narcotics.[11]

For institutionalized patients, the future was not especially promising. By the late nineteenth century the hospital was a place of last resort. Its patients often had long histories of behavioral signs, and many had been institutionalized on more than one occasion. Observations by early nineteenth-century psychiatrists that the longer the duration of the disease, the less the chances for recovery, seemed to hold true for the latter part of the century as well. The bulk of patients discharged as recovered tended to be among those with a relatively brief institutional confinement. Of 310 patients discharged as recovered from all Pennsylvania hospitals in 1876, 90 percent had been institutionalized for no more than a year, and 62 percent for six months or less. Moreover, the bulk of this group of patients had shown no symptoms for more than six months preceding their commitment. Those who recovered tended to be between the ages of 20 and 40; the chances for recovery declined with advancing age. Those who failed to recover or improve to the point where they were able to leave were likely to remain in a mental hospital or local welfare facility for extended periods. After examining American and British statistics for a thirty-year period, John B. Chapin estimated in 1877 that of every hundred cases, based upon the number of admissions, 34 percent would recover by the end of one year, 29 percent would die, and 36 percent would remain at a stationary level. A certain proportion of the recovered group would also find their way back to an institution after suffering a relapse. The implications were obvious: mental hospitals, despite their therapeutic goals, were actually providing long-term custodial care for many of their inmates.[12]

III

Admission to a mental hospital in the late nineteenth century was a frightening experience for most patients. Cut off from familiar circumstances, they were thrust into a complex institution with its own behavioral norms. Mental hospitals, after all, were coercive institutions. A large proportion of their total population was involuntarily confined, and force—either in legal or physical form—was the primary means of confining patients and maintaining internal discipline.[13] To emphasize only the coercive aspects of hospitals, however, is to disregard not only the historical context in which they functioned, but also the degree to which their internal character was a function of a mutual interaction among physicians, staff, and patients. Indeed, the internal environment of mental hospitals was at least partially molded by the character of their inmates. Nor can it be assumed that mental institutions were monolithic and static; like other complex organizations they passed through a variety of stages.

The typical late nineteenth-century hospital was structured along authoritarian and hierarchical lines. At the peak was the superintendent. All decisions pertaining to hospital life, including care, treatment, or architectural changes, were subject to his approval, if only because medical treatment of the insane involved the creation of a new environment. Directly under and responsible to the superintendent were the assistant physicians. They supervised the departments and wards, and were responsible for the day-to-day care of patients. At the bottom of the managerial hierarchy were the nurses and attendants: this group represented the institution to the patients and remained in constant contact with them. In addition to the medical staff, most hospitals had a salaried force of employees performing a variety of administrative functions—purchasing supplies, processing paperwork—as well as those preparing meals and maintaining the physical plant.

In theory the mental hospital was presumed to be a harmonious and efficient social organization. Its staff, medical and supporting, shared the same goal; to serve the needs of patients in order to promote their recovery. In practice, however, few hospitals ever corresponded to this ideal. As with virtually all human institutions, the ability to control the environment was severely restricted by both internal and external constraints. What emerged instead was an institution that reflected the human condition, with all of its strengths and weaknesses.

The most significant element in shaping the character of mental hospitals was the nature of their patient population. The patients, more than the medical and attending staff, created the internal environment to which others reacted. Admittedly, patients were also affected by a partially coercive atmosphere in which they were deprived of many liberties and forced to conform to certain behavioral norms. But, as a group, patients were by no means quiescent or accommodating; their behavior sometimes revealed an inability or refusal to conform. The character of the hospital, then, reflected an uneasy and sometimes hostile relationship between patients and staff.

More so than at most institutions, the behavior of many inmates tended toward social disorganization, if not anarchy. The ward structure reflected this centrifugal tendency, for it corresponded with certain behavioral patterns that ranged from total withdrawal to bizarre and violent conduct. Much of the time and energy of the staff was spent in dealing with immediate problems relating to patient behavior. As a result, the therapeutic aims of many institutions receded into the background as its managers struggled to maintain routine, discipline, and order—traits that mark many functioning organizations that are mission-oriented.

Consider, for example, the problems posed by patients often described as the "filthy insane." Virtually all hospitals had their share of such persons, many of whom represented cases of long standing. Upon entering their wards in the early morning, reported Dr. Stephen Smith, who served as a State Commissioner in Lunacy in New York during the 1880s, "the sight was most repulsive, and the odors intolerably sickening. . . . Some of the patients were literally wallowing in their own excrements. They had besmeared their beds, their heads and faces, and even the floors and walls of their rooms." In some instances three or four attendants were required to overcome the resistance of such patients and to wash and dress them. The result was "unfavorable in every respect." Other patients lapsed into habits of uncleanliness, and the time and energy of attendants was spent restoring some measure of hygiene.[14] Patient populations included the excited and violent, on the one hand, and the senile and paretic on the other. In all these cases, the institution was forced to adjust accordingly.

The conflict between institutional routine and patient behavior often resulted in the use of devices to restrain violent and excited patients. According to the census of 1880 (which provided detailed data by state and institution), about 5 percent of patients in mental hospitals were restrained in some way. Strait jackets were used for 44 percent of these cases; muffs (21 percent), straps (22 percent), cribs (5 percent), and handcuffs (7 percent) accounted for the remainder. The employment of such devices demonstrated no clear pattern; neither geographic location nor demographic variables were significant factors. The key element may very well have been the attitude of the individual superintendent or previous institutional practices.[15]

During the 1880s certain states and institutions moved to limit if not to abolish the use of mechanical restraints. In Alabama Peter M. Bryce reported considerable success with the nonrestraint system; Alice Bennett reported comparable results at the Women's Department of the Pennsylvania Hospital for the Insane in Norristown. A survey of the frequency of restraint conducted in 1891 by Clark Bell, a lawyer opposed to the practice, hinted that restraint enjoyed diminished popularity among superintendents.[16]

Restraint was one of the most controversial issues in nineteenth-century psychiatry. In England John Conolly had transformed nonrestraint into a virtual crusade in the 1840s and 1850s. In the United States the issue became equally divisive, and involved such key figures as Isaac Ray and Thomas S. Kirkbride. To mid-nineteenth-century superintendents, the decision to employ restraint involved a pragmatic judgment. If patients threatened their own or the well-being of others, the practice was necessary and permissible. Others insisted that the authority of the superintendent had to be limited by a recognition of the inalienable rights possessed by all patients. Although the controversy remained muted in the decades before 1860, its presence served as a reminder that the potential for conflict between institutional needs and individual autonomy had by no means been resolved.[17]

By the late nineteenth century restraint had once again become a source of friction. To critics of mental hospitals—a diverse group drawn from the fields of law, medicine, welfare, and philanthropy—the use of mechanical restraint was the ultimate symbol of failure. Dr. Joseph L. Bodine, for example, charged that the practice of restraint was intended to reinforce patient conformity to organizational rules; the consequence was aggravation of the malady and the creation of "a hopeless lunatic." To others, mechanical restraint violated the rights of patients, ran counter to progressive psychiatric thought, disregarded empirical data pertaining to the effectiveness of the practice, and even reinforced the behavior that it was intended to inhibit or prevent. Still other critics pointed to the example of England, which claimed to have abolished the use of restraining apparatus with beneficial results for all concerned. When the distinguished British psychiatrist John C. Bucknill travelled through the United States in the mid-1870s, his critical comments about the secrecy with which mental hospitals were administered, the lack of adequate external supervision, and the commitment of his American brethren to the idea of restraint, aroused a fiery controversy on both sides of the Atlantic.[18]

Within the ranks of American hospital superintendents, restraint remained a sensitive issue. Virtually no psychiatrist defended its indiscriminate use. The consensus among most psychiatrists was that its abolition, although desirable in theory, was impractical. Indeed, some emphasized that institutionalization itself was a form of restraint. Others pointed to the need to restrain patients who represented a threat to themselves or others. A smaller group insisted that the practice was completely unwarranted.[19]

The context in which the debate took place, however, suggested that the differences between the contending parties were not as fundamental as they thought. Both were concerned with the effects of disruptive behavior within institutions. Those who favored its abolition insisted that the more effective means of management could diminish or eliminate such behavior, and that restraints actually promoted the very type of behavior that it was intended to eliminate. "I am led to believe," observed Alice Bennett after evaluating the experiment of discontinuing restraints at the Women's Department of the Pennsylvania Hospital for the Insane,

> that much of the paraphernalia of the approved hospital for the insane—heavily barred windows, massive immovable furniture and the like—has too much the tendency to surround the patient with an atmosphere of suspicion, against which he naturally places himself in an attitude of defense, or even of offense; and, further, that to a much greater extent than has been

supposed, these expensive material "guards" can be substituted by moral agencies, which shall encourage, rather than repress, self-respect and self-control, often dormant, but almost never wholly extinct. . . .

One thought comes to me in closing: There is no more inexorable law, nor one of wider application, than that "action and reaction are equal," each to each.[20]

Those who were opposed to the discontinuance of restraint, on the other hand, indicated that in certain cases an institution had no alternative. Undoubtedly there was an element of truth in the claims of both sides. Behavior of some individuals led to restraint; in other instances the use or threat of restraint proved to be counterproductive. In any case, the existence of the practice shed some light on the disorder within hospitals and the limits of the power of their managers.

The disintegrative tendencies within mental hospitals were also evident in the relationship between attendants and nurses, on the one hand, and patients, on the other. Unlike physicians who saw patients only briefly and often irregularly, attendants and patients were in constant contact, and the interaction between them generally shaped the character of the institution. The crucial role of attendants, in part, was simply a function of numbers. In 1894 the nine state hospitals in New York employed fifty-four physicians. The doctor-patient ratio in individual institutions ranged from a low of 1:107 at Rochester State Hospital to a high of 1:240 at Willard; the statewide average was 1:171. By way of contrast, these same institutions had about one attendant for every seven patients. Throughout the nation the proportion of attendants to patients was about 1:12, but the breakdown in sectional terms was revealing. The East had the most favorable ratio (1:9), followed by the West (1:12.6), the South (1:15.2), and the Pacific region (1:18.8).[21]

Cognizant of the crucial role of attendants, superintendents conceded that their caliber left something to be desired. Long hours, arduous duty in wards filled with difficult patients, and relatively low pay made it difficult to attract or to retain high quality personnel. The resulting high turnover rates further undermined institutional stability. Indeed, even the possible attraction of regular employment was not a sufficient inducement at a time when periodic economic depressions created either irregular employment or unemployment. "It is impossible," charged the

Tennessee Board of State Charities in words echoed by many, "to secure a cultured or refined person as attendant upon the insane for the compensation provided." A less than competent attendant corps, superintendents insisted, was responsible for the frequent cases of brutal treatment of patients and the inability to create and to maintain a desirable therapeutic environment. Over a five-year period, Pennsylvania hospitals summarily dismissed 215 attendants, or an average of 9 per year per institution. Such dismissals constituted a little over 7 percent of the total number employed. Nevertheless, that such action was taken only in extreme cases involving "personal assaults upon patients, or for harsh conduct and improper language" suggested that most institutions in the state and elsewhere faced serious problems. Indeed, the inability to recruit better replacements undoubtedly acted as an effective brake upon a more liberal dismissal policy.[22]

In order to upgrade the skills of nurses and attendants, some institutions began to experiment with training schools. The first such school was opened in 1882 at the McLean Hospital, a private institution affiliated with the Massachusetts General Hospital in Boston. Two years later Buffalo State Hospital in New York followed suit, and by 1895 more than thirty such schools existed in the United States. Previously nurses and attendants had received what amounted to on-the-job training. Schools provided such staff with a somewhat more structured course of study generally lasting about two years. During their working hours, students attended a prescribed course of lectures, which were supplemented by appropriate reading materials. A few schools experimented with entrance requirements, and most gave examinations in order to weed out incompetents. At the end of the two-year period, students received a diploma, which presumably led to higher status and pay as well as the prospect of promotion to supervisory positions. Although such hospital positions were open to men and women alike, the women predominated because males resisted nursing as a career.[23]

Generally speaking, the efforts to upgrade the quality of nurses and attendants did not meet with overwhelming success. Turnover rates remained high. More importantly, the brutal treatment of patients remained an endemic problem. In 1906 the Massachusetts State Board of Insanity reported that recruitment was becoming more rather than less difficult. "It has been barely possible at times during the past year," it noted, "to procure respectable persons enough to do absolutely necessary work in caring for patients and safeguarding against danger." High turnover rates, it noted, even forced hospitals to send agents to employment offices to search for employees. In a fourteen-month period no less than 861 different men occupied 241 nursing positions (an average of 3.6 persons per job); 737 women filled 318 jobs (an average of 2.3).[24]

Undoubtedly relatively low wages and long hours acted as a deterrent to improvement of staff quality. Equally significant was the fact that work in a mental hospital for most individuals was difficult and at times unpleasant. Nurses and attendants cared for patients with a variety of needs: some were unable or unwilling to maintain personal hygiene; some were physically debilitated and infirm; and some behaved in seemingly bizarre ways. The result was either sporadic levels of hostility, conflict, or neglect— all of which worked at odds with institutional goals. Some outstanding nurses and attendants managed to surmount the problems that they faced and dealt with patients in a way that fostered close and trusting relationships. Others managed self-control and performed their duties in a responsible manner. But a few resorted to violent and brutal methods. To enforce discipline they employed extralegal sanctions, including the ducking of patients in water and other forcible disciplinary measures.[25]

In some extreme cases such staff actions resulted in the death of patients. Most of the cases receiving publicity did not involve systematic degradation of inmates, but rather an immediate emotional response by some attendant. In one instance a large and powerful paretic male was confined in separate quarters because of the dangers that he posed to others. Although the superintendent had left orders that no person was to enter the room alone, an attendant did so to clean up the room. A violent struggle ensued after the patient attacked the attendant. A second attendant, hearing the struggle, entered the room. The first attendant, according to the report, "being enraged, kicked and jumped upon the patient, inflicting comminuted fractures of the lower jaw-bone, fracture of a rib and extensive bruises and lacerations of the face, neck, shoulders and chest." Eventually the patient died, and the attendant was indicted and brought to trial.[26]

Superintendents and officials were by no means unaware of or insensitive to brutality and neglect. Whenever evidence of such behavior came to light, the erring attendant was usually dismissed. Nevertheless, the problem remained tenacious, for it involved complex human relationships. "Attendants are human and their work is arduous and exacting," noted a state supervisory board. "Some patients are trying, to the last degree; taking a malicious delight in annoying the attendants, and even taking advantage of the knowledge that they cannot be held accountable." A few institutions experimented with more open wards and greater personal liberty. These measures sometimes helped, but they did not eliminate the harsher aspects of institutional life. Violence, moreover, went in two directions, and patient attacks upon staff were not uncommon. A number of superintendents (including George Cook and John P. Gray), assistant physicians, and attendants were wounded or lost their lives as a result of patient assaults.[27] The human frailties of patients, attendants, and physicians created a precarious balance that was easily upset; the threat of disruption and disintegration was ever-present.

Although superintendents were concerned with interpersonal relationships within their hospitals, they were less sensitive to the social distance that separated them from their patients. Social, educational, and ethnic differences often created barriers to the development of close and trusting relationships. Superintendents in general were relatively well educated, came from a predominantly Protestant culture, and were overwhelmingly native born. A large proportion of patients, on the other hand, came from a very different social and cultural milieu. In 1880, for example, more than 15,000 out of nearly 41,000 patients in mental hospitals were foreign born. Even though the anti-immigrant sentiment that was so prominent among psychiatrists before the Civil War diminished toward the end of the nineteenth century, the social distance between doctor and patient often inhibited close personal relationships. When added to the paternalistic character of mental hospitals, social and class differences contributed still further to the disintegrative tendencies that lay immediately beneath the facade of institutional stability.[28]

Staff-patient relationships were not the only element that shaped the character of an institution; equally significant were relationships among patients. The ward system itself was a recognition of this fact. Assignments of patients to wards were not simply based on behavior and prognosis, but took into account such elements as race, ethnicity, education, and age. It was assumed that the behavior of patients was not totally unrelated to their backgrounds. Racial stereotypes, for example, produced friction among patients in those institutions that did not rigidly segregate whites and blacks. The superintendent of the Arkansas Lunatic Asylum observed that racial "incompatibility" often resulted in conflict among patients. "In this expression no discrimination is intended," he added. "It is only meant that each should be assigned to circumstances and surroundings that would be more agreeable and congenial to both, and therefore much more likely to conduce to desirable results in the treatment of their special maladies."[29]

Strict racial segregation, in fact, did not always guarantee harmony. One former patient recalled an instance in which a white patient wandered into an area reserved for black inmates and began to abuse them verbally. One black patient struck the white man and began to pursue him. The white patients, "though lunatic to a man, with the exception of the keepers, at this occurrence seemed to feel all the rancor of racial hatred rising within them. So long as their fellow-lunatic was so manifestly in the wrong they had shown no disposition to interfere with a chastisement so justly inflicted. But to see a white man fleeing before a negro foe, and the latter audaciously pursuing him into the midst of his friends, was too much for their self-control." The result was a violent fight involving patients and attendants.[30] Similarly, age, ethnic, and educational differences, which no ward system could completely overcome, also produced conflict among patients.

Most institutions attempted to offset the disorganization and monotony of hospital life by employing patients. Work was regarded as a critical element in creating a therapeutic environment. Inaction was considered harmful even to the normal mind, according to most psychiatrists, and in mentally ill persons its results were devastating. Wherever possible hospitals assigned male patients to their farms or to do maintenance work. Female patients were generally given household tasks such as sewing and cleaning, thereby reinforcing the sex-based division of labor characteristic of the larger society that had created a separate sphere for women in the home and effectively barred them from entering many occupations. Although patient labor had some minor impact on institutional finances, economic considerations played a decidedly minor role. Virtually no one suggested that patients be required to work in order to pay for their upkeep and thus relieve the fiscal burden on the state. On the contrary, work was important because of its therapeutic effect; financial gains were simply a desirable but not a necessary byproduct.

Work, however, never proved the hoped-for panacea. Many hospitals lacked facilities for other than routine labor. Attempts to induce legislatures to appropriate funds for the construction of workshops were often unsuccessful. Despite support from the state's central regulatory agency, the Michigan legislature turned down requests for funds for workshops. Equally important, many patients, for reasons of physical condition or age, were unable to work. Out of a total patient population of 4,944 in 1890 in all Pennsylvania hospitals, only 1,886 (39 percent) were employed. The hospital at Norristown had the highest proportion of employed patients (48 percent); the Dixmont hospital the lowest (11 percent).[31]

Compounding the problem of disintegrative tendencies within mental institutions was the imbalance between the numbers of patients and the capacity and quality of the physical plants to sustain them. During the 1880s a tenuous balance seemed to exist between total hospital capacity and the actual number of patients. A study by the Pennsylvania Committee on Lunacy in 1883 found that mental hospitals, which had facilities for 51,913 patients, had a total population of 51,815. This balance, however, was more apparent than real. In most states admissions, over which officials had little control, threatened to overwhelm the institutions. The desired balance between admissions and discharges was a fiction, if only because institutional populations were composed largely of chronic cases confined for long-standing periods of time. Few states had hospital facilities that were not strained. Crowding, in turn, intensified internal problems among patients and between staff and patients. Deteriorating physical plants, which resulted in part from the behavior of patients and the reluctance of states to improve or to replace existing facilities, exacerbated the problems of crowding. Two decades after it opened in 1833, the trustees of the Worcester Lunatic Hospital condemned the original plant as obsolete and recommended that it be replaced. Yet the institution remained in existence for an additional century despite its obvious deficiencies.[32]

To alleviate crowding, most hospitals resorted to a variety of practices. Some patients were discharged and sent back to their communities; some were transferred to local welfare facilities; those who did not have a legal residence were returned to other jurisdictions; and some were paroled on a trial basis. Oftentimes the result was a cycle of admissions and readmissions, with the availability of space playing a crucial role.

Most institutions, in fact, developed various legal subterfuges to minimize the effects of crowding. Parole was a case in point.

In New York State, for example, superintendents (excluding those in New York City and Kings County) did not have the legal right to discharge patients; actual power remained in the hands of boards of managers or judicial officials. Before taking such action, officials had to receive a written certification by the superintendent that the patient in question had recovered, or was incurable or harmless. For a variety of reasons, superintendents found the system slow and cumbersome, and some were reluctant to certify future behavior. But if the law restricted discharges, it said nothing about paroles. Hence superintendents proceeded to parole patients and then to forget about discharging them. In Pennsylvania a similar situation developed. In 1883 the legislature authorized parole for hospital patients not to exceed thirty days, provided that it was advantageous and that no harm would follow. Superintendents not only used the procedure liberally, but also renewed paroles until either the patient recovered and was finally discharged, or else was forced to return to the institution. When the Pennsylvania Attorney General ruled that parole could be extended only if the patient was returned to the hospital for an examination, its use declined precipitously. Families were usually reluctant to spend the time and money involved in travel to and from the hospital.[33]

The system of parole did in fact alleviate crowding in the late nineteenth century. It also provided hospitals with a legal means of demonstrating to patients that—as a Rhode Island agency put it in describing a new law authorizing parole in 1898—"self-control" would be rewarded and that sequestration "is but a means to an end, and that end, restoration to their homes."[34]

IV

Just as the experiences of individual patients differed, so too did institutional care vary widely in quality. In the early 1890s the average annual expenditure per patient at fifty-three hospitals was $179. There were, however, significant regional differences. Five Southern hospitals spent $129, as compared with $200 at Eastern and $167 at Western institutions. Nor were these differences simply a function of differential living costs. The Alabama Insane Hospital spent $24 per patient per year for food, as compared with $80 at one of the Ohio state hospitals. Similarly, staff-patient ratios and quality of physical plant varied in the extreme, depending upon the level of funding authorized by the legislature.[35]

In general, there were significant regional differences among hospitals. The South provided a lower standard of care as compared with other sections. In 1875 Alabama, Louisiana, Mississippi, North Carolina, South Carolina, and Tennessee each had one mental hospital, and as a group spent less than their Northern or Western counterparts. Southern hospitals also allocated funds along racial lines; facilities provided for white patients at the same institutions were superior to those given blacks. In 1884 the superintendent of the Alabama Insane Hospital noted that his institution had ample room for whites, but lacked sufficient and adequate facilities for blacks. Even when Southern states set up separate institutions for blacks, expenditures were not equal. In 1907 North Carolina spent $155 and $185 per patient per year at each of its white hospitals, but only $111 at the Goldsboro institution, which was restricted to black patients. Southern superintendents often acknowledged, directly and indirectly, the relative inferiority of their hospitals. When seeking a superintendent of nurses at his proposed training school, Dr. J. W. Babcock of South Carolina offered the position to a woman nearing completion of her training at the Massachusetts General Hospital in Boston. "As compared with Northern hospitals," he frankly conceded, "there will be many obstacles to contend with, as you can readily understand."[36]

Even greater differences existed between state mental hospitals and similar institutions established by urban governments. The origins of this dual system dated back to the early nineteenth century. When states established the first mental hospitals, they located them in the geographical center of the state to provide equal access to residents. In practice, however, hospitals tended to draw a disporportionate number of patients from adjacent areas. Urban areas, on the other hand, were usually located along the coast or near navigable waterways at some distance from the geographical center. Consequently, many cities, including Boston, New York, Brooklyn, Philadelphia, Chicago, Cincinnati, St. Louis, Detroit, and Milwaukee, established their own municipal mental hospitals during the nineteenth century.[37]

Urban hospitals from their very beginnings provided a significantly lower quality of care than their state counterparts. Some cities built their mental hospitals adjacent to their welfare and penal institutions in order to use inmate labor. New York City employed its convict population as attendants for the mentally ill. Given rapid population growth, the absence of a mature gov-

ernmental administrative structure, and budgetary pressures related to other needs, public officials often paid little attention to
their mental hospitals. At the Lunatic Asylum on Blackwell's
Island in New York in 1877, the superintendent was the only paid
medical officer for its more than fourteen hundred female patients
crowded into quarters designed for slightly over nine hundred
persons. Consequently, the institution faced severe problems: the
crowding created a disruptive environment; the absence of employment reinforced high levels of conflict and tension; and the
lack of effective supervision resulted in relative chaos. A decade
later the situation had changed but little. Conditions were hardly
different in the Kings County (Brooklyn) institution. Its superintendent insisted that in some respects convicts were more con-
tented than his patients. "If one thinks for a moment," he noted,

> they must realize how they would feel if they were locked up
> in an asylum, month after month, and perhaps year after year,
> without any occupation whatever, and very little liberty. This
> is a most distressing condition for the insane to be in, and it is
> one of the principal reasons why patients are unhappy, and
> always wanting to go out, because it is worse than prison, for
> in prison they have to work.

Nor did patients find a more hospitable environment at the Philadelphia Hospital, which was part of the municipal almshouse,
or at institutions in Cincinnati and St. Louis.[38]

Few institutions, however, could match the dismal conditions
at the Cook County Lunatic Asylum in Chicago. The origins of
this Asylum dated back to the 1850s when it was part of the
county poorhouse. In 1870 a new brick building for two hundred
insane patients had been constructed, and during the remainder
of the decade the institution's rapid growth paralleled Chicago's
rise to prominence. Before 1883 the Asylum received relatively
little publicity. In that year, however, Dr. S. V. Clevenger, one of
the more colorful figures in late nineteenth-century psychiatry,
was appointed as a special pathologist. At the beginning Clevenger
set about to gather patient data, a task made difficult because of
the destruction of institutional records during the great Chicago
fire of 1871.[39]

Within six months Clevenger realized that the inner workings
of the Asylum were far different from the impressions left after
brief and superficial visits. Lice abounded; patients died without
receiving medical attention; and restraints were used indiscrim-

inately and without any controls upon attendants. Whiskey and drugs were freely prescribed, and a serious drug addiction problem existed among patients. There was even evidence that the superintendent and a female supervisor were having an affair. The appointment of a new medical superintendent shortly after Clevenger arrived made little difference: the warden, who had political connections, controlled the domestic and financial management of the institution. Nor were conditions the result of inadequate funding. In 1884 the Asylum received an allocation of $332 per patient per year, as compared with $184 at the four Illinois state hospitals. Clevenger ultimately resigned his position and induced the Chicago Citizens' Association to undertake an investigation. With the cooperation of the state Attorney General's office, a number of county commissioners were first indicted and then convicted of corruption and theft.[40]

Considerable variations were also common among hospitals in a particular region and even within a given state. In some cases long-established traditions—some harmful to patients, some beneficial—accounted for institutional differences. In other cases leadership proved a crucial factor in molding the character of the institution. In still others the demographic composition of the patient population set the tone within the hospital. But, whatever their deficiencies, hospitals at the very least provided thousands of patients with a guaranteed subsistence level that was often superior to the level they would have confronted in their community. Indeed, institutionalized patients were shielded from the threat of starvation that grew out of the high unemployment that prevailed from the 1870s to the 1890s.

V

Although the proponents of institutional care for the mentally ill seemingly carried the day, their triumph was less than complete. Despite large investments made by states in constructing and maintaining mental hospitals, the number of patients exceeded capacity at any given moment. Nor was the quality of care and treatment equal, either within states or among regions. Most importantly, the tensions between patients, physicians, and attendants always inhibited the full realization of the goals embodied in the founding of institutions. From the very moment that hospital care became the accepted norm, therefore, American society faced new and puzzling dilemmas relating to the care of the mentally ill. Was institutional care as effective as its proponents claimed? Were there more effective solutions to this seemingly intractable social and medical problem? Was it necessary to impose limits on the autonomy and authority of the young but influential specialty of psychiatry? Similarly, to what extent was it desirable to permit public regulatory agencies to intrude into the internal affairs of hospitals? And who would represent the interests of the mentally ill? That such questions were even raised suggested that definitive answers were not yet available.

CHAPTER TWO

American Psychiatry: A Specialty Adrift

PSYCHIATRY, more than any other branch of medicine, originated in and was linked to institutions. Indeed, private practice in psychiatry was almost nonexistent during the nineteenth century. Unlike other physicians who maintained a private practice even when associated with clinics or hospitals, psychiatrists were not able to follow this pattern. Their specialty was institutionally based, and the overwhelming majority of them were public employees. Even specialization in mental disease led inevitably to a career in a mental hospital. Most physicians, whether apprenticed in a doctor's office or trained in a medical school, were never exposed to mental illness before deciding to take up psychiatry as a career. Employment as an assistant physician in a mental hospital was usually their introduction to the world of the insane.

This place of origin of American psychiatry was of crucial importance; it meant that psychiatric thought and practice were to a marked degree molded and shaped by a unique kind of institutional setting. Explanations of the etiology, symptoms, and prognosis of mental disease reflected not only the social background and medical training of physicians, but their experiences within mental hospitals. Just as the first generation of institutional psychiatrists in the 1830s and 1840s felt impelled to offer broad explanations of mental illness and rationalizations of institutional care and treatment, so too did their successors in the latter half of the century.

Although the language and metaphors of institutional psychiatrists between 1830 and 1880 were not fundamentally dissimilar, a new social context altered their significance. In the early period psychiatrists and their medical brethren shared similar views about the nature of disease and health. Toward the end of the century, on the other hand, medicine and psychiatry were following divergent paths. After 1880 the general hospital began to assume its modern form, and authority slowly shifted from lay trustees to physicians. This trend mirrored the transformation of the general hospital from an institution providing care for socially marginal groups to one reflecting a new emphasis on science and technology and catering to more affluent groups capable of paying the high costs involved.[1] Increasingly physicians spoke of medicine in terms of a biologically oriented science; the metaphors of health and disease took on a new meaning. Although practice changed far less than rhetoric, it was clear that in the future medicine would identify with science and technology.

Psychiatry and psychiatric institutions, on the other hand, did not undergo a comparable transformation. In the emerging world of scientific medicine, therefore, institutional psychiatry appeared to be the vestigial remnants of a premodern age, and the mental hospital a welfare-like institution far removed from the mainstream of medical practice. To many leaders of the new medicine, the psychiatric understanding of disease was based on vague metaphysical speculation that could not withstand scientific scrutiny. Slowly but surely psychiatrists became aware of the growing chasm between themselves and other physicians. Ultimately their marginal status would make them receptive to the kinds of innovations that would change the nature and location of their specialty. Before we analyze its transformation, however, it is first necessary to describe the nature of psychiatry in the closing three decades of the nineteenth century, when the differences between its members and the medical profession first became evident.

I

Although the education of physicians was undergoing significant changes in the last quarter of the nineteenth century, the path to a psychiatric career remained as it always had been. After completing a course of study either as an apprentice or at a medical school, the young physician, either through accident or design, received an appointment as an assistant physician in a mental hospital. James M. Keniston, for example, in his last year at the Harvard Medical School, was selected as Dr. John W. Sawyer's assistant at the Butler Hospital in Providence, Rhode Island. He had become interested in the field when he heard some lectures on insanity by the superintendent of the McLean Asylum. At the time of his appointment, he confessed that he "had never seen an insane person, as no clinical demonstrations were given." Nor had he ever visited a hospital for the insane. Keniston's experiences were by no means unique; most psychiatrists, including

Richard Dewey and William Alanson White, entered the specialty the same way.[2]

A position in a mental hospital offered certain advantages. It provided a young physician with a decent and stable salary at a time when neither the income nor status of practitioners were particularly attractive. In addition, the diverse patient population provided an unparalleled opportunity to develop diagnostic skills and medical techniques. Many general practitioners began their medical careers in a mental hospital. For those who elected to remain in the specialty, the possibility of becoming a superintendent, with its high levels of compensation, was an added inducement. Of 153 appointments to hospital superintendencies between 1875 and 1892, 93 had prior institutional experience, 76 were assistant physicians, and 103 had an institutional affiliation at the time of their appointments. Mobility in the field, on the other hand, was becoming more difficult. Between 1845 and 1854 the ratio of assistant physicians to appointments was 2.5:1; between 1885 and 1892 (when the total number of appointments to superintendencies rose from 21 in the earlier period to 78), the ratio increased to 10.7:1.[3]

Once in a hospital, the young physician quickly discovered that lack of training in psychiatry was not a serious impediment. Psychiatric disease categories were protean; a specific diagnosis had little or no meaning insofar as the patient was concerned. The organization of wards, for example, reflected behavioral patterns rather than disease categories. "I soon learned," Keniston recalled, "that giving a name to a given case of mental disease was relatively unimportant." Within two weeks of his arrival at Butler, Keniston was placed in full charge of the wards. His only psychiatric training consisted of some reading in texts by John C. Bucknill, D. H. Tuke, John Conolly, and Wilhelm Griesinger. To a considerable extent, psychiatry consisted of managerial and administrative chores. "The medical officers of our institutions have an immense number of miscellaneous duties; indeed, their medical duties, pure and simple, form but a small part of what devolves upon them—office work, business routine, and correspondence, with various administrative labors, consume a vast amount of time," wrote Richard Dewey in 1878. His article, in fact, was appropriately entitled "Management of the Insane." There were few differences between the strictly medical aspects of institutional practice and private practice.[4]

To care for and treat patients, however, required some justification or theoretical perspective about the nature of mental disease. Virtually all psychiatrists agreed that insanity was a disease of the brain, which in turn was the organ of the mind. To believe otherwise presented formidable problems. If the mind (often equated with the soul) could become diseased, it might conceivably perish. The immortality of the soul, upon which Christian faith depended, would thereby be denied. Yet to reject the dependence of the mind upon the brain might have meant falling back upon metaphysical concepts of human behavior that were incompatible with the assumptions of modern science. A physical disease, of course, did not rule out environmental, emotional, or social factors. Such factors, nevertheless, had to influence the brain through specific physiological mechanisms involving the reflex action of the nervous system or the blood supply. Heir to a holistic medical legacy, most psychiatrists believed that a malfunction in any vital organ could ultimately affect the brain and lead to insanity. "The nerves," observed the superintendent of the Northern Hospital for the Insane in Wisconsin,

> given off from the great central nerve mass, extend by many fibres to heart, lungs, stomach, kidneys, etc., each being intimately connected with the other, and each affected by disturbance or disease of the other, reacting one upon the other; thus, the influence of the disease of any organ upon the brain is incalculable, and if, by prolonged departure from a healthy condition of the organs of the body, that are thus intimately connected with the brain, not only by means of the nerve fibres but also through the instrumentality of the circulation of the blood; the same blood that washes a diseased lung, liver or kidney, bathing the delicate nerve-cells of the brain, it is not to be wondered at that the brain eventually succumbs to the double influence, and gives expression to its abnormal state, by inducing abnormal acts.[5]

The staunchest proponent of a somatic interpretation of insanity was John P. Gray, superintendent of the New York State Lunatic Asylum at Utica from 1854 to 1886 and editor of the *American Journal of Insanity*. A deeply religious figure, Gray was a firm believer in free will and the immortal character of the human mind. The capacity to choose between good and evil was essential to the concept of a moral universe, and Gray never doubted the existence of immutable moral laws that transcended time and place. He rejected therefore the philosophies of idealism and materialism; the former separated mental functions from the physical being of humanity, and the latter reduced all phenomena to purely physical explanations. Idealism posited a deranged mind independent of physical disease, a view that implied that the mind was not immortal. Correspondingly, materialism reduced behavior to bodily functions, thereby negating individual responsibility. Both approaches denied the idea of God and free will.

To avoid the pitfalls of idealism or materialism, Gray turned in part to Scottish common sense or moral philosophy. This school accepted both the concept of an objective physical reality and the belief that human beings possessed innate moral faculties independent of the material world. To Gray insanity required the presence of cerebral disease. "Disease," he insisted, "is what we have to deal with," and disease could not affect the mind but only the brain. Sensing a possible inconsistency, Gray conceded that the relationship between the mind and brain was "inexplicable" and might remain a "mystery." Indeed, his thinking was based on a selective blend of materialistic and idealistic concepts, for he abhorred any kind of determinism. Gray rejected explanations based on heredity, on the grounds that they negated free will and undermined individual responsibility. This position brought him into conflict with many colleagues at the trial of Charles Guiteau, the assassin of President James Garfield. Gray's commitment to a somatic explanation also led him to appoint a special pathologist at Utica to undertake post-mortem examinations to illuminate the pathology of insanity. By this means, he hoped to provide detailed knowledge about the presence of cerebral disease based on empirical data.[6]

The somatic concept of mental disease for most American psychiatrists represented both an act of faith and a starting assumption. With the exception of a few cases in which autopsies revealed the presence of a brain tumor or other abnormalities, most psychiatrists conceded that existing techniques failed to reveal any significant differences between the brains of normal and abnormal persons. "In the pathology of mental diseases," admitted Charles F. Folsom, ". . . it must still be said that, except in dementia and paralysis, we know very little of the pathological conditions of the brain *giving rise* to insanity beyond the fact that they probably are chiefly cortical and diffuse rather than local."[7]

Given their inability to demonstrate a relationship between anatomical changes and behavior, psychiatrists tried to identify the presence of mental disease by observing external symptoms.

In this respect they were no different from other physicians. Prior to the specific germ theory of disease, most medical men defined pathological states in terms of such external and visible symptoms as fever. To be sure, inferring pathology by focusing on symptoms created serious intellectual and scientific problems. Although disagreeing on the diagnosis of symptoms, few physicians questioned this approach. No other alternative seemed available. To late nineteenth-century psychiatrists disease was a given; the inability of their patients to function, combined with severe behavioral symptoms, was sufficient evidence of the presence of disease.

Nowhere were the intellectual and scientific dilemmas of psychiatry more pronounced than in the efforts to adopt a common nosology. Most psychiatrists recognized that a precise classification system would not only illuminate the course and development of a specific illness, but might also make possible the identification of those conditions that determined health and disease. Yet what kind of system could encompass all cases? There was awareness that a nosology based on etiology was superior to one based on symptoms, but absence of conclusive empirical data made the formulation of such a system virtually impossible. In the mid-1880s an international effort to define an acceptable classification system was begun. A variety of plans was presented, but all had obvious defects. The venerable Pliny Earle pointed to the obstacles that prevented the adoption of any system. "In the present state of our knowledge," he noted, "no classification of insanity can be erected upon a pathological basis, for the simple reason that, with but slight exceptions, the pathology of the disease is unknown. . . . Hence, for the most apparent, the most clearly defined, and the best understood foundation for a nosological scheme for insanity, we are forced to fall back upon the symptomatology of the disease—*the apparent mental condition*, as judged from the outward manifestations." To Earle the oldest, simplest, and most practical classification system of mental illness (mania, monomania, melancholia, dementia, and idiocy), therefore, remained of value.[8]*

* Many contemporary critics of psychiatry (particularly those who adhere to the concept of "deviance") emphasize the absence of any definitive proof that physiological processes "cause" mental disease. They infer that mental hospitals are performing a penal function in isolating deviants from the rest of society. Neither the premise nor the conclusion, however, is necessarily valid. The fact of the matter is that the way in which psychiatry historically defined mental illness was (and is) not fundamentally different from the way in which medicine historically defined disease.

In describing and interpreting the nature of insanity, psychiatrists also attempted to shed light on its etiology. The existence of a classification system based on external symptoms clearly complicated the problem and made it virtually impossible to demonstrate meaningful relationships between causal factors and the presence of particular behavioral signs or symptoms. The difficulties that impeded etiological clarity, however, did not inhibit discussion or speculation. The social and cultural role of medicine required that all medical practitioners provide some explanation of disease processes. Moreover, the rise of an ideal of scientific medicine in the late nineteenth century intensified demands for rational explanation, which were mirrored in the introduction of antisepsis in the 1870s and the popularization of pathogenic specificity in the 1880s. Psychiatrists were not untouched by such trends, and they attempted to provide explanations in order to reassure the public that mental diseases involved rational rather

---

Before the specific germ theory of disease, all physicians—psychiatrists and generalists—defined pathological states by describing them in terms of external and visible symptoms. This process was inevitable, if only because neither the prevailing technology nor theory could establish a relationship between biological mechanisms and external symptoms. To be sure, a classification system based on external symptoms created serious intellectual and scientific problems. Was fever, for example, one disease state or many? While often disagreeing on specifics, few physicians questioned the practice of defining disease by observing symptoms; no other alternative was available. Nor was there any tendency to argue that individuals with a high fever were social deviants because their immediate condition (mental as well as physical) differed significantly from that of the population at large. Indeed, there are numerous examples in contemporary medicine where physicians define pathological states even when patients appear to be in perfect health.

To maintain that psychiatric and medical definitions of disease are not fundamentally dissimilar is not to reject the view that the concept of disease is dependent in part on a series of nonscientific or external variables. With the possible exception of a number of infectious diseases, most pathological states are still described in terms of symptoms rather than etiology. Admittedly, there is a difference between defining disease in terms of behavioral signs, on the one hand, and physiological symptoms, on the other. But that difference may not be of fundamental significance, particularly if little or no distinction is made between behavior and physiological processes. In fact, we know relatively little about what is designated as mental illness, and that makes it difficult to prove or to disprove its existence. Moreover, in many cases it is not feasible at the present time to establish the validity of psychiatric disease categories. Schizophrenia, to cite one example, may be, in fact, what "fever" was before 1870—a general inclusive category describing a multiplicity of diseases. Assertions about the existence or nonexistence of mental illness represent in large measure acts of faith which reflect commitments to a particular course or courses of action.

than irrational and random elements. A scientific etiology also provided hope, if only because understanding could be translated into the kind of behavioral modification to prevent disease. "A terrified popular imagination still pictures insanity as some mysterious and monstrous incubus, coming from distant regions of darkness to crush out human reason," Mary Putnam Jacobi informed members of the American Social Science Association in 1881. "In reality, however, insanity means a complex multitude of morbid states, varying indefinitely in form and intensity, but all composed of elements which preexist in health. This fact affords a basis for prophylaxis, for it indicates the possibility of detecting these elements and, to a certain extent, of anticipating their morbid combinations."[9]

Generally speaking, late nineteenth-century etiological concepts reflected broad social perceptions and prevailing cultural values. Like their predecessors earlier in the century, most psychiatrists believed that insanity grew "out of a violation of those physical, mental and moral laws which, properly understood and obeyed, result not only in the highest development of the race, but the highest type of civilization." When referring to "laws," psychiatrists were not endorsing a deterministic universe; law was rather a moral construct that stipulated, but did not necessarily require, ideal forms of behavior. The mind itself functioned along an unbroken continuum; there was no sharp line of demarcation between normal and abnormal mental activity. One merged into the other, and both depended upon the physiological condition of the brain. Good health, insisted Henry P. Stearns, the influential superintendent of the Hartford Retreat, was simply a condition in which the brain's involuntary functions were "normally performed and under the control of the will"; when the brain deviated from this state, either because of inherited or acquired influence, the result was an "abnormal mind."[10]

In the psychiatric literature of this era, discussions of etiology tended to be protean and nonspecific in character. If there was no sharp distinction between normal and pathological states, it seemed evident that insanity involved an internal relationship between the individual and the environment. The nature of that relationship, however, remained hidden from view. "The life of every individual," observed Walter Channing, "is so secret and deep that often no one can divine the processes that go on from year to year and lead to outward action." Given the immense difficulties in tracing the inner life history of a person, Channing fell back on an explanation which emphasized external predisposing causes. Mental illness could be caused by several conditions: the harmful effects of the increasing demands of modern civilization; the migration from abroad of individuals already well along the road to degeneracy; an inherited predisposition to disease; and the role of such factors as occupation and marriage. Nor were Channing's etiological theories unique; virtually every discussion emphasized external elements. The list of causes seemed endless: addiction to alcohol, drugs, tobacco; sexual excesses; improper nutrition; inadequate housing; misdirected education; uterine and ovarian diseases; and moral or psychological causes, including domestic difficulties, grief, anxiety, adverse circumstances, business failure, pecuniary difficulties, sudden fright, worry, and mental overwork.[11]

Few psychiatrists, however, thought that the causes of insanity operated equally on all individuals. Like others, they believed that susceptibility was in part determined by race. This was particularly true of psychiatrists in the South, the region where the majority of blacks lived. To many (but not all) of these physicians, emancipation had led to a sharp increase in the incidence of insanity among former slaves. Blacks, insisted Dr. J. D. Roberts of North Carolina, were "essentially of an emotional character," and the abolition of slave discipline simply permitted them to indulge their passions and appetites unrestrained by the reason that was characteristic of whites. "As a slave," Dr. J. M. Buchanan of Mississippi wrote, "his passions and animal instincts were kept in abeyance by the will of his masters." Freedom, in other words, had brought debauchery and disease to blacks. Building upon an earlier medical tradition that assumed major anatomical differences between blacks and whites, some physicians assiduously collected brains from deceased insane blacks in an effort to identify the relationship between physiological structures and mental disease.[12]

In a superficial way the etiological constructs of the 1880s differed but little from those a half century before. Yet a new social context was beginning to alter the meaning of older concepts. Before 1850 etiological thought had expressed hope and optimism. Even if disease were the product of individual misbehavior and/or environmental factors, its course could be reversed by appropriate treatment. The very justification for hospitalization was phrased in terms of the need to break with those associations that produced disease and to create a new and more appropriate milieu.

Although conceding that moral treatment was ineffective if disease was of long-standing duration, antebellum superintendents believed that the overwhelming majority of acute cases of insanity could be cured.

By the last quarter of the nineteenth century, however, the optimistic attitudes of the earlier era were slowly giving way to more pessimistic views. The decline in religious authority, the growing importance of more secular modes of thought, periodic economic depressions that created unemployment and fostered class strife, an apparent increase in crime and degeneracy, the growing concentration of economic power, and the unchecked flow of immigrants who were considered undesirable—all combined to give rise to a new and less hopeful climate. Moreover, the mounting number of chronic cases in mental hospitals and the consequent decline in the ratio of recoveries offered further evidence that the claims by the older generation of cure were untrue. In the 1870s and 1880s Pliny Earle, one of the original founders of the AMSAII, undertook a series of retrospective studies that disputed earlier statistics. Earle charged that the reports of recoveries were grossly exaggerated: the proportion of cures represented the ratio of recoveries to cases discharged rather than to cases admitted; readmissions had been disregarded; and many individuals had "recovered" on more than one occasion. He concluded that the older claims of high curability rates were not sustained by the evidence, and that the percentage of reported recoveries was declining because of the increase of cases in the chronic and degenerate category.[13]

The growing pessimism among psychiatrists and social activists was especially evident in the new ideas regarding heredity. In the early nineteenth century hereditarian ideology was far less deterministic. Its proponents accepted the Lamarckian view that acquired characteristics could be inherited, and that inheritance involved tendencies and predispositions rather than fixed and immutable qualities. Environment, therefore, remained the decisive element in determining whether a predisposition to disease would become operative. Toward the close of the nineteenth century, on the other hand, explanations of heredity began to be presented in new ways, even though the belief in the inheritance of acquired characteristics persisted. Although pessimistic in nature, hereditarian ideology became increasingly popular. It endowed public policy with the presumed sanction of science; it justified the use of governmental authority to contain ostensibly anti-social persons; and it offered reassurance to a majority of Americans by suggesting that their biological endowments gave them the capacity to survive and even to prevail.[14]

Although no psychiatrist attempted a systematic formulation of the role of heredity, most stressed its pervasive importance. In 1883 Henry P. Stearns devoted an entire chapter in his book to "The Insane Diathesis," which he defined as "a nervous system so sensitively constituted, and illy adjusted to its surroundings, that when brought in contact with unusually exciting influences, there may occur deranged instead of natural mental action, and it becomes more or less continuous instead of evanescent." Stearns conceded that a predisposition did not have to become operative, but his emphasis on prevention indicated an underlying pessimism. Others related heredity and race. Walter Channing, for example, listed "the race-character of the population" and "hereditary predisposition" as the two leading causes of insanity. In his eyes, race was still a social and cultural category; he linked race and heredity to the unchecked immigration into the United States of "a distinct pauper class" representing "the most degenerated foreign element." Not all immigrants fell into this category, Channing admitted, and many were able to make a successful adjustment to their new environment. Nevertheless, he insisted that foreigners were contributing to the increase in insanity.[15]

Most psychiatrists accepted the centrality of heredity. Only John P. Gray rejected hereditarian formulations, largely because they were incompatible with individual responsibility and free will.[16] Commitment to hereditarian explanations of insanity were not necessarily pessimistic, if only because the belief persisted that most behavioral characteristics were acquired rather than innate. But in reality, hereditarian concepts assumed a more rigid meaning in the 1880s. Mental hospital populations by then were composed of large numbers of chronic cases with long histories of institutionalization. Moreover, discussions about social policy generally took place within a framework dominated by the conviction that pauperism, crime, and degeneracy were all related.[17] Indeed, the very legitimacy of mental hospitals was on occasion expressed in pessimistic tones. The Massachusetts State Board of Lunacy and Charity—one of the most influential public agencies in the country—mirrored the growing mood of despair when it called attention to the fact that recoveries from insanity were far less frequent than once believed. "The utility of our hospitals and asylums," it added in revealing words, "must not be tested by holding them to any impossible standard in this respect. The protection of the community from the harm and loss which the insane inflict, if left at large; the protection of the insane themselves from great sufferings of various kinds; the relief of families that would otherwise be burdened beyond their strength, by the care of insane relatives; these and other benefits which our Massachusetts hospitals and asylums confer, are an evidence of their great utility, both past and present."[18]

Psychiatric explanations about the nature and etiology of mental disease were in many respects little different from the views expressed about disease generally by physicians in private practice. Nevertheless, by the 1880s and 1890s the identification of specific pathogens and the growing significance of bacteriology had begun to reorient American medicine. The result was a vague perception that psychiatric theory was dated, and that psychiatrists were growing apart from their medical colleagues. As early as the 1870s institutional psychiatrists encountered hostility from other physicians who continuously alluded to the low quality of asylum doctors. "When vacancies occur in the medical staff," the *Boston Medical and Surgical Journal* noted in 1878, "accomplished men hesitate to assume positions of such drudgery, and . . . properly trained men are wanting to take the offices when they are offered. . . . The present system, at least, cannot long stand against the current which is pushing forward so rapidly to advance all branches of medical knowledge."[19] This comment was echoed in other medical journals.

II

Paradoxically, the extensive literature on the nature and etiology of mental disease had relatively little relationship to psychiatric practice. Superintendents who published extensively were themselves administrators of complex institutions and for the most part were immersed in the routine of hospital management. Their lack of concern on such matters did not spring from defects in their character or indifference to suffering. The size and structure of their institutions, the amorphous nature of treatment, and the absence of specific knowledge about mental disease meant that the imperatives of the hospital as a social system became the dominating factor. The omnipresent danger of social disorganization caused by the tensions arising out of the social distance between physicians and patients, as well as by the unpredictable character of patient behavior, only compounded the problem. Concern for the welfare of specific patients often came into conflict with the larger goal of maintaining order within a complex social institution.

Under such circumstances the dominance of managerial and administrative concerns was hardly surprising. Many elements within psychiatric thought—the nature of disease, the role of heredity—seemed irrelevant to the daily institutional routine. The vagueness of etiology and the inability to locate the somatic changes that allegedly accompanied disease patterns meant that psychiatric practice had little direct (or indirect) relationship to practice. The concept of moral treatment itself was largely synonymous with the creation of a specific environment that would promote recovery. That patient behavior—including interaction among patients themselves as well as with staff—would mandate certain controls led to the presupposition that superintendents would focus on managerial issues. Richard S. Dewey clearly understood this situation. In his discussion of mental hospital needs in 1878, he identified five general areas of concern in managing the mentally ill: means of employment and recreation for patients; the degree to which confinement and restraint were necessary; the effect of asylum routine on patients; the treatment of patients by attendants; and the relation of the hospital to the public, to its officers and employees, and to the advancement of knowledge.[20]

This disjuncture between theory and practice was also mirrored in the nature of late-nineteenth-century concepts of psychiatric research. Most practitioners accepted as an article of faith the idea that further progress in psychiatry lay in scientific research. If insanity was a somatic disease, then a detailed knowledge of the brain and nervous system was absolutely necessary. In this respect, American psychiatrists were profoundly influenced by European medicine which emphasized a chemical-physical approach to disease after 1850. Rudolph Virchow's celebrated cellular pathology was instrumental in pointing medicine in the direction of uncovering diseased organs and cells. The doctrine of cerebral localization reinforced the belief that lesions probably were the cause of insanity. Indeed, Theodore Meynert attempted to classify all mental disorders on the basis of anatomy; mental conditions were simply symptoms of an underlying pathology. "In view of the necessity of starting from anatomical facts," Meynert wrote in the Introduction to his famous *Psychiatry*, "I have endeavored, in every case, not only to give due weight to the structure of the brain as the fundamental basis for the various forms of disease, but have endeavored, with the same end in view, to insist upon and to explain every visible symptom exhibited by the patient."[21]

But if American psychiatrists adhered to the ideal of research, they also recognized the seemingly insuperable obstacles that had to be overcome. In the two decades following 1830, asylum physicians had performed autopsies in an effort to link symptomatology and brain lesions. The absence of concrete results led to a virtual abandonment of a practice that strained an already over-burdened medical staff. In a paper delivered at the meetings of the American Social Science Association in 1881, Walter Channing pointed to the absence of any serious pathological work in most mental hospitals. He attributed this situation to a lack of time, interest, and training. The direction of medical education and administrative demands on the medical staff precluded any serious pathological study in the field, "despite the opportunity for brilliant work." Adolf Meyer, who subsequently became one of the most influential psychiatrists in the country, had a much harsher characterization of medical research. "Science in America," he wrote shortly after migrating from Switzerland to the United States, "is nothing but an advertisement." Meyer described a chair in one of the better American medical schools as being equivalent of the veterinary school in Zurich some two decades earlier. Nor did his experiences at the Kankakee hospital in Illinois or the Worcester hospital in Massachusetts seriously alter his evaluation of psychiatric research. Meyer's complaints were echoed by some of his American colleagues. The majority of superintendents, wrote Henry M. Hurd, had a "rather inadequate conception of what is involved in a high class of pathological work and seem to feel that the analysis of urine and occasional blood examinations constitute the most useful part of the work."[22]

Generally speaking, there was little dissent with these negative evaluations. Critics nevertheless tended to oversimplify the situation as it existed. The first pathologist at an American mental hospital was appointed by John P. Gray at the Utica institution in 1869; other institutions slowly followed suit. Pathological studies of the structure and function of the brain and central nervous system, however, provided rather meager results. Research, therefore, had little impact on the lives of institutionalized patients. During Meyer's six-year tenure at the Worcester hospital in the late 1890s, he helped to reorganize the institution and to create a pathological department that served both as a research and training center. Although the enthusiasm and morale of the medical staff probably rose, the impact on patients was at best limited, if only because research and therapy were not necessarily related. Equally significant was the fact that research on occasion came into conflict with the goal of achieving a higher standard of medical care. The Illinois Board of State Commissioners of Public Charities observed in 1880 that the duties of medical officers in hospitals were arduous and time-consuming. Although it favored greater emphasis on research, its members also noted that "the study of the living insane patient is of far more value than the study of the same patient when dead. . . . But if so, how can time be taken from the regular duties of a superintendent or assistant physician, for pathological research, without loss to his living patients, who require his care?"[23]

III

By the 1870s and the 1880s American psychiatry occupied a marginal position. Its practitioners stood between two worlds. On the one side was a world of institutions created during the early part of the century. These hospitals were products of a culture in which moral and religious concepts were of primary significance. Moreover, the difference between medicine and religion was vague; both were concerned with the spiritual and physical well-being of the individual. Much of medical thought reflected a particular understanding of the natural laws that governed the universe. Health and illness were simply indicators of the degree to which individuals conformed to or deviated from such laws. In this sense a physician who pursued a career in psychiatry differed but little from their counterparts in general medical practice. The leaders of early and mid-nineteenth-century psychiatry—including Isaac Ray, Thomas S. Kirkbride, Luther V. Bell, Amariah Brigham, and Edward Jarvis—were an integral part of the medical profession generally.

During the second half of the nineteenth century traditional medical practice as well as concepts of disease had begun to change. Increasingly medicine located its roots in a biologically oriented science aided by a new kind of technology. Although psychiatrists had grown increasingly discontented with their institutional setting, they were as yet ill-prepared to join the new world of scientific medicine. Pressure for change, both from within and without, would slowly force a reorientation of the specialty. By the turn of the century a new concept of psychiatry had begun to emerge.

CHAPTER THREE

The Transformation of Psychiatry

ALTHOUGH MEMBERS of an established specialty in the late nineteenth century, psychiatrists found themselves under attack from a variety of individuals and groups, including other physicians, social activists, lawyers, state regulatory agencies, and former patients. On occasion it appeared that critics were determined to undermine the legitimacy of institutional psychiatry which an earlier generation had forged. Such hostility posed a serious threat to the continued vitality of the specialty. In reaction to widespread criticisms, psychiatrists began to redefine the foundations of their specialty. By the turn of the century psychiatry would no longer be identified exclusively by its administrative character or institutional location. On the contrary, its practitioners would now begin to identify themselves and their work by a renewed commitment to the study and treatment of mental diseases rather than the care of individual patients. As psychiatrists inadvertently minimized their role in providing care for chronic patients, the mental hospital began to lose its central position. At the same time psychiatrists slowly pushed the boundaries of their specialty outward into the community and attempted to broaden its function and role. When the process of change had run its course, American psychiatry had emerged in a new form.

The transformation of psychiatry was not an isolated development, but paralleled changes in other occupations. Traditionally, the term "profession" applied only to law, religion, and medicine, and was inseparably linked with moral and religious values. By the late nineteenth century, on the other hand, the concept of a profession had taken on an entirely new character. Although many of the new professional organizations that came into existence dealt with such familiar issues as admission and conduct of members, their basic goal was far more inclusive; they wanted to shape the environment in which they existed. In this sense professionalization was part of the process that gave rise to a new social order in which centralized structures and organizations, centralized decision-making processes, and values associated with modern science and technology profoundly altered the lives of the American people.

I

The initial assault on institutional psychiatry came from former patients who alleged they had either been committed illegally or treated harshly. Such attacks were not altogether new. Robert Fuller, a former patient, had attacked the very legitimacy of the McLean Asylum in 1833. In the succeeding three decades, former patients published critical remarks about hospital life, but most of these accounts were seeking to reform rather than to abolish hospitals. The sporadic patient exposés published before 1860, however, had little impact, if only because there was little disposition to question the necessity of institutional care of the mentally ill.[1]

During the 1860s this situation abruptly changed as states began to reexamine public policies toward all dependent groups and to establish external regulatory agencies. Under these circumstances, critics of mental hospitals found a wider and more sympathetic audience. The best-known foe of institutional psychiatry in the 1860s and 1870s was E.P.W. Packard. In 1860 she was committed to the Illinois State Hospital for the Insane by her husband and by the probable cooperation of Dr. Andrew McFarland, the superintendent. This action was taken under the provisions of an earlier statute that permitted the confinement of married women and invalids without the procedural safeguards available to other adults. Following her release after a three-year stay, Packard launched a crusade to secure legislation to safeguard the rights of patients and to restrict the authority of hospital officials. In attacking the arbitrary nature of commitment proceedings, Packard implicitly criticized a legal system that in theory if not in practice subordinated wives to their husbands. Her protest was evidence of the growing assertiveness of many mid-nineteenth-century American women.

An effective crusader, Packard induced a number of state legislatures to undertake detailed investigations of conditions within mental hospitals. Her first victory came in 1867 when Illinois enacted a personal liberty law that provided for jury trials in sanity hearings. Subsequent efforts in the 1870s and 1880s led to the passage of similar legislation elsewhere. Some states established visiting committees with powers to inquire into conditions at mental hospitals. Others permitted insane patients to write freely to whomever they pleased without prior approval or censorship. The first law giving patients letter-writing rights without any censorship was passed in Iowa in 1872; other states, including Massachusetts and Pennsylvania, enacted comparable statutes.[2]

The immediate reaction of most hospital superintendents was negative. They viewed such legislation as an attack on their professional autonomy and competency as physicians. Such laws, they insisted, were detrimental to the vital interests of the patient because lay persons were intruding upon the delicate doctor-patient relationship. Isaac Ray—author of a classic work on the medical jurisprudence of insanity and an acknowledged leader of the specialty from the 1830s to the 1870s—condemned the patient correspondence laws as "anomalous & utterly indefensible" and enacted in a "high-handed manner against evils not shown to exist." The boxes in which patients deposited their letters were under the jurisdiction of an outside board. Did the members of such a board possess judgment superior to that of hospital officers, Ray asked? "The only possible reply," he added, "is, either that, 'we can't trust you to do the right thing,' or that, 'we know better how to manage these things than you with all your long experience.' The boxes themselves would be a standing proclamation to the patients that the officers were unworthy of their confidence, and they must look to the outside Board for protection against the Superintendent, assistants, & Trustees who are combined for the purpose of depriving them of their liberty."[3]

In 1875 Ray introduced a series of resolutions at the meetings of the AMSAII, which passed with only two dissenting votes. The resolutions denied that any sane persons were being incarcerated. To endow supernumerary functionaries with supervisory authority over mental hospitals, the resolutions declared, would result in great harm to the institutions. And to permit patients to send unopened correspondence might result in considerable embarrassment for the individual and deprive the doctor of a means of gaining valuable information about the patient's mental outlook.[4]

Although the controversy over patient correspondence laws initially aroused considerable heat and contributed to the distrust of psychiatrists, the issue proved ephemeral. Once the novelty of writing letters wore off, few patients availed themselves of the privilege. Shortly after the Massachusetts law took effect, the materials in letter boxes for a three-month period for all state hospitals included seventy-five letters and half a bushel of trash. The letters themselves, conceded the secretary of the Board of State Charities, revealed nothing that warranted an investigation. Most of the wrongs complained of "were purely imaginary—generally ascribed to spirits, occult forces, influences in the air." With the passage of time, fewer and fewer letters were deposited by patients.[5]

By the 1880s and 1890s the letter-writing controversy had largely disappeared from view. Nevertheless, the disappearance of a particular concern in no way resolved larger questions about the mutual duties and obligations of patients and physicians. In the nineteenth century the authority of the institutional psychiatrist virtually had no legal constraints. This is not to imply that they were free to do as they chose. On the contrary, informal norms and standards of conduct of the specialty acted as important regulators of professional behavior. Such norms were based on a model that assumed deferential and paternalistic relationships. In this sense the authority of psychiatrists was derived not merely from their presumed training and knowledge, but also from their social class affiliation. A century later the transformation of values, behavioral norms, and legal standards would alter the context of relationships within institutions, but these changes would reflect an entirely different social order.

II

The letter controversy was quickly overshadowed by the implied and actual criticism levied against institutional psychiatry by a broad and loose coalition made up of charity reformers, members of state boards of charity, and urban "neurologists." The individual members of this coalition shared few common interests, but each, for different reasons, was opposed to institutional psychiatry even though the changes they suggested were fundamentally dissimilar.

The first group—the charity reformers—were legatees of a religiously based philanthropy whose roots had been established in the early nineteenth century. Their religious commitment had been reinforced by a faith in the Baconian form of science, which emphasized the collection and analysis of data and the formulation of general propositions that might serve as the basis of social policy. They had also modified their earlier dedication to voluntarism; in such states as Massachusetts, New York, and Penn-

sylvania they had begun to turn to administrative and bureaucratic solutions to deal with the problems of dependent groups.
Massachusetts led the way in 1863 with the creation of the nation's first Board of State Charities. Within little more than a
decade nearly a dozen states had followed suit. These early organizations reflected the belief that public welfare, if it was to be
contained, had to be placed on a more "scientific" basis, a view
that implied the imposition of greater controls upon public policy
in general and an uncoordinated system of individual institutions
in particular. In 1874 individuals from such boards from four
states met jointly with the members of the American Social Science Association, an organization created by Franklin B. Sanborn
and the Massachusetts Board of State Charities. The two groups
founded the National Conference of Charities and Corrections
(NCCC), which later emerged as the professional organization of
social workers.[6]

Although concerned with larger policy issues, the state boards
and the NCCC could hardly avoid involvement with mental hospitals. After all, these institutions represented the largest social
welfare investment made by states during the nineteenth century.
Generally speaking, neither the state boards nor the NCCC challenged institutional psychiatry directly or openly. Moreover, institutional psychiatrists attended the annual meetings of the NCCC.
Yet the very issues considered by the NCCC—the structure and
organization of hospitals, institutional and noninstitutional alternatives for the care of the mentally ill, appropriate modes of
hospital supervision—all implied that the existing state of affairs
was less than satisfactory and that changes were required.[7] The
fact that policy issues were being considered by individuals who
were not psychiatrists implied a loss of autonomy and control.
The resolutions introduced by Ray in 1875 at the meetings of the
AMSAII had tacitly acknowledged this point.

A much more serious challenge to the authority of institutional
psychiatrists came from the ranks of a group of urban practitioners
affiliated with the new specialty of "neurology." Neurology had
developed in Europe about the middle of the nineteenth century,
when investigators began to deal with psychopathology in terms
of the relationship between local structure and function. Those
physicians identified with the new specialty in the United States
had become interested in wounds involving nerve tissue during
the Civil War. By the 1870s they had broadened their interests to
include a wide range of "nervous" conditions, including the psy-

choses and neuroses as well as strictly somatic diseases involving the brain and central nervous system. Unlike the founders of institutional psychiatry—many of whom were identified with pietistic Protestantism and moral issues—neurologists tended to identify themselves with the world of science and especially European scientific medicine. Although they treated such amorphous conditions as dyspepsia, insomnia, and general malaise, they also dealt with organic disorders, including paralysis, hematomas, cerebral embolisms, locomotor ataxia, and chorea. Neurologists were concentrated for the most part in a few urban areas in the East. In the course of time they succeeded in establishing professorships for nervous diseases in New York City's most prestigous medical colleges, formed local organizations, and eventually a national association.[8]

Unlike their psychiatric counterparts, neurologists had no institutional base. There was no formal provision in the specialty for affiliation with a mental hospital, few of which were located in urban areas. Nor had the general hospital yet assumed its modern form; its philanthropic character and patient population rendered it unsuitable for neurologial practice. Neurologists usually established private practices and served as consultants to other physicians. Their clientele was relatively affluent, and they rarely, if ever, came into contact with the kinds of persons committed to public mental hospitals.

The specialty's concern with the brain and central nervous system, nevertheless, implied a certain competency to deal with mental disease. Some neurologists, including Edward C. Spitzka, were trained in Europe, where the distinction between neurology and psychiatry was vague, and where brain anatomy and physiology were stressed. But even if the neurological and psychiatric interpretations of mental illness were not fundamentally dissimilar, the social context of their respective practices remained far apart. In the introduction to his book on insanity in 1883, William A. Hammond (who served as Surgeon-General in the Union army during the Civil War and then helped to found the new specialty of neurology) thought it essential to mention the fact that he had never served as a mental hospital superintendent, a fact that presumably disqualified him to write on the subject. In defense he pointed to his teaching experience on "Diseases of the Mind and Nervous System" in four New York City medical colleges. Conceding that he had not seen as many cases as the average mental hospital superintendent, he observed "that a single case thoroughly studied is worth more as a lesson than a hundred that are simply looked at, and often from afar off." "The medical student who dissects one human body," Hammond added in what surely was intended as a slur, "is likely to learn more of anatomy than the janitor who sees hundreds of corpses brought to the dissecting-room."[9]

Before 1876 neurologists expressed relatively few criticisms of institutional psychiatry per se. The second issue of the *Journal of Nervous and Mental Disease* specifically disclaimed any intention to compete with the older *American Journal of Insanity*. Nevertheless, at the first meeting of the American Neurological Association (ANA) in 1875, there was an effort to bar superintendents of mental hospitals from becoming members. By 1878 open warfare had erupted between some neurologists and institutional psychiatrists. In March of that year Edward C. Spitzka gave a paper at the New York Neurologial Society, which was published the following month in the *Journal of Nervous and Mental Disease*. Spitzka, who was not noted for his restraint of language, insisted that the study of insanity—a disease that involved lesions—should be considered "a subdivision of neurology." He then went on to castigate institutional psychiatrists for their scientific ignorance and lack of knowledge of cerebral anatomy. After reading their reports he was

> inclined to believe that certain superintendents are experts in gardening and farming (although the farm account frequently comes out on the wrong side of the ledger), tin roofing (although the roof and cupola is usually leaky), drain-pipe laying (although the grounds are often moist and unhealthy), engineering (though the wards are either too hot or too cold), history (though their facts are incorrect, and their inferences beyond all measure so); in short, experts at everything except the diagnosis, pathology and treatment of insanity.

Spitzka then charged that the AMSAII was largely responsible for the sad state of affairs. Its members were "deficient in anatomical and pathological training, without a genuine interest in their noble specialty, [and] untrustworthy as to their reported results." He proposed the unification of psychiatry and neurology, with the latter playing the dominant role in mental hospitals even though its members would remain visiting physicians. "When I have used the terms ignorance, charlatanism, insincerity, and neglect," he added, "I have employed them because no other words could characterize so aptly the conditions to which I found it necessary to allude in the course of this inquiry."[10]

Within a month a committee of the Neurological Society recommended a crusade on behalf of "asylum reform"—one that involved the prohibition of mechanical restraint. Although not all neurologists endorsed this move, the Society clearly was on a collision course with institutional psychiatrists. The conflict within weeks became even more heated. A committee of the Medico-Legal Society of New York, which included Hammond and Spitzka, petitioned the New York legislature to investigate its state mental hospitals, particularly the Utica asylum. Hammond also published an anonymous editorial critical of John P. Gray and Utica. Dr. Eugene Grissom, superintendent of the North Carolina state asylum, replied to these attacks several weeks later when he read a widely publicized paper at the AMSAII attacking Hammond. Grissom charged that Hammond cared more for high fees than for intellectual consistency, and that his views were atheistic. Although Grissom's intemperate remarks were criticized, it was evident that the breach between the neurologists and psychiatrists was wide. Throughout the rest of 1878 the conflict became even more vituperative. When Spitzka published a bitter reply to Grissom's paper, both the medical and popular press were drawn into the controversy.[11]

The following year Hammond was invited to present his views before the New York State Medical Society. He began by charging that asylum officers, to legitimate their authority, had deliberately fostered the idea that insanity required institutionalization. Rejecting this claim, he insisted "that the medical profession is, as a body, fully as capable of treating cases of insanity as cases of any other disease, and that in many instances sequestration is not only unnecessary but positively injurious." Hammond went on to say there was "nothing surprisingly difficult, obscure or mysterious about diseases of the brain which can only be learned within the walls of an asylum." Questioning the scientific competency of institutional psychiatrists, he insisted that there were no lunatics "no matter how dangerous or troublesome, who would not be better cared for under the family system than within the walls of any lunatic asylum." Hammond qualified this generalization by conceding that severe or chronic cases could best be managed in a physician's home—a common practice in the nineteenth century. At the same time, he admitted that public institutions would be required for the poor. Hammond also urged that asylums be staffed and organized in the same manner as general hospitals, with a corps of visiting physicians.[12]

The controversy continued to rage between 1879 and 1882. In New York a state legislative inquiry took testimony from partisans on both sides; the final report conceded there were cases where patients had been mistreated, but rejected allegations of systematic and generalized abuses. Hammond and Spitzka continued to publish bitter attacks on their asylum counterparts. In one sense the neurologists were arguing for the legitimacy of their specialty. If insanity were a somatic disease, why could not ordinary physicians, assisted by neurologists, treat such conditions when the case warranted it? What justification did asylum physicians and the AMSAII—an exclusive organization that admitted only superintendents—have for their virtual monopoly over the care and treatment of the mentally ill? Why was American psychiatry, as compared with its European counterpart, backward and unscientific? Curiously enough, Hammond and Spitzka found relatively little support among their fellow neurologists. Many disliked the extreme nature of the charges, and disassociated themselves from the struggle; others were reluctant to carry on intraprofessional disagreements in public.[13]

In a deeper sense, however, the participants on both sides were not yet fully aware of the context and implications of their differences. Both groups were confident of their ability to understand and treat mental illness—a confidence scarcely justified by the facts. The neurologists, for the most part, had little contact with the patient population in institutions. The patients whom they saw in private practice tended to have problems which were of a different order of magnitude than those in mental hospitals. Institutional psychiatrists, on the other hand, never fully recognized the disjuncture between their theoretical views and their actual practice. On occasion some individuals would concede their lack of knowledge, but the specialty as a whole tended to rationalize its activities in terms of medical expertise. Indeed, the self-image of institutional psychiatrists precluded legitimation of a purely caretaker role. The conflict came to a close without resolving many of the questions that had been raised. By the mid-1880s the issues raised by Hammond, Spitzka, and others had all but disappeared from debate.

The conflict, however, revealed much about both groups. For one thing, it showed the weakness and vulnerability of institutional psychiatrists. Critics may have been in error when they accused asylum physicians of scientific incompetency, but they were correct when they pointed to the growing isolation of the specialty and the AMSAII from the field of medicine in general. For most neurologists, on the other hand, the question of institutional care became increasingly irrelevant. Moreover, the difficulties encountered by Spitzka and Hammond in their efforts to clarify the nature and etiology of mental illness fostered a spirit of caution. During the remainder of the century neurologists increasingly avoided psychiatric diseases and emphasized organic disorders. At the same time they institutionalized their specialty within general hospitals and medical schools. In doing so, they created alternative career choices for those interested in "nervous and mental diseases." Their urban location and private practice enhanced the attractiveness of the specialty, which slowly but surely became associated with a new technological and hospital-based medicine. The split between neurology and institutional psychiatry, as a matter of fact, was an aberration insofar as neurologists were concerned. For psychiatrists, however, institutional weakness and isolation from general hospitals and medical schools would slowly force a change in direction.[14]

III

Out of the controversy over patient rights and the attack on institutional psychiatry came the founding of the National Association for the Protection of the Insane and the Prevention of Insanity in 1880. There were several reasons why a national organization of this kind came into being at this time. Americans for several decades had been debating the issues of individual and civil rights for blacks and women, and the heightened concern with rights began to extend to other groups as well. The involvement of the legal profession added a further dimension as lawyers, judges, and physicians came into conflict over legal issues arising out of medical practice. It was precisely at this time that Thomas M. Cooley, one of the most significant legal thinkers of the late nineteenth century, turned his attention to the rights of the insane.

In a case that reached the Michigan Supreme Court in 1879, Cooley raised questions about the authority of medical superintendents of mental hospitals. He rejected the claim that a superintendent, acting in good faith, was immune from prosecution if confinement of a patient continued after the restoration of sanity.

"The rule of law," Cooley insisted in an evenly divided court, "no less than the rule of justice, is that he who commits the mistake shall bear the consequences. . . . Purity of motive should protect the officer against excessive damages, but individual rights must have settled and definite rules of protection, and cannot be left to depend upon the opinion of an officer as to what he may or may not do in abridging them." Two years later, using none of the invective employed in the conflict between neurologists and psychiatrists, Cooley published a temperate analysis that was by no means unfriendly to physicians. He noted, nevertheless, that the professional training of physicians inclined them to oppose investigations of their activities or of legal proceedings in commitment cases. After an extended analysis of the issues, he concluded that the patient's right to a trial to determine sanity or insanity was "unquestionable." "No certificate of a physician," he added,

> however honestly given, can determine the fact, for the physician possesses no part of the State judicial power. His fiat cannot be "due process of law," to deprive any man of his liberty. Those who act upon it may use it as an item of evidence in making out good faith, but it cannot protect them if it proves mistaken and untrue, and no legislative power could make it protect them. In England, a Parliament unfettered by constitutional restraints may give protection to those concerned in the confinement of a sane person, in reliance upon such a paper, if it shall be deemed wise to do so; but American legislatures exercise a delegated authority, and the power to legislate away the liberty of the citizen without the opportunity of a hearing has not been confided in them.[15]

In such an environment, it was hardly surprising that unchecked state authority and, by indirection, psychiatric autonomy, would be challenged.

The founding of the National Association for the Protection of the Insane and the Prevention of Insanity grew out of the hostility in New York City generated by the attacks on psychiatry by Spitzka, Hammond, and others. In 1879 an unsuccessful attempt had been made to replace the state's single lunacy commissioner with a three-member commission. An outgrowth of this effort was a public meeting in New York City in December, 1879. Among the participants were several civil service reformers, and Spitzka and George M. Beard (who had gained fame a decade earlier for his description of "neurasthenia"). The meeting adopted several resolutions, including one that urged the creation of a lunacy commission and another that called for a national organization devoted to the protection of the insane. In July, 1880, Beard, together with Drs. J. C. Shaw (superintendent of the King's County Lunatic Asylum in Brooklyn), Nathan Allen, and E. C. Seguin, presented papers at a special session on lunacy at the NCCC. The appearance of new forms of insanity, the increase in incidence, the helplessness of the insane, the necessity for public regulation, and the importance of raising the standard of care, Beard argued, made a new organization imperative. Such a society, he added, would disseminate knowledge about insanity, including its prevention, and above all, obtain *"universal recognition of the fact that it is no disgrace to be crazy."* Allen's paper dealt with hospital supervision, Seguin's with the right of the insane to liberty, and Shaw's with the practicability and value of nonrestraint.[16]

On July 1, 1880, the Association came into being. Although the preamble to its constitution acknowledged the existence of the AMSAII and the NCCC, it found both organizations inadequate. The AMSAII was a "professional and technical organization," and the NCCC dealt with many dependent and criminal groups as well as the mentally ill. The new organization, by way of contrast, brought together laypersons and professionals concerned with the insane. Its goals were broad: to encourage psychiatric and medical research; to develop an enlightened public opinion on the nature and treatment of insanity; to formulate an appropriate public policy; to work for legislation that would strengthen state supervision and secure the rights of patients; and to reduce public distrust by narrowing the differences between mental and general hospitals. The new organization, precisely because of its inclusive nature and broad objectives, was designed to appeal to a wide constituency. By noting specifically in its preamble that many insane persons did not require institutionalization, it placated neurological critics of psychiatry.[17]

The founding of the National Association initially met with considerable approval by medical and lay groups. A number of hospital psychiatrists also joined the organization, which held several meetings and confidently commenced publication of the *American Psychological Journal* in 1883. But within a year the organization was all but defunct. The loss of several leaders by death and resignation undoubtedly was a setback. There were other reasons, however, for its failure. Despite efforts at conciliation, the controversy between superintendents and their critics had never abated. The trial of Charles J. Guiteau for the assassination of President James A. Garfield in 1881 and 1882, for one thing, exacerbated existing differences. Gray appeared as a witness for the prosecution, and Spitzka for the defense. Such internecine warfare led some physicians to have second thoughts about the wisdom of discussing medical issues in a public forum. In early 1881, moreover, Dorman B. Eaton—who gave up a successful law practice to devote himself to the abolition of the spoils system and the transformation of city government—used the pages of the *North American Review* to launch an extreme attack on mental hospitals. Entitled "Despotism in Lunatic Asylums," the article condemned the closed nature of asylum management and noted the opposition of its officers to "inspection and publicity." In asserting the rights of the public, Eaton was implicitly bringing into question medical authority and legitimacy. Even neurological critics of hospitals had never acknowledged lay authority. Their central demands provided for neurolological participation in mental hospitals and a greater emphasis on outpatient practice, neither of which lessened medical control. In its first issue in 1883, the *American Psychological Journal* had called for cooperation between hospital psychiatrists and the organization. In that same year Spitzka conceded the necessity of institutional care and admitted that some of the agitation pertaining to restraint had "overstepped the bounds of legitimate criticism and reform." "Scientific zeal and integrity within asylums," he added, "will prove far better guarantees of humanity to the insane than associations of dilettante and newspaper editorials."[18]

The failure of the National Association for the Protection of the Insane and the Prevention of Insanity, however, had deeper roots. Its early hostility toward the AMSAII had been based on two beliefs: that hospital officials represented the major obstacles to constructive progress; and that medical science had already created the means for effective change in the treatment of the insane. Neither of these beliefs had a sound basis in fact. Hospital superintendents, to be sure, employed exaggerated rhetoric in validating their own claims. Yet beneath their rhetoric lay certain realities that effectively limited the courses of action open to them. The size of institutions, their physical plants, staff, and activities were dependent upon external influences. Their internal character, as we have already seen, was in large part shaped by the nature of their patients. Virtually no individual denied that hospitals had serious problems—including the superintendents under attack—but few persons were ready to concede that quick solutions were at hand.

The meeting of the AMSAII in the spring of 1881 illustrated the ambiguous position of institutional psychiatry. The opening remarks were given by Dr. Orpheus Everts, whose rhetoric was as colorful and exaggerated as those whom he attacked. Yet his words—precisely because they represented internal psychiatric perceptions—provided a critique regarding the allegations of institutional abuse. Everts noted that the total number of deaths and recoveries was always less than the number of admissions. The result was an "inevitable accumulation of the chronic and incurable class" which contributed to the negative reputation acquired by hospitals. He had only harsh words for lay reformers and their neurological allies. Everts pointed to several considerations all but overlooked: American hospitals did not differ in fundamental respects from their English and European counterparts; the existence of abuses (which he conceded) and the selection of unqualified superintendents had never been condoned; the parameters of the authority of superintendents could not be precisely stipulated "because the conditions which he has to meet can not be anticipated"; the debates at the AMSAII had always been open and dissent was common; and hospitals were already under constant surveillance by public officials. Moreover, the alternatives to institutional care were not necessarily in the interests of patients. "More insane persons," he insisted, "are ill-treated, injudiciously restrained, neglected and otherwise abused while among friends in the family relation, than suffer from similar treatment in the least reputable insane hospital in America, proportionately considered."[19]

Evert's defensive tone was reflected in the responses of his colleagues. Charles H. Hughes, a former superintendent and editor of the new *Alienist and Neurologist*, emphasized the differences between theoretical constructs regarding mental illness and the lessons derived from actual patient contact within institutions. His meaning was obvious; few critics had any actual hospital experience. Richard Gundry of the Maryland Hospital for the Insane, on the other hand, thought that "the best means of reform is to let the light in every place." He was ready to listen to those individuals having no institutional affiliation. His comments did not please Gray, whose position and views as editor of the *American Journal of Insanity* made him the favorite target of critics.

Gray specifically rejected Gundry's proposals, and the Association failed to take any positive steps.[20]

Although critics of institutional psychiatry persisted throughout the remainder of the nineteenth century, their tone became less strident and harsh. The invective of the late 1870s and early 1880s diminished markedly. As the dangers of unrestrained debate mounted, a decided effort was made to reduce the tensions growing out of underlying differences. In 1883 John B. Chapin, who was often in disagreement with his fellow superintendents, warned his colleagues that the continuing controversies were destroying public confidence in mental hospitals. "So virulent and persistent have been the assaults of various kinds, and so deep-rooted is the prejudice against what is called the asylum system that public confidence is well nigh destroyed." The appeal by critics to public opinion, Chapin noted, distressed the families of relatives in institutions; it deterred young physicians from entering the specialty; and it ignored "the restraining and conservative influences of professional comity and courtesy which should govern the relations of medical men toward their professional brethren." Even more significant, mental hospitals were now regarded "as objects of suspicion; as convenient places for the 'incarceration' of persons by designing relatives, and lunatic prisons, proper only for the detention of the criminal and dangerous insane." Chapin did not reject state supervision, but preferred a cooperative rather than an adversarial relationship. He also condemned the appeal by physicians to "outside . . . tribunals illy prepared by technical training to render judgment."[21]

Fear of conducting professional debates in public was not the only factor that resulted in a decline of the politics of confrontation. Equally significant was the fact that policy discussions continued to be conducted within the framework of institutional care. This being the case, all parties recognized that it was not in their interest to undermine public confidence to the point where the legitimacy of mental hospitals would be endangered. In addition, the differences between institutional psychiatrists and critics rarely involved diametrically opposing beliefs. Even the neurologists who advocated outpatient treatment never suggested that hospital care was unnecessary. In the end, responsibility for deciding policy issues increasingly shifted to legislatures and external regulatory agencies, thereby diminishing the authority of superintendents and professional organizations such as the AMSAII. The transformation of American psychiatry that began in the 1880s also diminished some of the differences that had created seemingly irreconcilable tensions.

Two examples illustrate the less strident atmosphere of the late nineteenth century. The first involved the discussion of commitment laws. During the Guiteau trial in 1881 and 1882, friction between the legal and psychiatric professions had increased. By the end of the decade and in the early 1890s, both groups were still debating commitment procedures, but in a different spirit. Although disagreements abounded, there was relatively little disposition to characterize opponents in harsh terms. Similarly, when Clark Bell, president of the influential Medico-Legal Society of New York, challenged the continued use of restraints in the early 1890s, he went out of his way to solicit comments from proponents as well as opponents. Bell observed that much of the controversy had been "a delusion," and insisted that the motives of the early superintendents were "as pure and as good as those who preceded and who succeeded them." There were far fewer differences between both schools than appeared at first sight, he added. Bell's conciliatory approach could hardly offend even those with whom he disagreed.[22]

The muted reaction in 1894 to S. Weir Mitchell's address to the American Medico-Psychological Association (formerly the AMSAII) was symbolic of the new era. In that year Mitchell, the eminent neurologist, was invited to address the organization on its fiftieth birthday. He first refused because he intended to be critical. When the invitation was renewed, he agreed to speak. Mitchell first sent out letters to more than two dozen colleagues soliciting their views about American mental hospitals. Most were critical of but not hostile toward their institutional colleagues. Even Spitzka expressed the belief that the condition of American psychiatry had "improved in every respect," and he paid homage to figures such as Luther V. Bell, Isaac Ray, Thomas S. Kirkbride, and others. In his address Mitchell compared psychiatry to other medical specialties and found it wanting. Psychiatry, he said, remained isolated from medicine. "You were the first of the specialists," he added, "and you have never come back into line. It is easy to see how this came about. You soon began to live apart, and you still do so. Your hospitals are not our hospitals; your ways are not our ways. You live out of range of critical shot; you are not preceded and followed in your ward by clever rivals, or watched by able residents fresh with the learning of the schools." Mitchell went on to deplore the absence of a spirit of scientific inquiry in mental hospitals; the widespread distrust of asylum therapeutics; the psychiatric disregard of any responsibility to educate the public about the dangers of insanity and its treatment; and the great role of political considerations in hospital management and administration.[23]

Yet when Mitchell completed his lengthy address, the delegates elected him an honorary member. Subsequent discussions of his remarks in both the deliberations of the Association and the medical literature remained muted. Walter Channing, who published a formal reply, observed that "nearly every point taken up by Doctor Mitchell has in some form been discussed by those having the care of the insane." Another superintendent was equally emphatic when he wrote that "nothing new has been brought forward; and not only that, but everything demanded in the address, has in more practical form been clamored for steadily, by hospital officers, during the past ten years."[24]

IV

The absence of any major controversy following Mitchell's address indicated that the criticisms of and challenges to psychiatric legitimacy had already had some impact on the specialty. But the changes in American psychiatry that began in the late nineteenth century were not simply the products of external criticism; they represented also a response to its increasingly marginal status. For much of its history psychiatry had been an administrative specialty; superintendents were involved in providing care for patients in large and complex institutions. The rationalization of such activities in predominantly medical terms was in many respects synonymous with a demand for autonomy. Admittedly, the freedom of superintendents to do as they wished was never total, in part because of the constraints imposed by state legislatures. Yet psychiatry had considerable freedom during the nineteenth century to shape mental hospitals; the most significant limiting factor was the nature of their patient population.

Beginning in the 1860s, states moved to rationalize and centralize all of their welfare functions. In so doing they created a nascent regulatory apparatus whose activities began to impinge on the autonomy of hospital superintendents. The determination of policy began to shift toward the state, and superintendents found their authority shrinking as external regulations slowly widened in scope. When the AMSAII took issue with public supervisory activities in 1875, the Illinois Board of State Commissioners of Public Charities reacted with firmness. Expressing "great respect" for hospital superintendents, the Board nevertheless doubted "whether outsiders are not quite as competent to judge of the results of treatment and of the effect upon the community as the superintendents are." "We do not think," its members added in telling terms, that superintendents "should be allowed to dictate legislation, nor do we believe that it is good policy for them to oppose intelligent and honest supervision and inspection by legally constituted authority." The AMSAII, furthermore, was "attached to the present system," and its members were incapable of conceiving of "necessary innovations." Indeed, the establishment of public charity boards should have been welcomed by the specialty because they could help to solve the difficulties facing the "most perplexed" superintendents. The Illinois board was explicit, and its reaction was by no means atypical.[25]

The fact that mental hospitals were public institutions presented an additional threat to psychiatric autonomy. As public employees, superintendents were both appointed by and responsible to others. Given the nature of their position, it was inevitable that many would function in a political way. From a psychiatric perspective, of course, the care and treatment of the mentally ill was presumably apolitical. The determination of strictly medical concerns should not be determined by external political authority. The rejection of external supervision in 1875 was reinforced nineteen years later when the American Medico-Psychological Association (AMPA) adopted a series of resolutions intended to insulate hospitals from politics. The resolutions urged the selection of superintendents "solely on professional grounds" and with tenure "during good behavior or competency." Authority to appoint subordinate officers would remain in the hands of the superintendent, and assistant physicians would be selected after successfully passing an impartial civil service examination.[26] In effect, the specialty reaffirmed its long-standing demand to control the selection of the professional staff in mental hospitals.

During the late nineteenth century superintendents as a group emphasized the degree to which their careers and institutions were subject to the vagaries of politics. Dismissals of hospital physicians after elections for public office invariably brought charges of political manipulation and favoritism. The specialty attributed many of its problems to the growing politicization of hospitals in the late nineteenth century. "Partisan politics," wrote Dr. Henry

Smith Williams in the *North American Review*, had "become influential in the conduct of the asylums in which the dependent insane are cared for. The baleful effects of this custom are as yet fully understood only by those persons who have had opportunity to view the subject as it were from the inside. The public at large is still in ignorance of the real bearings of the matter; hence the continuance of the evil."[27]

The dismissal of superintendents was often attributed to partisan politics when such was sometimes not the case. Personnel changes occasionally reflected new policy decisions, or a desire to have more sympathetic individuals in charge of public institutions, which, after all, were supported by public funds. In other instances dismissals were accompanied by charges of incompetency or illegal behavior. Williams' arguments, for example, were rejected by a distinguished group of Philadelphia physicians, who insisted that his description of the insane department of the Philadelphia Hospital was grossly inaccurate.[28]

The dismissal of Richard Dewey, superintendent of the Illinois Eastern Hospital for the Insane at Kankakee between 1879 and 1893, illustrates the difficulty of offering any simple or clear generalizations on this issue. His firing was widely attributed to the desire of the newly elected governor, John P. Altgeld, to replace officials identified with the Republican party. Altgeld, on the other hand, insisted that his action was based on evidence of patient abuse, financial mismanagement, and partisan political activity. Adolf Meyer, then on the medical staff of the hospital, had a distinctly unfavorable impression of the institution and felt that political considerations had played a role in its operations.[29]

Shortly thereafter Altgeld appointed S. V. Clevenger as the new superintendent. Clevenger was a well-known activist who had come to public attention after his exposé of conditions at the Cook County Insane Asylum in the mid-1880s. Upon assuming office, he was presented with a request by a prominent member of the state legislature to appoint specific individuals to responsible positions. There was additional political pressure when a subsequent request alluded to the institution's forthcoming appropriation. Clevenger was not averse to appointing Democrats to replace Republicans, provided they were competent, but he had distinct reservations about the individuals recommended. Within three months of his appointment Clevenger found himself in conflict with the trustees, who resisted his decision to dismiss one physician and several nonmedical employees. Eventually the trustees insisted that Clevenger take a "vacation" for health reasons, and then forced him to resign. Meyer believed that Clevenger was attempting to introduce the principle of civil service reform, but "met resistance and finally broke down, so that he was considered insane even by his friends." Others felt that he was an alcoholic who exhibited "delirious delusions."[30] In short, it is difficult to determine whether or not Clevenger's dismissal was justified on professional grounds.

Equally significant, the social composition of institutional psychiatry had changed, thus weakening the earlier commitment to binding principles. In the early 1870s hospitals began to employ female physicians to deal with female patients. By the end of the century as many as 200 women had worked in mental hospitals. In 1900 38 institutions employed 41 female physicians, although 23 were concentrated in Pennsylvania, New York, and Massachusetts, where state legislation called for the appointment of female physicians. Social rather than medical forces were largely responsible for the growing number of female doctors in mental hospitals. The differentiation of sex roles in the early nineteenth century had created a semi-autonomous "woman's sphere" which presupposed a world in which women could offer each other a kind of intimate friendship and companionship unavailable in a male-dominated society. Related to this attitude was the belief that female patients might be more open and receptive to physicians of the same sex, especially in cases where sexual considerations were involved in mental disease. Such attitudes were by no means unique to psychiatry, but cut across several fields. Some women, for example, succeeded in persuading states to create separate prisons for women, staffed exclusively by other women. At the same time nineteenth-century feminism sought to modify the rigid sex roles that had circumscribed the lives of women. By the second half of the century women were slowly beginning to move into the professions, including medicine. The breaking of professional barriers was not easy, as Mary Putnam Jacobi's famous attack on exclusionary practices in 1882 demonstrated.[31]

Opposition to the employment of female physicians within mental hospitals on the whole was not intense, in part because hospitals were already structured along sex lines. Although resistance was by no means absent, male physicians were receptive to the idea that female patients might be more responsive to female physicians. Those who rejected the intellectual equality of the sexes were prone to accept the moral and emotional superiority of women—a belief that helped to open hitherto closed doors. In some states male physicians played a leading role in breaking down discriminatory practices. Hiram Corson in Pennsylvania fought for passage of a state law mandating the appointment of a female superintendent for the female department with co-equal authority with her male counterpart. Although the law that passed permitted but did not mandate the change, the Norristown State Hospital adopted the new system and selected Alice Bennett for the position. At the Harrisburg hospital, on the other hand, Margaret Cleaves was placed in a subordinate position to the male superintendent, thus defeating the purpose of the legislation.[32]

Within hospitals female physicians encountered difficulties because of their sex. Males received higher salaries, and chances of promotion for a woman to a superintendency were nil. The very presence of women, however, tended to break down the homogeneity of the specialty, even when therapeutic and theoretical differences were unrelated to sex roles. A woman on occasion emerged as a prominent dissident. Alice Bennett, who enjoyed more autonomy by virtue of her position, for example, became a proponent of nonrestraint; she was one of the small group of institutional psychiatrists who belonged to the National Association for the Protection of the Insane. Most female physicians—precisely because of their subordinate status—could hardly offer the kind of loyalty to the specialty then demanded. The fact that many women left institutions for private practice was indicative of their general dissatisfaction.[33]

<h2 style="text-align:center">V</h2>

The seeming decline in psychiatric autonomy slowly led the specialty to redefine its character. Beginning in the 1880s the AMSAII began to alter its membership requirements, modify the founding principles adopted in 1851 and 1853 regarding the structure and administration of mental hospitals, and eventually to change its name. All of these actions symbolized the shift away from administrative and managerial issues and toward a greater concern with mental disease itself rather than with the care of insane patients.[34]

One of the first indications of change came in 1884, when the AMSAII appointed a committee to consider the possibility of opening membership to assistant physicians. The following year a three-member committee, headed by Pliny Earle and including Orpheus Everts and John Curwen, reported their views on the matter. A seemingly minor concern, the issue of membership was in many respects crucial. In the past the Association, as its name indicated, had limited its membership to superintendents concerned with managerial and administrative issues. To open membership to assistant physicians, on the other hand, implied a shift toward medical and scientific concerns that would change the orientation of the specialty. The committee emphasized the institutional origins of psychiatry, the fact that early superintendents were among the few persons knowledgeable about the care of the mentally ill, and the limited number of assistant physicians who had been in the field. By way of contrast, there were considerably more than two hundred assistant physicians by 1885, some of whom had greater experience than those above them. Moreover, many assistants had a superior medical education and would eventually become superintendents. Earle and his colleagues therefore recommended that assistant medical officers with five years' continuous service in one or more hospitals be admitted to membership in the Association.[35]

During the ensuing discussion the obvious question of a change in the name of the Association arose. Earle suggested that the AMSAII become known as a "medico-psychological society"—a title "based upon the objects of the society" rather than on the professional status of its members. A vigorous debate followed, for it was clear that many members recognized that a change in name implied a change in function as well. Although Earle and Curwen, two of the older members, favored the change in name, Gray and the majority were opposed. A change might undermine tradition and blur the distinction between psychological and administrative functions. When motions to rename the Association failed, a resolution passed making assistant physicians ex-officio members. Admission of assistant physicians had the added virtue of giving the Association a means of encouraging states to select experienced men as superintendents, and thereby confirming a selection process under the aegis of the specialty.[36]

The change in membership, however modest, was a harbinger of things to come. Two years later a committee was appointed to report on the "propositions" of the Association (a series of policy resolutions codified in 1851 and 1853 and published as a body in 1876). Generally speaking, these propositions were concerned with the construction and organization of hospitals, and emphasized the managerial and administrative character of the specialty. In 1888 the committee reported back to the Association. The original propositions, noted its members, had been the work of Kirkbride and Ray. Without implying direct criticism or disrespect, the committee suggested that the time had come for the Association to adopt a new stance. It introduced a series of resolutions which, taken as a group, implied a fundamental shift in the nature of the specialty. All hospitals for the insane should be constructed to facilitate "individual treatment," and to be more in keeping with modern general hospitals. The report distinguished between mental hospitals and chronic facilities—a position that was diametrically opposed to the views of the founding fathers. The impending break with tradition was also evident in the recommendation dealing with the qualifications of superintendents. They were now expected to be "physicians, thoroughly educated in the sciences, and experimentally successful practitioners of medicine." The committee, in addition, accepted the principle of external inspection by the state.[37]

After a lengthy discussion the Association declined to endorse the new principles or reaffirm the older ones. The sentiment of the members was that the AMSAII should not commit itself to a binding set of principles that would be inappropriate for future generations. Even Pliny Earle, who was present when the original propositions had been adopted, conceded in a letter that the principles were obsolete and engendered a belief that the Association was "practically averse to progress in improvement." The failure to take any action suggested that the propositions were virtually a dead letter and reflective merely of an era when construction and management of institutions had been the primary concerns. By implication, the members were also hinting that their specialty was headed toward a quite different future, even though the outlines of that future were unclear.[38]

Three years later Edward Cowles, superintendent of the McLean Asylum—an institution that symbolized the new "scientific psychiatry"—reviewed the history of the Association and paid homage to its founders. The time had come, Cowles concluded, for the specialty to move in a new direction. He insisted that the primary purpose of the AMSAII was "the promotion of the study of all subjects pertaining to the care and treatment of the insane." After noting that only 132 out of 271 members were superintendents (102 were assistant physicians with five or more years of service), he proposed a series of changes intended to transform the organization into a more effective institution for the "advancement of its scientific work."[39]

The comments of Henry M. Hurd of the Johns Hopkins Hospital—the most influential medical institution in the nation—proved revealing. Hurd insisted that the time had come to change both the name and functions of the Association. In the past the AMSAII was composed of men "who were here simply because they were superintendents of asylums." The organization now needed members not only with managerial abilities, but persons "familiar with mental diseases and competent to investigate the problems which come up in connection with the treatment of those diseases."[40]

The AMSAII in 1892 heeded Cowles's suggestions. It changed its name to the American Medico-Psychological Association (AMPA). At the same time, a new constitution was adopted that stipulated that the object of the organization was "the study of all subjects pertaining to mental disease, including the care, treatment, and promotion of the best interests of the insane." Active membership was conferred upon all superintendents, and associate membership was reserved for assistant physicians. An assistant physician, however, became eligible for full membership after three years of experience.[41] In his famous presidential address three years later, Cowles defined the new psychiatry in terms far removed from the generation of Kirkbride and Ray:

> The alienist, as a psychologist, is a general physician who is a student of neurology, and uses its anatomy and physiology; but he does a great deal more, for he must include all the bodily organs. . . . He is being aided by the more promising contributions from organic chemistry; and bacteriology. . . . Thus it is that psychiatry is shown, more than ever before, to be dependent upon general medicine.[42]

These structural and organizational changes by no means implied an immediate clinical shift. In 1895 a group of younger dissidents, including Adolf Meyer, formed an Association of Assistant Physicians of Hospitals for the Insane—an organization whose members were concerned with scientific rather than managerial issues. Although the organization never became a significant force, its very establishment was indicative of the belief, as L. Pierce Clark put it, "that the great majority of the medical men . . . in State Hospitals have a much less desire to progress along strictly scientific lines than most of us can conceive." The organizational changes, nonetheless, were indicative of the subsequent transformation of the specialty. Between 1874 and 1884 sixteen papers dealing with treatment of the mentally ill were given at the meetings of the AMSAII; in the following decade this number doubled. The content of papers after 1884, moreover, reflected a new interest in pathology, physiology, and pharmacology, and a willingness to experiment with surgical and endocrinological treatments of insanity. All of these approaches had relatively little in common with mid-nineteenth-century moral therapeutics.[43]

VI

By the 1890s the transformation of American psychiatry was well underway. As the specialty came under criticism in the preceding two decades by individuals committed to "scientific" medicine, its members became increasingly dissatisfied with what appeared to be an outmoded and obsolete emphasis on managerial concerns. Ultimately they began to reorient their specialty. An earlier generation had emphasized managerial and administrative aspects and in so doing had made the care of institutionalized patients the primary goal. Their colleagues of the late nineteenth century, by way of contrast, were as much concerned with disease as they were with individuals, and slowly the former replaced the latter as the central concern.

The emphasis on pathology, of course, reflected the general reorientation of medicine that was altering the social role of physicians in the late nineteenth century. As medicine became identified with bacteriology and other biological and physical sciences, its practitioners created a new doctor-patient relationship. More and more patients assumed a passive position, especially as physicians justified their dominant role in terms of their special training and knowledge. Imbued with the ideals of European, and especially German, science, American physicians created a new institutional complex that placed the modern general hospital and an increasingly elaborate technology at the center of medical practice. To those entering psychiatry, it appeared that the specialty had to change its ways if it was not to become a backwater.[44]

In changing the nature of psychiatric practice, however, activist physicians unwittingly made the mental hospital the focus of their dissatisfaction. Institutional psychiatry thus came to represent the past, and the new "scientific" psychiatry the future.

That the new psychiatry offered no therapies that were demonstrably effective, or that its concept of mental disease for the most part rested on a vague faith in future progress, was all but unheeded. In the identification of the mental hospital as the enemy, the stage was set for the subsequent emergence of private practice and outpatient work, a development that constituted a sharp rejection of the earlier approach. The result was the beginnings of an implicit abandonment of institutionalized patients, who constituted by far the bulk of the identifiable mentally ill.

CHAPTER FOUR

The Search for Public Policy

ALTHOUGH INSTITUTIONAL psychiatrists perceived of themselves as the prime molders of mental hospitals, the reality was quite different. The care and treatment of the mentally ill involved far more than the actions of psychiatrists or even the reactions of patients, if only because more than 90 percent of all patients were in *public* institutions. To a significant extent, therefore, patients, psychiatrists, and hospitals were subject to external authority exercised through legislative and executive agencies and mechanisms. Although public agencies and officials seemed far removed from the daily activities of mental hospitals, their actions and decisions often had a pervasive and enduring impact.

During the last quarter of the nineteenth century, state governments were deeply involved with policy issues relating to dependent groups. The widening role of the state, in part, reflected the decline of an older system of poor relief whose antecedents could be traced to fifteenth- and sixteenth-century England. The English system, which was codified during the reign of Elizabeth I, was based on the belief that public order required appropriate mechanisms for the relief of poverty and dependency. These legal codes gave fiscal and supervisory responsibility to local communities for dependent persons within their jurisdiction, and also facilitated the setting up of private trusts by individuals. In America during the nineteenth century a number of developments combined to undermine this system of poor relief that had existed for nearly three centuries: economic and industrial changes, geographical mobility, a growing and increasingly heterogeneous population, the emergence of new family structures, recurring business cycles, and the concentration of population within large urban centers.

A growing awareness that traditional mechanisms no longer met current needs led to the creation of a complex institutional structure in America during the first half of the nineteenth century. State involvement in welfare, however, was not based initially on a systematic and comprehensive analysis of existing

problems nor on the future consequences of any particular policies. Indeed, many policy decisions were ad hoc responses to immediate circumstances. Public policy for the first two-thirds of
the nineteenth century was mostly the result an incremental
decision-making process. Intent and outcome were often unrelated, a situation that gave rise to new policy issues. In response
to their growing welfare functions, a number of states established
boards of public charities in the 1860s and 1870s in order to begin
the process of retrenchment.[1] The very existence of such semi-
permanent bureaucratic agencies, however, introduced a new dimension. The agenda for dependency-related discussions increasingly was set by public officials not directly involved with the
care and treatment of the mentally ill, a development that tended
to diminish the authority of institutional psychiatrists and make
them more receptive to new roles outside of mental hospitals.

Beneath the rhetoric that accompanied debates over the proper
configuration of public policy in the late nineteenth century lay
a number of complex and perhaps unresolvable dilemmas. At any
given time a specific proportion of patients admitted to mental
hospitals did not recover and tended to remain institutionalized
for long periods of time. The accumulation of such chronic cases
posed troubling questions for public officials, psychiatrists, and
families. Should the state continue to build and maintain large
and relatively expensive central hospitals for a growing mentally
ill population? Did the presence of large numbers of chronic patients undermine therapeutic goals? What kind of setting provided
the best safeguards against the abuse of patients and the most
efficient form of supervision? What level of government—local
or state—should assume fiscal responsibility for the care of the
insane?

The answers that were given to these and similar questions in
the late nineteenth century varied in the extreme and reflected
in part the occupational and professional perceptions of particular
groups. Psychiatrists for the most part tended to define the problem in traditional terms and emphasized the need for medical
autonomy. They feared that separate custodial institutions for
chronic patients would lead to a dual system for acute and chronic
cases that was susceptible to the kind of abuses that were common
before the founding of mental hospitals. Local officials were concerned with the costs of providing long-term care for chronic
patients, and often supported a state takeover of all responsibilities pertaining to the mentally ill in order to relieve their con-

stituents of the financial burdens involved. State officials feared that a division of authority maximized the possibilities for abuse and rendered supervision all the more difficult. They therefore moved toward the centralization and rationalization of authority in state hands, even while manifesting receptiveness to novel institutional forms that might control costs and at the same time provide humane care for patients. The response by each group was by no means irrational, but reflected in large measure their respective constituencies.

The adoption of particular policies often had unforseen consequences. This occurred not necessarily because of malevolence or incompetency—although neither was completely absent—but because of the ability of individuals and groups to alter the nature of their responses and thus to introduce new elements that had a bearing on the outcome. When states assumed full responsibility for the care and treatment of the mentally ill, for example, local officials saw advantages in redefining insanity to include aged and senile patients, thereby making possible their transfer from almshouses to hospitals and shifting the fiscal burden to the state. The result was a rapid increase in the size of mental hospitals and a change in their function. Similarly, when state officials strengthened bureaucratic and regulatory mechanisms, psychiatrists began to alter the nature of their specialty, thus diminishing their commitment to the institutionalized mentally ill. The confidence in the ready availability of solutions to existing problems, moreover, tended to perpetuate continuous dissatisfaction with the institutional configuration that existed at any given moment. Consequently, public policy often resembled the pendulum of a clock; when the pendulum reached one extreme, it could move only in the opposite direction.

The absence of any consistent *national* policy toward the mentally ill reflected a political culture in which regional and local interests played a dominant role. Responsibility and authority were centered in numerous state jurisdictions, where traditions and practices often differed. Equally significant, there was no organized national group capable of transforming the care of the mentally ill into a major political or public issue. Families of patients in mental hospitals had turned to institutionalization as a last resort; their involvement ended when a relative was committed. Patients without families, by way of contrast, lacked anyone to represent their interests. For the larger public the institutionalized mentally ill were virtually invisible. Under such circumstances public policy tended to be shaped by public officials or psychiatrists whose perceptions were molded by their own immediate concerns.

I

During the last quarter of the nineteenth century the problems posed by dependency and disease seemingly acquired a new sense of urgency. Recurring economic panics and depressions, labor unrest and violence, the arrival of new immigrants from Eastern and Southern Europe, and the fear that pauperism, crime, and degeneracy were on the rise, all combined to raise questions about the future of the republic. Although fear and doubt never became dominant, they remained underlying elements in the debates regarding social problems. Discussions at the annual meetings of the NCCC in the 1870s and 1880s, for example, centered on social policy issues. Delegates—most of whom were associated with state boards of charity—were concerned both with aiding needy and indigent persons, and with rationalizing what appeared to be a welfare system that lacked a clear and coherent foundation. It was not surprising that public policy regarding the mentally ill would become a subject of interest and controversy; mental hospitals constituted one of the major economic investments made by state governments in the nineteenth century.

In the two decades after 1870 the construction of new state mental hospitals proceeded at a rapid pace. Between 1850 and 1869 35 new state institutions opened their doors; in the succeeding two decades 59 others came into existence.[2] The difference was even more pronounced than these statistics indicated; hospitals built after 1870 tended to be much larger in size. Ironically, the very expansion in the number of state institutions only accentuated the uncoordinated and often contradictory nature of public policy. Initially the founding of hospitals had been based on the assumption that mentally ill patients could be cured within a specific period of time—generally assumed to be a matter of months—and that the discharge of recovered patients would create room for new admissions. This assumption proved inaccurate. Many patients failed to recover and tended to remain institutionalized for long periods of time. Faced with a seemingly insoluble dilemma, hospital officials pursued two strategies: they expanded the size of their institutions, and at the same time discharged chronic patients back into the local community. In many instances the absence of a supporting network forced local officials to place discharged chronic patients in almshouses.

For much of the nineteenth century, therefore, responsibility for the dependent insane was shared by state hospitals and local almshouses. In 1872 Michigan had 45 poorhouses providing care at one time or another during the year for 3,300 paupers. Of these, 584 were children under the age of sixteen, 402 were insane, 161 were idiots, 50 were blind, and 22 were deaf and dumb. "This is an aggregation of misery," complained the Michigan board, "which is at present committed to unskilled hands, with restricted facilities, entirely inadequate to its care."[3]

The situation in Michigan was hardly unique. Virtually all almshouses cared for a heterogeneous population; the only common characteristic of inmates was their dependent status. A survey of 7 New Jersey counties in 1893 revealed the presence of 125 insane paupers in local almshouses. Two years later another study found nearly 500 "incurable" persons in 29 almshouses—excluding the insane—suffering from such diseases as consumption, paralysis, palsey, epilepsy, cancer, Bright's disease, rheumatism, and heart disease, among other ailments. In 1882 about 1,800 inmates of county almshouses in Pennsylvania were insane. Massachusetts had an even more complex institutional pattern. In addition to those insane persons confined in local almshouses, the state had quarters for harmless and incurable insane paupers at the state almshouse in Tewksbury—a large institution that contained facilities for foundling children as well.[4]

As the number of chronic patients increased, some states began to experiment with other kinds of institutions. In 1869 New York opened the Willard Asylum, which was designed for chronic pauper insane persons previously confined in county poorhouses, and for insane persons discharged from state hospitals as incurable. The experiment hardly provided a panacea; Willard grew so rapidly that it was soon unable to accept all the state's chronic insane patients. Two years after it opened, the legislature passed a law authorizing the State Board of Charities to exempt any county from the requirement of sending chronic cases to Willard if the county provided proper buildings and had the means to care for such persons. By 1880 the Board had granted exemptions to 14 counties whose asylums held more than 1,200 persons. The Board also estimated that 758 other mentally ill individuals were cared for in nonexempt county poorhouses, the state law notwithstanding. The entire system left much to be desired, insisted William

P. Letchworth and Sarah M. Carpenter in their analysis of the chronic insane in exempted counties in 1881. Originally the exemptions were intended "as a *temporary measure*" until the state had constructed sufficient facilities of its own. Under these circumstances the counties affected had not made significant investments in their facilities, and many of the chronic insane suffered accordingly. The State Board of Charities was unwilling to order such counties to improve their institutions because the option of removing such patients to state hospitals did not exist.[5]

The rapid development of a two-tiered system for the care of the insane in the nineteenth century followed rapid population growth and a corresponding increase in the number of chronic cases. When the Census Bureau collected aggregate data in 1904, it found that more than two-thirds of the patients in mental hospitals had been there for a year or more, and nearly two-fifths for five or more years. The census data only confirmed the fears of those already involved with policy three decades earlier. "What are we to do with the chronic insane, and how are they to be supported?" asked Nathan Allen at the second meeting of the NCCC.

> Unless there are some means besides death, of eliminating and removing the incurable and the harmless insane from our lunatic hospitals, these institutions become filled up with a class of patients, very few of whom can ever be benefited by curative treatment. . . . After the insane have passed through the curative stages of treatment, without relief, and settled down into an incurable, harmless state, what is to become of them?[6]

Virtually every state at one time or other in the late nineteenth century confronted mounting numbers of chronic and harmless insane persons. The issue was most acute in the older and more populous states of the Northeast. The Willard Asylum in New York was but a harbinger of the future. After moving the Worcester hospital to a new location, Massachusetts converted the old plant into an Asylum for the Chronic Insane in 1877. Shortly thereafter the New York State Inebriate Asylum in Binghampton became a hospital for chronic mentally ill patients. Newer and less populated states faced the same problem.[7]

In addition to the growing number of chronic mentally ill persons, many states faced certain anomalies and contradictions related to the financial and administrative system that governed mental hospitals. At the time that mental hospitals were established in the early nineteenth century, the care of dependent groups was still a local responsibility. Building upon this tradition, most legislatures provided the capital funds for the acquisition of land and the construction of buildings. Operating expenses, on the other hand, were paid by a weekly charge levied on the community in which the patient resided. Patients from families with sufficient means were expected to pay their own way, thereby reducing the charges to their communities. For individuals with no fixed residences (migrants and immigrants), the state generally assumed the costs.

Such a system produced contradictory results. Since the charges for most patients were arbitrarily fixed by the legislature, hospitals often found themselves lacking sufficient operating funds. To make up the difference, private patients were charged sums higher than those paid by local communities. This practice then led some institutions to provide private patients with better accommodations and other privileges, which often created internal conflicts and jealousies. The entire system also ignored the different operating costs of institutions whose physical plants were not identical. Hospital care, moreover, was far more expensive than almshouse care—a situation that created an incentive for local communities to retain their patients rather than committing them to state institutions. Finally, the peculiarities of the system made it impossible to determine the comparative cost effectiveness of individual hospitals. In an elaborate study of the financing of charitable institutions in 1879, the New York State Comptroller recommended that all institutional receipts be paid directly into the state treasury; the legislature, in turn, would provide each institution with an annual appropriation based upon careful cost estimates. The "lack of system," he insisted, "is one of the serious defects in the present management of our charitable institutions, and until there has been substituted uniformity and clearness in place of the complications, diversities and imperfections of the systems now in use, there will always be unjust discriminations and occasion for misunderstanding and criticism."[8]

II

The concern for dependent groups was not a new phenomenon, as the founding of various institutions in the antebellum decades had demonstrated. During the last third of the nineteenth century, however, this concern began to assume a new form. The tradition of religious commitment to charity persisted. Increasingly, however, concepts of welfare were affected by a new-found commitment to a more scientific analysis. In practice this meant a shift away from a voluntary mode of dealing with dependent groups to administrative and bureaucratic solutions. Symbolic of this shift was the growing emphasis on the collection and analysis of quantitative data. Indeed, many of the individuals who played an important role in late nineteenth-century public welfare shared a radical faith that quantitative research, when combined with administrative rationality, could replace politics.

As long as dependency had remained a local concern, its visibility as a social and political issue was limited. But as states expanded their activities, the category of dependency gained a new dimension, if only because expenditures at the state level were reported in aggregate terms and thus became far more visible. Between 1863 and 1880, twelve states established boards of charity which helped to transform both the perception of the problem as well as the policies practiced. Members of these boards (located in such strategic states as Massachusetts, New York, Pennsylvania, Illinois, Wisconsin, and Michigan) introduced a new element, for they dealt with dependency as a *general* category. In a certain sense, comprehensive policymaking diminished the uniqueness of the mentally ill; they became one dependent group among many.[9]

At the time of their founding and during their early years, state boards of charity had relatively few regulatory functions. The laws that created them, however, gave them extensive data-gathering functions, investigatory authority, and, above all, access to the legislative and executive branches of government. In this respect they were strategically situated. Their proximity to data and their ability to define issues and to establish an agenda for discussion provided a firm base from which their members could expand their role and authority. Moreover, such boards were not perceived as the representative of any special group; their members claimed to speak for the entire community. The creation of the NCCC also gave individual members a national platform.[10]

The expanding role of the state boards of charity occurred at the very same time that the influence of institutional psychiatry was declining. Faced with both internal dissent and external criticism, the AMSAII was in no position to resist, and the structural changes between 1885 and 1892 only confirmed its lessening interest in the administrative and managerial aspects of hospitals. Consequently, the influence on policy that superintendents exercised between the founding of the Association in 1844 and the 1860s declined sharply. For better or worse, the destiny of the institutionalized mentally ill would rest in the hands of individuals whose authority was derived from their affiliation with the administrative organs of state governments.

Like others of their generation, the individuals who helped to transform public welfare in the late nineteenth century were acutely aware of the economic, demographic, and industrial forces that seemed to undermine an older social order and to render past practices obsolete. The solutions they advocated rested upon a confident faith that knowledge and administrative rationality could create comprehensive policies that would eliminate waste and inefficiency and yet meet the legitimate needs of dependent persons. "We, who belong to these State Boards," observed George S. Robinson of Illinois in 1881,

> should realize, and the public needs to be made to see, that the care of the dependent and defective classes of the population is a business. It needs to be learned and mastered as any other business does. . . . Both theoretical and practical knowledge is requisite. The care of the unfortunate is really a profession; it may almost take rank with the learned professions. . . . To develop it, to elevate it to its proper rank; to secure for it the respect of the public, especially of intelligent and able men; to show its extent, its capabilities, its necessity and utility—this is a large part of the peculiar function of State Boards of Public Charities. They have to consider not only the practical but the scientific aspects of the questions which command their attention, and they need to be thoroughly imbued with the scientific spirit.

"For the present," the President of the Wisconsin board noted in a private communication to Pliny Earle that same year, "our work is largely to bring order and system and economy out of chaos and its necessary concommitant, extravagance. We hope to accomplish this and then to be able to give not a little attention to the general methods of internal management."[11]

Faith in bureaucratic and administrative values, order, efficiency, and rationality was by no means limited to those concerned with public welfare. On the contrary, by the turn of the century many professional and corporate groups disenchanted with the alleged abuses and inefficiencies inherent in popular government shared a similar faith. They favored centralized decision-making in order to promote the processes of rationalization and systemization, and thus to enhance the presumed effectiveness of public and private institutions. The shift toward centralized control had profound consequences insofar as political authority and power were concerned, for it reflected the growing significance of large organizations and the newly emerging professions.[12]

The symmetry of the new organizational society, however, was never complete, if only because of the persistence of disagreements. Individuals and groups might share a generalized commitment to order, rationality, and efficiency. When it came to specific formulations, on the other hand, the unanimity that prevailed on general principles all but disappeared. The assumption of policy-making authority by state boards, for example, led not to the imposition of any single system, but rather to the development of diametrically opposing systems by different states and regions. No doubt the decentralized nature of the American political system helped to encourage diversity rather than unity. Equally important, administrative means were not always adequate for the tasks at hand. Few could quarrel with the goal of making the welfare system and its varied institutions function in an efficient and rational manner. But what was the precise meaning of efficiency and rationality? How could mental hospitals with thousands of patients be made to conform to a single and admittedly vague standard, given the centrifugal tendencies of most institutions? The confident articulation of broad goals concealed an underlying human inability to develop appropriate administrative means that could overcome the varied behavior of all groups involved with the mentally ill—private families, local and state officials, institutional administrators and staff, as well as the patients themselves.

Whatever the reasons, the earlier consensus on the desirability of care and treatment in centralized but relatively small mental hospitals began to break down toward the close of the nineteenth century. Given the fact that the number of individuals who were defined as mentally ill was not declining, most states still faced the necessity of finding new alternatives. In general, older states with large populations, an established tradition of public welfare, an elaborate system of mental hospitals, and an educated elite sensitive to newer scientific concepts and to the importance of administrative solutions were the ones most receptive to the possibilities of innovation. The search for new policies proved strongest in the Northeast and Midwest and weakest in the South and newer states of the West.

III

The tendency to experiment with administrative and bureaucratic solutions was most pronounced in Massachusetts and New York. Both states were among the first to establish central supervisory boards concerned with welfare and dependency, a move which ultimately ended the sharing of responsibility for the care of mentally ill between the state and local communities. Although the path that each followed differed, the results were strikingly similar.

That Massachusetts was among the first to alter traditional policies was understandable. The Bay State had pioneered in nineteenth-century welfare. Its policies had helped to legitimate the state mental hospital in the early part of the century. Massachusetts had also established the first Board of State Charities in 1863 and a State Board of Health six years later. The cultural and intellectual leadership of its citizens reinforced its political significance, and where Massachusetts led other states traditionally followed.

Massachusetts, however, was by no means a typical state. Its native aristocracy had long resented the Irish Catholic immigrants, who arrived in ever increasing numbers after 1830. Nativism played a far more profound role in the Bay State than anywhere else throughout the nineteenth century. To many native-born middle-class Protestants, the social problems that plagued their state were directly attributable to the influx of the lower-class Irish. From the 1850s to the 1870s, and even later, nativist sentiment played a prominent role in state politics. Indeed, many of its public institutions were structured in such a way as to separate native- and foreign-born inmates.[13]

During the 1870s the Massachusetts Board of State Charities grew increasingly pessimistic about the way in which the Commonwealth cared for its insane patients. Established for therapeutic purposes, Massachusetts public hospitals were in practice providing custodial care for large numbers of incurable paupers, many of whom were foreign-born. Moreover, the costs of constructing hospitals appeared excessive to many; the state spent more than $3,000 per patient to build a new institution in Danvers which opened in 1878. Indeed, many patients enjoyed a higher standard of living within a hospital than in the community, where many confronted the threat of starvation. Clearly, the Board concluded, the traditional practice of adding new facilities as the need arose had failed; a new departure was necessary.[14]

Although there was widespread agreement on the need for basic changes in the state's welfare policies, there was little unanimity on the form that such changes should take. From time to time the state modified its policy in an incremental manner. When the old Worcester hospital (opened in 1833) moved to a new location in 1877, the legislature authorized the conversion of an existing but obsolete physical plant into an asylum for the chronic insane. Such an action, however, was recognized as a temporary palliative. Between 1875 and 1877 the legislature authorized two broad studies of public policy, one of which resulted in recommendations that a separate board be constituted to supervise the care of the mentally ill, and that the financing of institutional care be equalized and centralized.[15]

After prodding by the governor, the legislature in 1879 created a new State Board of Health, Lunacy, and Charity, which superseded the older Board of State Charities and State Board of Health. The new Board was unable to avoid the political controversies that followed the election of Benjamin F. Butler as governor in 1880. By 1886 the experiment of a single board was ended. Public health advocates had always opposed the merger; they differentiated sharply between health and the administration of welfare.[16]

Despite all the turmoil, the administrative reorganization did not appreciably alter public policy. The new Board, like its predecessor, continued to link insanity, pauperism, and a belief in incurability. It even went so far as to question the propriety of allocating public funds for the care of incurable paupers. On the other hand, its members had few alternatives to institutional care. The one exception came in 1885, when the Board induced the legislature to authorize the boarding of quiet and harmless chronically insane persons in private homes, with the assistance of state funding. The previous year the Board requested and received a lengthy paper on the subject by Dr. Henry R. Stedman, superintendent of the Hartford Retreat. Stedman took cognizance of the constant increase in the number of incurable patients. Many of them, he noted, were quiet and harmless, and could "be adequately and economically provided for outside of establishments." After analyzing the Belgian colony for the insane at Gheel—

which centralized the care of such persons in a single community—and the Scottish system—which distributed chronic cases
in private dwellings—Stedman clearly preferred the latter. An
effective boarding system would permit the state to end the costly
policy of constructing large hospitals, while at the same time
providing home care of dependent insane persons.[17]

The program was launched in August, 1885. About two-thirds
of the sixty patients sent to private homes were females. Most of
the homes were located in farming and rural communities, where
the cost of living was lower and where families often needed
additional income. Three years later Stedman conducted a comprehensive study of the experiment. Although the peak number
of persons boarded out did not exceed 125, the results were generally favorable. The greatest obstacle to further expansion was
the hostility of local officials, who preferred less expensive almshouse care.[18]

In the two decades following 1885, the boarding-out experiment
never outgrew its modest beginnings. The number of patients
involved increased rapidly for the first three years, diminished
during the next five, and then remained relatively stable until
1900. Before 1902 an average of 35 individuals were placed in
families each year; the average number in homes during the entire
period was 116, increasing to 144 between 1902 and 1905. Women
constituted the bulk of those placed in private homes; in the first
sixteen years 402 females were boarded out as compared with
only 99 males. The disparity between the sexes was not accidental. Applications from families for women far exceeded those for
men—a disparity that undoubtedly reflected a concern that physically larger and stronger males were more difficult to control
than females. The average age of each patient was 46 years. Before
1903, 300 families participated in the program; only 4.8 percent
were subsequently judged to be unfit. Of the families which were
involved, 38.8 percent were engaged in farming and 28.4 percent
headed by housekeepers (90 percent of whom were widows). About
14 percent of the families were related to the patients, and only
one-third received any compensation. Home care was also less
expensive than institutional care. Maintenance costs were the
same for both, but in home care the state avoided the expenses
associated with a physical plant. Nor was the shift from institutional to home care seemingly disturbing to patients. Between
1885 and 1901, 455 persons were placed out once, 36 twice, 9
three times, and 1 four times. Ultimately 146 (29.1 percent) were

found to be unsuitable. The average period of residence in a family was slightly over three years.[19]

Given its modest success, why did not the boarding-out system expand in scope and provide an alternative to institutional care? Owen Copp, a member of the State Board of Insanity who monitored the program, emphasized that only the state had a vested interest in its expansion. Hospital officials were not eager to continue the experiment, he insisted. An expanded program would probably have led to the creation of a decentralized system which would have given them additional functions and responsibilities in their geographical area. Moreover, according to Copp, the obvious candidates for home care were quiet and harmless persons, and these were precisely the kind of patients that hospital officials preferred to retain. The advantages to the state were clear; the system reduced costs and decreased institutional populations. Such advantages, Copp noted, "have not always been so clearly manifest as to command aggressive, sustained and organized support."[20] The absence of an organized pressure group, in other words, was crucial.

Other obstacles to the home-care experiment existed as well. The bulk of families willing to accept patients were located in rural and farming areas, whereas patients were concentrated in urban areas. A significant proportion of the institutionalized population, as we shall see later, suffered from a variety of physical impairments associated with senility and disease, and therefore required hospital care. Nor were communities, especially in urban areas, eager to accept mental patients; the relative absence of any hostility to the presence of patients in rural areas was merely indicative of a less dense population. Psychiatrists also manifested little interest in family care, perhaps because the very concept of care was not directly relevant to their interest in associating their specialty with medical science. They recognized as well the significance of patient interactions and were perhaps fearful of the consequences of removing those inmates whose very presence was beneficial.

Despite these drawbacks, Massachusetts continued to place patients in homes whenever possible. After the adoption of state funding for all mentally ill persons in 1904, there was a modest increase in the number of home-care patients—although much of the increase was attributable to the growth of the institutionalized population. In 1902 about 1.5 percent of all mentally ill persons cared for by the state were in homes; by 1905 the figure rose to

2.1 percent and by 1914 had reached 2.4 percent. In 1914 the average number of patients in mental hospitals was 13,276, and the average number in homes was 319. Few states, it should be noted, followed Massachusetts in adopting home care. Many lacked the Bay State's geographical compactness, its elaborate and complex administrative structures, and its cultural and intellectual traditions. Patient parole was widespread, but both the intent and the practice differed from home care.[21]

Given the concern for rationality and efficiency, it was not surprising that Massachusetts would also seek administrative solutions to the seemingly intractable problems posed by mental illness. During the decade of the 1890s, pressure for change once again began to mount. Local communities, especially Boston, were seeking to reduce the welfare costs that had been imposed by a system that mandated local responsibility. A transfer of authority to the state meant that local communities would no longer have to meet the fiscal obligation of providing facilities for mentally ill patients. The medical profession generally, and psychiatry in particular, were unhappy with the fact that the treatment of insanity was linked with charity. Combined pressure from both led to the creation of a special commission by the legislature in 1896. The following year the commission urged the creation of an autonomous State Board of Insanity and the assumption by the state of fiscal responsibility for all mentally ill persons. Both changes, the commission insisted, would result in more uniform and economical treatment under the authority of the "most advanced expert knowledge" and the elimination of the settlement laws. In 1898 the legislature authorized the creation of a new board, and two years later mandated state responsibility for the mentally ill. January 1, 1904, was set as the date when the new system would become operative.[22]

In New York the move toward state care followed a somewhat different path. The opening of the Willard Asylum for the chronic insane in 1869 had failed, as we have seen, to reach the goals envisioned by Sylvester Willard. Two years after it opened, the state legislature was forced to grant exemptions to various counties, permitting them to retain chronic patients in county asylums rather than sending them to Willard, which was overcrowded. This modification, curiously enough, added to the authority of the State Board of Charities; in addition to inspecting state institutions, its members were empowered to grant or to revoke licenses for county asylums. In 1873 the legislature altered the structure of the Board when it created the position of State Commissioner in Lunacy, who was an ex-officio member and reported to the Board. The following year the Commissioner in Lunacy became autonomous, thus weakening the policy and supervisory role of the Board. The founding of the State Charities Aid Association in 1872 further complicated the administration of public charities. Although a private organization, the Association quickly developed a close relationship with the State Board of Charities because their respective memberships in part overlapped. By 1884 the Association had also created a special committee on the insane.[23]

During the first decade of its existence, the office of the New York State Commissioner in Lunacy neither produced policy changes nor came into conflict with local or state officials. Its uncontroversial nature was due in large measure to the first occupant, John Ordronaux, a physician and lawyer whose specialty was medical jurisprudence. Ordronaux believed that New York's relatively decentralized system of administration ought not to be altered; he opposed any diffusion of authority of the governing boards of individual institutions. The county rather than the state was the basic unit, he maintained, since local officials were in a better position to understand their constituents. State supervision was undesirable if it constituted "an encroachment upon the rights of the people of the counties." The best reforms, he insisted, "will always emanate from the bosom of the citizens of a county." In his view the Commissioner, as well as the State Board of Charities, should serve in an advisory role to those individuals entrusted with the responsibility of managing individual institutions.[24]

In 1882 Ordronaux was succeeded by Stephen Smith, a physician who had played a prominent role in the creation of New York City's Metropolitan Board of Health in 1866. On assuming office, Smith encountered a system that struck him as neither rational nor defensible. Some counties maintained institutions for the insane without legal authorization; other counties had been exempted from the operations of the Willard Act and had established their own asylums; and the counties of Kings, Monroe, and New York had the right to maintain their own institutions for both acute and chronic patients. Superimposed upon local institutions were the state hospitals.

Unlike his predecessor, Smith believed that the division of responsibility between the state and local community was nothing less than a disaster. In his very first report he urged that "poor-house care of the insane" be discontinued. Responsibility for the care and treatment of insane persons, he insisted, should belong to state asylums, each of which should have jurisdiction within a defined geographical district. Such institutions should provide care for both chronic and acute cases, with the former being housed in adjacent cottages. Smith conceded that county opposition to his plan would be intense, since state care was more costly than county care. Nevertheless, he opposed state assumption of all fiscal responsibility on the grounds that families and local communities had to retain their interest in and relationship with insane persons. Instead, Smith urged that families, counties, and the state share the burden of support, with the relative responsibility of each determining the precise formula. Above all, he later added, "a poor house should remain a poor house and not be converted into an asylum for the insane."[25]

In 1883 Smith drafted legislation providing for the gradual transfer of insane persons from almshouses to state insane asylums. His proposal met with immediate opposition from county officials, who were faced with the prospect of paying higher rates in state institutions. County officials argued that large centralized hospitals were especially susceptible to abuse. Local institutions, on the other hand, permitted the maintenance of family ties and were far more responsive to the communities in which they were situated. Nor did Smith receive support from state hospital officials; they did not wish to incur the hostility of the counties, nor were they enthusiastic about the prospect of admitting large numbers of chronic and disturbed insane persons who had been housed elsewhere. Although the bill failed, Smith succeeded in forcing a debate that centered around the principle of state responsibility for all insane persons. For the next few years he assiduously cultivated the support of the influential State Charities Aid Association and the State Board of Charities. Both had close relationships with the legislature. The State Board of Charities, moreover, was in a position to employ its investigatory powers to buttress the case for centralization. In 1888 its standing committee on the insane prepared a long and detailed report on conditions in state and county institutions. State institutions, the report claimed, were deficient because they lacked sufficient accommodations, and the exempted county asylums were deficient "in the means for classification, treatment and medical supervision." The former defect, the report noted, could be remedied by a judicious program of expansion. But the problem of the exempted county asylums was beyond remedy, and the state either had to abolish county care or restrict and regulate it.[26]

By 1888 the State Medical Society and New York Neurological Society had joined Smith's coalition. A bill was drafted that year by the State Charities Aid Association, mandating state care for mental patients, and was introduced into the legislature. Although it failed to pass, Smith achieved a significant tactical victory in 1889 when he persuaded the legislature to abolish his position in favor of a three-member State Commission in Lunacy. Implied in this move was the final separation of the issue of insanity from indigency, and a fundamental reorganization in the institutional care of the mentally ill. The Commission's first report indicated as much. Its members recommended that all insane in county poorhouses be transferred to state asylums at the earliest practical date (excluding New York and Kings County); that each state hospital be given jurisdiction over a defined geographical area; that the state erect "comparatively inexpensive buildings" at each of its hospitals; and that the state assume the entire costs of maintaining insane persons.[27]

Within a year after the establishment of the State Commission in Lunacy, the Smith coalition—consisting of the State Charities Aid Association (and particularly its founder, Louisa Lee Schuyler), the organized medical profession, and some of the members of the State Board of Charities—succeeded in inducing the legislature to pass what was known as the State Care Act. New York, in effect, rejected the division of responsibility for the care of the mentally ill in favor of greater centralization. Unlike Wisconsin— which made provision for chronic cases in county institutions— New York opted for large central institutions serving a wide geographical area. The argument that large hospitals were more economical and promoted better individual care because of more accurate classification of cases proved persuasive. Equally significant, the state accepted the premise that the care of the mentally ill should under all circumstances remain the responsibility of the medical profession.

The provisions of the State Care Act of 1890 were simple. All the exemptions granted since 1871 were repealed, and county asylums reverted to the status of poorhouse. The distinction between chronic and acute cases (which actually dated from the 1840s, when the managers of the Utica asylum were empowered to return chronic cases to local almshouses) was eliminated, and all hospitals (including Willard) were placed on an equal footing. The law required that all county institutions send their insane to state hospitals as soon as accommodations were available. Moreover, it divided the state into districts, and assigned one institution to serve its needs. New York, Kings, and Monroe counties were exempted from the act, since each maintained separate mental hospitals, but they were given the option of coming under the provisions of the law if they so desired. Each of these counties (which included New York City, Brooklyn, and Rochester) between 1891 and 1896 came under the law and transferred their institutions to the state. The acceptance by the state of financial responsibility for the insane implied the end of local authority. The passage of a law in 1893 providing for an addition to the state property tax—the proceeds of which were to be applied to the care of the mentally ill—hastened the transfer. Had New York City and Brooklyn continued to maintain distinct municipal institutions, their citizens would have faced the prospect of double taxation. Indeed, New York City instituted a suit against the state in 1895, claiming that it ought not be required to pay a state levy for the support of nonresidents, but the court rejected the claim. The financial pressure applied by the state was accompanied by pressure from the State Commission in Lunacy, which was seeking an administrative reorganization to separate the insane from other dependent groups and to concentrate authority within its own office.[28]

Centralization of responsibility for the mentally ill in Massachusetts and New York produced similar results. First, it tended to promote uniform standards of care and administration throughout the system. Individual institutions increasingly were forced to conform to common fiscal practices, record keeping, and regulations. The new bureaucratic structure also facilitated the achievement of specific objectives that were previously unattainable under a decentralized system where individual hospitals retained autonomy. By 1893, for example, the State Commission in Lunacy had secured legislation requiring each hospital to appoint a female physician to its staff at a fixed salary of $1,200 per annum. Both boards also moved to establish what amounted to autonomous institutes to be devoted primarily to medical and scientific research. The very existence of a public agency meant that the mentally ill were represented in the process of policy formulation.[29]

Secondly, the circumstances under which administrative changes were introduced tended to give psychiatrists a more important role within the state hospital systems in New York and Massachusetts than they had in many other parts of the country. In these two states the medical profession was far more advanced in status, prestige, and organization. Traditionally, physicians were deeply involved with social policy and health issues, and they had in both states greater access to sources of political authority. Consequently, social policy tended to reflect medical perceptions to a far greater degree than was true elsewhere. For this reason, state policy in New York and Massachusetts in the late nineteenth century was increasingly influenced by the growing psychiatric emphasis on disease per se rather than on the mentally ill as a dependent group. The New York State Constitution of 1894 even elevated the State Commission in Lunacy to the status of a constitutional body, thus placing it beyond the power of the legislature to terminate its existence. New York also vested in the Commission exclusive jurisdiction over all institutions for the insane.

John B. Chapin, the first superintendent of the Willard Asylum, was especially critical of the refusal of his psychiatric colleagues to countenance the concept of care for the dependent insane (as contrasted with treatment in a medical setting). Originally the concept of "state care" had simply meant "a plan for the transfer of the chronic class who were in poorhouses to 'state care' and supervision." By the turn of the century, however, it was construed to imply "a plan to place the acute and chronic classes on the highest plane of hospital care." This goal, Chapin insisted, was unnecessary and unrealistic; it would simply escalate costs in caring for the insane and lead to an inevitable reaction against psychiatry.[30] Chapin's comments, however, were largely ignored by his colleagues.

Thirdly, the transfer of fiscal responsibility to the state helped to promote a dramatic change in both the character of the patient population and size of hospitals. The source of funding, as a matter of fact, was probably the single most important element in determining the kind of institution in which mentally ill persons were placed. Throughout much of the nineteenth century, dependent persons received care in local almshouses. But when communities were no longer required to assume the burden of supporting mentally ill residents, officials, in effect, reclassified many aged senile persons. This move facilitated their admission to mental hospitals, thereby shifting the burden of support to the state.

In Massachusetts first-admission rates for males aged sixty and over rose from 70.4 (per 100,000) in 1885 to 279.5 in 1939-1941; the comparable increase for women was from 65.6 to 223.0. Rates for younger groups, on the other hand, remained fairly stable. The care of aged senile persons thus became an implicit function of mental hospitals during the early 1900s. By mid-century 40 percent of all first admissions to New York state hospitals were aged sixty or more, even though this group constituted only 13.2 percent of the total population. Moreover, the change in the age distribution of the institutional population contributed in part to the rapid increase in the average size of hospitals. Between 1900 and 1910 the aggregate institutional population in Massachusetts rose from 7,623 to 12,266 (62 percent); during this same decade the state's population grew by about 8 percent. In the four decades following 1900, the institutional population grew about three and a half times, as contrasted with a population increase of about two-thirds. Much the same occurred in the decade following the passage of the State Care Act in New York; the hospital population rose from 5,402 to 21,815. Since the establishment of new institutions tended to lag behind the growth in the number of patients, the average daily population of individual hospitals rose sharply. The average daily census of the Northampton hospital in Massachusetts was 576 in 1900 and 2,090 in 1940. Four of the Bay State's nine regular mental hospitals had an average daily census of about 2,300 on the eve of World War II. The pattern in New York was similar; by 1940 the state's thirteen regular mental hospitals had an average daily population of more than 5,400 each.[31]

IV

The decentralized nature of the American political system, variations in the composition and distribution of population, and differing social and cultural traditions and patterns of wealth ensured that public policy toward the mentally ill would not assume a monolithic form. Many states did not establish regulatory boards before 1900; others gave their boards quite different functions and authority. Even where Massachusetts and New York innovations were emulated, the results were not always the same. Illinois and Wisconsin, which established boards in 1869 and 1871, respectively, pursued somewhat different policies, despite the fact that their board members maintained close contacts with their North-eastern colleagues.[32] Wisconsin rejected the idea of centralizing care in large state hospitals to serve a wide geographical area, and moved instead toward a controversial decentralized system based on county responsibility. Illinois, on the other hand, experimented with the structure of mental hospitals in an effort to find more acceptable alternatives. Both states provided contrasting illustrations about differential responses to the problems posed by mental illness.

Wisconsin, which was settled much later than the older seaboard states, did not open its first public hospital until 1860, and prior to that time kept its insane in jails and local welfare facilities. The state, nevertheless, was receptive to the possibility of innovation. In 1871 the legislature created a State Board of Charities and Reform, with functions comparable to those exercised by the boards in Massachusetts and New York. Unlike the latter, however, the Wisconsin Board was caught up in the rivalries between the state's contending political parties. None of its members enjoyed the autonomy and access to the sources of authority possessed by their Eastern colleagues. The financing of institutional care also kept shifting. When the Wisconsin Hospital for the Insane opened in 1860, its patients were supported by the state. Six years later the legislature required that families with sufficient means assume financial responsibility for patients, and in 1871 shifted part of the fiscal burden back to the counties.[33]

Composed of unpaid members and caught up in political conflicts, the Wisconsin State Board of Charities and Reform remained a somewhat marginal organization. Its investigatory authority led it to take an increasingly critical view of large congregate hospitals. As early as 1876 its members urged the state to establish an asylum for chronic insane patients, a group that constituted about 80 percent of the total number of mentally ill persons. Those who were fortunate enough to be admitted to the two public hospitals, the Board noted, received care of high quality, but their presence interfered with the therapeutic needs of acute cases. Others who were less fortunate were confined in jails and almshouses, where a more heterogeneous mix of people made it difficult for officials to maintain order and to create a more humane environment. By 1880 the Board was openly critical of institutional psychiatry. If insanity was incurable—as many superintendents conceded—then hospitals were "proceeding upon wrong methods." Certainly public distrust was on the rise, its members observed, as the founding of the National Association for the

Protection of the Insane and the Prevention of Insanity indicated. Some alternative was clearly required for those patients "who are not benefited by any medicine, and to whom the galling restraints and dead monotony of the daily life in a hospital as usually conducted, are positively hurtful." The Board's position brought its members into direct conflict with the state's two superintendents, both of whom were lobbying for additional funds to expand the size of their hospitals.[34]

Originally the Wisconsin Board had endorsed a central facility for chronic cases along the lines of the Willard Asylum, but it slowly modified its position as its members began to perceive the advantages of smaller county asylums. In 1878 a bill embodying some of the Board's views was introduced into the legislature, but it was so modified that the Board eventually ruled that its provisions were applicable only to Milwaukee County. In 1880 the Board reintroduced the county insane bill, which passed the legislature but failed to become law because of a technical procedural violation. In 1881 the bill finally became law. Under its provisions, counties, with the prior consent of the State Board of Charities and Reform, were permitted to construct facilities for chronic insane patients. Specifications for the structure had to be approved by the Board, which was also given authority to transfer patients to such facilities. Each county received $1.50 per week per patient from the state. If a county elected not to construct such an asylum and another county had sufficient space, the county of residence was required to pay, in addition to the state subsidy, $1.50 per week. Shortly thereafter the Board adopted resolutions governing county asylums, including specifications for clean and well-illuminated facilities, occupational opportunities, and a limitation on the use of restraints. The asylum remained under lay management, but a local physician was given an investigatory and supervisory role.[35]

Shortly after passage of the law, a number of counties established their own asylums. By the end of 1888 sixteen such asylums were in existence with a total population of nearly 1,400. Most were located on small farms ranging in size from 80 to 350 acres. Inmates came and went as they pleased, and there were sufficient means for occupational work and amusements. Because of the proximity to their homes, patients often received visits from relatives and went home on leaves. The State Board of Charities and Reform, which was dominated by laypersons, exercised close supervision over the county asylums in order to prevent abuses.

Since the Board had an adversarial relationship with the super-intendents of the state hospitals (and had lost some of its authority to the State Board of Supervisors), its members had a vested interest in overseeing the success of their creation.

If the goals of the county system were to limit the growth of state hospitals and to remove the mentally ill from jails and almshouses, then the innovation was surely a success during its early years. In 1881 the total population of the two state hospitals was 999; 255 were in the Milwaukee County Asylum (a mixed institution); and 455 were in poorhouses and jails. Seven years later the two state institutions had 1,087 patients, the Milwaukee institution 338, and only 36 were housed in jails and almshouses. The difference was to be found in the population of the county asylums, which supported 1,389 persons. To put it another way, the population of the state mental hospitals had increased about 9 percent during a period when the total institutionalized mentally ill population had risen by about 62 percent.[36]

Despite its apparent success, the Wisconsin system (as it became known), proved controversial and was not widely emulated. A year after its creation, the delegates to the NCCC listened to a defense of the system by H. H. Giles, a member of the Wisconsin Board. Support came also from Franklin B. Sanborn, one of the most influential figures in late nineteenth-century welfare. Frederick H. Wines, on the other hand, conceded the advantages of the new system, but still preferred care in state institutions (albeit in a sharply modified version). Dr. Charles S. Hoyt, long associated with the New York State Board of Charities, opposed the Wisconsin system. Hoyt favored large state hospitals; he emphasized their economy, stable standard of care, access to medical treatment, and the ease with which they could be supervised.[37]

Although several members of the Wisconsin Board attempted to publicize the successes of the county system, their efforts did not meet with overwhelming success. They received sympathetic hearings at the meetings of the NCCC, but the concern of this organization with the mentally ill was declining as the interests of its members shifted to other problems. The AMSAII also failed to offer support or encouragement. Concerned with insanity as a disease rather than as a problem requiring care, its members were not inclined to look favorably upon an institution in lay hands. The Association traditionally had rejected the idea of confining mentally ill persons in local welfare institutions. Its members believed that the caliber of individuals who served as managers never approximated the quality of physicians who occupied hospital superintendencies. The Association was also acutely aware of the fact that local care, particularly in urban areas like New York City and Philadelphia, left much to be desired.[38]

Despite psychiatric indifference or hostility,[39] interest in the Wisconsin system persisted in the late nineteenth and early twentieth century. Precisely because Wisconsin provided a different alternative, supporters of state care tended to assume a hostile attitude. In the debate preceding and following the passage of the State Care Act in New York in 1890, the Wisconsin system was explicitly singled out for criticism. In the nearby states of Michigan and Minnesota, the experiment was followed with interest, even though neither state emulated their neighbor. Maryland developed a version of the Wisconsin plan, but its county asylums lacked facilities and funds and were never intended to function as part of an organized and comprehensive state system. Much the same was true in New Jersey, where county officials found that local asylums were far less costly than state hospitals. Since New Jersey counties were financially liable for the care of their residents in state institutions, they decided to establish their own asylums. State government in New Jersey, however, lagged behind its neighbors insofar as the growth of regulatory and supervisory agencies were concerned, and in this respect the state resembled the South rather than the Northeast. The absence of state supervision, therefore, gave New Jersey county asylums a quite different character. Finally, the Wisconsin system was sometimes confused with the more widespread practice of retaining insane persons in county almshouses or undifferentiated welfare institutions where hospital facilities were unavailable.[40]

The most enthusiastic endorsement of the Wisconsin system of county care came in Pennsylvania. Concern for the disposition of chronic cases was evident in the 1870s. In 1874 the Board of Public Charities was given authority to order the removal of insane persons in county welfare institutions if proper care and treatment was not readily available. The law, however, did not deal directly with the more thorny issue of the chronic insane. During the 1880s Pennsylvania's policy was inconsistent. The Committee on Lunacy, created in 1883 and responsible to the Board of Public Charities, opposed the Wisconsin system, but its parent board in 1888 ordered it to remove those chronic insane who were neither dangerous nor violent from state hospitals and to return them to their home counties. This policy would be consistent with the transformation of Pennsylvania's "asylums" into "hospitals." Three years later the legislature authorized the establishment of a new state asylum for the chronic insane. By 1894 the new institution, located in Wernersville, was so crowded that the Committee on Lunacy urged a second institution for the chronic insane.[41]

Resistance in the Pennsylvania legislature to new and costly expenditures for additional facilities, however, soon forced a change in emphasis. In 1896 the Committee on Lunacy, after an evaluation of the Wisconsin system, came out in support of dual county and state responsibility. Within a year the legislature had acted on the proposal. Under the provisions of the new law, counties, following approval by the Board of Public Charities, were authorized to erect facilities for the care of the indigent insane. The state, in turn, would reimburse counties at the rate of $1.50 per week per patient. The rationale was similar to that used in Wisconsin: the chronic indigent insane would be cared for near their homes in small institutions that provided maximum freedom and occupational opportunities; the state hospitals thus would not have to expand costly physical plants nor be diverted from their therapeutic mission. The supervisory role of the Board of Public Charities presumably precluded any violation of regulations designed to protect patients in county institutions. Many counties were quick to act; by 1898 sixteen had either authorized or constructed new buildings, or had improved existing ones in order to become eligible for the state subsidy.[42]

In both Wisconsin and Pennsylvania the county asylum system persisted for decades. By 1930 the thirty-six Wisconsin county asylums cared for 7,557 individuals, as compared with a total hospital population of slightly over 2,000. In Pennsylvania, on the other hand, the insane were about equally distributed among the state hospitals (12,713) and the licensed county asylums (12,117).[43]

How successful were systems that divided responsibility between county and state institutions? The answer to this question can be given only in ambiguous terms. Even contemporary observers were not united in their evaluations; their judgments generally reflected starting assumptions and individual perceptions. If, for example, the goal of institutionalization was psychiatric care and treatment, then the system was a clear failure. In his study of Pennsylvania institutions in 1915, Dr. C. Floyd Haviland commended the large state hospitals, but bitterly criticized the county asylums for their emphasis on care and custody rather than on therapy. In his eyes the county asylums had few, if any, redeeming features; the only argument in their behalf was that they provided less expensive care than central hospitals. Nor was it possible, Haviland wrote, to identify incurable patients with any degree of precision. Even if it were possible, he added, the best grade of custodial care was still provided in state hospitals. Haviland's comments received the support of other psychiatrists, including Owen Copp, superintendent of the Pennsylvania Hospital for the Insane. The Board of Public Charities, by way of contrast, was critical of Haviland's report. Two decades later a committee that evaluated Pennsylvania's hospital system reaffirmed Haviland's judgment.[44]

If, on the other hand, the goal was humane care for a group for whom all known therapies had failed, then the county system must be judged as having achieved some success. When the Secretary of the Pennsylvania Committee on Lunacy inspected the Wisconsin system in 1909, he concluded that nowhere in the United States were the insane "better fed, better housed, and better cared for." Conceding that the quality of the medical service was below that given to patients in state hospitals, he also noted that the chronic insane required "very little medical treatment." A study of the Pennsylvania system by a special committee came to a similar conclusion.[45]

The county system admittedly was not without its share of problems. The division of authority between state and county proved troublesome. Wisconsin is a case in point. At the same time that it established its county system, Wisconsin created a State Board of Supervisors (in addition to the State Board of Charities and Reform) to exercise fiscal control. Although the existence of two state agencies produced conflict, it also left the members of the State Board of Charities and Reform relatively free to devote their energies to the county system. Friction between the two boards, however, led the legislature in 1891 to abolish both and to create a new State Board of Control instead. Concerned with elevating the standard of care of the state hospitals, the members of the new Board were not as deeply involved with the county system as their predecessors, and lack of supervision led eventually to some deterioration of local institutions. Under these circumstances county officials began to play a more prominent role; their preoccupation with economy and efficiency often brought them into conflict with the superintendents of the state hospitals.

Some county officials even emphasized the profit-making potential of their institutions. Moreover, coordination between county asylums and state hospitals was sometimes lacking because county institutions frequently refused to accept patients with severe behavioral problems. Like most innovations, the Wisconsin system produced mixed results.[46]

At about the same time that Wisconsin introduced its county asylum plan, Illinois began to experiment with an alternative to the traditional mental hospital. As in Wisconsin, the impetus for change came from the Illinois Board of State Commissioners of Public Charities. Established in 1869, the Board, led by Frederick Wines, its young and energetic secretary, immediately began to consider alternatives to large centralized hospitals. Shortly after assuming office, Wines convened a conference on insanity and solicited the opinions of nearly every American hospital superintendent. Although the conference had no immediate impact and the two new state hospitals built in the early 1870s reflected prevailing psychiatric concepts, it was evident that there was a growing receptivity to structural innovation.[47]

Like other states, Illinois faced a seemingly insatiable demand for additional hospital accommodations. The opening of two new hospitals in 1872 and 1873 (in addition to the Illinois Hospital for the Insane) had not solved the problem; their combined capacity could accommodate only about half of the total number requiring care. "It is evident," Wines warned in 1876, "that sooner or later the state will be obliged to make additional provision for hospital treatment at public expense." Nor was he willing to support an enlargement of existing hospitals; the number of insane already housed under a single roof was too large, to say nothing of the excessive cost involved in expansion. In suggesting that the time was ripe for innovation, Wines explicitly rejected the dominance of traditional psychiatry as expressed in the program of the AMSAII. Conceding that the opinions of superintendents ought to receive a hearing, Wines nevertheless expressed doubt "whether outsiders are not quite as competent to judge of the results of treatment and of the effect upon the community as the superintendents are; and we do not think that they should be allowed to dictate legislation." Superintendents were too much "attached to the present system, which they have learned to administer, and the beneficial effects of which they have seen in their own experience, and they can scarcely realize the extent to which a certain dissatisfaction with the result exists in the mind of the community at large." "Necessary innovations," Wines added, were not likely to originate with superintendents, whose discussions and activities "is rather to produce uniformity in the system and a firm adhesion to it." Curiously enough, Wines never mentioned that many of his own charges of overcrowding in hospitals resembled similar criticisms made by the AMSAII, which with considerable reluctance had raised in 1866 the maximum recommended size of mental hospitals from 250 to 600.[48]

That Wines was seeking alternatives to large overcrowded hospitals was hardly surprising. During the 1850s some American superintendents visited Europe and described different institutional forms. A decade later Americans were debating the possibility of developing new institutions based on the model of the Belgium town of Gheel, where insane inhabitants were accepted and housed throughout the community.[49] When Wines assumed the position of secretary of the Illinois Board, he was in a strategic position to alter state policy. At his conference in 1869 he was influenced by the views of Dr. Andrew McFarland, then superintendent of the only state hospital in Illinois. McFarland had suggested that hospitals, in addition to large central structures, should have smaller detached buildings capable of housing forty inmates under the supervision of a married couple and several attendants. To Wines the advantages of such an arrangement were compelling; the therapeutic requirements of acute cases could be satisfied, while less costly facilities that maximized freedom and minimized restraint for quiet chronic patients would become available. Given his belief that continued construction of large hospitals (with costs that ran as high as $3,000 per bed) would lead to increasing deprivation among the mounting number of chronic cases, Wines seized upon the hope that very large but decentralized institutions could resolve the grave problems confronting states.[50]

Initially Wines was unable to persuade the legislature to permit experimentation with the two hospitals authorized in 1869. Much to his surprise, however, Illinois authorized a fourth public institution in 1877. That the new facility would not necessarily be a traditional one was evident from several key provisions in the legislation. None of the commissioners appointed to select the site could come from the eastern part of the state, where the hospital would be located; they were also forbidden to accept gifts made to secure a particular location. The plan adopted for the hospital had to be approved by the governor and Board of Public

Charities, a provision that gave Wines considerable leverage. The legislative committee, perhaps at the urging of Wines, had recommended that the new hospital leave open the mode of construction in the hope that the new trustees "may be able to ascertain and demonstrate the feasibility of a reform in this particular, by the adoption of the village plan of construction, with detached buildings, erected at less expense and affording a greater measure of comfort to the inmates than is secured by the existing plan of construction in this country."[51]

Following a visit to England and France in 1878, Wines returned, determined to break with past traditions. In a statement prepared for delivery at the meetings of the NCCC (and delivered by a colleague), Wines attempted to rally support and to undermine the AMSAII. He described that organization as "a close corporation . . . committed to a certain rigid, almost inflexible type of hospital building . . . characterized by two prominent peculiarities, viz., uniformity, verging upon monotony, and the ease with which each individual patient may be subjected to any degree of restraint approved by the judgment of the medical officer in charge." Strong opposition led to a minor compromise. The new hospital would have detached structures, but they would be so grouped that in the event the arrangement proved unworkable, they could be reconverted to approximate an orthodox institution. The following year Dr. Richard Dewey was appointed superintendent. A former assistant physician at the Elgin hospital, Dewey supported Wines and helped to design the new institution.[52]

The Kankakee hospital, when it finally opened for a small number of patients in 1880, had a traditional central building with wings radiating from each side. Each wing had six wards for 25 patients, or a total capacity of about 300. At right angles were smaller detached structures, each different from the other. The detached buildings were generally two stories high: the upper floor was divided into smaller sleeping stalls; the lower floors included day rooms and other facilities. The smallest had less than 40 patients; the largest, intended for disturbed, noisy, and violent patients, had space for 167. Most buildings were designed for no more than 50 persons. Construction proceeded over a period of years, and by the time Dewey left in 1893, the hospital had an average population of almost 1,900—nearly twice the number at the other three state hospitals. The central structure contained mild acute cases deemed to be curable, as well as violent patients whose behavior posed a threat to themselves or others. The detached buildings housed all others, including chronic persons whose behavior posed no problems.[53]

In its planning stage Kankakee was designed to resemble a small village, "highly organized, thoroughly policed, in admirable sanitary condition, and under complete control; but affording to its insane inhabitants a variety, a freedom, and a satisfaction not attainable in any hospital constructed upon the type now prevalent in the United States." Its advantages seemed compelling. Segregate hospitals, Richard Dewey noted, balanced "the personal needs of the inmate and the harmonious, efficient and economical working of the institution as a whole." Decentralization also diminished population density and reduced friction among inmates as well as creating a greater sense of responsibility among attendants. Besides the greater opportunities for individualized care, the segregate system was more economical; on average, detached buildings could be constructed for about one-third the cost of a congregate hospital. Finally, the size and economy of Kankakee provided an opportunity to meet the needs of the chronic insane, a group all too often overlooked despite their numerical significance.[54]

Did Kankakee live up to the expectations of its founders? Again, no clearcut answer is possible. Several years after its opening D. H. Tuke visited the hospital and had a favorable impression. "I saw with pleasure, one evening," he reported, "a number of patients sitting at ease under the verandah of one of these cottages, some of them, if not all, having been engaged in wholesome work on the farm during the day. There was an air of freedom and homeishness which is necessarily more or less lost in an ordinary asylum, especially when of giant proportions." The average number of patients under restraint, moreover, was less than 1 percent, which was below the national average.[55]

On the other hand, the original plan for the hospital proved defective in some important respects. Because of the possibility of failure, the detached buildings were located close to the main structure in order to permit them to be connected if the segregate idea was abandoned. The relative high population density vitiated in part the original goals. Like all institutions, Kankakee suffered from overcrowding; by 1912 nearly 2,900 patients lived in facilities designed to accommodate 2,200. Although the cottages had a homelike quality, the low per-capita construction allowance led to their subsequent deterioration. Nor was the freedom granted to the patient unqualified. About 10 percent of its patients in

1912 had "ground paroles." Under its terms they were forbidden to leave the hospital grounds without permission; they were also required to work at assigned tasks, return to their cottages in time for meals and curfew, and to observe all regulations.[56]

Undoubtedly Kankakee suffered during its first two decades from the political situation that led to the dismissal of Richard Dewey in 1893 and the brief tenure of S. V. Clevenger, his successor. After 1893 the hospital continued to suffer from a lack of continuity as a result of administrative changes.[57] Adolf Meyer, who was hired by Clevenger as a pathologist, spent two and a half unhappy years at Kankakee. Meyer's dissatisfaction was admittedly conditioned by his medical perspective; he believed that the state had an obligation to provide every insane person with "the benefit of treatment and supervision by a competent physician." Like many of his professional colleagues, he tended to judge Kankakee in medical and scientific terms and to slight its role in providing custodial care for chronic patients. His judgment of Kankakee after eighteen months on the staff reflected his medical background. "I have become more and more convinced," Meyer wrote to G. Alder Blumer of the Utica hospital,

that the atmosphere of the place shows little chance of being improved to such a degree as to make life satisfactory enough to spare energy for the work that I am longing for. Catering towards political effects, towards more show and granting insufficient liberty of action, the administration discourages progress along sound principles. The library facilities are poor and the whole mechanism of medical work little promising although much better than when I came here. My courses on neurology and mental diseases have certainly roused the interest of the Staff; but the ground does not promise much fruit as long as the simplest means for clinical observation and examination are absent! Not even electrical diagnosis is provided for! I am expected to do all the clinical microscopy, the lecturing and the path. work and all the scientific observation, and the result is that in no line the work becomes quite satisfactory to me.[58]

Although Kankakee represented somewhat of an improvement in patient care, its establishment did not provide a solution that was emulated elsewhere. Kankakee's growth came close to vitiating its original objectives. As the Board of Public Charities reported in 1898:

We have . . . constantly opposed from the beginning the unnecessary and unwise enlargement of our state charitable institutions, and upon principle we do not favor the congregation
of so many unfortunates in a single locality and under a single
management. But the experience of the board during the past
thirty years has taught us that the sentiment of the legislature
in opposition to the multiplication of institutions and scatter-
ing them over the State is so great and so persistent that it is
useless for us to insist upon our counter conviction in this
regard.[59]

V

In Massachusetts, New York, Wisconsin, Illinois, and Pennsylvania the effort to define public policy involved state boards of
charity, and the same was true in a few other states. But the
majority of states lacked comparable boards, and dealt with insanity in other ways. The South is a case in point. Generally
speaking, Southern hospitals provided the lowest quality of care,
if per-capita expenditures provide any measure. Clearly, the level
of expenditures cannot be attributed to the absence of state boards
of charity, for the relative poverty of that region played a far more
crucial role. The absence of such boards, however, had a profound
effect; there was no single agency or group to set an agenda for
policy debates. That the South lacked administrative agencies was
in part a reflection of a long tradition that gave state governments
in this region minimal responsibilities for the care of dependent
persons. It is true that North Carolina was among the earliest of
all states to establish a Board of Public Charities (1869), but it
became inoperative after 1873, when the anti-Republican state
legislature refused to make any new appointments after the terms
of the older members had expired. Even when some new members
were subsequently appointed in the mid-1870s, the Board was
unable to function for lack of funds. In 1889 it became operative
once again, but without any authority. Its impotence after that
date was reflected in its plea in 1890 for an appropriation of $1,000
to defray printing and mailing costs, the services of a secretary,
and the expenses incurred in making inspections and holding
meetings. In 1895 Tennessee became the second Southern state
to establish a State Board of Charities, but its failure to provide
any operating funds prevented it from doing much.[60]

In the newer states of the Far West ad hoc arrangements for the care of mentally ill residents were common. In 1867 Nevada concluded an arrangement whereby its insane citizens would be cared for by California in return for a quarterly payment of $85. Crowding in the Stockton hospital and the reluctance of California officials to accept more Nevada residents led to a comparable arrangement between the state and two private California physicians in 1871. It was not until the end of the 1870s that the state acquired land and began construction of its own hospital in Reno. Montana, on the other hand, concluded an agreement in 1873 with two private physicians, who constructed and operated their own facility, and, in turn, received a weekly per-capita payment from the state. The arrangement must have been satisfying to the proprietors; they lobbied against the establishment of a state institution in 1894, and emphasized the substantial construction costs that would be incurred by the state.[61]

Western states in time tended to emulate policies that were more common in the East and Midwest. Wyoming, for example, established a State Board of Charities and Reform in 1891, and shifted the support of insane patients from the counties to the state. Its title notwithstanding, the composition of the Wyoming Board gave it a somewhat different character; the Board was composed of the State Treasurer, Auditor, and Superintendent of Public Instruction, a group more concerned with fiscal management than with substantive policy issues. Colorado, on the other hand, founded a more traditional State Board of Charities and Reform in 1891. Its members immediately urged the legislature to end the practice of confining the acute and chronic insane, epileptic, feebleminded, and idiot in the single Insane Asylum at Pueblo. They called for the construction of a new facility modelled upon the cottage plan. Although the Colorado legislature concurred with the recommendation, it failed to appropriate sufficient funds. The Colorado Board meanwhile continued to stress the efficacy of the Kankakee model, and explicitly rejected the Wisconsin system.[62]

In other states the decentralized nature of American federalism and the strength of local and county government inhibited the growth of regulatory activities on the state level. New Jersey, in fact, actually invested a private organization with public functions. In 1883 the legislature created a Council of Charities and Corrections, and empowered it to investigate public institutions. Its main function, however, was to prepare a common set of statistics of inmate populations and comparable costs of maintenance. Lack of operating funds and opposition from local officials inhibited its work, and it shortly thereafter disappeared. In 1886 the legislature incorporated the Morris County Charities Aid Association and several other groups into a State Charities Aid Association with powers to inspect and to prepare annual reports. Lack of any subventions and a decentralized structure that left visitations and inspections to local groups rendered the organization relatively powerless. As late as 1903 Frederick Wines, then secretary of the New Jersey State Charities Aid Association, noted that its powers were "so circumscribed, that the grant is more nominal than real." Wines insisted that a voluntary private organization could not be a substitute for a state charities board, and he urged the state to act. When the legislature created a Department of Charities and Corrections in 1905, it simply provided for a single salaried commissioner with minimal functions (largely record keeping) to be assisted by an advisory board composed of the heads of state institutions.[63]

State boards elsewhere existed in name, but lacked authority. The Connecticut legislature acted in 1873, but its Board was largely inoperative for the better part of a decade. New Hampshire authorized its State Board of Health in 1889 to constitute a Board of Commissioners of Lunacy. Its only power was the ability to transfer insane paupers from county institutions to the state hospital for remedial treatment; such individuals could remain in the hospital as long as treatment was justified. The Board had no power to enforce a recommendation or to remedy defects. When a State Board of Charities and Correction was founded in 1895, it not only lacked a regular office, but found that the state hospital was exempted from any visitations.[64]

VI

The diverse and often conflicting responses by states to the social problems posed by mental illness reflected in part a political culture based on local and state boundaries. Although the Civil War had put to rest an extreme concept of state sovereignty, that conflict had not produced any support for the view that the national government should define or enforce social welfare policies. In a heterogeneous society possessing numerous centers of political authority and divergent cultures, traditions, and peoples, the absence of any single policy was not surprising.

That innovation usually took a managerial or structural bent was equally understandable. Recognizing the inability of psychiatry to provide effective medical therapies, state officials and individuals concerned with welfare revealed an affinity for organizational solutions. Such solutions, in turn, were reinforced by newer concepts of efficiency that were rapidly gaining in popularity in many other fields.

The assumption by state agencies of greater policy roles had significant consequences for the institutionalized mentally ill. The division of responsibility for the care of the insane between the state and community was further undermined. Slowly but surely the shift in the sources of funding led municipalities and counties to transfer their mentally ill from almshouses to state hospitals and to redefine senility in psychiatric terms. State officials offered little resistance, for they were cognizant of both the shortcomings of local welfare facilities and the problems of supervision in a decentralized system. Under these circumstances, it was hardly surprising that state hospitals would not only grow in size, but would assume greater responsibility for providing long-term custodial care for large numbers of chronic patients.

The growth of state authority and accumulation of chronic patients that presaged a shift in the function of hospitals also played a significant role in reshaping American psychiatry. Slowly but surely the specialty of psychiatry became alienated from its institutional origins. The transformation of the AMSAII between 1895 and 1892 was but a harbinger of the future. In the new world of scientific medicine, the traditional psychiatric emphasis on the acquisition of managerial and administrative skills and custodial functions seemed peculiarly obsolete. One result was a weakening of the link between mental hospitals and psychiatrists.

CHAPTER FIVE

The Quest for Psychiatric Authority

"How MARVELLOUS have been the changes that have brought us to the conceptions we hold to-day of the scientific principles that underlie our medical art," Edward Cowles told the Maine Medical Association in 1897. Cowles emphasized in particular two recent additions to psychiatric thought that held great promise for the future: the "toxic causation of disease" and the "new methods of investigating the anatomy and physiology of the nervous system." Taken together, both demonstrated that the treatment of mental disease was "being brought more closely than ever to common ground with general diseases."[1]

Cowles's remarks reflected the new confidence and optimism that seemed to be overtaking psychiatry in the 1890s and contributing toward its transformation in the early decades of the twentieth century. Implicit in his address was a repudiation of institutional psychiatry and of the pessimism that had accompanied the belief that insanity was for the most part incurable. The new psychiatry, by way of contrast, was affiliated with the recent developments that had altered general medicine and offered for the first time an opportunity to alleviate, if not cure, many of the ills which had for so long plagued humanity.

If Cowles's specific beliefs were not accepted by all his colleagues, most shared his faith that psychiatry and medicine stood on the threshold of a new era. Good health would soon become the norm and morbidity and premature mortality the occasional exception. Even Adolf Meyer, an individual who distrusted many of the systematic and theoretical explanations current in the early part of the new century, and who expressed at times a pragmatic empiricism, believed that the science of psychopathology had made remarkable strides. "The difficulty," he noted, "is getting those matters applied in the hospitals." Change would only come, he added, when "those who are willing to see an improvement band together and induce medical schools to do their duty, and make it possible to have a critical supervision over the existing

State hospitals, [and] demand better standards of promotion and of cooperation with the agencies that are at hand."[2]

The optimism and anticipation of future advances characteristic of early twentieth-century psychiatry was by no means unique. By then the fears and pessimism of the 1870s and 1880s had been superseded by a growing confidence in the ability to deal with human problems in a changing world. To Progressive activists of the early 1900s, whatever their ideological persuasion, the nation stood on the threshold of a new social and moral order. Disagreements of course, were by no means absent; the range of Progressive thinking was sufficiently broad to encompass fundamentally different analyses. Some Progressives believed that evil and pathological behavior flowed from the immoral circumstances in which individuals lived. For these individuals, the solution lay in the transformation of the environment. Other Progressives were less sanguine about their ability to produce desired behavioral modifications simply by improving the environment. They urged instead the use of coercive measures, including (but not limited to) the passage of legislation that would exclude allegedly "undesirable" immigrants, ban the use of intoxicating liquors, and provide for the involuntary sterilization of defective persons. Whatever their ideological persuasion, however, Progressives shared a modern faith that the destiny of humanity could be altered by conscious and purposive action.[3]

The dream of a transforming social redemption, which played such an important role in early twentieth-century Progressive thought, led psychiatrists to go beyond the institutions which had for so long been linked with their specialty. Some explored the physiological and biological roots of mental disease, some developed a more analytic psychiatry that incorporated Freudian insights; some attempted to integrate psychological and physiological phenomena to illuminate the inner workings of abnormal minds; some experimented with novel therapeutic approaches; and others reached beyond the boundaries of medicine to create a mental hygiene movement that sought to demonstrate the social utility and relevance of modern psychiatry.

Whether or not they were affected by new ideas, psychiatrists seemed to share a common optimism. Bernard Sachs, a distinguished New York neurologist and former pupil of Theodore Meynert, for example, refused to abandon the traditional belief that the key to mental processes lay in the discovery of anatomical mechanisms. Sachs conceded that psychiatry had "lain dormant for many years." On the other hand, there was "no other branch of medical science" that presented "as many interesting problems." "The past of psychiatry," he insisted, "has been full of discouragement; the present is involved in a maze of uncertainty, but the future is full of hope." Two decades later Charles G. Wagner, in his presidential address at the AMPA, specifically rejected the "mild pessimism" of some of his colleagues. "I regard the future of mental medicine as filled with golden promise," he told them in confident words. "Serious, thoughtful students of psychiatry are busily at work on problems of vital importance, and I venture to predict that within the period of a decade or two their labors will result in a much better understanding of the etiology, pathology, diagnosis and treatment of mental diseases than we now possess."[4]

Between the 1890s and 1920s American psychiatrists began to look beyond the institutions in which their specialty had been conceived. Influenced by the theoretical and institutional changes within medical science as well as by those social and intellectual currents that had given rise to efforts to change American society, they began to redefine not only concepts of mental disease and treatment, but the very context of their specialty. In so doing they implicitly posited a conflict between the traditional mental hospital and its function of providing custodial care for large numbers of chronic patients, and the imperatives of modern psychiatry. Although the majority of psychiatrists continued to be affiliated with mental hospitals, the thrust of their specialty was increasingly away from institutional practice. That internal ferment did not conclude in theoretical innovation or demonstrably effective therapies was little noticed. When the process of change had run its course, the traditional relationship between psychiatry and mental hospitals had begun to dissolve.

I

The optimism of early twentieth-century psychiatry was not accompanied by a shared consensus about the nature of mental disease. If anything, psychiatrists tended to divide into a bewildering variety of groups, each with its own set of assumptions and beliefs. Conflict rather than harmony was the norm as individuals attempted to legitimate their views by discrediting all others. Although the conflict was sharpest within the psychoanalytic movement and between psychoanalysis and more traditional psychiatry, it was by no means absent from the latter alone. Figures such as William Alanson White, superintendent of St. Elizabeths Hospital in Washington, D.C., and one of the most prolific writers of his era on psychiatric problems, attempted to act as a mediator and conciliator, but his efforts and those of others only toned down but never halted the hostilities and fragmentation within the specialty.

By the turn of the century the older psychiatric somaticism was under attack from a variety of sources. Somaticism, of course, was never completely rejected; to do so might have transferred medical concepts to the field of metaphysics. Critics of the older somatic style, however, could present strong counter-arguments: the absence of evidence demonstrating a relationship between lesions and abnormal behavior; a classification system that was both rigid and vague; an etiological scheme based on personal and superficial observations rather than on biological findings; an approach that ruled out the study and analysis of mental phenomena; the neglect of therapeutics that arose from a belief that many insane persons fell into the chronic patient category; and the failure to pursue systematic neuropathological and laboratory research.

The criticisms of traditional somaticism, however, did not reflect theoretical clarity nor were they based on the kind of empirical data that might be used to construct a new synthesis. American psychiatry remained a heterogeneous specialty, and a variety of different and often unrelated concepts appealed to different practitioners. Those psychiatrists who assimilated to one degree or another Freudian concepts into their thought generally had few links with public mental hospitals, where the overwhelming bulk of patients were concentrated; analytic and psychoanalytic psychiatry had its greatest influence in smaller private hospitals and private practice.

The disunity of early twentieth-century psychiatric thought was not due simply to the lack of a tradition of basic research or the relative weaknesses of American medical schools, as compared with European medical education, although both elements played a role. More important was the fact that the very concept of mental disease could not be separated from the deeper and more profound problem of explaining the nature of human beings in general and their behavior in particular. At one extreme were certain deterministic systems that reduced behavior to physiological mechanisms and ruled out independent thought or actions that did not have specific causal antecedents. More widely accepted, however, were eclectic models that posited a link between mental and biological factors. But the nature of such links remained shrouded in mystery, and the very concept of mental phenomena posed seemingly unresolvable theoretical difficulties.

In modern medicine the demonstration of a relationship between the presence of certain symptoms and a specific bacterial organism had led to the development of a new classification based on etiology rather than on symptomatology. The inability to pursue a parallel course left psychiatry with a classification system based on external symptoms that tended to vary in the extreme. Conclusive evidence that paresis (general paralysis of the insane) was actually the tertiary stage of a disease that began with a prior syphilitic infection offered a model for psychiatric diseases. Nevertheless, neither psychiatrists nor pathologists were able to identify other specific disease entities in comparable terms.[5] The formidable scientific and intellectual problems that created fundamental divisions among psychiatrists, however, did not lead to a generalized pessimism. Just as medical scientists had begun to illuminate the relationship between microorganisms and infectious diseases, so too could psychiatrists uncover the etiological factors that led to mental disease.

II

The career of Adolf Meyer, one of the most influential figures in American psychiatry from the 1890s through the 1940s, illustrates both the promise of the specialty as well as its problems. Born in Switzerland in 1866, Meyer studied at the University of Zurich under August Forel and received his medical degree in 1892. After migrating to the United States that same year, he obtained a nominal appointment at the University of Chicago, and then worked as a pathologist at the Kankakee hospital for nearly three years. Between 1896 and 1901 he occupied a similar position at the Worcester hospital in Massachusetts. Meyer then succeeded Ira Van Gieson as director of the Pathological Institute of the New York State Hospitals. When Henry Phipps offered to endow a new psychiatric clinic at Johns Hopkins in 1908, Meyer was chosen as its first director and received a professorship of psychiatry in the Medical School. Meyer remained in Baltimore until his retirement in 1941 and death in 1950.[6]

Trained originally in neurology, Meyer's psychiatric views changed considerably over the course of his long career. The two figures who exerted an early influence were Thomas Huxley and Hughlings Jackson. Huxley's contributions were threefold: his definition of science as organized common sense; his discussion of Darwin and Hume, which tended to stress the biological aspects of human problems; and his extreme parallelism, which made a mere epiphenomenon of the mind. Jackson's contributions were equally relevant; he played an important role in establishing the concept of "levels of integration" in the central nervous system—an idea that developed out of the evolutionary approach to biology. Although Meyer initially rejected the study of psychiatry, he soon began moving toward a biological and pluralistic concept of human beings that involved a rejection of Cartesian dualism.[7]

When Meyer arrived in the United States he was immediately drawn to the writings of three Americans—Charles S. Peirce, John Dewey, and William James. From Peirce, Meyer came to appreciate the role of independent thought and scientific logic in contrast to what he regarded as the contemporary European subjectivization of all sciences. Dewey and James, along with Peirce, contributed a basic sense of pluralism, or, in Meyer's words, "a recognition that nature is not just one smooth continuity in which isolated particles could tell us all there is to be known; that in physics, for instance, we have to learn that there are things which are discontinuous from each other in the sense of their occurring in quanta, and that with this recognition we have to work with space-time, not only space and time, and with functions and not only with statics." His understanding of pragmatism was conducive to the long and arduous task of collecting relevant data.[8]

Shortly after his arrival in Worcester, Meyer spelled out his underlying assumptions in an article in the *American Journal of Insanity*. In his eyes the fundamental principle on which psychiatry rested was the "biological conception of man." Neither a purely somatic nor a psychological approach would suffice by itself. "We must . . . ," he argued,

accept the statement that all mental activity must have its physiological side and its anatomical substratum in the forms of nervous mechanisms, combinations of cells, especially of the cerebral cortex. A disease of these cells and their processes means at the same time a *physiological* and a *psychological* disorder; destruction of these cells, a destruction of *physiological* and *psychological* "function." Further, we cannot conceive a disorder of the mind without a disorder of function of those cell mechanisms which embody that part of the mind.

Meyer conceded that the evidence to substantiate this point of view was incomplete, but he insisted that a multidimensional approach was probably the only fruitful one to pursue. All mental reactions had their physiological counterparts; conversely, purely psychical disorders, commonly called functional, were a disorder of the life of the brain, as was organic lesion. Even though physicians had not yet learned to see the changes in the cells and processes, they had to admit that a functional disorder was just as serious as any organic disorder.[9]

Meyer's importance was due in part to the fact that he served as a conduit through which European psychiatric innovations came to the United States. During a return visit to Europe in 1896 he spent six weeks at Emil Kraepelin's clinic in Heidelberg. Meyer also reviewed the famous fifth edition of Kraepelin's *Psychiatrie: Ein Lehrbuch für Studirende und Aerzte* and helped to disseminate its concepts in America. Kraepelin played a key role in transforming modern psychiatry. He attempted to integrate the clinical-descriptive approach, the somatic approach, and the course of a disease into a unified and coherent system. For much of the nineteenth century mental illness had been classified on the basis of an unproveable etiology or content of symptoms. Kraepelin, by way of contrast, attempted to diagnose mental illness by understanding its course and outcome. He singled out groups of signs as evidencing specific disease entities, such as dementia praecox and later the manic-depressive psychosis. Studying thousands of cases, he observed their life histories both before and after the advent of the disorder. The disease entity was then usually identified in terms of its eventual outcome. Dealing with a large mass of data, Kraepelin sorted out everything that individuals had in common, omitting what he regarded as purely personal data. In many respects he was concerned with the form rather than with the content of a mentally ill person's thought process, and helped to prepare the ground for the emergence of dynamic psychiatry, with its emphasis on the individual and the process by which mental disease developed.[10]

In later years Meyer grew dissatisfied with the Kraepelinian system because classification in lesser hands became an end in itself. At the turn of the century, however, the ideas of Kraepelin acted as a catalyst for change. Willing to borrow from others but rejecting all forms of dogmatisms, Meyer attempted to develop a genetic-dynamic approach to the problem of mental disorder. "Psychobiology"—the name he gave to his understanding of psychiatry—involved the integration of the life experiences of the individual with physiological and biological data. Eschewing both Comptean positivism and psycho-physical parallelism, he urged his colleagues

> to trace the plain life history of a person and to record it on . . . the life chart; the result is a record of a smooth or broken life curve of each one of the main organs and functions, and in addition, a record of the main events of the life of the whole bundle of organs, that is, "the individual as a whole" and of the facts which determined and constituted his behavior. . . .
>
> Psychobiology as thus conceived forms clearly and simply the missing chapter of ordinary physiology and pathology, the chapters dealing with functions of the total person and not merely of detachable parts. It is a topic representing a special level of biologic integration, a new level of simple units having in common the fact of blending in consciousness, integrating our organism into simple or complex adaptive and constructive reactions of overt and implicit behavior.[11]

Since every individual constituted "an experiment of nature," it was essential to develop as comprehensive a life history as was humanly possible. Beginning at Kankakee and continuing for much of his career, Meyer transformed the patient record; nothing was irrelevant. Before his arrival in Worcester, for example, patient records were kept in large bound volumes; entries were scattered throughout and tended to be extraordinarily brief. Oftentimes different physicians entered isolated observations months apart and frequently unrelated. Meyer succeeded in getting the hospital to keep individual patient records in a single folder. Thus *all* material pertaining to any patient—even those readmitted—was easily accessible.[12]

Influenced by Darwinian biology and by the concept of adaptation, Meyer stressed the interaction between organism and environment. The test of mental health was the ability of the individual to function efficiently. Mental illness, on the other hand, was largely a behavioral disorder involving defective habits; certain early experiences in a person's life produced inefficient adaptation in adulthood. A knowledge of disease patterns thus depended upon a full understanding of the life history of the individual. Although never rejecting a somatic etiology or the role of constitutional and genetic influences, Meyer tended to emphasize psychogenic factors. Consequently, he gave habit training a central position in the treatment of mental disease. Incorporating and disseminating some of Freud's and Jung's concepts into his own work before 1910, Meyer never became a convert to psychoanalysis. After 1910 he became increasingly critical of psychoanalytic oversystematization and its tendency to read meaning into all the simple facts of human life. Moreover, Meyer held to a "teleological psychology" (as compared with a psychology of "blind reaction") in which human behavior had a purposive element. Similarly, he disliked the Freudian emphasis on sexual factors and on the unconscious.[13]

Although stressing the rigorous collection of data, Meyer was unable to integrate facts and theory in a systematic manner. The articulation of a comprehensive theory always lay in a remote future. After delivering the first Thomas W. Salmon lectures at the New York Academy of Medicine in 1931 on psychobiology, Meyer never published them during his lifetime. He was unable to develop a comprehensive framework that could comprehend the data drawn from experience. Similarly, in his relationships with colleagues and students at Hopkins, he always resisted efforts to arrive at any firm or definitive conclusions. "Our New World environment," he wrote to William Healy in 1917, "has been too readily overawed by the formulations of Kraepelin, Freud and others, much to the detriment of the fresh and courageous pragmatism which is the sanest product of our best leaders. Our people are brought up in dogma and they are rarely satisfied without some dogma and many are tempted to bow. Why not swear allegiance to the rich harvest of fact and the dictations of its conclusions? I would not ask anyone to snub the systematizers; but they are always a side product, a side vision to me and not more." Meyer's hostility toward theory was reflected in the domineering position he assumed toward his students; Smith Ely Jelliffe once observed that Meyer had "put partly castrated pupils in professional chairs."[14]

Meyer's popularity and influence in the United States was in part derived from his institutional affiliation with Johns Hopkins. Much more significant, however, was his broad eclecticism, which gave him an ability to incorporate virtually every contemporary intellectual and scientific current into his thinking. That he had relatively few competitors within psychiatry reflected the weakness rather than the vitality of the specialty within the United States. Indeed, Meyer's psychobiology raised many more questions than it answered. Arthur O. Lovejoy, the distinguished philosopher, found Meyer's published views full of "obscurities," which he generously attributed to the mode of presentation rather than to the ideas themselves. But Lovejoy's specific critique was harsh. Meyer's effort to integrate mental and physical facts, he noted, failed to discriminate between their nature, or to say anything about logical inconsistencies and ambiguities. Nor was Lovejoy alone in raising questions. Edward B. Titchener, the eminent Cornell psychologist who along with Meyer participated in the famous conference at Clark University in 1909 during Freud's only American visit, suggested that Meyer was seeking "to plunge us back into the obscurities and confusions of fact." Since Titchener was seeking to construct a formal and rational system of psychology that rested on universal laws or generalizations dealing with the normal adult mind, he rejected what he regarded as Meyer's crude empiricism. Moreover, he insisted that Meyer was reverting to a "teleological interpretation" of science. "We are now in one of those waves of popular thought which sweep over countries from time to time," he noted, ". . . and the wave is strongest here in America . . . [and] shows itself in all sorts of related movements: in philosophical pragmatism, in the revival of Thomism in the Catholic philosophy, and in your and other men's psycho-biology. In essentials, it is a reversion to Aristotelianism, nothing more or less. The main difference is that the concept of substance has been largely eliminated from it: matter has become energy, mind has become the sum-total of mental processes, disease has become the sum-total of symptoms." Similarly, Edward J. Kempf, who served a brief institutional apprenticeship before moving toward the Freudian camp, also emphasized that Meyer lacked a theoretical framework. Kempf sharply criticized Meyer's "non-commital attitude" which inhibited "clear self-expression" and remained "inaccessible to direct analysis." And Walter B. Cannon, the famous experimental physiologist whose celebrated book in 1915 attempted to explain the function of emotional excitement in terms of bodily changes, defined the difference between himself and Meyer in 1931 in terms of the latter's need to offer "practical treatment." Cannon, however, despaired of finding "any community of interest between the physiologist and the psychiatrist," given the imprecision of psychiatric terminology and concepts. Lovejoy, Titchener, Kempf, and Cannon wrote from clearly defined positions; other individuals who read Meyer were simply unable to grasp the essentials of his position. The efforts that Meyer made to clarify his views invariably created only greater confusion.[15]

III

Other psychiatrists were by no means unaware of the scientific and logical impediments that seemed to be blocking progress in their specialty. The continuing debate over nosology, for example, indicated a current of uncertainty. In a textbook published in 1905 Stewart Paton conceded that classification in psychiatry and medicine differed; the former did not deal with "definite disease entities" (i.e., typhoid fever), where a demonstrable causal link was present. Nor had psychiatrists been able to establish a connection between lesions and behavior. The only rational method, Paton suggested, was one that took into consideration "all the possible facts bearing upon the case." His preferred nosology was a reflection of the problems faced by psychiatry. Paton recommended a system that divided diseases into the "defect psychoses"—psychoses due to autointoxication (which he admitted was unproved)—and the manic-depressive and dementia praecox groups (which were based on "symptomatology, course, prognosis, and termination, without regard to the pathological findings"). In his presidential address at the AMPA in 1907, Charles G. Hill echoed Paton. Classifications of mental diseases had become so numerous, Hill observed, that there was little room for addition, "unless we add 'the classifying mania of medical authors.' "[16]

Such imprecision of diagnostic categories led to endless debate. The need for statistical and epidemiological data, nevertheless, required some form of nosology. The data-collecting activities of federal and state agencies only magnified the problem; the existence of discreet categories made comparisons either impossible or meaningless. By 1917, therefore, the AMPA and the National Committee for Mental Hygiene (NCMH) collaborated to produce a uniform classification of mental diseases to overcome the existing disorganization which, as the committee noted, "discredits the science of psychiatry and reflects unfavorably upon our Association." The new plan, according to its defenders, "substituted system for chaos" and made possible the combination and comparison of data collected in different places at the same time and established a basis for the comparison of present and future data. The new classification was "elastic" and included a provision for revision at five-year intervals. The very adoption of a formal system based on statistical considerations, of course, illustrated the difficulties that impeded efforts to link concepts and hard data. Nor did the new system silence dissent, for continued dissatisfaction with particulars persisted. When Meyer resigned from the committee that developed the new classification, he informed E. E. Southard that he had "no use for the essentially 'one person, one disease' view." "I prefer," he added, "to speak of an individual *presenting* certain facts that we can do something with in the way of definite demonstration, and if possible, in the way of some prediction of a type of lesion, and along the lines of attack in the way of some therapeutic activity, and also along the lines of prognosis. Whether a person has a dozen such facts or only one, is to be a matter of demonstration and not of legislation."[17]

The amorphous nature of nosological systems was accompanied by an equally confusing debate centering on the nature of mental illness and its etiology. The fact that the specialty faced extraordinary scientific and philosophical problems did not go unrecognized. Paton, for example, conceded that the relationship between structure and function was shrouded in mystery, and he warned against coming to any premature conclusions. At the same time he drew encouragement from the fact "that the little we know at least is sufficient to show that paths along which the alienist must pursue his studies."[18]

Others were not as cautious as Paton. As practicing physicians, they felt obligated to provide answers that would meet both their internal professional needs as well as those of patients and a broader public. The explanations of mental disease and its origins that they advanced varied widely. E. Stanley Abbot suggested to his colleagues at the AMPA that the first problem was "not what *causes* insanity, but what *is* insanity." After a survey of the definitions offered by others, he presented his own; insanity was "a morbid condition of the mind which renders it impossible for the conscious individual to think, feel or act in relation to his environment in accordance with the standards of his bringing-up." Since insanity was a "*mental* disease," psychiatric research had to center on the study of mental phenomena and not physical conditions. A few years later H. A. Tomlinson expressed virtually an opposite viewpoint. Tomlinson insisted that all forms of insanity had a common basis; their apparent diversity was "dependent upon inherent physical conditions resulting in instability or defect" which operated "in accordance with the conditions in the environment of the individual affected."[19]

As a group, American psychiatrists remained highly eclectic and fragmented. Some, like E. E. Southard, continued to emphasize brain pathology; some found autointoxication as an important antecedent in the advent of mental disease; some investigated the blood as a possible lead; some pursued studies involving chemical analysis; some focused on the endocrine system; and others stressed the role of prior infections or malfunctions in the immunological system. Admittedly, many of these investigators reached negative rather than positive conclusions; these research projects reflected the nature of psychiatric thought. Those who pursued a somatic approach found certain models consistent with their belief; in the early twentieth century a good deal of attention was focused on paresis and pellagra. Whether these could serve as universal models for psychiatry, of course, remained problematic. Much the same held true for the renewed interest in the hereditarian origins of insanity. Those who believed in the significance of heredity generally argued by analogy because of their inability to delineate specific mechanisms involved in the transmission of disease from one generation to another.[20]

The concepts of Sigmund Freud had relatively little influence on American institutional psychiatry before 1920, particularly outside the Northeast. Those who entered the specialty by working in a mental hospital had had traditional medical training and were rarely exposed to psychoanalytic ideas. Many physicians with a neurological orientation tended to regard psychoanalysis as more of a cult than a branch of science. Yet in the decade preceding and following Freud's American visit, psychoanalytic concepts began to find a small but friendly audience. Meyer's initial reaction, for example, was reserved but not unfriendly; he saw a parallel between psychoanalytic concepts and his own emphasis on the uniqueness of the individual, the importance of their life history, and habit disorganization. The most prominent convert to Freudian ideas was William Alanson White, superintendent of St. Elizabeths, a large federal mental hospital in Washington, D.C. Possessing impressive psychiatric credentials, a prestigious institutional affiliation, and a personality that enabled him to mediate between opposing factions, White helped to legitimate and popularize both psychoanalysis and the belief that psychiatry would play a major role in preventing and resolving innumerable social problems. Nevertheless, early twentieth-century Freudian concepts had a far greater influence on culture and intellect than on medicine in general or on psychiatry in particular. The protean nature of Freudianism led individuals to give it a major role in preventing and resolving innumerable social problems.[21]

For the bulk of institutionalized patients, psychoanalytic therapy had little meaning. The number of mentally ill patients who were institutionalized would in any case have precluded its use within hospitals. Analysts, moreover, dealt mainly with what was known as the psychoneuroses; the hard-core psychoses remained largely outside psychoanalytic practice or theory. In 1911 and 1912 Edward J. Kempf of the Indianapolis State Hospital adapted Freud's passive free-association method in dealing with female schizophrenics, but Kempf was not typical of institutional psychiatrists. White attempted to introduce a psychologically oriented therapy presumably based on Freudian concepts, but he admitted that it was difficult to evaluate the results since the few psychotics who had returned to a "constructive and productive life" might have recovered in any case. He emphasized, however, that Freudian ideas had helped to raise staff morale and to develop a sense of optimism and hope. Yet Smith Ely Jelliffe, White's closest friend, collaborator, and a central figure in American psychoanalysis from World War I to his death in 1945, observed as late as 1940 that psychoanalysis "in a mental hospital is practically useless. One has not the time, nor are the patients in the main of the type for whom it can be used."[22]

The absence of any psychologically oriented therapies within mental institutions, however, did not imply therapeutic nihilism. On the contrary, therapeutic innovation was the rule rather than the exception, even though, as Charles G. Hill conceded in 1907, most therapeutics were "simply a pile of rubbish." The overwhelming majority of therapies (excluding the use of salvarsan for the treatment of paresis) tended to be nonspecific and empirical in character. Yet each therapy was usually supported by some rationale. Dr. Donald Gregg, of the influential Boston Psychopathic Hospital, in 1914 offered three justifications for medical intervention: first, such interventions served to combat in a direct way the processes causing a disease; secondly, it strengthened the patient's general resistance; and, finally, it reassured "the patient or his friends that something is being done for him in accordance with the idea that still lies deep-rooted in most human minds that for every disease there is some curative drug." In an analysis of six wards containing an average of 95 patients, Gregg noted that in a single month 877 orders for medical treatment had been given. The two medical therapies used most widely were hydrotherapy (39 percent) and eliminatives (38 percent). The remaining therapies were divided between stimulants (6 percent), packs (9 percent), and depressants (3.5 percent); miscellaneous approaches accounted for the remaining 3.5 percent. He also pointed to the availability of other interventions in the psychiatric armamentarium, including lumbar puncture to drain off excessive amounts of cerebrospinal fluid.[23]

The fact that nonspecific therapies dominated psychiatric practice was no aberration because the same held true for medical practice in general. Medical intervention reflected a shared faith between patient and physician that assumed it would be effective. The alternative belief in therapeutic nihilism was never seriously entertained, partly because physicians rejected an approach that might impair their social legitimacy, and partly because patients and families eagerly sought treatment.

Generally speaking, discontinuities between psychiatric theory and therapeutic intervention prevailed, but exceptions were by no means uncommon. The use of bilateral ovariectomy is a case in point. This operation was first popularized by Robert Battey, a Georgia surgeon, in the 1870s. He performed it on normal women to combat general and nonspecific nervous conditions and sexual disorders and to restore general health. By the 1880s bilateral ovariectomies (along with other surgical procedures on both male and female that involved sexual organs) were performed with increasing frequency. Most of the patients were middle-class females with vaguely defined symptoms who were not in mental institutions. The female nervous system, according to many physicians, was far more frail than that of her male counterpart, since it was largely dependent on her reproductive organs. A few physicians believed that woman's characteristics from puberty to menopause were controlled by the uterus and ovaries. If this was the case, removal of the ovaries might alleviate a variety of symptoms limited to women.[24]

During the 1880s Battey's operation was used only on rare and isolated occasions on insane women in mental hospitals. The widely held belief that a remote relationship existed between the ovaries and uterus, on the one hand, and insanity, on the other, led a few physicians to consider bilateral ovariectomy as an appropriate therapy where there appeared to be a conclusive relationship between female organs and mental disease. Interest in surgical intervention was far greater among physicians specializing in obstetrics and gynecology than among institutional psychiatrists. Just as "disease of the abdominal organs may favor insanity even by interference with nutrition alone," I. S. Stone told the Section on Obstetrics and Diseases of Women of the AMA in 1891, why was it not equally possible for "disease of the organs peculiar to women, which so much more than the corresponding organs in men, have to do with her physical and mental condition . . . cause psychical derangement." Prior to reading his paper, Stone wrote to twenty mental hospitals to determine the number of cases of insanity due to some disease of the pelvic organs of females. The overwhelming majority of those surveyed rejected the allegation that insanity in many females was traceable to pelvic disease, although none rejected the possibility that such a relationship might exist.[25]

Shortly thereafter Dr. Joseph Price, "in consultation with Dr. Alice Bennett" and with the approval of the trustees of the State Hospital for the Insane at Norristown, Pennsylvania, performed four ovariectomies at a separate annex ward and scheduled about fifty additional women for the procedure. Price was a firm believer in the efficacy of such intervention, and denied that the surgery was either brutal or experimental. The state's Committee on Lunacy, on the other hand, condemned the practice as "unwarranted and indefensible" and forced its discontinuance. Its members doubted that even a relative or guardian of an insane female possessed "the moral or legal right to give consent to the unsexing of the insane person. . . . What redress would such a person have, if, recovering her reason, she objected to her mutilated condition?" Support for the Committee also came from prominent members of the medical profession. "To erect a hospital, or propose one, where women were to be castrated in companies of fifties, with the hope of a cure of insanity," wrote John B. Chapin, president of the AMSAII, "would be generally regarded, in the present state of meagre knowledge upon the subject, as revolting." Although the belief persisted among some that insanity in women was attributable to their physiology, surgical intervention in mental hospitals was extremely rare, primarily because of opposition within psychiatry itself. In 1916 a psychiatrist who surveyed the relationship between his specialty and gynecology insisted that the belief that mental disease was due to genital disorders deserved to be regarded as "a superstition which must be lived down."[26]

Similarly, those psychiatrists who posited a causal link between focal infections and mental illness were prone to act on the basis of their convictions. Henry A. Cotton, a former student of Meyer at Worcester and superintendent of the state hospital in Trenton, New Jersey, became an ardent convert to the view that chronic, masked, or focal infections played a "very important role in the etiology of the psychoses." Persuaded that many infections spread from the teeth to other regions of the body (especially the tonsils, stomach, and lower intestinal tract), he came to the conclusion that the extraction of diseased teeth or removal of infected tissues represented an appropriate form of therapy. In a paper delivered at the American Psychiatric Association (APA) meetings in 1922, Cotton claimed striking success. According to his statistics, in the decade before 1918 about 37 percent of the patients recovered spontaneously; in the four succeeding years aggressive therapeutic intervention had raised the recovery rate to 80 percent.[27]

The reaction to Cotton's work among his psychiatric colleagues was generally negative. As early as 1919 White privately expressed the belief that the emphasis on infected teeth was "most unfortunate." Meyer was ambivalent; his introduction to Cotton's published Vanuxem lectures at Princeton University was noncommittal. J. K. Hall, one of the most prominent Southern psychiatrists, ridiculed Cotton as being infected with "red ants." Hall decried the false hopes raised by such work, to say nothing of its unsoundness. "The world has been overflowing for the last few years with lots of damn fool theories," he added, "and I think it important for the welfare of humanity that some of us doctors at least retain what little sense we have in trying to keep our feet on the ground." In the discussions at the APA meetings Edward Brush, former superintendent and editor of the *American Journal of Insanity*, noted that the surgical procedures used (including colostomy and colectomy) were both serious and dangerous; Cotton, he suggested, held preconceived ideas and shut out all evidence to the contrary. Other psychiatrists were equally critical, although a few favorable statements supporting Cotton were made. Most hospital superintendents accepted to some degree the theory of focal infections, but in most cases they responded by establishing dental departments.[28]

In light of the growing publicity, an investigation of Cotton's controversial practices was inevitable. As early as January, 1923, Dr. Augustus S. Knight, Medical Director for the Metropolitan Life Insurance Company and chairman of the Medical Committee of the state hospital in Morris Plains, expressed an interest and concern about Cotton's claims. One year later Dr. Joseph E. Raycroft of Princeton University, and a member of Trenton State Hospital's Board of Managers, thought that an investigation under the auspices of the Board might be desirable. Raycroft was generally favorable, and he believed that Cotton's work could withstand scientific scrutiny. Another physician and member of the Board was more dubious, partly because the institutional records were incomplete and partly because of the "undesirable notoriety" that would follow. Raycroft persisted, and ultimately contacted Meyer, who suggested that Dr. Phyllis Greenacre, his associate at Hopkins, spend part of the winter of 1924 and 1925 in Trenton. Greenacre's study, when completed, discredited Cotton's claims. She conceded that such surgery tended to quiet excited or aggressive patients. But the Trenton records were incomplete or inaccurate; procedures were undertaken without controls; and the statistical analysis was totally unscientific. Moreover, the more surgical detoxication was employed, the smaller the chances were for recovery or even survival.[29]

At the same time that Greenacre was preparing her study, allegations of patient abuse led to hearings before a joint legislative committee. Meyer was determined that the unfinished study would not become involved with a public investigation. In her testimony, therefore, Greenacre simply denied that she had witnessed patient abuse or encountered false records. When Greenacre completed her report, however, Meyer wanted Cotton to respond before the document was passed on. Initially Cotton was unable to do so because he suffered a breakdown following his appearance before the legislative investigating committee. He was found "wandering about the streets in Trenton" in a "confused and apprehensive" state. Subsequently he rejected all of Greenacre's documented claims. By 1927 the affair had come to an end, and the report was never made public. Indeed, the New Jersey Department of Institutions and Agencies was not persuaded by Greenacre's statistical analysis, and its inability or refusal to judge either Cotton or Greenacre led to no action being taken.[30]

Three years later Dr. S. Katzenelbogen of Johns Hopkins visited Trenton and found few significant changes. Many staff members, he reported, lacked even rudimentary psychiatric training, thus weakening any claims about improvement and recovery. The indiscriminate removal of teeth was not followed by replacement dentures, thereby causing dietary problems as well as the patients' feelings of shame about their appearance. Colectomies were routinely performed even when pathological evidence was lacking.

In most cases it was impossible to demonstrate the presence of septic foci in supposedly infected organs. Katzenelbogen concluded that many of the favorable therapeutic results that were claimed might simply be due to the fact that *something* was being done by the physician to the patient.[31]

Cotton resigned as Medical Director in 1930 after charges were made that while a state employee he saw private patients and maintained what was in effect a private hospital. Nevertheless, he remained at Trenton as Director of Research on a salaried basis until his death three years later. However, Raycroft and others, influenced by Greenacre, virtually halted the use of surgical procedures as a therapy for mental disease. Cotton, on the other hand, never changed his beliefs; in mid-1933 the *American Mercury* published an article in which he reaffirmed his claims of therapeutic success.[32] Interestingly enough, during the entire decade of the 1920s no person saw fit to challenge Cotton's authority or his right to prescribe aggressive therapies whose efficacy was not even remotely established and which enjoyed little support within the specialty. Nor was there any discussion of the relationship between ethical considerations and aggressive therapeutic interventions of questionable validity. Disagreements involving medical practice and ethics were regarded as an internal problem, the resolution of which precluded any external intervention.

IV

The ferment within psychiatry in the early twentieth century was also characterized by institutional changes. By the turn of the century two innovations had appeared: the research institute and the psychopathic hospital. The creation of such institutions arose from changes within medical science in general. To many observers it seemed that medical science was standing on the threshold of a new era. The specific germ theory of disease suggested an explanation that was empirically verifiable, and it pointed the way toward the development of specific therapies. Scientific and technological innovation had also created conditions that made possible the emergence of the hospital in its modern form. Before 1880 the small number of hospitals that existed offered care for the poor and socially marginal groups. After 1880 the hospital began to embody the scientific and technological imperatives that legitimated a changing profession as well as commencing to serve a more affluent clientele. Consciously or unconsciously, psychiatrists began to find in general medicine an appropriate model to follow. During the first two decades of the twentieth century, they began to push their own specialty in the direction of comparable institutional innovation.

Original scientific work, noted Dr. C. R. Bardeen of Johns Hopkins in 1899, was virtually impossible in the absence of an appropriate institutional structure. In Germany, for example, the most original scientific work was done in universities with close ties to mental hospitals. Lacking either German traditions or institutional arrangements, America suffered by comparison. To remedy existing defects, Bardeen proposed that every hospital retain a qualified pathologist with clinical and research responsibilities. Larger states, he added, should establish a "central laboratory" located near "some centre of intellectual activity" and "in active association with some university if possible." Such a laboratory would be a focal point for scientific activities; its functions would include research and training. Bardeen suggested that the newly created Pathological Institute of the New York State Hospital might serve as an appropriate model.[33]

Established in 1895, the Pathological Institute was given two mandates: to study the "causes and conditions that underlie mental diseases, from the standpoint of cellular biology," and to offer instruction in brain pathology to state hospital physicians. Its first director was Ira Van Gieson, who had been associated with the College of Physicians and Surgeons in New York City and who was regarded as an authority on histology and on the pathology of the brain and nervous system. Van Gieson had little regard for traditional institutional psychiatry. Indeed, the Institute was first located on Madison Avenue and Twenty-Third Street in New York City at a considerable distance from any mental hospital. Van Gieson believed that scientific investigation of mental diseases had to be "unshackled from the narrow circumscribed connections which have so long governed it." Similarly, psychiatry had to be liberated "from the confines of the asylum walls"; the very definition of problems belonged to the scientist rather than to the asylum physician. Van Gieson's goal was singular yet grand; he hoped to develop a correlation of sciences. "Different branches of sciences," he proclaimed, "must be co-ordinated and focussed together as a search-light on the mysteries of mental disease. They must all work hand in hand. They must be linked together and correlated, otherwise the whole aim of the work is defeated." Under his leadership the Institute was divided into six sections: psychology and psychopathology; normal and comparative histology of the nervous system; cellular biology; pathological anatomy, bacteriology and physiological chemistry; experimental pathology and hematology; and anthropology. Van Gieson himself was preoccupied with the relation of autointoxications to neural diseases.[34]

Despite Van Gieson's imposing vision, the Institute was soon embroiled in controversies. From the outset Van Gieson and the superintendents of the state hospitals were in disagreement. Van Gieson believed that research on normal functions and tissues had to take precedence over the pathology of insanity; the superintendents wanted the Institute to unify and centralize the pathological activities of state hospitals and to maintain an intimate relationship with clinical work. It was a classic struggle that pitted the ideals of pure science against the needs of active clinicians, and it occurred at a time when neither advocate could point to a body of relevant empirical data that validated a comprehensive theoretical structure. When the legislature threatened to withhold the Institute's annual appropriation in 1900, the parent State Commission in Lunacy appointed a committee composed of Edward Cowles, William T. Councilman, and G. Alder Blumer to undertake an investigation. Blumer solicited Meyer's advice, for by this time Meyer's work at Worcester had earned him national recognition. The committee's final report paralleled most of Meyer's suggestions. It urged that the Institute be reorganized to expedite its teaching function and to integrate its clinical, anatomical, and chemical research. The report insisted that the director must be trained in both pathology and clinical psychiatry, and that the Institute be relocated near a medical school and a small mental hospital.[35]

Van Gieson's response was bitter. He attacked his asylum foes in strong language and suggested that their medical training lacked a firm grounding in science, psychology, and philosophy. Given the fact that "the science of psychopathology" had not yet been worked out, how could the Institute undertake routine instructional duties? Moreover, psychiatry was so dominated by the asylum mentality "that no scientist can enter this universally supposed avatar of psychiatry without running the risk of having to mould his work befitting the conceptions of the officials." Privately Van Gieson was even more adamant. The basic issue, he wrote to Meyer, was between the freedom of psychiatry as a science versus bondage "to the rock of asylum superintendency which is general[ly] ignorant of genius and future expansion of scientific psychiatry." Meyer was also critical of part of the committee's report, which he regarded as overly vague. On the other hand; he was equally critical of Van Gieson. The foundation of the Institute, Meyer observed, proved too weak for its superstructure; and the hostility toward clinical psychiatry was unjustified.[36]

In the midst of the dispute, Dr. Peter M. Wise, president of the State Commission in Lunacy, solicited Meyer's advice. Unsympathetic toward Van Gieson, the Commission was already considering a replacement, and Meyer was an obvious candidate. The fact that Meyer's relationship with the superintendent of the Worcester hospital was strained only enhanced the possibility of inducing him to move. In a long memo exceeding sixty pages, Meyer spelled out some of his own views. The basic problem was that institutional medical work had failed to furnish a body of material which was required "before a medical science becomes digestible and teachable, and a basis for research." The focus of the Institute, insisted Meyer, had to be on the patient suffering from mental disease, and mental hospitals could provide the elements for research. A number of wards—akin to a psychopathic hospital—could be reserved for the Institute; a move to Ward's Island near the state hospital located there was also desirable. That hospitals had not taken advantage of research opportunities was obvious; but the absence of psychiatric training gave them a medical staff ill-equipped for their duties. To remedy this defect Meyer proposed some form of post-graduate study (an early version of what subsequently became a psychiatric residency). The ultimate goal of the Institute was to provide the state hospitals with adequately trained physicians, who in turn could contribute to the ultimate transformation of their institutions. "In this way," concluded Meyer, "it is hoped that a correlation can be made between the needs of the hospitals, the needs of medical education and the needs of psychiatry which longs for greater possibilities in applying the methods of medicine and the sciences."[37]

In 1900 Meyer, unpersuaded that the future of the Institute was secure, declined an offer to succeed Van Gieson. A year later he reconsidered and toward the end of 1901 moved from Worcester to New York.[38] He immediately reorganized the Pathological Institute and created three departments (clinical, chemical, and histological). His goal was to raise "the standard of medical work in the State institutions." Traditionally, Meyer noted, humanitarian and administrative duties dominated state hospital work. The general advancement of medicine and dissatisfaction with the "common indifference to psychiatric matters," however, had created a new situation. In order to alter prevailing institutional practices and to restore psychiatry to medicine, Meyer decided to visit each hospital in the state in order to review staff qualifications and to determine if purely administrative functions detracted from the maintenance of a "satisfactory standard" of medical care. During each visit Meyer proposed to study twenty-five admissions and an equal number of discharges as well as five cases in which an autopsy had been performed.[39]

During Meyer's tenure as director, the hostility between the Institute and state hospitals largely disappeared. Meyer's clinical emphasis and seemingly inexhaustable knowledge of medicine and psychiatry ensured a friendly reception, if only because he appeared in the vanguard of change. After his visit to Utica, for example, there was a notable surge in staff morale and a determined effort to translate recommendations into practice. The emphasis on individual patients was more congenial than the completion of statistical forms, noted the Utica superintendent in a letter clearly reflecting his admiration of Meyer. An ability to deal with more than five hundred male patients without restraint or hypnotics, wrote another physician, "was entirely due to the methods you instituted in showing me how to find out all there was to know about patients: my judgment was then clear to know what to do for them." The direct benefit to patients, on the other hand, was less evident (although many may have very well benefited from the greater attention paid to them); theoretical clarity and clinical innovation did not automatically follow. C. P. Oberndorf, who spent time at the Institute in 1909 and after, later recalled that where "Meyer's grasp seemed wanting was in the correlation of a wealth of laboriously ascertained facts with the meaning of the clinical picture that the patient presented. Facts without theory, just as theory without facts, are not enough."[40]

Nor was Meyer's tenure in New York without its problems. His hope of merging clinical and pathological work was on occasion frustrated by superintendents who felt their staffs not sufficiently large to permit the assignment of one physician to laboratory work. Other superintendents were reluctant to provide their staff with released time to attend instructional meetings. One individual was informed that satisfactory performance made it unnecessary to receive further instruction from Meyer. Finally, the passage of legislation in 1904 authorizing construction of a

Psychopathic Hospital in New York City embroiled Meyer in a conflict with state authorities and the State Charities Aid Association. Meyer opposed the construction of such a hospital on a site far removed from available transportation and so close to a large power-generating plant. He proposed instead that the institution be constructed adjacent to an existing state hospital. Provision for admission could remain in part with existing hospitals throughout the city, with adequate ambulance service to facilitate the transfer of patients. In effect, Meyer wanted to promote local involvement and to encourage a modification of "the still existing indifference of most of our general hospitals and physicians." With the exception of changing the name of the Pathological Institute to the Psychiatric Institute, Meyer found his new post more and more frustrating. The integration of psychiatry and medicine that he had hoped for floundered in the absence "of any definite policy." When Henry Phipps decided to endow a new psychiatric clinic at the renowned Johns Hopkins Hospital, Meyer enthusiastically accepted a position as director and professor of psychiatry.[41]

In 1910 August Hoch succeeded Meyer as director of the Psychiatric Institute, a position he retained for seven years. The work of the Institute under Hoch narrowed somewhat. Although continuing to offer courses at various state hospitals and to publish the *State Hospital Bulletin* (which first appeared in 1908), the Institute never became a driving force in integrating psychiatric institutions and practices with medicine and general hospitals as planned. Nor did it help to formulate and implement a cohesive state policy on matters regarding mental illness. Hoch himself introduced psychoanalytic concepts to a small group of physicians and pursued his own interest in psychological phenomena, but his influence on policy remained marginal. Under George S. Kirby, who succeeded Hoch in 1917, the Institute eventually became part of Columbia Presbyterian Hospital and Medical Center, thereby confirming its status as an educational, clinical, and research center.[42]

Only a few states followed New York's lead, and their experiences were somewhat similar. The Massachusetts State Board of Insanity in 1909 created a new position of pathologist. Responsible to the Board, the pathologist was to be entrusted with three general functions: first, to supervise the clinical, pathological, and research work in state institutions; second, to visit institutions periodically; and, third, to report to the Board on existing conditions and to make recommendations. The appointment of Elmer E. Southard to the position seemed to herald a new beginning. After receiving his M.D. from Harvard in 1901, Southard's ascent to fame was rapid. His reputation for originality and productivity was such that in 1909 he was appointed to the newly created Bullard professorship at the Harvard Medical School. An individual with extraordinarily broad interests, Southard had considerable influence over the careers of a group of younger psychiatrists and neurologists, some of whom achieved fame in their own right. Aside from nearly 200 papers and three books published before his death in 1920 at the age of forty-four, Southard was also one of the founders of social psychiatry and psychiatric social work.[43]

Despite his contributions to social psychiatry, Southard was essentially a somaticist in his interpretation of mental disease. Smith Ely Jelliffe recalled years later that Southard "made no clinical inquiries." "How often have I seen him in reality and in fantasy lightly palpating those hard areas of the cortex," Jelliffe added, "feeling—in more senses than one—here was the answer to all of the enigmas." By virtue of his reputation and varied positions in the Bay State, Southard was able to exert considerable influence upon the research undertaken. He himself began a massive comparative study of brains removed from the bodies of both normal and demented subjects in the hope of uncovering the relationship between brain structure and mental disease; others were quickly involved in the project. Indeed, he urged young physicians to "look beyond the individual patient. Not to see the woods for the trees, not to observe disease principles in the rush of individual patients, is the fallacy."[44]

In general, Southard's leads were followed at other Bay State institutions; the emphasis was on brain lesions or organic malfunctions. After 1913 considerable effort was devoted to syphilis, including its diagnosis through the Wasserman test and treatment by salvarsan. In that year Noguchi and Moore published their definitive findings; syphilis, caused by the treponema pallidum, led to brain lesions, which in turn gave rise to the symptoms and signs of paresis. For somatically trained psychiatrists like Southard, paresis was an ideal model for mental disease. Southard had long been interested in syphilis, given the high proportion of paretics in mental hospitals. The State Board of Insanity proved sympathetic and authorized an expansion of research into the problems of treatment and in 1915 appointed Dr. Harry C. Solomon as a special investigator in brain syphilis. Eventually nine other institutions were involved in the project. "No apology need be made for putting syphilis in the forefront of the routine problems of psychiatry in the institutions," Southard reported in 1917. Two years later he succeeded in persuading the state to rename his research laboratories at the Boston Psychopathic Hospital, where he also occupied the position of superintendent. Its new title was impressive (the Massachusetts State Psychiatric Institute) although—as he conceded privately—it was little more than a "name" with a "skeleton organization."[45]

Two years before Southard was appointed pathologist, Illinois established its own State Psychopathic Institute modeled after its New York counterpart. The President of the State Board of Charities, as a matter of fact, noted that if Meyer had been treated differently by Kankakee officials, the first such institute would probably have been founded in Illinois. Located at Kankakee, the new Institute was headed by Dr. H. Douglas Singer. Its functions reflected a desire to uplift the medical and scientific character of psychiatry and hospitals, and the Institute was charged with responsibility for normal laboratory work as well as for research and education. At the outset a small appropriation ($4,000) limited its effectiveness. By 1912 the budget had nearly tripled, and the Institute undertook the task of redressing the psychiatric ignorance of recent medical school graduates on the staff of public institutions. The geographical location, however, proved a hindrance, and eventually the Institute was transferred to the Chicago State Hospital, where it developed a working relationship with the University of Illinois College of Medicine.[46]

The enthusiasm with which the Illinois Institute was launched was not commensurate with its achievements. As late as 1923 its functions remained largely routine: making Wasserman tests for various state institutions; conducting studies on the metabolism of epileptics (which were admittedly unsatisfactory because the intake and output of patients were not controlled); examining brain specimens by the neuropathologist; and working with the school of psychiatric nursing. Pure research was rendered virtually impossible because the Institute did not control any of its own hospital beds.[47]

By 1914 another state—Wisconsin—had also established a Psychiatric Institute at the state hospital in Mendota. Emphasizing the study and treatment of syphilis, the Institute launched a "campaign of prevention" to educate the public about the need to treat the disease during its early stages and before lesions of the central nervous system or brain produced insanity. Subsequently, its staff began biochemical and metabolical studies designed to shed light on dementia praecox. The location of the Institute at a state hospital, however, proved less than ideal. W. F. Lorenz, the director, urged its transfer to the University of Wisconsin, which had already developed some working relationships with the Institute. "Scientific investigations," he noted in a veiled criticism of his hospital, "should be untrammeled and, if possible, should never be compelled to surmount the opposition of those who are without the technical knowledge and experience to properly appraise the value of the work." A university, on the other hand, provided a far more favorable environment for research and educational activities. Under such a jurisdiction, the Institute "would for all time be assured of the counsel, guidance and sympathetic direction of men scientifically trained." By 1925 the transfer had been consummated.[48]

In spite of the optimism with which they were launched, virtually none of these research institutes (including informal institutes such as the one at the State Psychopathic Hospital at the University of Michigan) lived up to expectations. Some individuals blamed American society for the failure because there was no national commitment to research. "Isn't it rather a commentary on the American manner of doing things that we go enthusiastically and busily about matters of hospital organization and bringing up recalcitrant states into line," observed Southard, "and do not so eagerly push the fundamental basis of progress?" The problem, however, was far more complex than he was willing to concede. Simon Flexner, director of the Rockefeller Institute for Medical Research (now the Rockefeller University), was dubious about even undertaking neuropsychiatric research; he virtually claimed "that there were no problems in a fit state for work." Southard emphatically rejected such a position, but his own work and that of others suggested that Flexner's observation was not wide of the mark. To concede its validity was to surrender the vision of a truly scientific psychiatry at a time when the prestige of scientific medicine was clearly on the rise. Nor were many practicing psychiatrists prepared to accept a caring or custodial model for their specialty; their vision of a new psychiatry which eradicated an age-old malady proved irresistible. Given the scientific and technological obstacles that impeded even a rudimentary understanding of many forms of mental illness, it seems unlikely that a determined and targeted research effort would have achieved spectacular results. Similarly, the emphasis on the educational function of institutes was rarely accompanied by a discussion of the precise results that should be disseminated among practitioners. If the answer to psychiatric problems lay in the future, how could a greater emphasis on education alter practice? When commenting on the "checkered career" of the New York Psychiatric Institute, Thomas W. Salmon, medical director of the NCMH, offered a suggestion to Southard that revealed the tenuous foundations that underlay much of psychiatric thought. "How desirable it would be for your institute and Kirby's to grow up side by side, each developing its own point of view but comparing aims, methods, work and accomplishments at frequent intervals! I suppose everyone will agree that the three chief functions of a psychiatric institute are research, instruction and public enlightenment."[49]

V

The second institutional innovation that embodied the psychiatric vision of a better future was the psychopathic (or reception) hospital. Before the turn of the century, the traditional mental hospital had served two functions: long-term care and treatment. Although often divided over the desirability of separate institutions for chronic cases, psychiatrists had never considered a kind of institutional modification—one that presupposed either the existence of hospitals that dealt with acute cases whose stay would be measured in days, or the creation of wards in general hospitals limited to the treatment of mental disease. Between 1890 and 1920, however, psychiatrists not only debated such possibilities, but moved to alter institutional arrangements.

The most significant elements hastening a reconsideration of traditional institutional forms were the changes within medicine in general and the transformation of the mental hospital in particular. The changes in medical education during this era merely reinforced the vision of scientific medicine. The famous report on medical education by Abraham Flexner in 1910 only confirmed the legitimacy of the changes that had already taken place, and offered assurance that future funding would in no way reverse or impair contemporary trends. Fearing obsolescence or irrelevance, psychiatrists sought to restructure the institutional basis of their specialty in a way that would promote their reintegration with scientific medicine. The psychopathic hospital seemed admirably suited for this purpose.

The origins of the psychopathic hospital date back to the closing decade of the nineteenth century. At that time there was growing concern over the treatment of mentally ill persons during the commitment process and prior to the time that they were actually institutionalized. Some states issued specific regulations to protect patients, and to avoid any incarceration in jails. Cognizant of the problem, New York City completed in 1879 a reception pavilion for the insane at Bellevue Hospital. Six years later general oversight of the unit was transferred to the superintendent of the municipal asylum. Commitment was limited to five days, and individuals were examined and processed on the basis of staff evaluations. Between 1888 and 1891, 7,669 persons were admitted to the pavilion, of whom 5,681 were sent to other asylums and the remainder either transferred to other institutions (893), discharged (969), or died (106).[50]

The step from a reception pavilion to the psychopathic hospital was a logical one. Just as acute diseases of the lungs or stomach were treated promptly at general hospitals, why could not acute cases of insanity be treated in special wards at general hospitals or in psychopathic hospitals modeled after general hospitals? Why was it necessary to wait until the mental disease was so advanced "as to satisfy a lay tribunal of the necessity or justification of the forcible deprivation of his [the patient's] liberty"? Why could not individuals in the early or acute stage of mental disease turn to a local institution which provided short-term and immediate treatment for voluntary patients, thus obviating in many instances the necessity for commitment to a state hospital?[51]

In 1899 a group of Albany physicians petitioned the county board of supervisors to erect a "building for the temporary care of insane patients." The petition was favorably received, and a law providing an appropriation of $18,000 for construction of such a facility at the Albany Hospital (a private institution) was passed. With a recently constructed physical plant, the Albany Hospital was in a position to use one of its pavilions for the treatment of mentally ill persons. The result was the establishment of Pavilion F (the Department of Mental Diseases of the Albany Hospital), which had an administrative structure comparable to that of other departments. Between 1902 (when the first patient was admitted) and 1907, Pavilion F admitted 1,031 patients. Of this number, 596 were sent home either recovered or improved, 316 remained stationary, 86 died, and 245 transferred to regular mental hospitals. Without such a facility, observed J. Montgomery Mosher, the attending physician, most of these patients "would either have had to be improperly treated at home, or would have been committed after a probably harmful development of the disease."[52]

Michigan, on the other hand, followed the German model when it established the Psychopathic Hospital at the University of Michigan in Ann Arbor. In 1901 the legislature appropriated $50,000 for a "Psychopathic Ward of the University of Michigan Hospital." Its title notwithstanding, the ward was in all respects a complete hospital in itself. Intended to serve as a central and unifying facility for the various state hospitals, it also had intimate links with the university-based medical school. Headed by Albert M. Barrett, who had been trained by Meyer at Worcester, the Psychopathic Hospital had four responsibilities which, taken together, differentiated it from regular mental hospitals: first, in its care, observation, and treatment of patients; second, the clinical and anatomical research; third, the instruction of medical students; and, fourth, the development of cooperative work with state asylums. Its admission policy was relatively flexible. In cases where the very question of insanity was at issue, or if insanity was due to physical conditions requiring the facilities of a general hospital, the legal commitment hearing could be continued for a period not exceeding thirty-five days. Provision was also made for voluntary admissions. In virtually all cases the prior approval of the director was required.[53]

During the first decade of the twentieth century interest in reception and psychopathic hospitals and wards grew. In 1907 Meyer observed that so many cities were interested in establishing such facilities "that to-day the problem is one of the most actual and commanding the greatest attention." Yet the optimistic hopes and expectations of the potential achievements of psychopathic hospitals did not lead to a dramatic increase in their number. Before 1920 only four institutions could be clearly identified in this category—Pavilion F, the Michigan Psychopathic Hospital, the Henry Phipps Psychiatric Clinic at the Johns Hopkins Hospital, and Boston Psychopathic Hospital. Of these four, Phipps and Boston Psychopathic were the most influential, and their history offers some instructive and revealing case studies.[54]

The Phipps Psychiatric Clinic came into existence as a result of a bequest from Henry Phipps in 1908, who agreed to provide sufficient funds to construct and equip a psychiatric division at the Johns Hopkins Hospital for sixty patients and to endow a professorship of psychiatry. Opened in 1913, the Clinic, under Meyer's leadership, quickly acquired a national reputation as a training and research center. Its prestige was also enhanced by the fact that it was part of the nation's most prestigious hospital and medical school. Between 1913 and 1919, the staff published nearly 100 papers in medical and scientific periodicals and books.[55]

Outward appearances notwithstanding, the Clinic faced serious internal difficulties during its first decade. Budgetary authority remained in the hands of the hospital's administration rather than the Clinic's director. The base of funding was Phipps's original and subsequent grants, and Meyer found it difficult to raise additional funds elsewhere. At one point Meyer considered the possibility of establishing a suburban branch that might increase the Clinic's revenue by attracting affluent patients unwilling to come to an urban institution, but the plan never materialized. By 1919 Meyer conceded that the Clinic was in "a state of marasmus due to inadequate feeding." "The past nine years," he wrote to David T. Layman in 1922, "have been an unduly heavy burden on me personally. To run a Clinic of this sort with less than one half the endowment which the New York Psychiatric Institute or the Boston Psychopathic Institute gets from the State for staff and laboratories—and that while everybody imagines I have practically unlimited funds for research, since naturally no public statement of the facts could ever be made—has been a very trying experience, borne by me largely out of loyalty to Mr. Phipps and to the Hopkins ideal." Meyer believed that neither William H. Welch nor Rockefeller's General Education Board understood or appreciated the new dynamic psychiatry and were wedded to the obsolete German emphasis on a research laboratory divorced from living patients.[56]

Other obstacles prevented the realization of Meyer's dreams. The relationship between Meyerian psychiatry and medicine had never been a happy one. Meyer emphasized the individual, whereas his medical colleagues outside psychiatry had less sympathy for such an approach. Nor was Meyer able to foster close links with other disciplines at Hopkins; intellectual and administrative differences precluded cross-disciplinary cooperation. Meyer's open-ended pluralism tended to produce eclectic-minded individuals hesitant to generalize about their specialty. As a system of thought, psychobiology was not always internally consistent or clear to those who attempted to grasp its essential meaning. "I am not sure," recalled Richard S. Lyman, who spent three years at Baltimore in the early 1920s, "how much of a philosophy, sufficiently rounded to be satisfying, was carried away by members of the staff at that time." The relatively small and select group of patients at the Clinic, moreover, was scarcely typical of the larger and more diverse population found at public hospitals generally. Phipps's reputation, therefore, was more a reflection of its Hopkins affiliation than Meyer's intrinsic achievements.[57]

Unlike the Phipps Clinic, the Boston Psychopathic Hospital was the product of strains and tensions within Massachusetts, which still retained the influential position in the field that it had enjoyed since the early nineteenth century. As early as 1906 L. Vernon Briggs, a young physician embarking on a career as a psychiatric activist, urged the establishment of an "observation hospital" for mental disorders in Boston; admissions would be largely limited to acute cases in the early stages of illness. At that time no state institution was located in Boston. Aside from the municipally owned Boston Insane Hospital, residents of the city had to be committed to state institutions located elsewhere.[58]

By 1908 Briggs persuaded the legislature to enact a law providing for the transfer of the Boston Insane Hospital from city to state jurisdiction. Shortly thereafter another law authorized the establishment of an observation hospital as part of the renamed Boston State Hospital. A crusader who disliked opposition and who tended to perceive those with whom he disagreed in conspiratorial terms, Briggs also launched a movement to abolish restraint and substitute occupational therapy in its place. His charges about alleged deficiencies in state hospitals led to an acrimonious public and private debate that quickly expanded to include the manner in which the state organized and financed its hospital system. The conflict became so heated that Meyer was called in to prepare a lengthy but vague report to the governor and Council on conditions. On the basis of his investigation, Meyer recommended a more decentralized structure.[59]

After much fanfare and numerous complications, the Psychopathic Hospital opened in 1912 as a department of Boston State Hospital under the direction of Southard. The new facility did not provide long-term custodial care, nor did it confine patients for extended periods. Instead it acted as a clearing house for Boston's mentally ill as well as providing intensive treatment for acute patients, who were either returned to their homes or admitted to one of the state hospitals for more extended treatment.

The institution was also intended as a center for research. Under Southard's leadership it acquired a national reputation. "The psychopathic hospital in a community," Southard informed the Section on Hospitals of the AMA in 1913, "is bound to be one of the most concrete sources of enlightenment as to psychopaths, and every society for mental hygiene, for sex hygiene, for the amelioration of alcoholism, for eugenics, should make it part of its business to help start a psychopathic hospital with its outpatient service in every community in which there is any hope for awakening social sense."[60]

At the outset Southard succeeded in recruiting an impressive staff that included Elisha H. Cohoon and Arthur P. Noyes in administration, Herman M. Adler and Abraham Myerson as the chief medical officers, A. Warren Stearns and Douglas A. Thom in the outpatient department, Robert M. Yerkes in psychology, Mary C. Jarrett in social work, Myrtelle M. Canavan in pathology, and Harry C. Solomon in therapeutic research. Its close relationship with the Harvard Medical School added still further to its reputation. Influenced by the seeming success of the Psychopathic Hospital, the legislature in 1917 authorized the Commission on Mental Disease (successor to the State Board of Insanity) "to develop, extend and complete a statewide system of psychopathic hospital service by establishing new hospital and out-patient units in suitable districts in connection with existing or future state hospitals under the supervision of said commission."[61]

The early experiences of the Psychopathic Hospital suggested that new institutional forms did not necessarily resolve older problems. From the beginning the relationship between the Psychopathic Hospital and its parent, Boston State Hospital, was beset with difficulties. In part, these difficulties reflected personality conflicts. More significant, however, was the respective focus of each institution. The Psychopathic Hospital was dedicated to research, Boston State Hospital to the care of patients. The two were not necessarily incompatible, but Southard found that the governing authorities believed that "the prime consideration was treatment of patients," a view that was not especially congenial to research. In addition, the Psychopathic Hospital provided a series of services to voluntary "non-insane" patients. Between 1913 and 1918 children under fourteen constituted 24 percent and adolescents 16 percent of the total outpatient clientele. Southard, together with Mary Jarrett, created what also became a model social service department that involved close cooperation between psychiatrists and social workers. Nevertheless, the out-patient department, Southard complained, was threatened by "the constant custodializing tendency in the Psychopathic Hospital, owing to the endeavor to keep the per capita of the Boston State Hospital as low as possible." Indeed, he added,

> recent conversations with numerous trustees of institutions in this state and elsewhere lead me to the view that the nature of the Psychopathic Hospital is still misunderstood. When its essential function of caring for the non-insane is not understood by those laymen nearest the heart of the psychiatric situation in Massachusetts, how can it be possible for the Psychopathic Hospital to execute its function with respect to voluntary admissions to the out-patient department, to the maximum?[62]

Southard's observation, of course, revealed more than he may have realized. For if the Psychopathic Hospital's "essential function" was the treatment of the non-insane, what was its relevance or relationship to the state hospitals providing care for thousands of mentally ill patients? Nor did the emphasis on research lead to therapeutic innovation; the treatment given patients differed but little from the treatment at orthodox mental hospitals. Given Southard's somatic views, the orientation, according to one of his successors, "was in many respects away from the patient, especially his immediate living problems. Enthusiasm was primarily for hydrotherapy, chemicals to control distraught behavior, and studies of metabolism, neuropathology, and syphilis of the nervous system with its dramatic neurological signs."[63]

For the staff of Boston Psychopathic Hospital as well as for families of patients, the institution served a significant function. The morale of the staff was generally high, partly because the endemic isolation of traditional mental hospitals was not a factor and partly because the institution's location promoted close contacts with medical school and general hospital personnel. Shortly after arriving at Boston Psychopathic, C. Macfie Campbell, later to become its director, observed that it

> is rather interesting meeting the other men such as Morton Prince, McDougall, etc., and a good deal of time is taken up with meetings which do not always bring in much of a return. Still more time is taken up in eating dinners in other people's houses. After this winter I expect to have a somewhat more regular programme and to have a little more time for work. As

to whether it will be possible to sit down and actually take up some definite piece of work within the coming year I am not quite sure. . . . Altogether conditions here are very attractive and any lack of returns will not be able to be attributed to poor opportunity.

Similarly, Boston Psychopathic remained popular with families fearful of traditional mental hospitals. The institution's special status and absence of large numbers of chronic patients facilitated the admission of patients by relatives. If conditions led subsequently to commitment to a state hospital, the family could take solace in the belief that it had exhausted all other alternatives, and that a thorough diagnosis had been made.[64]

In brief, the existence of Boston Psychopathic Hospital had relatively little impact on the institutional configuration for the mentally ill in the Bay State. The small scale of the institution, its somewhat different admission policy, and the absence of encouraging results precluded a role that would make it a harbinger of radical change. In 1921, nearly a decade after its opening and the year in which it gained independent institutional status, the hospital treated a total of 894 patients (4 percent of the total in public institutions); the daily average census was 58.9. More significant, of the 894 admitted, only 14 were discharged as recovered, 102 improved, 155 stationary, and 151 not insane. An additional 182 were transferred to other institutions, 14 died, and 122 were "nominally dismissed."[65]

VI

Paradoxically, the optimistic expectations of psychiatrists and the institutional innovations of the early twentieth century did not significantly alter the lives of thousands of institutionalized mentally ill persons. The relative absence of change went unrecognized, and most individuals (and particularly those identified with a professional group) tended to overestimate their ability to determine particular outcomes. Yet the illusion of power and knowledge often creates a perception of rapid change. Such was the case in the early twentieth century when a vision of a scientific psychiatry integrated with modern medicine stimulated both a search for new concepts and therapies as well as the creation of novel institutional forms.

For the general public the optimistic claims of psychiatrists were welcome, if only because they held out the hope of an eventual solution to the tragic problems associated with mental illness. Indeed, psychiatric ideology was less the product of an autonomous specialty than it was the reflection of the pervasive faith in science and rationality that constituted the foundation of much of early twentieth-century American thought. That ideology and reality were far apart mattered little. All societies, after all, require explanations to account for the unexpected or abnormal. Psychiatrists, like their medical predecessors and successors, provided both an explanation of behavior and a rationale for treatment. Had they rejected such a role, they might have fatally impaired their professional legitimacy and prepared the way for other groups willing to meet perceived social needs.

The transformation of psychiatry after 1900 had relatively little effect upon the bulk of institutionalized patients. In fact, the broadening of occupational opportunities for psychiatrists correspondingly reduced their commitment to institutional care. Benign neglect, in other words, weakened still further the legitimacy of state mental hospitals which, with some exceptions, were increasingly perceived by many psychiatrists as outmoded institutions left over from an earlier era. The role of caretaker for individuals who were socially marginal and who lacked either resources or families (or both) was frowned upon by a specialty that defined its mission in medical and scientific terms.[66]

CHAPTER SIX

The Mental Hygiene Movement

THE FERMENT within psychiatry at the turn of the century not only helped to reorient basic concepts and promote institutional change, but also laid the foundation for the emergence of what became known as the mental hygiene movement. Mental hygiene, of course, was a diffuse concept that meant different things to different persons. Whatever its meaning and significance, however, it reinforced the growing chasm between psychiatry and mental hospitals by focusing attention on noninstitutional populations and problems.

In a superficial sense, the early twentieth-century emphasis on mental hygiene was little more than a continuation of the nineteenth-century concern with prevention. In reality, there were fundamental differences between the concepts of mental hygiene and prevention. Mental hygiene was a product of "scientific" modes of thought wedded to the power of private organizations and public authority; nineteenth-century concepts of prevention reflected a world view based on an older religious tradition that emphasized natural law, free will, and individual responsibility. The contrast between these two approaches was especially evident in the careers of antebellum psychiatrists and their early twentieth-century successors. Prevention was derived from a synthesis of Protestantism, Scottish moral philosophy, and Baconian science, and the literature of prevention was designed to illuminate the causal relationship between behavior, on the one hand, and mental and physical disease, on the other. Responsibility for the prevention of disease, however, resided in the choices made by autonomous and free individuals; government and private organizations would educate individuals rather than dictate their behavior.

Early twentieth-century mental hygienists, by way of contrast, held different views. Disease was a product of environmental, hereditarian, and individual deficiencies; its eradication required a fusion of scientific knowledge and administrative action. Confident that they possessed the requisite knowledge to prevent as well as to treat pathological behavior, mental hygienists launched a broad-based crusade to create a better society. The destiny of the American people was no longer to be left to chance or to the decisions of atomistic individuals, but was to be purposively guided in a direction that enhanced the welfare and happiness of all citizens.

As members of a profession which they believed was destined to play an increasingly central part in the creation of a new social order, psychiatrists began to broaden their specialty. Unlike their nineteenth-century predecessors, many had been trained in neurology, which strengthened their ties with medicine. The emphasis on scientific research rather than on care and custody, on disease rather than on patients, and on alternatives to traditional mental hospitals was merely a start. More compelling was the utopian idea of a society structured in such a way as to maximize health and minimize disease. In an address before the New York Neurological Society on the eve of America's entry into World War I, Thomas W. Salmon outlined the future of psychiatry. In the past the isolation of patients in mental hospitals had also isolated those who studied the disease. The new psychiatry, on the other hand, had to reach beyond institutional walls and play a crucial part "in the great movements for social betterment." Psychiatrists could no longer limit their activities and responsibilities to the institutionalized mentally ill. On the contrary, they had to lead the way in research and policy formulation and to implement methods in such areas as mental hygiene, care of the feebleminded, eugenics, control of alcoholism, management of abnormal children, treatment of criminals, and to help in the prevention of crime, prostitution, and dependency.[1]

At the turn of the century the appealing but vague commitment to mental hygiene assumed several programmatic forms, including the creation of the National Committee for Mental Hygiene as well as a eugenics movement. Although different in character and objectives, they illustrate the receptivity of psychiatrists to new social roles and a hostility toward institutional career patterns, as well as a tendency to employ administrative solutions in an effort to prevent the propagation of such groups as the insane and retarded.[2]

I

The concept of prevention had long been embedded in psychiatric thought. Its amorphous nature and elusive content, nevertheless, precluded any clear relationship to the specific behavior of individuals. The advice offered by psychiatrists for much of the nineteenth century was largely conditioned by their cultural values and social position as well as their scientific concepts. The prevention of insanity, wrote Henry P. Stearns in 1883, had to come primarily "from the education of home and school life, and from the regulation of daily conduct in its relation to the brain; and, as the nervous system presides over and controls the body and its several members in the discharge of their functions, an understanding of its physiological action, at least in some degree, is of great importance to everybody." If Stearns's observations were typical—and there is every reason to believe that they were—then it is evident that late nineteenth-century prophylactic thought differed but little from the moral and didactic literature characteristic of that era.[3]

In his presidential address at the AMPA a quarter of a century later, Charles P. Bancroft spoke in similar terms. Psychiatry, Bancroft observed, had done little to enlighten the public about the genesis of mental disease. "The time has arrived," he added, ". . . when we should impress upon boards of health the importance of observing certain laws of mental hygiene in the school and home; and when finally the general practitioner should become so familiar with the antecedents of insanity that he can use his influence in correcting and diverting evil tendencies which, unchanged, are likely to result in alienation."[4]

Although the tone and content of Bancroft's remarks were traditional, the social context in which he spoke was beginning to change and infuse older generalities about prevention with new social consequences. Among the most significant changes were the creation of voluntary organizations and private foundations dedicated to the elimination and prevention of disease by the application of a combination of environmental changes and techniques to modify human behavior. The establishment of voluntary organizations deriving financial support from foundations with unprecedented resources was another development of major significance. Throughout much of the nineteenth century responsibility for the resolution of social problems rested with state and local governments and, to a lesser extent, with relatively small voluntary societies supported by private philanthropy. By the turn of the century, private foundations, including but not limited to those established by Andrew Carnegie and John D. Rockefeller, were beginning to assume a more important policy role. Their very presence suggested that, in the future, regional or national approaches to social problems would become more common. Such organizations had their greatest impact upon science and medicine, where funding was of critical importance in directing institutional development, education, and research in particular directions.

The transition from an amorphous concept of prevention to a mental hygiene *movement* offers an illustrative case study. When the National Association for the Protection of the Insane and the Prevention of Insanity was created in 1880, it lacked a sound financial base. Its title notwithstanding, the Association devoted virtually no attention to prevention, and within a short time went out of existence. The founding of the National Committee for Mental Hygiene (NCMH) in 1909, on the other hand, occurred in a quite different setting; its history provides an example of how structural changes can inform older concepts with new meanings, and how an organization and movement can in turn influence the lives of dependent groups such as the mentally ill.

The NCMH was indissolubly linked with the life and career of Clifford W. Beers. Born in 1876, he graduated from the Sheffield Scientific School at Yale in 1897. After holding several jobs in New York City, he made an unsuccessful suicide attempt which resulted in several broken bones and other injuries. After his release from a general hospital, his mental condition deteriorated. In August, 1900, his family sent him to Stamford Hall, a small proprietary institution specializing in the treatment of nervous and mental disorders and opium and alcohol addiction. After an eight-month sojourn at Stamford Hall, he was sent to the Hartford Retreat. When his family could no longer pay the high costs of a private institution, he was committed to the Connecticut Hospital for the Insane. Beers was finally discharged in September, 1903. By then he had spent more than three years in mental hospitals. His unpleasant experiences subsequently gave rise to a belief that fundamental changes in the structure and organization of such institutions were indispensable if they were to fulfill their therapeutic mission.[5]

Upon returning to New York, he was rehired by his former employer. Following a seemingly successful performance in the business world, he grew more and more elated and finally decided to write a book that would help others struggling with the problem of mental illness. His goal was nothing less than the creation of a movement to help "hundreds of thousands of men and women" by improving conditions in mental hospitals. What was required was a national organization supported by affluent individuals. Ultimately a cabinet level "Board of Health and Happiness" might be created within the federal government. Beers's own role became increasingly clear; he would write a book with an impact comparable to that of *Uncle Tom's Cabin* and ultimately become "the man behind the throne."[6]

Beers's elated state was such that his brother persuaded him to reenter the Hartford Retreat, where he prepared a document that ultimately served as the basis for his classic, *A Mind That Found Itself*. After a month he was discharged and returned to work. But his preoccupation with the cause to which he would devote his life was such that he took the advice of Joseph Choate and began writing his autobiography. His most enthusiastic backer was William James, the eminent philosopher and psychologist, who provided indispensable moral and financial support until his death in 1910. In early 1907 the firm of Longmans, Green and Company agreed to publish the book. Beers, however, decided to send his manuscript to a number of psychiatrists for comment. Since the book was indissolubly linked to the creation of an organization, he did not wish to alienate a group whose support he deemed vital.[7]

The initial reaction to Beers's manuscript was mixed. William M. McDonald of the Butler Hospital believed that Beers had "exaggerated" conditions and overestimated his objectivity. Although Beers was receptive to criticism and proposed to alter his manuscript, the changes failed to satisfy McDonald. Indeed, McDonald's response was couched in terms that suggested the presence of a chronic tension between the authoritative demands of physicians for autonomy and the expressed desire of lay persons to play a significant role in medical reform. McDonald particularly resented the insinuation that physicians had "done little or nothing toward the improvement of conditions." "When you have seen a mother's love and tenderness bring about the absolute destruction of a daughter's mind as I have seen it do," he added, "you will be less sure that amateurs could replace men who have made the subject of mental disturbance a life study. You might as well send a group of loving, tender and sympathetic men and women into our operating rooms to relieve appendicitis, acute peritonitis, to remove tumors, to stop hemorrhages, to amputate mangled and useless limbs." Beers was willing to consider further manuscript revisions, but insisted that his own state of mind and experience as a patient did not preclude a role as an accurate observer. The responsibility for institutional shortcomings and abuses rested with staff rather than inmates, he declared. The reaction of several other institutional psychiatrists was friendly but noncommittal.[8]

Beers was both perceptive and shrewd; he recognized that he had failed to gain the endorsement of any of the acknowledged leaders of psychiatry. When Stewart Paton suggested that he contact Adolf Meyer, Beers responded enthusiastically. In September, 1907, he sent Meyer the proofs of his book, and subsequently held four meetings lasting about fifteen hours and conducted an extensive correspondence as well. Meyer's criticisms were not unlike those of McDonald, but they were couched in friendlier language. He suggested, for example, that Beers omit some things and insert here and there "a remark which would point to the *hyper*critical attitude which you showed at the time and which was not especially judiciously balanced according to normal life." Beers made innumerable changes, but never altered in substance the allegations about the harsh treatment that he had received. Meyer eventually approved publication of the book even though he retained private misgivings, and subsequently wrote a favorable review for the *North American Review*. Meyer clearly hoped that Beers's energies could be constructively channeled. "I strongly feel that we hospital physicians have a rare opportunity in Mr. Beers," he wrote to a Connecticut superintendent. "It would be difficult to find a man with stronger convictions, and the point will be for those who have a wide experience to guide the energy that exists in him and to make the most of the opportunities."[9]

A Mind That Found Itself was finally published in 1908. Although others had preceded him in publishing exposés of institutional life, none approached the impact made by Beers's classic work. The book, as Norman Dain has pointed out, "combined the desire to expose, reform, and inform" without ever denying the fact that the author had been mentally ill. Nor were the criticisms directed against hospitals per se, but rather focused upon the sometimes insensitive and occasionally brutal treatment of inmates. By submitting his work to psychiatrists and other prominent figures, Beers also managed to endow it with reliability and sensitivity; under no circumstances could it be regarded as the work of a crank or unreliable witness. Couched in eloquent language, *A Mind That Found Itself* was a call for action to inaugurate a new beginning in the institutional care and treatment of the mentally ill.[10]

In Beers's mind the writing of a book was but a prelude to the formation of a national movement. In 1905 his ideas were vague; he wanted a national organization dedicated to the improvement of conditions, but one that rejected "yellow journalism or other sensational means." The improvement of mental hospitals was only one element in a more comprehensive plan that included wider dissemination of knowledge as well as help to those persons on the verge of a mental collapse. Insofar as financing was concerned, Beers was confident that support would be forthcoming from wealthy philanthropists cognizant of the significance of the movement. By 1907 Beers was writing about a "National Society for the Improvement of Conditions Among the Insane" that would represent both the institutionalized and noninstitutionalized insane, promote the establishment of modern hospitals, stimulate research, and form subsidiary state societies modeled after the State Charities Aid Association of New York. He undoubtedly agreed with William James, who criticized the ignorance of the public and the complacency of psychiatrists. James suggested that Beers and a national society serve as a "mediator between officials, patients, and the public conscience."[11]

Given their developing relationship, it was natural that Beers would turn to Meyer for advice. Meyer's response was encouraging; he proposed the formation of a Society for Mental Hygiene "to show our people better ways of healthy living, prevention of trouble, and efficient handling of what is not prevented." Meyer's suggestion for an organization devoted to "mental hygiene" actually introduced a new element; it deflected Beers's original emphasis on institutional improvement and directed it toward the far more amorphous goal of promoting mental hygiene. But, like most of his colleagues, Meyer never spelled out with any degree of clarity the precise content of such a concept. He was firmly persuaded as well that "hospitals with the medical staffs should be the leaders of such movements"—a view that would place psychiatrists in a position of authority.[12]

The deflection from institutional change to the promotion of mental hygiene represented a fundamental shift. A movement to promote health had replaced one concerned with improving the care and treatment of a specific group of patients. That prevention proved an attractive idea was understandable. To psychiatrists hygienic concepts opened up new vistas and shifted attention away from their custodial role and inability to cure admittedly vague disease entities. Prevention also had the virtue of hastening the reintegration of psychiatry and medicine, since it provided psychiatry with the mantle of a biologically oriented specialty and put it in step with other medical prevention movements. To the emerging profession of social work, seeking both identity and status, the movement offered the hope of collaboration with physicians on a more equal basis; the goal was not limited to the treatment of individuals, but involved as well the promotion of specific behavioral patterns within families and larger social groupings. The organizational mode was equally attractive in an era that placed great faith in formal structures that unified science and rational administration. Above all, the goal of prevention seemed certain to attract broad support from a public increasingly fearful of the seeming rise in syphilis and other venereal diseases as well as a high incidence of alcoholism. Mental hygiene, in other words, was so broad and inclusive that it aroused little opposition.

Even prior to his involvement with Meyer, Beers had begun to lay the groundwork for the creation of a national organization with constituent state societies. Although endowed with energy and initiative, Beers was often deferential in his attitude toward elite groups. His first concern, therefore, was to recruit a number of distinguished persons to serve as trustees. He contacted Frederick T. Gates, a former Baptist minister who was largely responsible for administering John D. Rockefeller's philanthropic enterprises. By the beginning of 1908 Beers had recruited more than twenty honorary trustees and nearly three dozen honorary members drawn largely from academic life, medicine and psychiatry, and social work. He was disappointed, however, in the seeming disinterest of individuals from wealthy backgrounds. Efforts to recruit such distinguished Americans as President Theodore Roosevelt failed. Refusing to be discouraged by transitory setbacks, Beers continued to push ahead. He accepted the suggestion of George McAneny, a New York reformer and president of the City Club, that the name of the organization be changed to the National Committee for Mental Hygiene and thus follow the model of the more successful National Child Labor Committee.[13]

During the first half of 1908 Beers began to encounter formidable problems. His approach to Rockefeller was rebuffed; his private finances were in shambles, and the hope of a paid position in the new organization was still a remote possibility. More importantly, his relationship with Meyer began to deteriorate. Meyer initially had been supportive of Beers's desire to create a national organization. By early 1908, however, Meyer had concluded that tactically it would be wiser to confine organizational activities to a single state where a successful demonstration project would serve as a model for other states to follow. Although not completely persuaded, Beers agreed to center his activities on his native state of Connecticut. By April he had prepared a preliminary prospectus for the soon to be created Connecticut Society for Mental Hygiene. Its goals were extraordinarily inclusive: the Society would serve as an educational agency dedicated to the improvement of conditions among the insane and the protection of the mental health of the community; it would fight against constant legislative investigations and replace them with a "commission of experts" who would prepare a plan for reform; it would appoint after-care committees to aid discharged patients; it would propose legislation governing private hospitals, improving the quality of attendants, and developing a model system for public hospitals; and it would promote the teaching of psychiatry in medical schools. Beers's prospectus left few problems untouched.[14]

Meyer's initial reaction was favorable, and in May, 1908, the Connecticut Society for Mental Hygiene was formally organized. From that point on relations between the two men deteriorated rapidly. Beers believed that at the state level mental hygiene societies should be organized and controlled by lay persons who would influence public opinion and indirectly create political pressure for more generous state funding. Meyer, on the other hand, insisted that psychiatrists had to be the dominant force; Beers was an individual whose talents could be put to effective use only if he were controlled by physicians. The personalities and characters of both men were so different that conflict and misunderstanding were perhaps inevitable. Beers had extraordinary if unfocused energy; his desire to ameliorate and improve conditions was unbounded. Meyer was meticulous and cautious; he tended to try and dominate all those with whom he came into contact. Because Beers lacked medical training, it was all the more important to Meyer that he be made to accept the advice and guidance of more knowledgeable and qualified persons. Meyer may have also felt that Beers's earlier history of mania might recur if he were left without proper medical supervision. In the summer and fall of 1908 another point of friction developed. Buoyed by the bequest of Henry Phipps to establish a psychiatric clinic at Hopkins and persuaded that *A Mind That Found Itself* had been a contributing factor, Beers began to entertain the possibility of approaching the philanthropist for funds for the proposed national organization. Meyer was unhappy about this development; he neither relished the prospect of an independent national organization which he could not dominate, nor did he want the new clinic which he would head to compete for future funding.[15]

During the late fall and winter Meyer and Beers continued to feud over the creation of a national organization. Beers envisaged a national crusade, while Meyer kept emphasizing the necessity for concrete work, albeit of an unspecified nature. Increasingly, Beers became more impatient. What was required, he wrote to Meyer in October, 1908, was "a plan of organization which will make it possible for the public and the medical profession to work in close harmony for the good of all." If hospital officials refused to cooperate, he warned, "the laymen identified with the Mental Hygiene movement would be well within their rights if they finally undertook an aggressive campaign which would force hospital officials in all States to measure up to the highest standard attained in the admittedly best hospital in any State." Meyer continued to discourage the formation of a national organization, and urged Beers to continue his fund-raising efforts in Connecticut not only to influence the legislature, but to undertake a survey of the facts upon which policy recommendations could be made. "The more I think over the matter the more do I see the immaturity of any scheme which appeals only to the sentiments and to the drumming up of an organization." Meyer also expressed the hope that "we shall not be 'launched' and 'financed' before we have formulated that mere bagatelle the work."[16]

Unable to stop Beers's momentum, Meyer finally acceded, and the NCMH was officially organized at a meeting in New York City on February 19, 1909, attended by eleven eminent individuals. A formal organizational structure was established, including an Executive Committee chaired by Meyer and made up of both prominent laypersons and psychiatrists. The stated goals of the organization reflected Beers's views: the NCMH would protect the public's mental health; promote research into and dissemination of material pertaining to the etiology, treatment, and prevention of mental disease; enlist the aid of the federal government; and establish state societies for mental hygiene. The implementation of these goals involved the establishment of aftercare programs, the development of effective modes of education, and the creation of a subdepartment of public health within the federal government. Concerned with funding, the founders decided to submit an appeal for funds to John D. Rockefeller. Even at this early date the shift away from the care of the institutionalized insane was evident.[17]

For the next three years the NCMH remained a largely paper organization. Had Beers's only concern with the institutionalized mentally ill remained constant, the organization might have been able to work toward concrete goals. By 1909, however, even Beers had been caught up in the enthusiasm for a broader and more inclusive movement. Meyer, who was forever seeking to restrain Beers, actually reinforced the growing commitment to mental hygiene despite the amorphous content of the term. Shortly after the founding of the NCMH, William James supported a proposal to change its name to the National Committee on Insanity. James agreed with Charles Strong that mental hygiene was a "flabby and evasive" and "misleading" term; the "real subject . . . is *Insanity*." Beers in this instance disagreed with James, who was without doubt his strongest supporter. His shift from his earlier concerns was evident in his reply. "But attacking insanity, as such, is but a small part of our work. Protecting *sanity* is the prime object." Meyer was even more emphatic in his opposition to change. The very use of the word insanity would be a "misfortune," and if mental hygiene were misunderstood it was time to show the public "that what is good in it implies no hocus pocus and offers plain and simple and strong and reliable help to success in living." Indeed, were the name change adopted, he was prepared to withdraw from the committee. Beers and Meyer prevailed, and the organization's name remained unchanged. It was already evident that a radical shift had occurred. Beers's original goal of forming an organization dedicated to the improvement of conditions among the institutionalized mentally ill was being subordinated to the goal of prevention.[18]

The absence of a concrete program was by no means the only impediment to the organization's success. Internal conflicts and persistent financial problems further impaired the effectiveness of the NCMH. The relationship between Beers and Meyer remained a troubled one. By 1909 Beers's personal finances were desperate. His hope, of course, was to be appointed to a salaried position as secretary of the NCMH, though initially he wanted to serve in that position without salary until the organization had sufficient funds. Meyer, on the other hand, was opposed to the employment of Beers by the Committee; he urged instead that

Beers confine his activities to Connecticut. In his eyes Beers was a layperson whose talents and energies had to be guided by professionally trained persons like himself. Nor did Meyer want Beers to develop an independent position even in a single state; the role that he proposed for Beers was limited to volunteer social work. In November, 1909, he advised Beers not to emphasize organizational issues, but rather to do "your best in collaboration with the hospital physicians, in learning to find out what they need and wish rather than in teaching them." A relatively modest salary for work at the state level would also restrain Beers's expansive tendencies. "To tell the truth," Meyer wrote to George Blumer regarding a salary for Beers, "I should not like to put him into a position in which he could flap 'eagle's wings' too freely. It would not be safe for him."[19]

Throughout 1910 the two men were on a collision course, and Meyer raised the possibility of resigning from the NCMH. Although Beers felt that such a move would be a misfortune, he insisted also that the NCMH was his own creation. He had made Meyer "its central figure" rather than the other way around, he claimed. For his part Meyer insisted that the differences between the two revolved around Beers's sense of unreality and fiscal irresponsibility. The issues were far more complex. To William James it was a case of "the ox and the 'Wild Ass' not working well in double harness." Meyer had been brought up "scientifically" and believed "in work accreting bit by bit in finished form"; Beers was an advocate of a "big movement." Meyer, James noted, would do little if left to himself; Beers was clearly the indispensable element in the movement. Certainly James was not far from the mark; in countless other relationships Meyer exhibited domineering characteristics and an inability to reach firm conclusions. "Psychiatrists," noted Beers in an obvious allusion to Meyer, "have an aversion to direct statement. Instead of saying that 'work will begin,' they say 'it seems about on the point of beginning.' Thus they play safe. If the world should come to an end before the actual beginning of the work, they can tell the angel Gabriel that they left no unfinished task on earth."[20]

That Beers was willing to defer to Meyer's leadership was incontrovertible. As Secretary of the Connecticut Society for Mental Hygiene, he brought together mental hospital trustees and members of the State Board of Charities, and calmed the fears of institutional psychiatrists by limiting the organization's activities to aftercare and public education. But Beers refused to accede to suggestions that he reduce the scope and significance of his work or to surrender his commitment to a national movement. His efforts to soothe Meyer's feelings or to change his convictions proved futile. In March, 1910, Beers wrote to James that Meyer seemed "unwilling to serve in a responsible position, without that absolute *power* which one of his temperament inevitably craves, yet invariably knows not how to use effectively." That spring the NCMH decided to raise funds in order to appoint a medical director and secretary, and thereby become a functioning organization. Privately Meyer opposed the decision, but the lack of support for his position led him to issue an impending resignation as chairman of the Executive Committee. Beers attempted to persuade Meyer to remain a member, but by the summer events had reached the point where a break was now all but inevitable. Meyer rejected Beers's fund-raising activities "for things which are not plain and concrete," and insisted that only a fundamental change in direction would cause him to withdraw his resignation. But when it became clear that, with the exception of Stewart Paton, he was isolated within the NCMH, Meyer severed all of his ties with the organization in December, 1910.[21]

While Beers and Meyer were engaged in conflict over their respective roles, the NCMH remained largely inoperative because of the inability to raise sufficient funds. During the first two years of its existence the Committee had no income. In early 1911 Beers was appointed Secretary at an annual salary of $3,000. Toward the end of the year, Henry Phipps agreed to give $50,000 to the NCMH for surveys and also offered an endowment for the same amount if an additional $200,000 could be raised from other sources. Phipps also provided Beers with additional funds that enabled him to repay most of his personal debts and become solvent for the first time in years. Although organizational finances would remain a chronic problem and occupy a good part of Beers's time, the NCMH could at least turn its attention to more substantive matters.[22]

II

In 1912 the NCMH opened permanent headquarters in New York City. The organization also employed Thomas W. Salmon, who was given the title of Director of Special Studies rather than Medical Director because funds with which to pay his salary were then limited to two years. Salmon was an individual whose reputation far exceeded his achievements. Born in Troy, New York, in 1876, he graduated from medical school in 1899. After failing in private practice, he joined the Public Health Service, and shortly thereafter was assigned to plan and to execute psychiatric examinations of immigrants at Ellis Island. Shocked by what he observed, he attempted to persuade the Public Health Service to improve physical conditions among the insane immigrants awaiting deportation, and proposed that examinations be administered abroad to preclude long voyages for those who would be denied admission. He also published several articles critical of the policy of unrestricted immigration to the United States because it contributed to the rising number of foreign-born patients in mental hospitals. His criticism of the Public Health Service resulted in suspension from duty, and eventually he was transferred to the Marine Hospital in Boston. In 1911 he took a leave of absence to work for the New York State Commission in Lunacy, and the following year extended his leave to join the NCMH.[23]

The formal appointments of Salmon and Beers raised pressing problems about the future course of the NCMH. The conflict between Beers and Meyers had transformed Beers's ideas from improving conditions in mental hospitals to a more general and amorphous goal of promoting mental hygiene. But the very use of the term raised troubling problems. Given the vagueness of psychiatric diseases and the absence of any clear and demonstrable etiology, how was it possible to determine what measures effectively promoted prevention? To admit such doubts or reservations would have undermined the scientific claims of psychiatry and other emerging mental health professions at a time when medicine and science seemed on the ascendancy. Consequently, the emphasis on prevention usually reflected social and cultural values rather than a body of empirical data. Alcoholism and syphilis were exceptions to the rule, but the NCMH never made them a central focus of organization activities. Leadership in the antiliquor movement and the crusade against prostitution was left to other groups and organizations.[24]

In seeking a clearly defined mission, Beers, William L. Russell, and August Hoch adopted a strategy typical of the Progressive era. The NCMH would undertake surveys of conditions among the mentally ill which in turn would "stimulate activity among the people of the States which have been studied." Such work would also leave the Committee "in a position to give expert advice and to assist in formulating plans for ameliorating the condition of the insane throughout the country." The social survey by this time had become one of the major weapons of Progressives. Undertaken by trained experts, such surveys would both shed light on problems and provide a prescription for action. The underlying assumption was that an intelligent and enlightened public would accept the guidance of a rational and scientific intelligentsia. Just as the Flexner report had been used to alter the structure of medical education, so state and local surveys would provide citizens with the knowledge required for effective action.[25]

Before the NCMH could undertake surveys, however, it had to develop sources of funding. Despite Beers's optimism, the task proved more difficult than he anticipated. Phipps's initial bequest of $50,000 helped, but his resources were limited. During the first decade of its existence, the NCMH directed a substantial part of its energies to fund raising. Between 1911 and 1921 the organization confronted no less than three crises that threatened to cut short its very existence. The first crisis was resolved by the Phipps grant; the second by a four-year commitment by Mrs. William K. Vanderbilt and Mrs. Elizabeth Milbank Anderson, who each pledged to donate $10,000 annually; and the third by an unrestricted grant of $100,000 in 1921.[26]

Prior to 1914 the approach to Rockefeller had been unsuccessful, and Beers's efforts to enlist the aid of Henry Ford had also failed. During 1912 and 1913 Beers continued to court the Rockefeller Foundation, which was already deeply committed to a number of medical projects. Although concerned with alcoholism and venereal diseases, Foundation officials were not prepared to offer financial support. When the Committee's funds were nearly exhausted, however, the Foundation offered to employ Salmon and assign him to the NCMH. Perhaps Salmon's social views and his published work on the relationship between immigration and insanity were congenial to Rockefeller and Foundation officials. Meyer was also supportive of Salmon, partly because he may have feared a recurrence of Beers's illness, and partly because of his own belief in the necessity for medical autonomy. Too much information, he wrote to a Rockefeller official in 1914, came from "reporters and prejudiced publicists." "The movement," he added, "naturally cannot be merely a layman's movement, and the scientific and critical foundation has to be furnished by the best of physicians. I should like to see Dr. Salmon get the proper independence and means at his disposal to quietly proceed and to take up in one region after another, and to accumulate and publish a body of facts which will permeate our medical administrators and make its impression on the thinking persons among the people who want to get information." The Foundation offer was initially rejected, but between 1915 and 1918 the Foundation granted funds to pay Salmon's annual salary of $7,000. It also provided $85,050 for surveys, $47,500 for studies dealing with the psychopathology of crime, $42,500 for war work—including elimination of the unfit for military service, and the care and treatment of those who might or did become mentally disabled in order that they return to active duty or civilian life—and gave preliminary funding for the effort to develop a uniform statistical reporting system for mental diseases.[27]

The earliest surveys sponsored by the NCMH were completed in 1915 and covered South Carolina, Texas, Tennessee, and Pennsylvania. Most surveys focused directly on conditions among the institutionalized mentally ill. It was hardly surprising that three were of Southern states; there was general agreement that the quality of care and treatment in that region was considerably below that found elsewhere. South Carolina was perhaps typical. For years Dr. J. W. Babcock (one of the earliest figures to call attention to the relationship between the dietary disease of pellagra and insanity), superintendent of the State Hospital for the Insane at Columbia, had been prodding the legislature to improve conditions. A legislative committee in 1910 not only conceded the accuracy of his complaints, but recommended the sale of the hospital and the erection of a new one. Nothing was done, and the conflict with Governor Cole Blease led to Babcock's resignation in 1914. After his election as Governor and even before being inaugurated, Richard I. Manning requested the NCMH to undertake a survey. Salmon then secured the services of Arthur P. Herring, Secretary of the Maryland Lunacy Commission, who completed a critical report in early 1915. At Manning's urging, the legislature authorized a $600,000 expenditure to reconstruct the hospital's physical plant and to restructure its internal administration; it also provided for a separate colony for black insane persons in order to free additional space for white patients. The sum allocated for maintenance, however, remained stable, rising from a daily per capita cost of 50¢ in 1914 to only 52¢ in 1916. Nor did the hospital gain autonomy, for Manning subsequently refused to reappoint Babcock as superintendent even when urged to do so by United States Senator Benjamin R. Tillman. Tillman was furious, and seconded Babcock's judgment of the Governor's mental capacity. "He is a high 'grade imbecile,'" observed Tillman in unrestrained language, "or rather he is a well born imbecile who happened to have good forbears. To sum up . . . he is a damn fool and a damn rascal too."[28]

Other surveys had mixed results. The Texas legislature appropriated $400,000 for a new hospital and $200,000 to remodel an abandoned prison and to add one new building for the use of black patients. In Tennessee the Board of Control seemed receptive to proposed changes, but noted that improvements could be made only when sufficient funds became available. In Pennsylvania C. Floyd Haviland's investigation provided ammunition to those who hoped to abolish the mixed system of state and county care. The formation of state societies for mental hygiene sometimes followed NCMH involvement, though the effectiveness of such organizations was often questionable. The underlying assumption embedded in all of the early studies was that accurate data would inevitably lead to the introduction of needed reforms. Such hopes were hardly justified by the results.[29]

Salmon, however, was not content to limit the Committee to surveys of the institutionalized mentally ill. His vision of psychiatry transcended the institutional context that had for so long been the foundation of the specialty. In effect, he wanted to expand the functions of psychiatry and to merge it with a broader movement committed to the resolution of a variety of social rather than strictly medical problems. Much of the National Committee's work, Salmon conceded in 1917, related to the care of the institutionalized insane. "But this is not of our choosing," he added, even while noting that the NCMH could not ignore the dismal institutional legacy left from the nineteenth century. Reflecting a confident and expansive mood, he insisted that the role of twentieth-century psychiatry was to extend its frontiers in order to make "schools and prisons . . . the chief fields of efforts and not the institutions for the so-called insane." Salmon also seemed to decry the fact that by his definition there were only 150 psychiatrists in the entire nation. This number, however, did not include "physicians engaged in the care of the insane, but . . . men who practice the science of psychiatry."[30]

Salmon's remarks were by no means idle chatter. On the contrary, he had already begun to redirect the NCMH in a new direction. Not all of the early surveys conducted under the auspices of the NCMH were traditional in character. In 1914, for example, the Committee sponsored a study of Springfield, Illinois. Although concerned with commitment laws, the need for psychiatric wards in general hospitals, almshouse care, aftercare, and the state mental hospital, the investigation devoted an equal amount of time to mental defectives and alcoholics. Two years later Aaron J. Rosanoff supervised an extensive study of mental disorders in Nassau County, New York. The shift in emphasis was profound, for Rosanoff and his staff were not concerned with determining the percentage of insane and feebleminded in the population. They deliberately adopted instead a twofold classification that sought to reveal the degree to which "social maladjustments" were due to mental disorder. In addition to traditional medical categories, they dealt with a large number of "sociological" categories, including truancy, sexual immorality, vagrancy, criminal tendency, dependency, drug addiction, and domestic maladjustment. The conclusions of this study were striking; the bulk of individuals requiring psychiatric treatment were not in institutions. Rosanoff and his colleagues called upon state officials to develop "a comprehensive policy of mental hygiene" with an appropriate administrative structure. Because of "arbitrary limitations" on psychiatry that were "based on old legal and academic conceptions," most states had archaic policies that fell "far short of the best that modern society could afford." The line between the mental hospital and the community, Rosanoff told his colleagues at the AMPA in 1917, was artificial and pernicious; the state hospital had to be placed in "closer touch with psychiatric problems arising at large in its district, and make available for the community unrestricted psychiatric consultation and advice."[31]

At about the same time, Herman M. Adler, chief of staff of Boston Psychopathic, agreed to undertake an even more extensive study of Cook County in Illinois, where Dr. William Healy's work with juvenile delinquents had already broadened the traditional boundaries of psychiatry. In focusing on a heterogeneous population that included psychopathic delinquents, truants, vagrant children, prostitutes, and alcoholics, Adler deliberately blurred the line of demarcation between mental abnormality and mental health. Mental problems, he observed, included "both the problems of the insane and feebleminded and the problems of the social failures." Adler was particularly critical of the traditional but narrow institutional approach, and urged the adoption of policies that minimized the role of mental hospitals and made the entire community the focal point of psychiatrists and of other mental health professionals. In planning to meet community needs for dealing with mental problems, he recommended that "the emphasis should be laid upon provision for supplying the highest grade technical service and that the institutional factors and questions of buildings can be delegated to minor consideration." The bulk of the study was devoted to the problems of children and adults; the institutionalized mentally ill were largely ignored.[32]

Before America's entry into World War I, the NCMH's energies tended to be directed largely toward improving conditions for the institutionalized mentally ill. In addition to its state surveys, the organization published in 1912 a compilation by John Koren of all state laws relating to the insane, and five years later issued an updated revised edition. In 1917 and 1918 it worked hand in hand with the AMPA to develop a uniform system of statistical reporting for mental hospitals in order to collect data that could be aggregated and compared.[33]

Slowly but surely, however, Salmon began to redirect the organization. Beers proved a willing supporter, perhaps because of the bitter taste left by his earlier involvement with Meyer. Against the wishes of those who wanted to emphasize surveys and the collection of data, Beers fought for the establishment of a new journal to popularize the cause. He prevailed despite the anger that some of his methods had aroused. The initial issue of *Mental Hygiene* appeared at the beginning of 1917, with an announced aim of publishing material for an educated but general audience. "It is our hope," the editors wrote,

> that MENTAL HYGIENE will prove equally useful to the highly trained worker in psychiatry or psychology, the physician engaged in preventive medicine, the teacher seeing in education preparation for life, the magistrate concerned not only with the consequences but the causes of the offense before him, the parent seeking knowledge of the mechanisms by which character is built, and the student of social problems desirous of understanding the complex fabric of organized society through knowledge of those factors which mould the mental lives of individual men and women.[34]

With the return of Salmon from military service at the end of the war, the outward thrust of the NCMH grew even more pronounced. "There is an unparalleled opportunity," wrote Salmon in an unsuccessful effort to get financial support from the Rockefeller Foundation, "for us to be of constructive service in helping states formulate their programs not only with regard to feeble-mindedness and insanity but to the mental factors involved in delinquency, dependency, prostitution and the like and, above all, in suggesting to school authorities the required machinery for recognizing and meeting the needs of psychopathic children." When Stewart Paton criticized the NCMH for its failure to integrate biology and psychiatry, Salmon conceded that the organization had not engaged in laboratory research. But he insisted that the organization's "social research as to the manner in which people are behaving themselves in the communities and the relationship of certain mental factors to this behavior should not all be lightly dismissed by calling it 'propaganda.' "[35]

Between 1919 and 1922 Salmon helped to alter the character of the NCMH and to establish a variety of programs involving work at the community level. The Rockefeller Foundation, however, was reluctant to become involved with social-action projects that might prove controversial; it preferred to support medical education and research. In rejecting some of Salmon's suggestions, Edwin R. Embree, the Foundation's secretary, noted in April, 1921, that his organization's support of state surveys "had in mind not only and not so much the effect which would be produced in the states concerned, as a demonstration of the value of such studies." By December Embree spoke about diminishing Rockefeller support for the NCMH, and he urged its leaders to seek other sources of support. Salmon, however, was not to be dissuaded. Despite his conflict with Beers and his subsequent resignation to accept a professorship at Columbia University, he helped to push the Committee in new directions. In 1921 the NCMH obtained support from the Commonwealth Fund for the creation of a Division on the Prevention of Delinquency. In turn the Division founded a number of child-guidance clinics as demonstration projects. These clinics were to represent the major thrust of the activities of the NCMH during the 1920s. With the financial assistance of the Rockefeller Foundation, the Committee also established a modest fellowship program for psychiatrists, psychologists, and psychiatric social workers.[36]

Salmon's departure in 1922 made little difference; the NCMH did not restore its initial goal of improving conditions among the institutionalized mentally ill to a paramount position. Frankwood E. Williams, Salmon's successor as Medical Director, was concerned with other problems. In 1925 he sent an application to the Rockefeller Foundation dealing with the "psychopathology of dependency." The NCMH proposed to undertake a study aimed at demonstrating that dependency in many instances was not the result of lack of "proper opportunities" or "misfortune," but rather grew out of the inability of the individual "to accept those opportunities that have come to him or to meet the exigencies of living with any degree of adequacy, due to an inherent intellectual inadequacy in himself, to a mental or nervous disease that has taken away what adequacy he may once have had, or to personality, psychopathological in type, that would make adequate adjustment to situations . . . exceedingly difficult—in some cases impossible." The proposal for $30,000 was immediately rejected by Embree, who insisted that such a study "should more properly be supported by an organization having a general interest in social matters and social welfare." The Foundation, he added, restricted its activities to studies "having a definitely biological bearing."[37]

The NCMH, of course, in theory had never modified or abandoned its commitment to the mentally ill. Its cooperative venture with the AMPA to create a uniform statistical reporting system for mental hospitals proved a success, and in the early 1920s the United States Bureau of the Census assumed full responsibility for the system, thereby ensuring its continued existence. In practice, however, the Committee's deepening involvement in activities not directly related to the mentally ill diminished any role that it might have played in modifying public policy dealing with the mentally ill. The change in orientation was dramatically demonstrated in the nature of its mental hygiene surveys. The earliest postwar studies in North Carolina and Missouri were traditional and resembled in most respects their prewar predecessors. Those completed in 1921 and after, on the other hand, were of a quite different character. The Maryland Mental Hygiene Survey, for example, was requested by the Baltimore Alliance of Social Agencies, the State Board of Education, as well as by the Maryland Lunacy Commission. Fewer than ten out of a total of ninety-six printed pages of the final report dealt with the mentally ill; the bulk of the material was concerned with studies of children and mentally deficient persons. Much the same was true of surveys in such places as Wisconsin, Arizona, Kentucky, Rhode Island, South Carolina, North Dakota, Texas, Cincinnati, Staten Island (New York), and New York City. Indeed, the latter study focused exclusively on hospital and dispensary outpatient departments, public schools, social agencies, courts, and protective agencies.[38]

The transformation of the NCMH was reflected in the subsequent career of Beers, who remained the driving force for the first fifteen years of its existence. Admittedly, much of Beers's time was spent in a seemingly endless quest for funds. But by the 1920s Beers was directing his energies toward the creation of an international organization that paralleled the NCMH. In 1930 the First International Congress on Mental Hygiene met in Washington, D.C. Beers's efforts had brought together over 3,000 participants from forty-one nations. Although the conference was attended by a number of distinguished psychiatrists and psychoanalysts, the actual impact of the event was less than clear. During the 1930s Beers grew even more remote from the concerns of his earlier career. Ironically, he was admitted to the Butler Hospital in Providence in 1939 when he became mentally ill again and remained institutionalized until his death in 1943 at the age of sixty-seven.[39]

Privately it was not uncommon for individuals to express serious reservations, if not doubts, about the contributions of either the National Committee or its constituent state societies. In 1936 Dr. Henry B. Elkind, the Medical Director of the Massachusetts Society for Mental Hygiene, conceded the difficulty of evaluating the work of such organizations. "There is little question," he added, "of the ability of psychiatry and mental hygiene under favorable circumstances to help in the adjustment of individuals who are unhappy, or in difficulty of one sort or another, or suffering from mental disease; but to enlarge that statement to include the promotion of public education for individual unhappiness is to go beyond what mental hygiene is now able to accomplish." Similarly, Meyer expressed a longing for a mental hygiene division "which shall be in a position to give an honest account of its actual work without having to swell the unfortunate noise and propaganda that has become necessary to maintain the salaries and professionalism of so many half-doctors and new 'professions' under the name of mental hygiene, and under the praise of unattainable panaceas."[40] Others called into question the very legitimacy of the mental hygiene movement. "Its capacity for creating a need," observed Maxwell Gitelson, a future president of the American Psychoanalytic Association, "has developed far in advance of its capacity for meeting the developed need."[41]

That the NCMH chose to focus on problems other than those presented by the institutionalized mentally ill was hardly surprising. Years of criticisms of mental hospitals had exacted a heavy toll, and psychiatry as a medical specialty had little to gain by identifying itself with such institutions. Just as twentieth-century psychiatry began to look outside of institutions, so too did the NCMH, as well as comparable state and local societies, seek wider horizons. Prevention was an attractive alternative, partly because of its broad appeal, and partly because the treatment of mental disease offered little encouragement. Although the NCMH had a strong representation of hospital psychiatrists in its early years, they had never constituted the driving force within the organization, and as they retired they were replaced by individuals with quite different concerns. The emphasis on child guidance during and after the 1920s was especially compatible with a larger society increasingly fascinated with the problems of youth and of prevention. Frankwood E. Williams even attempted to redefine mental hygiene by identifying it with infantile sexuality and the developing psyche of the infant. During the 1930s the NCMH devoted a good deal of energy to psychiatric education and to establishment of a specialty board. Finally, the concept of prevention paralleled the mature development of a professional spirit in psychiatry; prevention gave psychiatrists an important role in both individual and social reconstruction. By 1930 it was not uncommon to hear claims that psychiatry could make important contributions to industry and education. By that time the APA had a Social Problems Section, and in 1939 a group of psychiatrists attempted to organize an Association for the Psychiatric Study of Social Issues.[42] As professionals and laypersons embraced an all-inclusive mental hygiene movement, they implicitly ignored or abandoned the institutionalized mentally ill.

III

The NCMH and its constituent state societies represented the relatively hopeful and benign side of the mental hygiene movement. Those associated with these and similar organizations believed that prevention was the most effective way of dealing with mental disease, given the intractable nature of the malady. Mental hygiene, however, had another and very different side. Whereas many of its supporters emphasized hope and looked forward to a time when science would find an appropriate cure, others were less confident. Fearing that an alleged increase in degeneracy in general and in mental illness in particular threatened the biological well-being of the American people, they supported a variety of interventionist measures, including marriage regulation, immigration restriction, and involuntary sterilization.

Although interventionist measures to limit the spread of alleged degenerates did not become significant until after the turn of the century, their antecedents dated back many decades. Throughout much of the nineteenth century fear of and hostility toward persons defined as socially undesirable was common. In some cases this hostility tended to be directed toward minority ethnic groups; in other cases the object of concern was a more vaguely defined class of individuals whose character defects presumably reduced them to a dependent state. Nevertheless, the element of fear was overshadowed by a religiously based optimistic activism and faith that individual will and volition could surmount character imperfections. A plastic interpretation of heredity (which assumed that inherited characteristics could be modified by environmental changes and transmitted to future generations) tempered social antipathies.

After 1880, on the other hand, a more pessimistic tone began to emerge. Increasingly hereditarian formulations were expressed in a harsher terminology that rejected environmental solutions and substituted coercive measures in their place. Although few accepted the distinction between inherited and acquired characteristics, a prevailing pessimism led many to conclude that degenerate traits were fixed and immutable; what was required were solutions that inhibited their spread to the rest of the population. The growing hereditarian vogue gained even greater credence because it appeared to be phrased in scientific terminology that explained social phenomena and at the same time served as a guide to action.

During the last two decades of the nineteenth century, the elements of fear and hope, optimism and pessimism, began to find expression in a nascent eugenics movement. Basing their action upon the proposition that fixed inherited traits determined character, eugenicists set out to encourage the multiplication of the "fit" and to discourage the propagation of the "unfit." A particular version of Darwinian biology and a new interpretation of race that substituted heredity for culture as the defining element helped to rationalize the claims of the eugenicists. In a society whose foundations seemed threatened by social tensions related to economic depressions, class conflict, rising levels of violence, and bureaucratically structured organizations whose activities seemed to submerge individual achievement, eugenicists offered an explanation and a guide to remedial action.[43]

Fear that foreign governments were using the United States as a receptacle for infirm, crippled, and mentally ill persons as well as for criminals strengthened a growing desire to end unrestricted immigration. The NCCC, which represented state boards of charity and generally included some institutional psychiatrists, had standing committees on immigration and alien paupers and criminals, and during the 1880s supported legislation to reduce the migration of such persons to the United States. In 1882 Congress enacted one of the first statutes designed to limit immigration by applying a principle of selectivity. Among its provisions was a stipulation that convicts, insane persons, idiots, and individuals unable to care for themselves without becoming a public charge would be excluded, but deficient enforcement procedures vitiated the statute's intent.[44]

During the 1890s eugenical concepts gained wider support. In 1896 Connecticut became the first state to pass legislation regulating marriage for eugenic purposes, and other states quickly followed suit. Many of these early laws forbad the marriage of insane persons. Eugenicists, however, recognized that such laws had only a limited effect. Persuaded that further inaction would threaten the very foundations of American society, they began to promote a variety of policies, including greater segregation of the feebleminded, immigration restriction, and the sterilization of defective individuals. The Immigration Restriction League, founded in 1894 by a group of young New England Brahmins, was a harbinger of things to come. This organization brought together individuals from the intelligentsia, from business and academic life, whose activities reflected prevailing eugenic and racial concepts.

Before 1921 immigration restrictionists won only limited victories. Nevertheless, sentiment for action, fueled by individuals and organizations hostile to the new immigration from Eastern and Southern Europe and promoted by an Anglo-Saxon intelligentsia with a growing affinity for racial concepts, continued to increase. Although success would not come until after World War I, the movement helped to disseminate eugenical concepts.[45]

One of the muted themes of restrictionists was that immigration bore a disproportionate responsibility for the increase in insanity and other forms of degeneracy that threatened the biological well-being of the American people. This allegation, however, drew relatively little support among those involved with the care of the mentally ill after the turn of the century. Before that time Eastern officials—especially those in New York and Massachusetts (states that had high concentrations of immigrants and well-developed hospital systems)—propounded the view that immigration regulation or restriction would diminish insanity and pauperism. In 1914, by way of contrast, Spencer L. Dawes (a Special Commissioner of the Alien Insane in New York) prepared a report that utilized age-corrected data. Dawes avoided any discussion of the relationship between immigration and insanity. He recommended instead that the federal government assume financial responsibility for the alien insane, since under existing statutes the national government had jurisdiction over admission and deportation of aliens.[46]

In general, psychiatrists provided only marginal support for the restrictionist cause. Fascination with racial categories led some to measure the susceptibility of particular groups to insanity, but the results were rarely conclusive. In 1880 Edward C. Spitzka analyzed data pertaining to the insane by race, but he found that each had its own peculiar configuration, and hence could offer no policy recommendations. Shortly thereafter, James G. Kiernan, who first stimulated Spitzka's interest in the subject, concluded in a more nativist vein that one-seventh of all immigrants were paranoics, and he urged action to exclude such individuals. Subsequent psychiatric studies of the relationship between race and mental disease rarely offered clear-cut results, if only because a below-average percentage in one disease category was often accompanied by an above-average figure in another. With some exceptions, many of the psychiatric investigations of mental disease among immigrants concluded that the stress of a new and strange environment rather than innate factors was responsible for a high incidence. Even Salmon, an individual who first came to prominence because of his work on immigration and insanity, tended to emphasize an environmental rather than an exclusively racial etiology.[47]

After 1900 the development of more sophisticated techniques of statistical analysis called into question the allegation that immigrants provided a disproportionate share of admissions to mental hospitals. When the institutionalized population was analyzed in terms of the age distribution of the entire native and foreign-born population, for example, the relative proportion of immigrants in hospitals declined precipitously. The hospital population was composed entirely of individuals over the age of twenty. Yet a large proportion of the native white population was under the age of twenty, whereas a much smaller proportion of immigrants was less than twenty. The census of 1910 noted that unadjusted mental hospital admission rates for native-born white Americans was 57.9 (per 100,000), as compared with 116.3 for foreign-born whites. If the respective age distribution for each group was taken into account, the corrected figures would be 91.2 for the former and 123.3 for the latter. "The age difference," conceded the authors of the census, "probably goes further than any other factor toward explaining the contrast between the native white and the foreign-born white in respect to the proportionate numbers admitted to hospitals for the insane," and they suggested that other differences between the two groups might be accounted for by sex distribution or by urban-rural residence. Increasingly, the validity of statistics suggesting that immigrants were responsible for a rising incidence of mental disease encountered formidable challenges from individuals employing age-corrected data.[48]

Between 1909 and 1914 the AMPA as well as individual members attempted to influence Congressional deliberations pertaining to immigration. Their concern, however, was not with the restriction of immigration generally, but rather with more effective inspection of immigrants to determine their sanity. Since the overwhelming majority of members were affiliated with state institutions, their interest in the subject grew out of the fiscal problems of supporting the alien insane with public funds. In 1914 the Association adopted a resolution endorsing a bill under consideration in the House of Representatives which provided for a more effective "detection, exclusion and deportation of mentally and physically defective aliens, and in a general improvement in the character of our immigration." Two years earlier the AMPA had also appointed a Committee on Applied Eugenics, but its report in 1913 focused on heredity rather than immigration.[49]

The debate over immigration restriction led eventually to the passage of three major pieces of legislation between 1921 and 1927, all of which applied a system of national quotas based on earlier population distributions. These laws were intended to limit the numbers of immigrants as well as to reduce the proportion from Eastern and Southern Europe. Support was provided largely by individuals and organizations active in the eugenics movement or committed to racial interpretations of culture. Those involved with the mentally ill, on the other hand, were largely concerned with the fiscal issues relating to mental hospitals, and were in general not associated with racial concepts. A few psychiatrists, including Meyer, permitted their names to be used by the Eu-

genics Committee of the United States of America, an organization chaired by Irving Fisher and including such prominent
racial theorists as Madison Grant. But when sent a report by the
organization's Committee on Selective Immigration, Meyer responded in negative terms. Would it not be wiser, he noted, for
such a report "to put forth a rather modest acknowledgment that
a great deal of the trouble may lie in our actual unpreparedness
in this country to assimilate the unusual." The report was less
than honest when it suggested a return to the level of 1890. "It
would not quite do," he continued, "to say publicly that we are
afraid that we have too many Catholics, and Hebrews, and Greeks,
and Turks to suit ourselves, which of course any group of people
have a right to say." "All this," concluded Meyer,

> I say only to suggest that a frank admission of what is back of
> the report would be just a little more worthy and promising of
> improving the understanding, rather than giving the appearance
> of scientific support to matters which after all are just a little
> bit too frankly human and not strict science. One might for
> instance say that to meet these so-called undesirables the whole
> system of requirements could be raised for the whole number.[50]

IV

The individuals who took an active role in promoting the cause
of immigration restriction were primarily concerned with the
alleged threat posed by large numbers of individuals from Eastern
and Southern Europe who shared neither the racial traits nor the
culture of Americans; the mentally ill were of only marginal
significance. Those who promoted involuntary sterilization, on
the other hand, were determined, in order to prevent the widespread dissemination of undesirable traits, to prevent the mentally ill, feebleminded, and criminal population from reproducing
themselves. The inspiration for such preventive measures as sterilization initially came from modern eugenics. In England Sir
Francis Galton laid the foundations of eugenics by attempting to
demonstrate that human abilities were inherited and that inherited traits were not subject to environmental influences. Galton
also developed statistical techniques (including the correlation
coefficient) in order to demonstrate that children approached the
mean more closely than their parents.[51]

By the turn of the century, eugenicists were seeking to harness the authority of the state to the theory of heredity. Specifically, they urged the passage of legislation that would prevent socially undesirable groups from propagating themselves, thus raising the quality of the nation's genetic pool. Salpingectomy (cutting and tying the fallopian tubes) and vasectomy (cutting and tying the vas deferens through a slit in the scrotum) were perfected in the 1890s, thus making sterilization possible without having to resort to the far more drastic procedure of castration. The availability of seemingly simple and safe surgical procedures, when combined with a pessimistic view of heredity and an abiding faith in the ability of human beings to control their own destiny, helped to give rise to a eugenics movement to improve the biological character of the American population by preventing the further breeding of undesirable groups.

The harsh hereditarian formulations assumed programmatic forms during the 1890s, when a nascent eugenics movement was in the making. Some emphasized education, some urged the passage of laws regulating marriage, and some promoted more effective segregation of the biologically unfit. Each of these alternatives, however, had drawbacks: education did not always give rise to the anticipated results; laws regulating marriage did not preclude sexual contacts resulting in pregnancy; and complete segregation was both difficult and expensive because of the numbers of individuals involved. Sterilization, on the other hand, had the virtue of overcoming such shortcomings: it was inexpensive, simple and relatively safe, irreversible in nature, and its benefits were clear and direct. To many activists concerned with the welfare of the American people, the case on behalf of sterilization was compelling; the harm to the individual was minimal and the advantages to society great. Indeed, sterilization was not incompatible with the Progressive movement's emphasis on social reform before World War I.[52]

As early as 1897 a bill was introduced in the Michigan legislature providing for the sterilization of the feebleminded and of certain criminals, but it failed to pass. In Pennsylvania a somewhat similar bill passed the legislature in 1901 and 1905, only to meet with an executive veto. The eugenicists were finally successful in 1907 when Indiana passed a law providing for the mandatory sterilization of confirmed criminals, idiots, imbeciles, and rapists when recommended by a board of experts. In the succeeding ten years, fifteen other states enacted some form of comparable legislation. Most of the laws applied to the mentally ill as well as to other groups who were regarded as biologically undesirable. By 1940 a total of thirty states had enacted at one time or another statutes that provided for the sterilization of individuals confined in state institutions.[53]

The absence of a visible national movement to promote sterilization was striking. Unanimity on the desirability of the practice was absent in the medical, legal, and scientific professions. Nor was there a central organization directing the drive to secure enactment of such laws. To be sure, the Eugenics Record Office, founded in 1910 as a center for eugenical research and as an agency for the dissemination of propaganda, provided some national cohesion, but it could hardly be termed a pressure group on this issue. Nor did the NCMH support sterilization, if only because knowledge about heredity was too fragmentary to justify the practice. The absence of a national movement, however, did not prevent some significant successes. As a matter of fact, the decentralized nature of the American political system probably facilitated the passage of sterilization laws. In states that enacted legislation, the driving force was either an individual or small groups associated with public institutions (mental hospitals, schools for the feebleminded, and prisons), state boards of charity, private welfare organizations, or institutions of higher learning where biological doctrines offered scientific sanction for political activism. The fact that institutional populations were in no position to dissent, that an effective opposition was absent, and that the formation of a national political coalition was unnecessary, aided passage of such laws in the face of broad public apathy and ignorance.[54]

Between 1907 and 1940, a total of 18,552 mentally ill persons in state hospitals were surgically sterilized. The number was not equally distributed among the states, as the statistics in Table 6-1 demonstrate. More than half of all sterilizations were performed in California alone, which, together with Virginia and Kansas, accounted for nearly three-fourths of the total. Clearly, the experience with sterilization was a function of the state in which patients resided, and the practices within that state. Neither total population of the state, age distribution, or any other apparent variable explains these differentials.[55]

Among psychiatrists there was no clear consensus on the wisdom or desirability of sterilization. Most shared a belief that heredity played a role in the etiology of insanity, but their understanding of heredity tended to be protean and general rather than specific. In 1913 the subject arose at the meetings of the AMPA.

TABLE 6-1
STERILIZATION IN STATE INSTITUTIONS UNDER STATE LAWS, 1907-1940

State	Mentally Ill			All Others*
	Male	Female	Total	
Alabama	0	0	0	224
Arizona	10	10	20	0
California	5,329	4,310	9,639	4,929
Connecticut	19	337	356	62
Delaware	206	71	277	333
Georgia	6	68	74	53
Idaho	2	10	12	2
Indiana	213	177	390	643
Iowa	83	91	174	162
Kansas	1,035	724	1,759	645
Maine	0	10	10	180
Michigan	71	234	305	1,840
Minnesota	113	266	379	1,501
Mississippi	135	320	455	68
Montana	16	20	36	150
Nebraska	53	90	143	245
New Hampshire	24	166	190	240
New York**	0	41	41	1
North Carolina	90	150	240	777
North Dakota	123	174	297	237
Oklahoma	70	232	302	168
Oregon	287	321	608	842
South Carolina	0	0	0	35
South Dakota	0	0	0	577
Utah	44	43	87	165
Vermont	1	12	13	199
Virginia	976	1,365	2,341	1,583
Washington	141	245	386	281
West Virginia	0	18	18	28
Wisconsin	0	0	0	1,156
Total	9,047	9,505	18,552	17,326

* The bulk of individuals in this category were feebleminded; a much smaller number included several mixed groups, such as habitual criminals.
** New York's law was declared unconstitutional, repealed, and never reenacted.

The previous year Hubert Work, the organization's president, delivered an address that emphasized the need for "prophylactic psychiatry" and favored sterilization. The organization promptly established a Committee on Applied Eugenics with Work as chairman. The following year the Committee delivered a report that urged a judicious combination of both segregation and sterilization of mental defectives. The latter practice, it noted, neither harmed the individual nor was it imposed for retributive reasons. The delegates accepted the report without signifying approval or disapproval, but the discussion indicated that many were favorably disposed.[56]

Support for sterilization tended to be strongest among officials of state welfare agencies. In many (but not all) instances, hospital superintendents were supportive. William D. Partlow of Alabama was clear and incisive in his beliefs. "For many years," he wrote to E. S. Gosney (co-author of *Sterilization for Human Betterment*), "I have advocated the sterilization of certain types of constitutional hereditary deficients, including feebleminded, insane, repeating criminals, chronic drug and alcoholic addicts, epileptics, etc." Indirect assistance was often provided by psychiatrists who emphasized the role of heredity and lent their name and influence to the Eugenic Record Office and by a committee organized by Harry H. Laughlin ("Committee to Study and to Report on the Best Means of Cutting Off the Defective Germ-Plasm of the American Population"). E. E. Southard, for example, urged eugenical research and took an active part in the work of the Eugenics Record Office.[57]

Even though the majority of institutional psychiatrists favored eugenic concepts and at the very least were silent on sterilization, opposition was not absent. William A. White, whose influence within the specialty probably equalled that of Meyer, was unalterably opposed. In a balanced analysis of "Eugenics and Heredity in Nervous and Mental Diseases" in 1913, White summarized existing theories of heredity. Taking note of the split between the Neo-Lamarckians and the Neo-Darwinians (the former accepted and the latter rejected the inheritance of acquired characteristics), he also distinguished between hereditarian and environmental influences in the development of the individual. Insisting that the state of knowledge precluded state-mandated sterilization, White refused to sanction the legitimacy of the practice. Privately his views were even more inflexible. The Mendelian hypothesis, he observed, could not be applied to human beings, since "unit characters are vague and indefinable and nobody knows what they mean." State sterilization commissions, moreover, operated in an arbitrary and casual manner. When invited to address a tri-state conference on the subject of prevention and sterilization, White expressed his opposition in no uncertain terms. "I do not believe that there is the slightest particle of justification for the mutilating operations that are being advocated ... and if I should happen to talk in Baltimore at your meeting I should unhesitatingly denounce the sterilization propaganda."[58]

White's views were echoed by a minority of psychiatrists and others who insisted that eugenics was based on unscientific extremism. The Illinois State Charities Commission was one of the few state agencies to call attention to the extremism of eugenic advocates, some of whom were bringing ridicule upon a science that deserved more (although the Commission never specifically referred to sterilization). Abraham Myerson, whose influential study of the inheritance of mental diseases raised serious doubts about the validity of hereditarian concepts in psychiatry, opposed sterilization because available data did not justify its use. Meyer was somewhat more circumspect in his views, but was not persuaded that sterilization (which he once described as "merely an act of power and force") was a panacea. Smith Ely Jelliffe was dubious of the soundness of eugenic concepts in general, a view echoed by Jacques Loeb, the distinguished biologist. J. K. Hall, the most influential Southern psychiatrist of the 1920s and 1930s, also ridiculed the claim of sterilization advocates. "Some better method of preventing human diseases will have to be thought of than human sterilization," he concluded in a pithy and sarcastic tone. "There could never be another flood—if all the water were dried up; nor another sun-stroke—if the sun were blotted out. Sterilization of the human being primarily prevents begetting or conceiving children. The prevention of disease in an unconceived child—is almost inconceivable."[59]

By 1934 the controversial nature of sterilization led the American Neurological Association to appoint a committee to undertake a broad study; a grant from the Carnegie Foundation provided financial assistance. Chaired by Abraham Myerson, the Committee included three other physicians and a genetic consultant. A year later the Association accepted a preliminary report, and in 1936 an expanded version was published in book form by the Macmillan Company.[60]

Myerson was not neutral; his opposition to sterilization was a matter of public record. At the very time of his appointment, he had given a paper at the Association's meetings that was sharply critical of Harry H. Laughlin, one of the nation's outstanding advocates of sterilization. Skeptical of the accuracy of data pertaining to heredity, Myerson warned of the potential threat. "Logically," he declared, "any group that becomes dominant in the United States may declare all others alien to the fourth generation and only the persons whose prolific ancestors came over in the remarkably small Mayflower can qualify as members of the American race. . . . The dominant group may go on to declare that persons of the diverse types should be sterilized or prevented from procreating." Myerson insisted that neurologists and psychiatrists had an obligation to oppose legislation of the kind advocated by Laughlin since it posed a threat to "freedom and individuality." Myerson's opposition was not unqualified, however, for he favored "limited sterilization laws."[61]

After surveying existing legislation and the relative noncompliance in most states, the ANA committee summarized the arguments employed by supporters of sterilization. It specifically rejected the allegation that insanity and feeblemindedness was increasing, and called attention to such factors as changing age distributions and other demographic variables which in turn gave rise to larger institutional populations. After an examination of the existing literature, the committee concluded "that not much scientifically valid work had been done on the subject of the inheritance of the diseases." Its members staunchly opposed involuntary sterilization, but endorsed voluntary sterilization for selected diseases "with the consent of the patient or those responsible for him."[62]

Prior to 1940 the debate over sterilization rarely focused on ethical or moral issues. The Catholic Church was a notable exception; it officially opposed involuntary and voluntary sterilization on the ground that both violated natural law. To most proponents and opponents of the practice, however, the underlying issue was whether or not scientific knowledge about heredity made sterilization legitimate. Medical autonomy and authority were issues taken for granted. To the overwhelming majority of psychiatrists, patients played a passive role because they lacked the knowledge or judgment to make medical or scientific decisions. Nor were psychiatrists unique in their beliefs or behavior; the same attitudes were characteristic of the medical profession as a whole. Moral and ethical concerns emerged only after revelations about the use of sterilization in Nazi Germany became public knowledge and thus altered the framework in which the debate took place. Before 1940 there was relatively little disposition to question the degree to which medical and scientific authority ought to be constrained by ethical and moral considerations. Indeed, a study of sterilization by the United States Public Health Service in 1940 specifically eschewed any analysis of other than scientific and legal issues.[63]

V

Between 1900 and 1940 a self-conscious mental hygiene movement replaced an older prescriptive and didactic tradition. Amorphous in form, the movement was based on a union of science and social activism and reflected a pervasive confidence in the ability of human beings to prevent disease and other social ills. Nor did mental hygienists limit their activities to the problem of mental illness; many were involved in education, child guidance, and the modification of behavior generally. Indeed, the emphasis on prevention grew in intensity because access to funding was facilitated by new philanthropic foundations that were playing an increasingly significan: role in American society. In 1911 John D. Rockefeller helped to make possible the establishment of the Bureau of Social Hygiene, which was incorporated two years later and supported the study of prostitution, venereal disease, delinquent females, and the relationship between moral problems and law enforcement. The Bureau was only one of many similar organizations, all of which shared to one degree or another a utopian vision of a society in which disease was the exception rather than the rule.

For the institutionalized mentally ill, the mental hygiene movement had less than positive consequences. The NCMH, originally intended to improve the quality of hospitals, assumed other roles. In so doing it inadvertently overlooked the interests of a group unable to speak on its own behalf. Nor was there significant opposition within the Committee to policies that looked away from the already mentally ill. Many psychiatrists welcomed a role that seemed to enhance their professional identity by emphasizing prevention rather than care. Ironically, psychiatrists—who could have played a crucial role in creating greater sensitivity for the welfare of the institutionalized mentally ill—chose instead to pursue other ends.

CHAPTER SEVEN

The Invisible Patient

DURING THE EARLY decades of the twentieth century a new spirit of optimism seemed to transform American psychiatry. Psychiatrists increasingly looked to the future, when novel therapies and new preventive techniques would reduce if not eliminate the incidence of mental diseases that devastated individuals and their families. To be sure, occasionally voices were raised against this confident mood. "Sad as it is to make the confession," noted Dr. I. S. Wechsler in a paper delivered to an audience of neurologists and psychiatrists in 1930, "the fact remains that, despite accumulation of knowledge, the ultimate cause or causes of nervous and mental diseases is unknown. There are a great many theories but few facts. Their very profusion not only is in inverse ratio to our knowledge but is an actual confession of ignorance or merely a verbal cloak." "All of us still are children before the great unknown," he concluded, "and it ill befits us to play the role of high priests." Wechsler's warning, however, was atypical; most of his colleagues were firmly persuaded that a new era was about to begin in scientific medicine.[1]

By focusing upon mental disease as an abstraction, psychiatrists for the most part either ignored or else lost ight of their institutionalized patients and the realities of their world. Patients became, in effect, virtually invisible entities. Yet the character of the patient population was crucial to any understanding of the nature and function of mental hospitals. These institutions after 1900 increasingly began caring for aged persons and individuals suffering from a variety of diseases and conditions, most of which required custodial care rather than treatment by specific therapies. The focus on disease largely deflected any effort to understand the needs of hospital patients. Even when a vague awareness of the patient population developed during the 1920s and 1930s, neither psychiatrists nor public officials—each of whom defined the problem in terms of their own preconceptions and concerns—were prepared to adjust their own roles to patient needs. Equally significant, the character of mental hospitals increasingly reflected the chronic nature of their patients. After World War II hospitals came under sharp attack because of their allegedly repressive character. Yet the growing hostility toward institutional care was often based on ignorance about patients and an inability to appreciate the significance and importance of custodial care.

I

Between 1903 and 1940 the number of mentally ill patients in state hospitals increased almost fourfold from 150,000 to 445,000. Such aggregate data, however, tell us little about the kinds of persons in institutions. Who was likely to be confined in a mental hospital? What circumstances led to their commitment? Did the nature of institutional populations remain constant or change over time? In what ways did patients influence the structure and functions of hospitals? And what were the realistic alternatives, if any, to hospitalization?[2]

One of the most striking characteristics of the institutional population in the decades after 1900 was the relative and absolute growth in the number of aged patients—particularly those sixty years or older. Before 1900 elderly people, generally speaking, were not confined in mental hospitals in significant number. This was true even in cases where marked behavioral symptoms were in evidence.

Two factors were responsible for the small number of aged patients. First, the number of individuals aged sixty and over, relative to the total population, was relatively small. In 1860 only 4.3 percent of the population was sixty or over; in 1900 and 1940 the comparable figures were 6.4 and 10.4 percent, respectively. In absolute terms the change was even more striking. On the eve of the Civil War only 1,348,000 persons were sixty or over; between 1900 and 1940 the number rose from 4,872,000 to 13,748,000. Second, when aged persons were destitute or without families willing or able to provide care, they were generally sent to local almshouses. Throughout most of the nineteenth century almshouses served as undifferentiated welfare institutions; among their main function was the care of aged dependent persons, many of whom were senile.[3]

Between 1880 and 1920 the almshouse declined in significance as a public institution. Admissions fell from 81,412 in 1904 to 63,807 in 1922 (a drop from 99.5 to 58.4 persons per 100,000). At the same time that admissions declined, the number of indigent aged individuals in almshouses rose sharply. In 1880 33.2 percent of the almshouse population was sixty and over; in 1904 and 1923 this group accounted for 53.1 and 66.6 percent of the total, respectively. During this same period the number of aged mentally ill in these institutions declined precipitously from 24.3 percent in 1880 to 5.6 percent in 1923 (Table 7-1). The decline, however, was more apparent than real, for the number of aged mentally ill persons committed to hospitals was rising steadily. What occurred, in effect, was not a deinstitutionalization movement, but rather a transfer of patients between different types of institutions. The shift, moreover, was less a function of medical or humanitarian concerns than a consequence of financial considerations. As states began to adopt and implement the principles of state responsibility for all insane persons in the late nineteenth and early twentieth century, local public officials seized upon the fiscal advantages inherent in redefining senility in psychiatric terms. If senile persons were cared for in state hospitals rather than in local or county almshouses, the burden of support would be transferred to the state. To many families, confinement in a mental hospital may have been preferable to almshouse care. Not only did hospitals provide better care, but paradoxically enough the stigma of insanity—especially if an aged person was involved—may have seemed less than that of pauperism.[4]

During the latter part of the nineteenth century the proportion of aged persons in mental hospitals mounted rapidly. Although reliable national data are not available, statistics from individual states and hospitals reveal the magnitude of the change. In many states, including Alabama, Kansas, Massachusetts, and Washing-

TABLE 7-1
MENTALLY ILL PAUPERS IN ALMSHOUSES, 1880-1923

| Year | Total Population | Total Almshouse Population | Mentally Ill Paupers | | Percentage of Mentally Ill Persons in Almshouse Population |
			Admitted During Year	Enumerated on a Given Date	
1880	50,155,783	66,203	—	16,078	24.3
1890	62,222,250	73,044	—	16,440	22.5
1904	81,792,387	81,764	3,375	8,432	10.3
1910	91,972,266	84,198	1,847	3,518	4.2
1923	109,248,393	78,090	2,091*	2,052	5.6

* During 1922. Unfortunately, the census provided no data on the age distribution of mentally ill paupers in almshouses.

ton, the percentage of patients aged sixty and over rose between
300-400 percent.[5] In New York, to offer a specific illustration, 18
percent of all first admissions to state mental hospitals in 1920
were diagnosed as psychotic either because of senility or arteriosclerosis. By 1940 this category accounted for nearly 31 percent
of all first admissions. During this same period the average age
at first admission rose form 42.69 years to 48.47. The trend toward
an older population continued even after the end of World War II
(Table 7-2).[6] Nor was New York unique in this respect. Between
1916 and 1925, 16.3 percent of all first admissions to Warren State
Hospital in Pennsylvania were sixty-five and older; the comparable figure for 1936-1945 was 23 percent (if the data included
aged fifty-five and over, the respective figures would be 29.3 and
36.2 percent). The data for Illinois and Massachusetts reveal a
similar pattern.[7]

Such statistics show that mental hospitals were to some extent
serving as old-age homes for elderly people suffering from some
sort of physical or mental impairment. A breakdown of the 800
patients aged sixty-five and over in Massachusetts in 1900 (who
represented 13 percent of the total hospital population) revealed

TABLE 7-2
FIRST ADMISSIONS TO NEW YORK STATE HOSPITALS, 1919-1921 AND 1949-1951,
CLASSIFIED ACCORDING TO AGE

Age (years)	1919-1921 Number	Percent	1920 Percent Age Distribution of Population for N.Y.S.	1949-1951 Number	Percent	1950 Percent Age Distribution of Population for N.Y.S.
Under 15	72	0.4	29.7	689	1.4	22.6
15-19	963	4.7	7.9	1,871	4.0	6.1
20-24	1,812	8.9	8.9	3,187	6.8	7.3
25-29	2,386	11.8	9.4	3,612	7.7	8.1
30-34	2,336	11.5	8.6	3,314	7.1	7.9
35-39	2,388	11.8	8.1	3,367	7.2	8.0
40-44	2,003	9.9	6.7	3,158	6.7	7.6
45-49	1,771	8.7	5.9	2,998	6.4	7.0
50-54	1,513	7.4	5.1	2,989	6.4	6.6
55-59	1,190	5.9	3.7	2,935	6.3	5.6
60-64	1,085	5.3	3.0	3,155	6.7	4.6
65-69	907	4.4	} 4.7	3,350	7.1	3.6
70 and over	1,877	9.2		12,227	26.2	5.0

that 127 of these 800 (14.4 percent) were confined to their beds; 211 (24 percent) were unable to maintain minimum personal hygiene; 215 (24.4 percent) were helpless and had to be cared for like infants; and 272 (27.5 percent) had no friends or acquaintances.[8]

The number of aged persons in state hospitals obviously varied over time and by geographical location. The increase in the aged population in the two Wisconsin state hospitals between 1875 and 1920 was relatively modest (from 11.9 to 15.1 percent); the county care system, however, provided an alternative institution for the aged insane. Within a single state, wide variations among institutions were not uncommon. In Massachusetts in 1932 the average age of first admissions committed by the courts was 48.6 years. But individual hospitals showed widely diverging patterns: the highest average age was 54.4 years (Boston State Hospital); the figures for Taunton State Hospital, Grafton State Hospital, and Boston Psychopathic Hospital were 50.1, 41.7, and 39.1, respectively.[9] Despite institutional variations (which were related to varying rates for death, discharge, and retention), it is clear that the aged constituted a substantial proportion of the total hospital population. By the late nineteenth century age-specific admission rates of older persons began to rise markedly as compared with admission rates for younger persons. In their classic study of rates of institutionalization covering more than a century, Herbert Goldhamer and Andrew W. Marshall found that the greatest increase occurred in the category of sixty year olds and over. In 1885, age-specific first admission rates in Massachusetts for males aged sixty and over was 70.4, and for females 65.5 (per 100,000). By the beginning of World War II, the corresponding figures were 279.5 and 223.0 (Table 7-3).[10] A study of Warren State Hospital in Pennsylvania covering 1916-1950 showed a similar pattern (Table 7-4).[11]

Why were aged persons confined to mental hospitals? Communities hardly could perceive them as threats to personal security. Nor could it be said that the function of institutionalization was to alter their behavior or to provide them with restorative therapy. "The question of the care of the aged is one that will confront us always," noted one superintendent who conceded that no effective treatment was available.[12] Mental hospitals, in fact, assumed the function of old-age homes, partly because of the lack of alternatives. The decline in mortality rates among younger elements of the population, in addition, led to a relative and ab-

TABLE 7-3
MALE AND FEMALE AGE-SPECIFIC FIRST-ADMISSION RATES
PER 100,000 POPULATION, MASSACHUSETTS, 1885 AND 1939-1941

	1885		1939-1941	
Age	Male	Female	Male	Female
10-19	22.0	15.0	57.2	42.8
20-29	96.4	75.0	124.2	91.1
30-39	111.0	107.9	159.9	108.2
40-49	110.0	108.1	164.0	106.0
50-59	102.9	78.8	174.5	117.3
60-	70.4	65.5	279.5	223.0

TABLE 7-4
AVERAGE ANNUAL RATE OF FIRST ADMISSIONS PER
100,000 POPULATION, WARREN STATE HOSPITAL, PA., 1916-1950

	1916-25	1926-35	1936-45	1946-50
Total Age Adjusted	51.6	57.9	68.2	76.5
Total Crude	43.7	54.1	68.3	79.1
Under 15 Years*	1.5	5.3	6.4	3.0
15-24	28.8	39.8	47.5	49.7
25-34	80.0	71.4	78.6	84.1
35-44	73.0	84.7	92.1	102.0
45-54	68.5	88.5	98.6	104.6
55-64	81.7	88.9	103.1	117.4
65-74	106.4	116.0	149.5	177.7
75-	176.2	185.7	289.2	398.7

* Using as a base the population 10-14 years of age.

solute increase in the number of the aged, thus giving rise to the social problems associated with an aging population.

Older persons ended up in mental hospitals for a variety of reasons. Some had no family to care for them, or, in other instances, families lacked sufficient means to offer care. Other aged individuals, especially those who exhibited strikingly abnormal forms of behavioral patterns, were institutionalized because relatives were unwilling or unable to assume responsiblity for them. For some indigent aged persons, the mental hospital provided the only means of survival.

The use of mental hospitals as homes for aged senile persons did not go unnoticed. The New York State Commission in Lunacy in 1900 called attention to the increasing numbers of such cases in mental hospitals—a development in part associated with the passage of the State Care Act of 1890. Its members noted that only almshouses provided care for dependent aged persons who exhibited aberrant behavior. Mental hospitals, on the other hand, were in a position to provide an environment that included food, shelter, and personal care. Members of the Commission, however, refused to endorse any legislation that precluded the admission of "dotards" to mental hospitals.[13]

Generally speaking, public officials saw no obvious solution to the dilemma presented by aged senile persons. Some proposed that counties or families assume fiscal responsibility; others urged the construction of separate buildings at mental hospitals; and yet others insisted that sons and daughters be forced by law to meet their responsibilities toward parents. Admittedly, most state welfare officials never addressed the problem apart from the larger issue of dependency, and therefore were often criticized for their passive acceptance of the status quo. A study of Illinois state hospitals in the early 1930s emphasized in disapproving tones the degree to which mental hospitals were serving as old-age homes. A major problem, the report noted,

> is the presence of increasingly large numbers of old people— primarily not mental cases—but described in medical parlance as "senile." Social revolutions, radical changes in housing and living problems, the growth of urban life, and countless other factors have tended to force the old man and woman from their homes. Simultaneously there has been a failure in the State of Illinois on the part of the counties to adequately meet this problem, which under our political and statutory law is their responsibility.
>
> The state mental hospital, organized for quite other purposes, has become their only haven. The state hospital, organized to provide more than mere shelter, offers a more expensive form of care than would otherwise be the case were such cases concentrated on the same scale. An illustration of the enormity of this difficulty is found in the Chicago State Hospital, which today is being converted into a huge infirmary, with nearly seventy percent of its 4,000 patients aged or infirm, suffering from no psychoses which would be beyond the capacity of the old-fashioned detached city cottage or rural home or of a well-managed county home.

Whether or not senility should be defined in psychiatric terms was largely beside the point; the necessity for caring for such persons was obvious to all. The structure of public financing and the fact that hospitals for the most part provided better care than almshouses combined to thrust upon mental institutions an increasing responsibility for the welfare of aged and senile persons.[14]

Psychiatrists, of course, were sensitive to the problems posed by aged patients, if only because their institutions were increasingly involved in providing care. After 1900 articles dealing with senile dementia and arteriosclerosis appeared regularly in the medical literature in an effort to distinguish between pathological and aging processes. Implicit in psychiatric thought in these decades was a belief in an inevitable life process that concluded with senility (although not all were equally affected). The uniform nosology developed by the AMPA in 1918 to enhance the collection of statistical data separated the senile psychoses from psychoses with cerebral arteriosclerosis, even though for some psychiatrists the distinction was not especially meaningful. During the 1920s and 1930s studies of the relationship between age and mental diseases became more common. By 1940 discussions of mental hospitals rarely omitted mention of aged patients. The subject was deemed sufficiently important for the Public Health Service to convene a conference on "Mental Health in Later Maturity" in early 1941. Five years later the distinguished British psychiatrist Aubrey Lewis addressed himself to the problem of aging and senility, which he described as a "Major Problem of Psychiatry."[15]

Most psychiatrists, nevertheless, were ambivalent in their attitudes toward aged patients. Their training and socialization led them to emphasize the pathology of mental life, whereas senility involved in part natural and inevitable physiological processes. Disease, at least in theory, was amenable to therapeutic intervention. Aging, on the other hand, gave rise to conditions requiring the kind of humane care that had little or no relationship to medicine or science. Consequently, the majority of psychiatrists dealt with the problem of senility in medical rather than in social terms. Cognizant of the growing number of aged persons in mental hospitals, they rejected the custodial role and insisted that such groups did not belong in mental hospitals. As Dr. Charles G. Wagner of the Binghamton State Hospital noted in 1900:

We are receiving every year a large number of old people, some of them very old, who are simply suffering from the mental decay incident to extreme old age. A little mental confusion, forgetfulness and garrulity are sometimes the only symptoms exhibited, but the patient is duly certified to us as insane and has no one at home capable or possessed of means to care for him. We are unable to refuse these patients without creating ill-feeling in the community where they reside, nor are we able to assert that they are not insane within the meaning of the statute, for many of them, judged by the ordinary standards of sanity, cannot be regarded as entirely sane.

Although sympathetic toward the plight of the aged, many psychiatrists believed that alternative provision for their welfare was required. "It is unjust to the patient and to the State," noted an Idaho superintendent in 1926, "that the only place open to such individuals is in a State Hospital." His Nevada counterpart observed more than a decade earlier that hospitals could offer at most "a good home and pleasant environments," but both, he concluded, could be provided at a lower cost in an alternative setting. The reaction of Lawrence Kolb, a psychiatrist who played a significant role in the development of federal policy toward drug addiction, was typical. Kolb noted in 1941 that mental hospitals were "increasingly overburdened by aged patients for whom nothing can be done"; nevertheless, he insisted that it was "economically unwise and therapeutically unsound to take care of all dementing old people in hospitals." The question posed shortly after 1900 by Robert M. Elliott at the quarterly conference of the New York state hospital psychiatrists was largely ignored. Elliott had conceded that hospitals accepted patients other than the aged senile whose condition was not amenable to therapy. Were not the aged "entitled to the State's bounty" along with other insane persons? "If they are not to be received by the State hospitals, what shall be done with them?"[16]

II

The task of describing the institutionalized mentally ill population with any degree of accuracy is almost impossible. Hospital data were often published at irregular intervals; the absence of firm and consistent reporting categories precluded systematic and detailed analaysis; and a nosology based on symptoms rather than on etiology rendered it extraordinarily difficult to describe the patient population in other than demographic terms. Some of the surviving data, nevertheless, suggest that mental hospitals cared for a substantial number of patients, in addition to aged senile persons, whose behavioral peculiarities were related to an underlying somatic etiology.

Patients suffering from syphilis are a case in point. Before the widespread use of penicillin and other antibiotics, insanity resulting from syphilis accounted for substantial numbers of admissions to asylums. Syphilis, of course, was a disease with a long history. By the late fifteenth or early sixteenth century it appeared in acute epidemic form. At that time many of its victims died before tertiary manifestations could develop or become apparent. In the nineteenth century a number of physicians described general paralysis of the insane (or paresis), but the relationship between this condition and syphilis remained obscure. After 1850 accumulating evidence showed that paresis was the tertiary stage of a disease that developed from an earlier syphilitic infection. In the tertiary stage, massive damage to the central nervous system or brain by the *treponema pallidum* (the organism responsible for syphilis) resulted often not only in bizarre behavior but in dramatic neurological symptoms, paralysis, and eventually death.[17]

Before 1900 data on the incidence of paresis are unreliable. A survey by A. E. Macdonald in the 1870s revealed that few mental hospital reports identified paresis in their classifications of insanity. Using available institutional data, Macdonald discovered that males provided the bulk of admissions, and that the proportion of paretics to the whole number of admissions differed according to geographical region. Paretics accounted for 4 percent of male and 0.9 of female admissions in the East, for the Middle States 8.6 and 0.4 percent, for the West 1.7 and 0.2 percent, and for the South 1.1 and 0.1 percent. His findings, although implausible because of the unreliability of the data, nevertheless suggested that paresis was not of major significance insofar as patients in mental hospitals were concerned.[18]

By the early years of the twentieth century, the situation was markedly different. Between 1911 and 1919, for example, about 20 percent of all male first admissions to New York State mental hospitals were cases of general paresis (the comparable rates for females during this period being about one-third that of men). This group, in absolute terms, was composed of 5,615 males and 1,517 females. Between 1920 and 1931 the total number of paretic first admissions climbed to 10,190. After 1925, however, first admission rates began to decline. By 1940 paresis accounted for 9.4 percent of male and 3.2 percent of female first admissions.

Many other states had rates comparable to those of New York. Nationally, 9.2 percent of all first admissions to state hospitals in 1933 were cases of general paresis; by 1942 that figure had fallen in 8.3 percent.[19]

Whether the seeming rise in the incidence of paresis in the early twentieth century was due to more accurate observation and reporting, or to the development of a more stable relationship between parasite and host that increased the number of tertiary cases, cannot be answered in light of surviving sources. Certainly the introduction of the Wasserman test at most mental hospitals provided a fairly reliable (but not infallible) technique for determining the presence of the *treponema pallidum*. The development of the collodial gold test by Lange in 1912 and the demonstration by Noguchi and Moore of the presence of the syphilitic organism in paretic brains in 1913 added more elements of reliability to the statistics of this disease.[20]

Given the nature of the disease, few households were willing or prepared to cope with paretic persons. Since general hospitals lacked separate facilities to care for patients in the tertiary stage—persons who could survive for as long as five years in this condition—responsibility for providing care for them devolved upon mental hospitals. Paretic patients in general differed in age from those classified as psychotic either because of senility or arteriosclerosis; the former were usually over thirty years of age and under sixty. Of 8,186 males admitted to New York State mental hospitals as paretics between 1920 and 1931, 2,565 (31.3 percent) were aged 30-39, 3,000 (36.6 percent) were 40-49, and 1,664 (20.3 percent) 50-59; only 6.9 percent were over sixty and 4.6 under thirty. Despite the relative absence of aged persons among paretic patients, the prognosis was decidedly negative. Between 1913 and 1922, 87.7 percent of all first admission paretics in New York State died during their confinement. In 1920, for example, 825 such cases were admitted for the first time. Of this number 322 (39 percent) died in less than six months, 113 (13.7 percent) between six and eleven months, and most of the remainder between one and four years after their admission. For reasons that are not completely clear, death rates by 1931 among this group had declined sharply and the trend toward greater longevity became pronounced. For the bulk of these patients, the hospital provided custodial care as well as some form of medical care similar to the care offered in many general hospitals.[21]

Generally speaking, at least one-third and probably a half or more of all first admissions to state mental hospitals represented cases where behavioral symptoms were probably of known somatic origins. In 1922, 52,472 persons were admitted to state mental hospitals for the first time. Of this number, 3,356 were without evidence of any psychoses; they were admitted because of epilepsy, alcoholism, drug addiction, psychopathic personality, or mental deficiency. Of the remaining 49,116 first admissions, 16,407 suffered from a variety of identifiable somatic conditions, including senility, cerebral arteriosclerosis, general paresis, Huntington's chorea, pellagra, and brain tumors. Between 1922 and 1940 the proportion of individuals admitted for the first time with such somatic conditions increased from 33.4 to 42.4 percent. If we assume that a significant proportion of individuals in the functional categories also suffered from a variety of conditions with a somatic origin—an assumption that may be warranted from other present-day data—it is evident that mental hospitals provided care for a patient population with severe physical as well as mental problems. The fact that the somatic group had higher death rates (as compared with the lower death rates for the functional psychoses) suggested that the diagnoses were not inaccurate. In 1940, for example, the somatic group accounted for 19,357 deaths out of a total of 31,417 (or 61.6 percent).[22]

There were, of course, significant regional variations in the distribution of diseases. Pellagra—a disease caused by a dietary deficiency and often accompanied by behavioral symptoms—was generally confined to the South. Between 1930 and 1932, the State Hospital at Goldsboro, North Carolina—which was limited to

TABLE 7-5
FIRST ADMISSIONS TO STATE MENTAL HOSPITALS, 1922-1940,
BY PSYCHOSES OF KNOWN SOMATIC ORIGIN

	1922	1926	1930	1935	1940
Total first admissions	52,472	52,793	62,738	72,438	79,449
with psychoses	49,116	50,090	57,534	65,201	69,511
without psychoses	3,356	2,703	5,204	7,237	9,938
psychoses of somatic origin	16,407	18,235	22,511	25,275	29,445
percentage of psychoses of somatic origin (based on total first admissions with psychoses)	33.4	36.4	39.1	38.8	42.4

black patients only—reported no less than 19 percent of its admissions were due to pellagra.[23]

A significant proportion of the total institutionalized population, in other words, were persons suffering from a variety of physical disabilities that also involved behavioral symptoms. Whether or not the mental hospital was the appropriate place for them was beside the point; most of these patients required some form of comprehensive care that few, if indeed any, homes could provide.

Viewed from an international perspective, seeming national differences in incidence rates of mental disease concealed different practices and policies. In Norway, for example, the incidence rate of first admissions up to the age of forty between 1928 and 1932 was slightly higher than the rate within the United States. Beyond the age of forty, American rates rose sharply, whereas the Norwegian rate showed a gradual decrease. This did not imply, however, that the pattern of mental diseases was different. Before World War II, the United States committed many of its senile aged groups to mental hospitals. In Norway, on the other hand, such patients were boarded out to their own families, to other families, or sent to special institutions for the aged.[24]

What about the thousands of other mental patients who apparently did not suffer from known somatic diseases? Who were they and why were they institutionalized? Of those identified as psychotic but not suffering from identifiable or known physical disabilities, the overwhelming majority were diagnosed either manic-depressive, schizophrenic (dementia praecox), or alcoholic. In 1922 these three groups accounted for 44.4 percent of all first admissions; by 1940 the percentage had declined to 39.2 percent (Table 7-6).[25] These categories present obvious problems, partly because of their etiological and descriptive vagueness. It is possible to delineate some of the demographic characteristics of these three groups. Nevertheless, it is by no means certain that such characteristics were linked with the nature of the disease or condition of the patients.*

* After 1900 a large body of demographic data on the institutionalized mentally ill became available. The federal census in 1904 and 1910 conducted extensive surveys on the subject and beginning in 1923 published annual compilations. New York and Massachusetts, in addition, established their own statistical agencies to gather statewide data. Much of this data was subjected also to more critical analyses by the application of sophisticated statistical techniques. The results were often surprising. Males, for example, had higher first-admission rates than

TABLE 7-6
PERCENT DISTRIBUTION OF PSYCHOSES OF FIRST ADMISSION TO
STATE HOSPITALS, 1922-1940

	1922	1926	1930	1935	1940
General paresis	10.1	9.3	8.7	9.1	8.6
Cerebral arteriosclerosis	6.2	8.4	11.2	13.4	15.5
Senile	10.4	11.0	10.2	9.1	9.9
Alcoholic	3.7	4.5	4.6	5.1	5.1
Manic-depressive	16.5	15.5	15.0	13.8	10.5
Schizophrenia (dementia praecox)	24.2	23.6	22.7	23.0	23.6
All other psychoses	28.9	27.7	27.6	26.5	26.8

The nature of the patient population in mental hospitals, however, is not a completely unknown entity. Although it is probably impossible to determine the precise reasons for the institutionalization of patients or to categorize the nature of their condition with any degree of accuracy, it is possible, by using available data, to suggest some reasonably informed guesses. To be specific, discharge, retention, and mortality rates indicate that hospitals were caring for two distinct groups. The smaller group was composed of individuals who appeared to benefit from brief periods of confinement and were thereafter able to return to their communities

females, though there were significant differences between groups of psychoses according to sex. Thus females had higher rates of first admissions with senile psychoses, manic-depressive psychoses, and involutional disorders, whereas males had higher rates of psychoses with cerebral arteriosclerosis, general paresis, alcoholic psychoses, and dementia praecox. Rates of first admission were lowest in the younger age groups and rose steadily to a maximum in old age. Rates of mental disease were lowest in rural populations, and higher in urban areas. The differences in first-admission rates between immigrants and native born, when corrected for age distribution and urban-rural residence, did not prove to be significant. Blacks had higher first-admission rates than whites, but largely because of syphilis and alcoholism. Unmarried, widowed, and divorced persons had higher first-admission rates than married individuals. Rates for migrant persons, when adjusted for age, sex, and race, were far higher than for nonmigrant persons.

The relevance of such data for an understanding of the nature and etiology of mental illness, however, remains unclear, if only because correlation cannot be equated with causality. Moreover, the focus of this book is upon the mental hospital as an institution, the relationship between patients and psychiatrists, and the development of social policy. For these reasons, I shall not attempt to offer any speculative remarks about the nature and etiology of mental disease in terms of age, sex, marital condition, race, place of residence, and educational background.[26]

and resume their lives. The larger group was composed of individuals with severe mental and physical difficulties who required assistance.

Several contemporary studies published in the 1930s shed some light on the kinds of patients hospitalized during the second and third decades of the twentieth century. In 1931 Raymond G. Fuller and Mary Johnston conducted a retrospective study of all first admissions to New York state hospitals in terms of outcomes. They initially selected three periods for intensive anaalysis: 1909-1911, 1914-1916, and 1919-1921. The history of every person admitted during each of these periods was followed through until mid-1928. According to the Fuller-Johnston study, between 1909 and 1911, 2,481 patients admitted for the first time to mental hospitals were schizophrenics, 1,579 were manic-depressives, and 1,104 were alcoholics. The medical histories of these groups were quite dissimilar. The manic depressives and alcoholics had a much more favorable prognosis; 59.7 of the former and 62.7 of the latter spent less than a year in hospitals, whereas the comparable figure for schizophrenics was 27.4 percent. The average total duration of hospital confinement for each group also revealed wide variations; the manic depressives and alcoholics averaged 2.9 and 3.2 years, respectively, and the schizophrenics 8 years. Similarly, 64.0 percent of alcoholics and 62.0 of manic depressives had a favorable report on the last recorded outcome. But for the schizophrenics the percentage dropped sharply to 25 percent. For those patients who did not improve or recover within six months of admission, the prognosis grew steadily bleaker. No less than 722 out of the 2,481 schizophrenics admitted between 1909 and 1911 remained in the hospital for the full sixteen years covered by the study.[27]

Put differently, Fuller and Johnston calculated that of every 100 first admissions, about 35 were discharged as recovered or improved, 7 remained unimproved, 42 died in the hospital, and 16 were still in the hospital when the study ended. Of those institutionalized for less than a year, about half were discharged as recovered or improved, three-eighths died, and one-eighth were discharged but declared unimproved. Although the average duration of hospital confinement was 49.2 months, the median was only 11.4 months. Of those who were below the median, the average duration of confinement was only 3.7 months; the other half averaged a stay of 99.6 months.[28]

Employing some of the same data as well as additional New York State data, Benjamin Malzberg found that the mentally ill had far higher mortality rates than the general population. In 1930, for example, the mortality rate among patients with mental disease was approximately five times that of the general population—even though there were great differences in the rates among specific age groups (Table 7-7). The leading causes of death in rank order were as follows: diseases of the heart, pneumonia, paresis, tuberculosis, arterial diseases, and nephritis. Within specific psychiatric categories, there were again wide variations. Malzberg found that the ratio of deaths among patients diagnosed as schizophrenics compared to the standardized death rate of the general population of the state was about 2.3:1; the ratio for manic depressives was 5.7:1; cerebral arteriosclerosis 11.4:1 (compared on the basis of population aged 45 and over); general paresis 14.8:1; and alcoholic 4.8:1.[29]

The high death rate among patients was generally a result of admission policies rather than of conditions within hospitals. Many patients, Malzberg observed in language echoed by others, were admitted "almost at the point of death." Treatment in such cases was "without effect," and admissions served "the purpose

TABLE 7-7
MORTALITY RATES OF PATIENTS WITH MENTAL DISEASES
IN NEW YORK STATE HOSPITALS, 1930

Age (years)	Average Annual Death Rate Among Patients with Mental Disease*	Annual Death Rate in General Population of New York State**	Ratio of Death Rate Among Patients to That of the General Population
20-24	49.8	3.2	15.6
25-29	42.6	3.7	11.5
30-34	40.4	4.5	9.0
35-39	42.7	5.6	7.6
40-44	48.4	7.8	6.2
45-49	54.1	11.4	4.7
50-54	63.4	16.5	3.8
55-59	78.0	23.6	3.3
60-64	110.2	34.6	3.2
65-69	143.3	48.8	2.9
70-74	207.1	70.8	2.9
75-79	280.0	106.8	2.6
80-84	357.5	156.3	2.3
85 and over	382.8	241.1	1.6

* per 1,000 exposures.   ** per 1,000 population.

of merely relieving relatives or friends of onerous duties." Death rates as well as recovery rates tended to be highest in the twelve months after admission. In 1922 23.5 percent of all deaths occurred among individuals institutionalized for less than two months, and 48.3 percent for less than a year. Although the latter figure fell to 44.2 percent by 1940, it was clear that in many cases patients with terminal illnesses were being sent to mental hospitals. No doubt the fact that public mental hospitals did not charge for their services made them a better alternative than general hospitals. This was particularly true because the overwhelming majority of families were not covered by medical insurance plans prior to 1940. The experience of the New Jersey State Hospital at Marlboro, which opened in 1931, seemed to contradict the New York and national data; its statistician reported in 1933 a mortality rate of only one-quarter of that of New York institutions. In this instance, the exception merely proved the rule. Marlboro received its patients as a result of transfers from other public hospitals rather than from new admissions. Patients with long histories of confinement tended to have far lower death rates than newly admitted patients.[30]

III

The character of patient populations was a critical variable for mental hospitals. Although psychiatrists and public officials tended to emphasize therapy as being of prime importance, the fact of the matter was that hospitals were fulfilling a quite different role. Simply put, they were providing custodial care for dependent persons. Indeed, the debate as to whether certain groups (such as the aged senile) belonged in mental hospitals was beside the point; some form of care for such patients was required, irrespective of the setting in which it was provided. That mental hospitals offered custodial care was not a novel development. State governments, after all, traditionally funded such institutions, and early and mid-nineteenth-century psychiatrists always insisted that the care of the chronic insane was a legitimate function of mental hospitals. But the decline and eventual disappearance of the almshouse (an institution that provided care for poor elderly persons) in the early decades of the twentieth century created a void. Given the absence of alternative sources of funding from the federal government or private sector as well as the shift away from community responsibility, it was not surprising that families and local officials turned to mental hospitals to meet a perceived need.

For much of the nineteenth century, by way of contrast, the patient population of mental hospitals was composed of large numbers of acute cases institutionalized for less than twelve months. Although national data are lacking, a sample of individual institutions reveals that their custodial function had not yet become paramount. The experiences of Worcester State Lunatic Hospital—the oldest and most influential public institution in Massachusetts—were instructive. In 1842 (a decade after its opening), 46.4 percent of its patients had been hospitalized for less than a year; only 13.2 percent had been in the hospital for five or more years. In 1870 the comparable figures were 49.6 and 13.9 percent. Nor was Worcester atypical. In 1850 41.1 percent of patients at the Virginia Western Lunatic Asylum had been hospitalized for less than a year and 29.6 percent for five years or more; the respective figures for the California Insane Asylum in 1860 were 40.2 and 0.1 percent. Although exceptions were by no means uncommon—the Northampton State Lunatic Hospital in Massachusetts from its beginnings included high proportions of chronic cases—most hospitals before 1890 included large numbers of patients who were admitted and discharged in less than a year.[31]

After the turn of the century the pattern began to be reversed as the proportion of short-term cases fell and long-term cases increased. In 1904 27.8 percent of the total patient population had been confined for less than twelve months. By 1910 this percentage had fallen to 12.7, though it rose to 17.4 percent in 1923. The greatest change came among patients institutionalized for five years or longer. In 1904, 39.2 percent of patients fell into this category; in 1910 and 1923 the respective percentages were 52.0 and 54.0 (Table 7-8).[32]

Although data for the United States as a whole were unavailable after 1923, the experiences of Massachusetts during the 1920s and 1930s were perhaps typical. Between 1917 and 1933 first admissions to the state's mental hospitals increased from 3,658 to 4,554 per year. The total number of admissions, in other words, rose by 75 patients each year. At the same time the average annual increase in the total patient population was 441. This increase was due largely to the fact that hospitals retained patients who failed to recover or improve. Between 1929 and 1937 the average length of hospital confinement rose from 8.9 to 9.7 years. Put in a slightly

TABLE 7-8
LENGTH OF TIME SPENT IN MENTAL HOSPITALS BY PATIENTS, 1904-1923
(PERCENTAGE DISTRIBUTION)

Years	1904	1910	1923
Under 1	27.8	12.7	17.4
1	8.7	8.2	9.3
2	6.9	7.8	7.6
3	5.7	6.3	6.2
4	4.7	5.5	5.3
5-9	16.4	20.1	19.8
10-14	10.5	12.7	12.8
15-19	6.2	8.4	8.4
20 and over	6.1	10.8	13.0
Unknown	7.0	7.5	0.2

different way, out of every 1,000 first admissions in 1937, 167 were returned to the community and 86 died; for readmitted persons the respective figures were 113 and 35. The most astonishing statistic was the total number of patients retained in hospitals; 746 out of every 1,000 first admissions and 851 out of every 1,000 readmissions remained institutionalized at the end of one year.[33]

By the 1930s nearly 80 percent of the available beds in Massachusetts hospitals were occupied by chronic patients. What accounted for this situation? Neil Dayton, Director of the Massachusetts Division of Statistics, suggested two possible explanations, although he expressed no opinion as to their validity. First, the receptivity of society to absorb recovered patients had diminished markedly, and families were unwilling to accept discharged patients. Second, recovery from disorders necessitated longer stays in the hospital.[34] In retrospect, neither explanation seems especially persuasive. There is little evidence to support the claim that communities and families were less willing to accept recovered patients. Indeed, the steadily increasing numbers of patients in hospitals probably increased pressure to discharge persons as quickly as possible. Similarly, none of the data indicated any change in the pattern of treatment that lengthened the period of confinement.

Given the imprecision of diagnostic categories and other surviving data, it may be impossible to account fully for the changing pattern of admissions, retentions, and discharges. Certain facts, however, stand out. First, hospitals were receiving a high percentage of patients suffering from severe somatic conditions, many of which were not amenable to demonstrably effective medical interventions. The high death rate that followed the onset of institutionalization, as well as other evidence, suggests as much. Second, the rapid increase in rates of hospitalization in the older age groups indicates, in part, the presence of persons with severe physical problems that precluded any reasonable hope of recovery. Third, the growth of the resident population in mental hospitals was *not* a function of a greater incidence of mental disorders, but rather reflected the changing age distribution of both the general and patient population and the decline of almshouses.

It is true that other institutions could have assumed the responsibility for caring for certain groups that were sent to mental hospitals. Alternative patterns of care, however, did not develop in the decades prior to 1940. The few states (especially Wisconsin) that had developed a dual system of functionally specialized institutions remained the exception rather than the rule. The persistence of the mental hospital grew out of a combination of circumstances. In the first place, the thrust toward state care hastened the decline of county and local institutions such as almshouses. As the fiscal role of states expanded and as the number of aged persons rose, local officials began to perceive of the financial advantages of redefining senility in psychiatric terms and sending aged people to mental hospitals. Although hospital officials had grave reservations about the wisdom of transferring aged and dependent senile persons to their institutions, they were in no position to turn such patients away. The absence of either an institutional alternative or proven and effective methods of care for such aged persons created a need, and subtle but powerful social pressures forced mental hospitals to meet this need. Secondly, there was no groundswell of support for the creation of a decentralized system that would include a large number of small community institutions. Local care in the nineteenth century was generally equated with neglect, and the quality of care in state hospitals, whatever their shortcomings, had always been higher. Moreover, the association of state mental hospitals with psychiatrists and other physicians had given these institutions a certain legitimacy that their local counterparts lacked. Supervision in a centralized system also appeared more effective than in a decentralized system and therefore less susceptible to abuse. Finally, the very existence of mental hospitals discouraged any further exploration or consideration of other alternatives.

IV

Curiously enough, neither psychiatrists, public officials, nor involved laypersons were fully cognizant of the extent to which the role and character of mental hospitals were being altered by a changing patient population. There was general agreement that too many patients had become "institutionalized" and hence were destined to spend the rest of their lives as pitiful guests dependent on public largesse; that brutality and neglect were endemic; that deteriorating physical plants and inadequate care were common; that lethargy, neglect, and overcrowding had reduced mental hospitals to the status of inadequate poorhouses. In a famous exposé in 1947, Frank L. Wright expressed a commonly held view of institutional care.

> Inadequacy, Ugliness, Crowding, Incompetence, Perversion, Frustration. Neglect, Idleness, Callousness. Abuse, Mistreatment, Oppression. These have been the principal characters in the drama of the preceding chapters. They have always dominated the center of the stage.[35]

Wright's comments, of course, implied a generalized public callousness or indifference toward the fate of the mentally ill. Although not without justification, such criticisms were in some respects wide of the mark. That substandard conditions existed in many mental hospitals was indisputable; inadequate appropriations in many states and regions were characteristic. Nevertheless, the problem was far more complex. As we have already seen, hospitals cared for an overwhelmingly chronic population whose behavioral disorders were often related to an underlying somatic pathology. The presence of so many of these patients contributed to the depressed and deadening atmosphere present in so many institutions. Physicians, but especially nurses and attendants who spent most of their working hours in close contact with such individuals, could hardly maintain high morale and enthusiasm, given the tragic condition and often bizarre behavior of their patients. Indeed, the character of the patient population strengthened the centrifugal forces that were always present, and conflict and disorganization often lay directly below the surface at many institutions.

It is conceivable that efforts might have been made to experiment with alternative forms of care that might have mitigated, even if they could not eliminate, the more depressing aspects of institutional care for chronic patients. Admittedly, custodial care could rarely promote recovery. But recovery for the bulk of chronic cases was largely beyond the realm of possibility; such diseases and conditions as paresis, senility, or Huntington's chorea were not amenable to any known therapy, nor was home care an acceptable alternative. Chronic patients required care above all; their specific medical needs were no different from the needs of sane but ill persons.

Despite the fact that the hospital population was composed of large numbers of chronic cases with an underlying somatic pathology, those individuals and groups involved with the mentally ill continued to stress the primary importance of therapy.[36] Given their professional self-images, psychiatrists and other mental health workers were unable to accept a role in which care rather than treatment was paramount. The vision of a therapeutic hospital was sufficiently powerful to sway many laypersons, especially those who helped to mold images in the popular media. Even Albert Deutsch, author of a classic work on the history of the mentally ill published in 1937, tended to emphasize the therapeutic as contrasted with the caring or custodial function. His powerful indictment of mental hospitals, which appeared first in the daily press and then in book form in 1948, was based on the proposition that the "Ideal State Hospital" should operate as a "therapeutic community." Deutsch, however, had relatively little to say about the thousands of patients for whom therapy was not a viable alternative.[37]

The disjuncture between image and reality would ultimately have a profound impact upon mental hospitals, for it would call into doubt their very legitimacy. For most patients, on the other hand, the mental hospital remained the only institution that provided such basic necessities as food, clothing, and shelter. This is not to suggest that other modes of care could not have been developed. It is only to insist that specific historical circumstances led to the creation of a particular kind of institution that adapted itself to a changing constituency.

CHAPTER EIGHT

Dilemmas of Control:
Accountability versus Autonomy

BY THE TURN OF the century the division of responsibility between
local communities and states for the care of the mentally ill was
coming to a close. The assumption of fiscal responsibility left
state officials in a position to establish a more unitary policy.
Freedom to establish policy, however, was not itself a central
issue. Much more significant was the manner in which states
chose to exercise an authority which they had always possessed
but not always used.

Throughout the nineteenth century state legislatures acted only
intermittently in dealing with the mentally ill, and usually only
in response to immediate problems. Normally their actions were
limited to the establishment of new hospitals, expansion of existing ones, fiscal appropriations, and occasional investigations.
There was little if any effort to engage in systematic and long-
range planning, if only because of high turnover rates among legislators and the absence of permanent committee structures. Access to data was often limited by the fact that there were no
permanent state agencies to collect or to analyze statistical materials. Finally, the concept of planning—generally a function of
the executive branch of government—was all but nonexistent.

During the last few decades of the nineteenth century, the
founding of central state agencies altered the organizational context in which policy was established. In addition to gathering data,
these agencies had investigatory functions and responsibility for
formulating recommendations concerning public policy. Increasingly, state officials served as the intermediaries between the
governor and legislature on the one hand and individual mental
hospitals on the other.

After 1900 many states began to experiment with new structures. The pervasive faith in rational administration and scientific
management that was so characteristic of the Progressive era led
to the adoption of new organizational forms that were intended
to maximize efficiency and accountability. Public officials often

equated rational administration with policy; the distinction between means and ends was generally absent. At the very same
time the goal of institutional psychiatry was increasingly expressed in terms of the need for medical and professional autonomy. The result was protracted conflict between state governments and a medical specialty whose past was intimately linked
with public institutions. Curiously enough, the heated and often
acrimonious conflict over structure—which in practice became a
central policy issue—was in some respects not directly relevant
to the needs of institutionalized patients. There was, as we shall
shortly see, little relationship between the quality of care in mental hospitals and particular structural forms. Indeed, the debate
over structure tended to deflect attention away from the problem
of providing care for a patient population that in the twentieth
century was composed of chronic cases with a somatic pathology
and for whom demonstrably effective therapies did not exist.

I

Those who favored administrative solutions for the problem of
mental illness confronted a system that appeared to be dysfunc-
tional. For much of the nineteenth century local communities
were required to reimburse hospitals for the operating costs incurred in caring for their residents. Consequently, states had little
incentive to develop a system designed to control expenditures.
The growing number of foreign-born persons and high rates of
geographical mobility, however, made it increasingly difficult to
maintain a system based on fixed legal residences. State governments slowly but surely began to assume the costs previously
paid by local communities. By 1917 only about a dozen states
still insisted that counties contribute funds for the support of
patients; the remainder accepted financial responsibility, even
though families were still required to pay for all or part of the
charges if they had sufficient resources. In practice the overwhelming majority of patients were supported by the state, since
few had resources or relatives to pay the high costs associated
with long-term care. In New York, for example, nearly 90 percent
of all patients between 1918 and 1940 were supported at state
expense.[1]

At the same time that the fiscal role of the state was expanding,
American society was being transformed by new economic and
technological forces. If the benefits of industrialization were wel-

come, the process of change that altered human relationships appeared to many to threaten the foundations of the social order. Traditional concepts of morality seemed obsolete, and representative government, with its decentralized decision-making process, appeared wasteful. Decision-making in the new order, on the other hand, increasingly reflected the process of rationalization and systematization, which in turn was related to modern science and technology. The so-called systematizers claimed that they were restoring an earlier social order. In fact, however, they were weakening the traditional and decentralized decision-making process by enhancing the role of new groups of "experts" whose authority was derived from their presumed knowledge and impartiality.[2]

By the late nineteenth century the structure of government had begun to change. At the local level there was a shift away from ward representation toward citywide elections and adoption of a city-manager form of government. Proponents claimed that the new system would end favoritism and corruption, but it also became clear that "impartial" decision-making involved a transfer of authority away from the community. At the state level a centralizing process had set in even earlier. Although the state boards of charity established during and after the 1860s implied a diminution in the autonomy of local institutions, the actual authority of these boards was generally limited to investigatory functions, data collection, and policy recommendations. Their members had virtually no budgetary or administrative control. In succeeding decades, however, a number of states created new boards and reorganized existing ones. These new agencies were staffed by salaried persons who believed that the application of scientific modes of analysis to social issues could lead to the development of a rational and efficient system. In effect, the decision-making systems characteristic of new business corporations became a model for government reorganization. Faith in administrative rationality was so pervasive that systematizers often concluded that efficiency and policy were one and the same. They assumed that efficient administration would *ipso facto* create humane and effective public policies to deal with the mentally ill and other dependent groups.

Wisconsin, for example, had founded a traditional State Board of Charities and Reform in 1871. Like others already in existence, the board lacked fiscal authority, and its members did not receive compensation for their services. A decade later the legislature created a second and parallel agency, the State Board of Supervisors, with sharply expanded authority. The new law abolished all boards of trustees of individual institutions, appointed a business manager at each, and gave the board budgetary power. The existence of two competing agencies created jurisdictional conflicts, and in 1891 the legislature abolished both and established a State Board of Control.

The new agency, as its title suggested, had sharply expanded authority. Its powers included the right to "maintain and govern" all state institutions, to supervise many county and private institutions, and to appoint superintendents and executive officers. The intent of the legislation was to reduce the costs of welfare by creating a more efficient administrative structure. Ultimately the Board was instrumental in placing many employees under civil service, thereby insulating institutions from direct political control and reinforcing a greater degree of professional autonomy. Isolation from politics, however, did not give individual institutions greater leeway, if only because the Board's budgetary power gave its members a dominant position. James E. Heg, a prominent Wisconsin figure who had been a superintendent and had served on both a local board and the State Board of Control, noted that under the Wisconsin system a superintendent was "simply an executive officer to carry out instructions, but . . . not encouraged to originate any policy himself."[3]

Within about a decade, seven other states had adopted the Wisconsin model. Four were in relatively new and sparsely populated states (South Dakota, Wyoming, Washington, and Arizona); three were in more established states (Kansas, Iowa, Minnesota). In some states the board of control represented the first effort to rationalize and centralize a system of independent institutions; in others boards of control replaced preexisting boards of charities.[4]

In general, boards of control—which were more powerful than charity boards—were more common in states that lacked established traditions or institutions. In New York and Massachusetts, for example, hospital superintendents had always played significant roles in the formulation of public policy, even though conflict between themselves and state legislators and officials was common. Despite the fact that both states pursued rationalizing and centralizing policies, efforts to establish control boards proved unsuccessful. In 1909 Governor Charles Evans Hughes urged the New York legislature to create a Board of Fiscal Control with authority over salaries and purchases, thereby creating a uniform state system. His recommendation led to a study of methods of fiscal control by the powerful State Charities Aid Association, but the Association opposed a board of control. "It seems clear," the study noted, "that centralization as such is not necessarily economical; that such opportunities for economy as are afforded by centralization have thus far been but very incompletely realized; that in a number of its most important contracts the State has shown bad judgment in its specifications and a woeful laxness in supervising deliveries under the contracts."[5]

Boards of control were, for the most part, absent in the older and populous states of the East; they were more prevalent in the newer and less developed states of the Midwest and Far West, less encumbered by older traditions and institutions. Rhode Island broke with its neighbors in 1912. It founded an autonomous Board of Control and Supply with jurisdiction over all finances at the same time that it maintained its Board of State Charities and Corrections. The result was protracted conflict. "Will it be found," the Board of State Charities and Corrections queried, "that the prime objects of the institutions are sacrificed to business control and we reach the stage of commercialized charity?" By 1917 the legislature had abolished both boards and substituted a Penal and Charitable Commission in its place. Rhode Island, however, was the exception that proved the rule in the East.[6]

Boards of control reflected the early twentieth-century faith that public decision-making was most effective when isolated from politics and under the control of individuals and groups whose authority was based on their special training and expertise. The new boards also replaced local governing boards of individual hospitals, thus furthering the shift of responsibility away from local communities. Those who favored such boards also took it for granted that rational administration was more efficient. In Minnesota, for example, the state auditor was the first to propose the establishment of such an agency. Shortly thereafter a commission was appointed by the legislature. In urging action, its members noted that existing boards of control "have eliminated controversy from the question of dividing the state's bounty and prevented legislative combinations for that purpose." After favorable action by the legislature, the new board offered its congratulations and emphasized the benefits that accrued to the people by a change from the "obsolete to the progressive." The more profound issue of the relationship between representative government and autonomous public agencies was all but ignored.[7]

Curiously enough, the powers of boards of control were rarely used to alter public policy or to introduce changes within individual hospitals. Sometimes the most significant effect was the effort to equalize institutional expenditures within a given state. Members of such boards for the most part accepted the dominant paradigm: mentally ill persons were to be treated in hospitals under the control of qualified psychiatrists; lay people, including board members, lacked the competence to decide medical or scientific issues. The focus of such boards was rather on the financial management of hospitals and on the need to bring public policy into harmony with those methods developed in private business. Shortly after its creation, the Arizona Board expressed dismay at the fact that the insane asylum had no "uniform system of records and accounts," and urged the legislature to adopt such a system. "The most progressive states," noted its Kansas counterpart, "are creating boards of control and making a systematic study of such matters, and taking the state institutions out of politics and putting them upon a humane and business basis."[8]

Although the concept of efficiency was pursued in theory, in practice it proved to be elusive. A few years after North Dakota had created a board of control, one of its hospital superintendents criticized the use of per capita cost as a measure of efficiency. It was, he insisted, "impossible to establish a uniform standard." A mental institution that housed patients in a central building had lower heating costs than those with individual buildings constructed on the cottage plan; a hospital that cared for chronic patients required fewer attending physicians; and a hospital with a modern laboratory and hydrotherapy apparatus obviously had higher costs. Under the circumstances it was not surprising that "per capita cost"—which was often used by boards of control as the basic standard for measuring efficiency—was "not a consistent term" and meant "one thing in one place and another elsewhere." The Wisconsin Board of Control, as a matter of fact, was never able to equalize per capita expenditures. In 1923 the weekly per capita cost at its three state hospitals averaged $5.92, $8.83, and $9.33, respectively.[9]

Boards of control proved most effective in sparsely populated states having comparatively few institutions. But this proved to be true only because the change in administration was more nominal than real. In states with large populations and a variety of welfare and penal institutions, centralized control exacted a price. Economy and efficiency tended to become ends in themselves, and little attention was paid to specific institutional needs and human wants. Boards of control also created new costs associated with regulation, and their changing membership impaired policy cohesion and continuity. Their involvement in the internal administration of institutions tended to limit the flexibility and effectiveness of superintendents. The abolition of local boards staffed by individuals drawn from the community in which the institution was located further diminished public interest. Finally, the autonomy of boards of control also raised questions about a system in which an agency evaluated its own effectiveness. Only six years after creating a board of control, Minnesota reestablished a board of charities to act as a state board of visitors to mental institutions and thus to ensure independent inspection procedures.[10]

If boards of control did not become the dominant organizational model, their very existence indicated widespread interest in structural reorganization. To many Progressives rationalization and centralization of state government was but a prelude to the development of more effective preventive and rehabilitative policies. The seeming diversity, if not chaos, in the organization of state government only confirmed the necessity for change. As late as 1913 twenty-one states had boards of charity and/or corrections. In several of these states, notably New York and Massachusetts, jurisdiction over the mentally ill fell elsewhere. Twelve states had boards of control, although one state (California) had a separate Commission in Lunacy. Seven states had no central governing authority whatsoever. Of these, three were in the South (Alabama, Georgia, and South Carolina), one in the East (Delaware), and three in the West (Idaho, Nevada, and New Mexico). The pattern in the remaining states was mixed.[11]

By the early twentieth century a number of states began to experiment with new kinds of administrative systems to bring order out of apparent chaos. Two similar, but competing, models emerged. The first involved the centralization of welfare administration within a unified department of public welfare with jurisdiction over all dependent groups, including the mentally ill. The second involved the creation of an autonomous state agency with the sole responsibility for mentally ill persons which reported directly to the governor.

Not surprisingly, the very same states that were reponsible for innovation during the nineteenth century tended to lead in the twentieth. Illinois is a case in point. In 1906 the governor of Illinois proposed that the state consider unifying the management of public institutions and possibly establishing a board of control. The old but still influential State Board of Charities opposed such a reorganization. For nearly three years a debate raged over the proper shape of public charity administration. In 1909 the legislature finally adopted a compromise measure. Under its provisions a new Board of Administration was given authority to appoint and discharge employees under civil service rules, to contract for all supplies, and to administer public institutions. All local boards of trustees were abolished. To avoid the pitfalls of extreme centralization, on the other hand, a State Charities Commission was given the authority to inspect, criticize, and recommend policies for state charitable institutions. Similarly, a measure of local autonomy was retained, since each institution was required to have its own board of visitors responsible to the Charities Commission.[12]

The new system, however, survived for only five years. In 1917 the newly elected Governor, Frank O. Lowden, threw his support behind the recommendations of the legislature's "Efficiency and Economy Committee," which had been established three years earlier. The Committee had been especially critical of the large number of "independent" agencies within state government and their unchecked authority to spend public funds. The absence of "effective centralized control or responsibility," it charged, simply led to "waste and expenditure." The result was the passage of a Civil Administrative Code, which completely revamped the structure of state governments by reducing the more than one hundred boards and commissions to nine principal agencies.

The reorganization created a single Department of Public Welfare with an appointed Director. Under the Director were a number of subordinates: an assistant Director; three Superintendents responsible for charities, prisons, and pardons and paroles; a fiscal supervisor; a criminologist; and an alienist. The alienist served as an advisor to the Superintendent of Charities, who, in turn, was responsible for the state's mental hospitals. In practice the Department always selected a psychiatrist for the position of alienist, even though the law did not require specific qualifications. The legislature also retained the principle of investigating institutions and policies by an independent board that reported directly to the governor. The failure to fill vacancies or provide an appropriation, however, rendered this last provision useless. The new Department of Public Welfare, noted an Illinois periodical concerned with institutional issues,

> will save thousands of dollars in salaries and wages, traveling expenses, office supplies and the like, and without doubt will perform the work in a more efficient manner.
>
> This will be the first experiment on so large a scale of the one-man power in the administration of public institutions from which politics have been eliminated and into which it has been sought to place men on the sole basis of merit and experience.[13]

Faith in the redemptive power of structural reorganization was by no means confined to Illinois. Organizational change in one state often stimulated others to follow suit. Ohio was an example. In 1898 Ohio adopted a law forbidding county institutions from accepting any insane patient after 1900. Lack of space forced the legislature to extend the deadline. But as the state accepted greater fiscal obligations, it began to expand its authority. In 1911 Ohio emulated Illinois and created a bipartisan Board of Administration which superseded all local governing boards of public institutions and effectively concentrated authority in state hands. By 1913 the Board of State Charities had been absorbed into the new agency. For nearly a decade Ohio's welfare and penal institutions remained under this system. In 1921, however, the legislature enacted an "emergency" measure abolishing the Board of Administration and replacing it with a Department of Public Welfare under a director. The new law was modeled after the one enacted in Illinois, since the purchase of supplies as well as the construction and repair of buildings was given to a different agency.[14]

During the 1920s a number of states moved to establish agencies similar to that of Illinois. The titles often differed, but the direction was similar. North Dakota created a Board of Administration in 1919 with jurisdiction over all penal, charitable, and educational institutions. In 1921 Missouri abolished all local institutional boards and transferred their authority to a State Eleemosynary Board. That same year California founded a Department of Institutions and limited the functions of local boards to inspection and advice. By 1932 unified welfare departments in one form or another existed in twenty-six states, and seventeen had two or more agencies. Only five remained without any central agency.[15]

The thrust toward unification and centralization was relatively uneven. Some agencies were hampered by laws which did not give them administrative control or an appropriation that enabled them to carry out specific functions. In 1924 the Montana State Board of Charities and Reform received an appropriation of $400 for the entire year. Although Colorado reorganized a relatively weak State Board of Charities and Corrections into a State Department of Charities and Corrections, it failed to strengthen the limited powers of the new agency. The Georgia State Board of Public Welfare, created in 1919, had virtually no responsibilities pertaining to institutional care of the mentally ill. The Louisiana State Board of Charities and Corrections, founded in 1905, was inactive for at least ten years. In 1921 it was reconstituted and survived in an attenuated form until 1938. North Carolina established a State Board of Charities and Public Welfare in 1917. Composed of three representatives from each state institution, the board never functioned as a state agency; its members were concerned largely with the unique problems of their own institutions. In 1921, therefore, the legislature restored separate and independent boards for each public institution. New Jersey divided authority between local institutional boards and its Department of Institutions and Agencies, founded in 1917. The result was frequent conflict, which limited the authority of the central administration.[16]

The movement to centralize and rationalize the administration of public institutions, however, did not always take the same form. Some states, including Massachusetts and New York, created autonomous agencies whose jurisdiction was limited to the mentally ill. Such states were clearly in the minority. The fact that Massachusetts and New York adopted this organizational form was significant, however, since both were widely regarded as acknowledged leaders in the field.

That Massachusetts and New York never unified the administration of their public institutions was not an accident. Both had organized and powerful medical groups, and their influence played a decisive role in differentiating health and welfare. In Massachusetts the experiment of unifying health and welfare by merging the State Board of Health and Board of State Charities in 1879 proved short-lived; by 1885 the legislature had separated them and created a State Board of Lunacy and Charity. The movement to end the division of responsibility for the insane between state and county finally led to the creation of an autonomous State Board of Insanity in 1898. During the debate over reorganization the state's medical societies had argued that mental hospitals should remain under medical control. Moreover, as Dr. Walter Channing noted, the earlier experiment of a single charity board with jurisdiction over health and welfare had proved less than successful because the board "had to scatter its forces in so many directions" and was unable to deal effectively with the particular needs of the mentally ill.[17]

The new State Board of Insanity was composed of five appointed members, at least two of whom were to be "experts in insanity." In turn, the Board appointed an executive officer who was also required to be a psychiatrist. Local boards of trustees were retained, although they reported to the new agency. The Board had the right to pass upon the construction of new and repair of existing facilities, to transfer patients, to prescribe statistical forms and accounting procedures, and to supervise and inspect all mental hospitals, private and public. Subsequently the Board gained the right to veto appointments of superintendents and to license private mental hospitals.[18]

The organizational pattern established even before the turn of the century in Massachusetts was never reversed. In 1916 a Commission of Mental Diseases replaced the State Board of Insanity, but retained the same authority. When a constitutional convention recommended consolidation of more than one hundred departments into twenty divisions, a new Department of Mental Diseases was one of them. This Department came into being when the new constitution went into effect in 1919. In 1938 its name was changed to the Department of Mental Hygiene. The same law required that the Commissioner and Assistant Commissioners be diplomates* in psychiatry of the recently created American Board of Psychiatry and Neurology.[19]

New York followed a similar path. In 1873 the legislature established the position of State Commissioner in Lunacy within the State Board of Charities. The following year the office was made independent. The major change, however, came just prior to the passage of the State Care Act of 1890. As a result of the lobbying of Dr. Stephen Smith (then State Commissioner in Lunacy), a number of medical societies, and the State Charities Aid Association, the legislature abolished the position and created a salaried three-member State Commission in Lunacy. One of its

* In a medical context a diplomate is a physician qualified to practice in a specialty by virtue of training, experience, and certification (usually after passage of an examination) by a specialty board.

members had to be an experienced psychiatrist, the second a lawyer, and the third a "citizen of reputable character." The Commission exercised general supervision and oversight of the lunacy statutes, and regulated all matters pertaining to the welfare of the insane. The State Board of Charities, which lost considerable authority, noted in a somewhat critical vein that the new Commission stood for "centralized power of the most absolute character." The slow accretion of fiscal responsibility simply strengthened the power of the Commission. In 1893 the "estimate system" was adopted. All hospitals were required to present detailed financial estimates of their needs at stated times to the Commission, but the Commission had authority to revise and approve them.[20]

The original legislation retained local boards of managers but made them responsible to the Commission. In 1902, however, the legislature abolished local boards and transferred their authority to the Commission. Provision was made for the establishment of a board of visitors, which made monthly inspections of hospitals and reported its findings to the Governor and Commission. Opposition to this change quickly surfaced. The State Charities Aid Association was critical; it insisted that the presence of local boards stimulated public involvement and interest and also provided security against abuses. By 1905 the legislature had reversed itself and reestablished local boards. Nevertheless, the right to appoint superintendents remained with the Commission, subject to the approval of the local board of managers. Ultimately the organizational structure that came into existence in New York during the late nineteenth century remained largely unaltered in its essentials. In 1912 the State Commission in Lunacy became the State Hospital Commission, and in 1926 its title was changed to the Department of Mental Hygiene. The changes in titles were significant; they reflected both the effort to redefine the problem of insanity in medical terms and the more recent preoccupation with mental hygiene. The substantive changes, however, were relatively minor.[21]

The New York and Massachusetts patterns, though not widely emulated, had considerable influence. Many states that initially opted for a unified welfare department quickly found that centralized control created its own unique problems. In practice, the means to realize the alleged benefits of a centralized system were simply not available. Less than three years after the establishment of the Ohio Department of Public Works, its Director urged the state to reestablish its predecessor agency (Board of Administration). The needs of individual institutions differed, he noted, and a central agency under one individual could not provide "the care, attention, and study" to which 25,000 state wards were entitled, "not to mention economic waste to taxpayers resulting from lack of proper supervision." The following year the Director repeated the criticism of his own agency to a gathering of managing officers of state institutions. Twenty-one of them, including eight superintendents of mental hospitals, promptly petitioned the legislature to restore a modified Board of Administration.[22]

To obviate the problems that followed extreme centralization, some states established semi-autonomous divisions within a unified welfare department with limited responsibility and authority for the mentally ill. Pennsylvania, for example, had long functioned with this kind of system. In 1883 the "Lunacy Law" required the Board of Public Charities to appoint five of its members to serve as a Committee on Lunacy, with powers to supervise, inspect, and license. In 1887 the Board formally asked the legislature to transfer its authority pertaining to the mentally ill to the Committee. But the measure failed in the House of Representatives after it had passed the Senate. Individual institutions remained under the control of local boards of managers or trustees, who also selected the superintendents.[23]

In line with the movement to rationalize and centralize state administration, Pennsylvania created a Department of Public Welfare in 1921. The Department was organized in four divisions, one of which—the Bureau of Mental Health—retained roughly the same functions and authority as its predecessor. But since the Bureau lacked administrative authority over state or county institutions, its actual impact on policy was negligible. The Board's activities were confined to occasional inspections of hospitals, the transfer of patients between institutions, the coordination of courses for assistant physicians, and mobile community mental hygiene clinics. Eventually the clinics were transferred to the state hospitals, each of which was assigned a specific geographical territory. The Board developed a comprehensive plan in 1929 to modernize the state's hospitals, but the depression of the 1930s destroyed any hope of funding.[24]

Other states attempted to follow a parallel course. In 1921 the North Carolina State Board of Charities and Public Welfare created a Bureau of Mental Health and Hygiene. The authority of the new division, however, was minimal, since the state as a whole functioned under a highly decentralized system that left authority in the hands of independent institutional boards. The attempt to centralize had an even more checkered history in Virginia—the state with the most comprehensive system of state hospitals in the South. After 1902 each hospital had its own three-member board of directors, all of which came together in a General Hospital Board to supervise the system. The creation of a State Board of Public Welfare in 1922 and the establishment of a Bureau of Mental Hygiene within the larger agency did little to alter the situation, since the Bureau's functions were largely limited to clinic and outpatient work. Dr. J. K. Hall felt that the General Hospital Board (on which he served) had "no other purpose than to hear the report of the operation of each hospital read by the superintendent of the respective hospital." Hall insisted that the lay character of the Board (only two of fifteen members were physicians) contributed to its general ineffectiveness. To him "laymanization" was synonymous with "ignorization." The creation of a new State Hospital Board with Dr. Hugh C. Henry as the Director of State Hospitals in the late 1930s did not satisfy Hall. The office held by Henry had been created by administrative edict and lacked legal standing; the Board could therefore dismiss him at any time. Similarly, all of the Board members could be appointed and removed at the pleasure of the governor, a provision that simply politicized and layicized a body that in Hall's opinion should have been dominated by qualified psychiatrists.[25]

By 1940 even Illinois had moved toward creating a separate administrative structure to govern its mental hospitals. A committee of the Chicago Institute of Medicine, after surveying the state's charitable institutions, concluded that a separate and distinct public department should be created to administer state hospitals. Recognizing that legislative action would be slow because new costs would be incurred, the Department of Public Welfare took administrative action on its own and established an internal Division of Mental Hospitals as a first step in early 1940.[26]

II

To what extent was the Progressive faith in administrative rationalization and centralization justified by actual results? Did states with central structures develop more effective policies than those without such structures? Was one form of administration more efficient than others? Were levels of conflict in any way related to particular organizational forms? Was institutional care and treatment in any way a function of structure? What was the relationship between the nature of public policy and administrative systems?

Generally speaking, administrative rationalization had a far smaller impact than its advocates anticipated. Centralized agencies found it relatively simple to promulgate uniform rules and regulations that theoretically would enhance institutional effectiveness. It was, however, far more difficult to ensure compliance. This proved to be the case if only because behavioral adaptations by both staff and patients in many instances circumvented the intent of such regulations. Nor were central boards ever able to develop effective supervisory apparatus to ensure institutional compliance. Claims to the contrary, administrative techniques never approached the ability of thousands of individuals to ignore or to alter regulations that appeared to be unreasonable or inappropriate.

Centralization occasionally facilitated certain kinds of policies. The outstanding example involved the policy of deporting to other jurisdictions nonresident insane persons who had been committed to mental hospitals. Such a policy grew out of the decentralized political structure of the United States, which in turn affected the financing of public welfare. For much of American history, public welfare, following English precedents, was a local and private responsibility. Each community was expected to care for its dependent citizens. Large-scale immigration to the United States of relatively impoverished individuals and high rates of geographical mobility created an entirely new category of dependent persons who, in theory, were not eligible to receive public aid because they failed to establish legal domicile in a community. Such individuals became known as "alien paupers" or "state poor" in the nineteenth century, and fiscal responsibility for them rested with the state. Fear that foreign nations were "dumping" dependent and undesirable persons on American shores led some states to create new agencies to ensure that immigrants would not become public charges. In 1847 New York established a Board of Commissioners of Emigration and in 1851 Massachusetts did the same with a Board of Alien Commissioners. Both of these boards were predecessors of their respective state board of charity. Between 1854 and 1863 the Massachusetts Board removed 774 persons from state hospitals and returned 398 to their communities of origin.[27]

That New York and Massachusetts were among the first to develop systematic policies to diminish the number of dependents cared for at public expense was not surprising. Not only did both states lead where others followed, but both also received a disproportionately high percentage of immigrants during the nineteenth century. As a result, the New York legislature in 1880 gave the State Board of Charities the right to deport crippled, blind, insane, and other infirm paupers. During 1881 45 such persons were sent abroad; by 1895 the number reached 261. The numbers, though small, were significant in terms of policy. In 1893 and 1895 the legislature empowered the State Commission in Lunacy as well to deport alien and nonresident insane persons. Within the Commission a State Board of Alienists assumed operational responsibility for enforcing the law; in 1912 it was renamed the Board of Deportation. In 1894 the Commission removed 13 alien and 7 nonresident insane persons; the high came in 1912, when the figures reached 1,172 and 582, respectively. The number declined until after the end of World War I, when there was a brief resumption of large-scale immigration. Between 1894 and 1940 the Commission deported a total of 15,214 insane aliens and removed 20,994 nonresidents from mental institutions. Massachusetts pursued similar practices in regard to its nonresident insane. In 1898, for example, the State Board of Lunacy and Charity returned 110 insane persons to other states and 201 to foreign countries. In the three preceding decades, a total of 5,550 mentally ill individuals were removed to other jurisdictions. Under the new State Board of Insanity the number of deportations fell. Between 1898 and 1908 the Board deported 1,160 persons, an average of a little over 100 per year.[28]

The growth in the number of state agencies and the relative ineffectiveness of federal legislation pertaining to the exclusion of certain categories of dependent immigrants increased interest in deportation as a policy. By 1900 a number of states had enacted laws mandating the deportation of aliens and nonresidents. After the turn of the century the practice became even more common. Some states formalized the procedures by creating specific offices. The Illinois Board of Administration included a Department of Deportation, and its successor Department of Public Welfare employed a "State Deportation Agent." Minnesota first created a "Deporting Agent" as part of its Board of Control, and subsequently upgraded the position by expanding it into a full-fledged Bureau. Many states also concluded interstate agreements to exchange dependents. Thus, as long as responsibility for the care of the mentally ill was borne by states, each one attempted to minimize its costs.[29]

Despite the popularity of the policy, deportation never involved large-scale transfers. Legal barriers existed, including residency laws that varied from state to state and region to region. Although the NCCC discussed the desirability of a uniform settlement law for all states, no action was ever taken. Moreover, deportation proved a two-way street; states both received and deported insane dependent persons. "If all States do this work," a Minnesota official observed in 1898, "what will be gained?" His state, he observed, would benefit because in the long run the tide of immigration was toward the West. Yet in 1940 Ohio succeeded in deporting only 54 out of 67 persons it believed to be nonresidents, while at the same time accepting 86 insane persons from other states and rejecting 32. Most states were less scrupulous than Ohio in reporting data. In 1939 the California Department of Institutions published a table that listed the alleged savings to the state. Between 1923 and 1929 4,160 insane individuals and 2,987 delinquents were deported at a savings of slightly more than eight and a half million dollars. The table, however, did not balance the savings by the costs incurred as a result of deportation into the state. Moreover, it failed to emphasize that in 1939 the 262 insane persons who were deported constituted only about 1.2 percent of the total hospital resident population. Given fixed hospital costs, the actual savings were not statistically significant.[30]

Although the effectiveness of deportation as a policy was undoubtedly facilitated by the existence of a central agency, the relationship between organizational structure and policy was at best obscure. The examples of New York and Massachusetts are again instructive. Both had autonomous departments whose authority was limited to the care and treatment of the mentally ill. Their achievements were widely admired, and both were often held up as models. Their uniform statistical systems contributed to the further development of psychiatric epidemiology, and the contributions of Benjamin Malzberg and Horatio Pollock in New York and Neil Dayton in Massachusetts during the 1920s and 1930s proved of enduring value. In both states legislative appropriations for institutional care were well above the national average. In 1931 the average per capita cost of maintenance in mental hospitals in the United States was $291, whereas the comparable figures for New York and Massachusetts were $392 and $366, respectively. A decade later Massachusetts surpassed New York, but both remained above the national average.[31] In Massachusetts the State Board of Insanity established outpatient departments at all mental hospitals. Both states created extensive internal networks to share experiences, train its medical staff, and disseminate information. Both were staunch advocates of the importance of research; in New York the Pathological Institute and in Massachusetts the State Pathologist and Boston Psychopathic Hospital had high reputations.

Similarly, states that lacked effective central structures appeared to have far lower standards of care. The smallest per capita expenditures were found in the South, where states usually had weak or nonexistent central agencies. In 1931 Virginia spent an average of only $177, North Carolina $163, Mississippi $183, and Alabama $193 (see Tables 8-1 and 8-2). Dr. J. K. Hall, who devoted considerable time and effort to induce Virginia to establish a separate agency under psychiatric control, believed that structural reorganization was a sine qua non for progress. Psychiatry in the South, he observed in 1936, was "still in a medieval state." Virginia, Hall informed Douglas Southall Freeman, the famous newspaper editor and historian, "needs a Commissioner of Mental Hygiene to deal with the problem as a state problem, and to activate, direct, and coordinate such work as is now being done in mental sickness." "So long as psychiatric administration [in Virginia] remains so thoroughly laymanized," he wrote three years later, "just so long, in my opinion, will psychiatry remain static."[32]

Yet it is difficult to attribute differences between states to varying administrative structures. During the nineteenth century New York and Massachusetts pioneered in social welfare even before they created elaborate administrative systems. Their higher expenditures for the care and treatment of the mentally ill were not unique, for both ranked near the top in other categories as well. Moreover, Wisconsin, which functioned under a Board of Control rather than under a department under psychiatric domination, had higher average per capita expenditures than either New York or Massachusetts. Oregon, with a similar structure, on the other hand, was fourth from the bottom. Indeed, tradition rather than structure was the most significant determinant of both the quality and quantity of institutional care. Massachusetts and New York had long-established traditions whose roots went well back into the nineteenth century (if not earlier) and preceded particular

TABLE 8-1
AVERAGE PER CAPITA EXPENDITURE FOR MAINTENANCE AT
STATE MENTAL HOSPITALS, 1931-1940 (DOLLARS)

	1931	1940		1931	1940
United States	291	301			
New England	—	388	East South Central	—	172
Maine	358	305	Kentucky	153	147
New Hampshire	378	383	Tennessee	219	158
Vermont	300	287	Alabama	193	200
Massachusetts	366	425	Mississippi	183	265
Rhode Island	303	303			
Connecticut	336	356			
			West South Central	—	202
Mid-Atlantic	—	377	Arkansas	192	194
New York	392	398	Louisiana	250	180
New Jersey	495	395	Oklahoma	216	199
Pennsylvania	310	291	Texas	214	216
East North Central	—	297	Mountain	—	262
Ohio	202	203	Montana	262	—
Indiana	236	202	Idaho	182	258
Illinois	281	272	Wyoming	264	220
Michigan	311	482	Colorado	239	276
Wisconsin	466	501	New Mexico	185	243
			Arizona	224	—
West North Central	—	231	Utah	247	258
Minnesota	203	213	Nevada	185	267
Iowa	239	221			
Missouri	237	267	Pacific	—	267
North Dakota	282	237	Washington	245	238
South Dakota	324	241	Oregon	201	179
Nebraska	231	247	California	238	291
Kansas	229	199			
South Atlantic	—	269			
Delaware	483	380			
Maryland	261	233			
Washington, D.C.*	693	666			
Virginia	177	189			
West Virginia	181	178			
North Carolina	163	158			
South Carolina	281	264			
Georgia	226	204			
Florida	312	265			

* Federal Government

TABLE 8-2
STATE MENTAL HOSPITALS AND ADMINISTRATIVE SYSTEMS, 1939

Individual Board of Trustees appointed by Governor	Arkansas, Connecticut, Delaware, Louisiana, New Hampshire, North Carolina, New Mexico, Utah
Single central Board of Trustees for all hospitals	Alabama (self-perpetuating), Mississippi, South Carolina
Single central Board of Trustees for all public institutions	Missouri
Board of Control	Iowa, Kansas, Minnesota, Nebraska, North Dakota, Oklahoma, South Dakota, Texas, West Virginia, Washington
Central Board composed of Governor and cabinet	Arizona, Florida, Montana, Nevada, Oregon, Wyoming
State Department of Mental Health or Hygiene	Massachusetts, New York
State Department of Welfare	California, Colorado, Georgia, Idaho, Illinois, Maine, Rhode Island, Tennessee, Vermont
State Department of Welfare with a sub-department for mentally ill	Indiana, Kentucky, Ohio, New Jersey, Pennsylvania

NOTE: Maryland had a conglomerate structure that cannot be classified.

structural forms. Wisconsin's Progressive tradition dated from the 1890s, and transcended the issue of the mentally ill.[33]

The South, by way of contrast, spent less on its dependent groups, both in the nineteenth and twentieth centuries. Once again, it is difficult to explain its consistently below-average ranking by the absence of central administrative structures. The lower expenditures for social welfare in the South was in part a function of the region's widespread poverty. Nor was the practice of segregating black mentally ill patients related to particular administrative structures; such policies reflected the general pattern of race relations in that region. Conversely, the absence of segregation in the North grew largely out of the small number of black patients, and in a few hospitals segregation was imposed if the number warranted the practice. Irrespective of their regional affiliations, psychiatrists tended to share a common belief in the existence of innate racial differences, a view that shaped their attitudes and practices toward black patients.[34]

In their comprehensive study of regional differences in the 1920s and 1930s of the institutionalized mentally ill population, as a matter of fact, Joseph Zubin and Grace C. Scholz minimized the importance of administrative structures. Variations in per capita costs, they concluded, reflected "variations in care rather than variations in economical administration." Regions that provided "more adequate care" tended to spend "more per capita."[35]

III

That organizational structure did not directly explain policy, however, is not to imply that structure was of no significance. As a matter of fact, debates over structure were often the occasion of bitter and protracted conflict between public officials and institutional psychiatrists. Officials were preoccupied with cost effectiveness, while psychiatrists focused on professional autonomy. The competing claims of both groups tended to submerge from sight the nature of the patient population and their particular needs. Public policy, therefore, was defined in terms of structure and authority rather than substance.

As psychiatry emerged as a self-conscious specialty in the nineteenth century, its members began to seek the right to establish standards to govern the institutions in which they practiced. Yet their autonomy was curtailed by virtue of their status as public employees—a situation that placed them in a somewhat unique position as compared with their medical brethren who were overwhelmingly in private practice. Precisely because of their dependent status, institutional psychiatrists were constantly forced to defend themselves against allegations that seemed to impair their professional legitimacy.

Toward the end of the nineteenth century, as we have already seen, the specialty had begun to change. Nevertheless, the internal transformation did not resolve the ambiguous position of most practitioners, the overwhelming bulk of whom remained in institutional practice. When the AMPA published a list of its members in 1895, 190 gave an institutional address and 61 a private address. Those with private addresses, however, included neurologists, psychiatrists who had retired from hospital practice, and some who held organizational positions. By 1940 1,458 members still gave an institutional address, although the number providing a private address (which was not necessarily identical with private practice) had risen to 841.[36] It was understandable, therefore, that structural issues remained of major significance to a specialty with intimate connections to state government.

Recognizing the inevitability of some form of public control, most psychiatrists favored the New York and Massachusetts model of an independent agency whose jurisdiction was limited to the mentally ill and whose director was a qualified psychiatrist. They argued that the high quality of public institutions in both states grew out of a unique administrative structure that seemed to maximize professional independence and personal satisfaction. Such perceptions, however, stemmed more from sheer numbers than from any conclusive data. New York and Massachusetts had a large and influential medical profession, as well as the highest concentration of psychiatrists in the nation. In 1910, for example, 39.7 percent of the membership of the AMPA (excluding foreign members) were concentrated in New York and Massachusetts; in 1923 the comparable figure was 36.7 percent. In 1910 37 states had fewer than ten members each, 7 (plus the District of Columbia) had between 10 and 19, and only 5 states had 20 or more members.[37]

Since few states had a critical mass of psychiatrists to justify a separate agency for the mentally ill, the demand for autonomy generally took a different form. Even before the turn of the century the AMSAII and AMPA had gone on record favoring a civil service system that would protect mental hospitals from political control. As the specialty grew in size, the demand for autonomy assumed new forms. In 1922 the newly reorganized APA created a Committee on Standards and Policies that attempted to emulate the AMA's Council on Medical Education and Hospitals. Two years later the Committee prepared a list of minimum standards for mental hospitals, most of which related to the internal organization of institutions. The Committee urged that the superintendent be an experienced and qualified psychiatrist with unlimited authority to dismiss employees who failed to discharge their duties. It suggested that all mental hospitals have adequate medical staffs, modern treatment facilities, and an outpatient department. Its members, however, were also sensitive to the importance of external constraints, and their demand that the "positions and the administration of the institution must be free from control by partisan politics" was endorsed by the parent association.[38]

As a preliminary step, the Committee proposed that the APA send out a questionnaire to all mental hospitals. The information gathered would be used to formulate a set of minimum standards, which, in turn, would become the basis for grading the performance of hospitals. H. W. Mitchell, superintendent of the Warren State Hospital in Pennsylvania, expressed enthusiasm for the proposal, since psychiatrists would be able to report "fully the difficulties encountered in their local work, or the unfavorable features of state control or supervision." The context in which the Committee functioned suggested that the demand for freedom from "political" control included an organizational structure in which both key decisions and evaluation mechanisms would remain in the hands of psychiatrists. Although the Committee sent out a questionnaire and reported back to the meetings of the APA in 1925, lack of funds aborted the hope of developing hospital standards.[39]

Between 1927 and 1933 the APA took no further action. In 1934, however, the Committee on Standards and Policies proposed that a more modest study be undertaken of the "various types of governmental agencies charged with the management of public institutions for mental diseases." Its report noted that the highest standard of care existed in states where central agencies were "free from political entanglements." The Committee was particularly critical of boards of control whose members had broad duties relating to many dependent groups and lacked "specialized knowledge in the prevention and treatment of mental disability." Its members clearly preferred the organizational structure that existed in Massachusetts and New York.[40]

After a survey of all states in 1935, the Committee developed a three-class rating system, which was published as part of its report to the annual meeting of the APA. Class A included states in which central boards were composed of qualified psychiatrists or laypersons selected on the basis of ability rather than as a reward for political service. Class B was composed of states where political considerations were important but did not adversely affect patients. Class C consisted of states where "standards of care must inevitably suffer from political practices." In any case, the Committee reiterated its belief that a central board be headed by a trained and reputable psychiatrist.[41]

On the basis of reports from all regions, the Committee prepared a report that was circulated in manuscript form, but never published. The document made it clear that the New York plan of organization was worthy of emulation, since its standards were "of the highest" and were "free from politics." Twenty-two states and the District of Columbia appeared in the "A" category, nine in the "B," and nineteen in the "C." In general, New England and the Mid-Atlantic region led the nation, since all eight states were in the "A" group; all other regions received mixed ratings.[42]

The importance that psychiatrists attributed to particular types of central regulatory structures, however, often was not justified by the results. Massachusetts was a case in point. Since the turn of the century, responsibility for overseeing a far-flung system of institutions had remained with an agency whose jurisdiction was limited to the mentally ill and mentally deficient, and its head was always an eminent psychiatrist. Dr. George M. Kline, a former president of the APA, served as Commissioner of the department from 1916 until his death in 1933; he was followed by Dr. James V. May, another former president of the APA and superintendent of Boston State Hospital for more than fifteen years. May's tenure was brief, and in mid-1934 he was succeeded by Dr. Winfred Overholser, a veteran of seventeen years' service in the state hospital system. Massachusetts, moreover, had a powerful and eminent medical profession as well as a large psychiatric community. The state also ranked second behind New York between 1895 and 1940 in terms of APA members. Neither the size and prestige of the specialty nor the existence of a separate and highly regarded Department of Mental Diseases, however, could insulate the mental hospital system from state government. Between 1936 and 1938 both the Department of Mental Diseases and a number of state hospitals were enmeshed in a conflict that demonstrated the vulnerability of the specialty and the limits of its authority and independence.

This conflict revolved around James Michael Curley, who was inaugurated as Governor early in 1935. One of the most colorful and controversial figures of his era, Curley had a checkered political career that included four terms as Mayor of Boston, one as Governor, and a term in federal prison for influence peddling. One of the last of the great urban political bosses, Curley's political strength derived from his links with a lower-class constituency for whom he provided both services and jobs. In mid-1936, just as Overholser's term was about to expire, Curley visited several wards at the Boston State Hospital occupied by some elderly women who appeared untidy. Curley refused to permit any of the physicians to accompany him, and he ignored Dr. May, who had returned to the superintendency following his brief service as Commissioner of the Department of Mental Diseases. That same day Curley—who was then running as the Democratic candidate for United States Senator—denounced conditions at the hospital and suggested that May and Overholser resign. "The real object," insisted Dr. Arthur Ruggles, superintendent of the Butler Hospital in Rhode Island, "is not to reappoint Overholser." Curley, he added, "is a dangerous enemy." Overholser conceded that some of Curley's allegations about lack of food, linen, and clothing, as well as unsanitary conditions, were true, but attributed them to a cut in appropriations rather than to any deliberate actions on May's part.[43]

Several months later Curley lost his bid for United States Senator, but he nominated Dr. David L. Williams to succeed Overholser, whose term had expired. Williams was neither a psychiatrist nor a member of the APA; he had previously been in charge of a Veteran's Hospital laboratory in Bedford. His appointment aroused fierce opposition among psychiatrists. The reaction was exacerbated when Curley, using an obscure clause in a state law, conferred on the Department of Mental Diseases the functions previously performed by the trustees of Boston State Hospital. Williams removed May from office, and May then retired from state service. Williams eventually appointed Dr. Harold F. Norton, who was thirty-five years old and had been on the hospital's staff for three years, as superintendent.[44]

Early in January, 1937, Charles F. Hurley succeeded Curley as Governor, and immediately restored to the trustees of Boston State Hospital their lost authority. The trustees promptly voted to remove Norton from office, on the grounds that he lacked experience. Norton issued a public statement describing the "shocking conditions" in the hospital. Roy G. Hoskins, Director of Research at the Memorial Foundation for Neuro-Endocrine Research at the Harvard Medical School, believed that Norton had "chosen to put all the dirty linen on the clothesline in the front yard" in order "to save his own official hide." Hoskins admitted nevertheless that during May's tenure as Commissioner "matters got rather badly out of hand." Overholser believed that Norton was competing with the press "in attempting to prove that his is probably the worst institution in the United States, if not in the world." "The high professional level of his action," added Overholser ironically, "may be gathered from the fact that he has taken an obvious delight in showing newspaper reporters and camera men through the institution, pointing out particularly mattresses which were said to be torn and sheets which were dirty, although some of my informants who visited the institution were thoroughly impressed with the fact that Dr. Norton seemed to know exactly which bed to go to and that the whole affair savored very strongly of a staged show." When the new governor decided to hold a hearing, the trustees of the hospital resigned and a new board was appointed.[45]

A week before Hurley took office, the Council of the APA directed its Executive Committee to prepare a resolution dealing with the situation in Massachusetts. The Executive Committee in turn unanimously expressed "deep concern" and insisted that the interests of the mentally ill could "only be served when those in authority encourage continuity of service and insist on recognized professional qualifications and breadth of experience." In his inaugural address, Hurley took note of the controversy as well as the request by the Department of Mental Diseases for what a special commission described as a "staggering sum" for renovation and new construction. Hurley proposed that the legislature authorize an investigation. "Specifically," he noted,

> there is reason to believe that the proper care of the mentally sick, for which the Commonwealth holds itself duly responsible, is gradually being extended into fields where we cannot sensibly assume responsibility. There is in the public mind an ever-growing tendency, which has been deliberately fostered and directed, to throw upon the care of the Commonwealth many who should and could be cared for at home. The practical distinctions between the insane, the neurotic, the moronic, and the retarded are being obscured, to all intents and purposes, so as to favor the shifting of humane responsibility for the care and upbringing of all these types from the home to state institutions. Theory and practice are being most plausibly confused in the elusive name of science.

Given the fact that the Department of Mental Diseases absorbed about 25 percent of the state's income, as well as the budgetary pressures engendered by the greatest depression in American history, the legislature concurred in the governor's recommendation, and authorized the establishment of a special commission.[46]

In April 1937 the Governor appointed seven members to the new commission, which included six laypersons and one psychiatrist. By the end of the year the group sent a report to the legislature that absolved the state's mental hospitals of any wrongdoing. The report was critical, however, of the Department of Mental Diseases, which during the long tenure of Dr. George M. Kline "had become a one-man affair." Moreover, the new Commissioner had not performed the duties of his office, allegedly because of illness, but actually because Hurley had already inaugurated removal proceedings against him. The commission therefore recommended that the Department of Mental Diseases be superseded by a Department of Mental Health headed by a commissioner and including two associate commissioners, two of whom (including the former) be diplomates of the American Board of Psychiatry and Neurology. The power to appoint and discharge superintendents was to be transferred from local boards to the new commissioner. Finally, the commission proposed that the legislature authorize a still broader study of the problems of the mentally ill.[47]

The commission's recommendations were not received with enthusiasm by the psychiatric community. Overholser, who by this time had been appointed to succeed the recently deceased William A. White as superintendent of St. Elizabeths Hospital in Washington, D.C.—a move widely perceived as a vindication of his position—was critical of the commission. Its members had not asked him to testify. The nonmedical composition of the group, according to Overholser, was evidence of its political character. This view was seconded by Ross M. Chapman, then president of the APA. Chapman was also hostile to the proposal that the Commissioner be given the power to appoint superintendents. "With a politically minded, unsympathetic and ruthless Governor and a subservient commissioner," he noted, "the effectiveness of the state hospitals could be destroyed almost overnight." "The whole affair," Overholser insisted, "is a dirty mess and the reputation of Massachusetts, or such little as it has left, is being blasted in grand shape."[48]

Throughout 1938 the ferment continued unabated. When the state auditor launched an independent investigation of alleged mismanagement and a seemingly high number of violent deaths in state hospitals, he came into direct conflict with the Governor. The legislature meanwhile had agreed to continue the work of the commission, which, in turn, arranged for an independent study of the state hospitals by the Mental Hospital Survey Committee. Both the commission and the Survey Committee vindicated the public institutions even though they proposed a number of modifications. But before the commission completed its report, the legislature enacted a law creating a Department of Mental Health. The law gave hospital trustees the right to appoint and remove superintendents subject to the approval of the commissioner. This provision, along with another stipulating that the commissioner, assistant commissioner, and superintendents be diplomates of the American Board of Psychiatry and Neurology, won approval of the psychiatric community.[49]

Because of the Bay State's prominent role, the internecine warfare between 1936 and 1939 received national publicity. Yet the situation in Massachusetts was not unique and was repeated elsewhere on frequent occasions. Even New York was not exempt. In 1913 the removal of the secretary of the State Hospital Commission led to allegations of political interference. The people of the state, noted William L. Russell, had to decide whether or not "the medical needs of the patient are to be the controlling consideration," and this could only be assured by professional rather than lay control.[50]

In practice the effort to resolve the contradictions between professional autonomy, on the one hand, and public accountability, on the other, was rarely successful. The absence of any central administrative structure in North Carolina, for example, created its own unique problems. In 1928 Dr. Albert Anderson, superintendent of the state hospital in Raleigh for more than fifteen years, was indicted by a Grand Jury on fifteen separate counts alleging malfeasance in office, theft, cruelty toward patients, and the use of patient labor on private property. The investigation was initially launched by an assistant attorney general and the Commissioner of Public Welfare. Because of inaction by either the Governor of the state or the hospital's board of directors, the case went before a jury. Eight of the counts were dropped after the testimony was presented. Anderson was found innocent on five and convicted on two counts of using patient labor in both his private hayfield and forest. The State Supreme Court threw out both convictions, ruling that the charges did not constitute a crime, and that the case should have been investigated by the hospital's directors. Anderson insisted that his use of patients on his farm "was openly done and without any attempt at concealment, and . . . for the sole purpose of benefiting the patients." He also denied "any actual or intended profit." Dr. J. K. Hall, Anderson's nephew, conducted a vigorous private and public defense, charging that the entire affair represented an effort to bring "official medicine . . . under the domination of lay people." "The cold fact," he added in his monthly column in the influential *Southern Medicine and Surgery*,

> is that those who undertake to deal with the mentally abnormal subject themselves eventually to the dangers of assault—assaults upon their bodies and upon their motives and their characters. The history of psychiatric work in North Carolina certainly, and throughout the country probably, is a confirmation of that statement. Criticism originating in a mind occupied by high motives is beneficent and helpful, but springing from any other source criticism is malignant and destructive.[51]

That the tensions growing out of autonomy and accountability were not easily resolved was evident from a study of mental hospital administration conducted by the Mental Hospital Survey Committee in 1937. Dr. J. G. Wilson, a senior surgeon with the Public Health Service, prepared for the committee a study of the relationship between politics and state hospital administration. At the very outset Wilson noted the variations in administrative structures, but conceded that the situation could not be analyzed in strictly medical terms. Law and administration differed, and he conceded that the particular method of state control was not especially important. Two key elements—"public opinion" and the "personality of the superintendent"—could not be quantified nor an accurate weight assigned to each, even though both were of major significance. After a survey of conditions in the various regions, Wilson reported that political interference was strongest in the West South Central and Pacific states, and least pronounced in New England, the West North Central, and Middle Atlantic states. Admitting that legal guarantees were in practice not a sufficient protection against "political" interference, Wilson nevertheless placed primary emphasis upon the degree to which the superintendent enjoyed security in office.[52]

Although the reaction to Wilson's report was generally favorable, the comments of Winfred Overholser and Louis Casamajor raised questions about the relationship between structure and autonomy. "Once again," noted Overholser, "we come down to the proposition that it is the men who administer the laws who determine their efficiency, and not the laws themselves," and he urged the Committee to "seriously consider giving this fact full publicity." In turn, Casamajor, an important and influential figure in New York neurological and psychiatric circles, wanted to know more about the "subject of political interference in our State Hospitals." "We assume," he observed, "that political interference runs parallel with inefficiency of management and inadequacy of medical care. I should like to know just how close this parallel really is."[53]

Without doubt strictly political elements played a role in some states, where appointments were based on party affiliation alone. On the other hand, some hospital superintendents were themselves deeply involved in state politics, which tended to weaken their claims for the necessity of autonomy. Admittedly, the line between representing the interests of the hospital to the legislature and partisan involvement was vague. In 1932, for example, William D. Partlow managed to persuade the Alabama legislature to exempt in part his institution from a newly imposed centralized purchasing system, a position that brought him into direct conflict with the governor. Partlow insisted that independence was necessary in order to protect his hospital against the "vicious determination and unholy designs on the part of the central administration." A few years later, however, his influence led Lister Hill, who was seeking to succeed to the seat in the United States Senate vacated by Hugo Black, to solicit his support. Partlow saw nothing peculiar in the request, and made his support conditional on a platform committed to "Americanism, American institutions, traditions and principles and in every way against the trend toward Communism."[54]

The underlying issues, of course, were far more complex. If psychiatrists gained independence from public control, by what standards would they be judged, and who would assume the role of judge? Could state governments, which were legally and financially responsible for the welfare of dependent groups, abrogate their responsibilities without providing some form of supervision and control? That such dilemmas were not easily resolved was demonstrated in a paper given by Overholser at the APA meetings in the spring of 1939. Overholser generally defended some form of central control, particularly in states with large hospital populations. He thought the Massachusetts and New York model of an independent department headed by a qualified psychiatrist most desirable, but conceded that in smaller states such an organization was probably unnecessary. He also defended the wisdom of retaining local boards with advisory rather than operational authority, to serve as a buffer against political interference. The virtues of a central agency in Overholser's eyes were clear; it could facilitate nondiscriminatory budgetary allocations, the collection of uniform statistics, rational planning, efficient purchasing, the maintenance of high and equal standards for personnel and medical care, the supervision and licensing of private hospitals, and the development of a statewide system of outpatient facilities. At the same time Overholser quoted with approval the resolution adopted by the AMSAII in 1875 "that any supernumerary functionaries endowed with the privilege of scrutinizing the management of the hospital, even sitting in judgment on the conduct of attendants and the complaints of patients, and controlling the management, directly by the exercise of superior power or indirectly by stringent advice, can scarcely accomplish an amount of good sufficient to compensate for the harm that is sure to follow." Alluding indirectly to his experiences in Massachusetts only a few years before, he observed that "human nature has not changed greatly since the time of the founding fathers!" In other words, his concept of state control implied that the exercise of authority had to be vested in psychiatric hands, a view that many public officials were not prepared to accept. Nevertheless, Overholser's paper was enthusiastically received by his colleagues. This was so even though the claim that professional autonomy would enhance the quality and effectiveness of care and treatment was not supported by any compelling body of evidence. The success of centralized control, observed Nolan D. C. Lewis, depended upon the personality of the individual in charge. "An absolute monarchy isn't a bad type of government," he added. "If you have a good king who lives long enough it will be successful. If physicians . . . are in the hands of spoilsmen, then your central system fails."[55]

The centrality of the debate over structure and control was magnified by the absence of any external pressure group representing the interests of the mentally ill institutionalized population. Although patients clearly influenced the character of hospitals through their behavior, they were generally silent and inarticulate when it came to broad issues of public policy. With the exception of an occasional "exposé" of hospital conditions by former patients (and not all of these were unfavorable) or an occasional journalist, the mentally ill never became an independent pressure group. During the 1930s there were isolated attempts to establish associations of former patients. In 1931 L. Cody Marsh, a psychiatrist on the staff of Worcester State Hospital, raised the possibility of founding such an organization. "I can't escape the conviction," he wrote to Clifford W. Beers in an effort to solicit moral and financial support, "that if so-called insanity is to be baptized with respectability, which is now the case with formerly untouchable things such as tuberculosis, cancer, and leprosy, the patient himself must be willing to come out into the open and admit that he has suffered from mental disease without any sense of shame or apology." William A. Bryan, superintendent of the Worcester hospital, was favorably inclined and attempted to organize a "community council" made up of representatives from various religious and social welfare organizations, in the hope of easing the transition from institution to community. Bryan was also supportive of Marsh's recommendation that former patients who had made a successful transition be provided with a public forum in order to break down existing prejudices toward individuals who had recovered.[56]

Marsh's project, however, apparently proved a failure. Beers was not enthusiastic. Most people, he noted, considered a mental breakdown "a sort of disgrace" and regarded recovered patients "with some suspicion." He therefore questioned "whether the organizing of ex-patients, even those who may be willing to join such an organization, will be in their interest." Marsh apparently alienated his colleagues, and subsequently was discharged from state employment upon the initiative of George M. Kline, the Commissioner of Mental Diseases. Marsh then moved to Boston and attempted to organize a society of "progressive psychiatrists" to remove patients from state hospitals and board them in the community. Harry C. Solomon, who played a prominent role on both the state and national psychiatric scene for more than half a century, dismissed Marsh as a "muck-raking, paranoid sort of individual." Other isolated attempts were also made to form an organization of ex-patients before 1940, the most significant occurring in Illinois with the founding of the Recovery Association of Former Patients. These societies, however, were concerned less with policy and structural issues and more with easing the transition from hospital to community and combatting the stigma attached to mental illness.[57]

IV

To a considerable extent, therefore, the relationship of mental hospitals to the state reflected in part the competing interests of public representatives and institutional psychiatrists. Neither of these groups were unconcerned with patients, but both tended to define the problems in terms of their own backgrounds and allegiances. Influenced by the Progressive faith in rationalization and centralization, many states experimented with a variety of administrative structures designed to maximize efficiency and accountability. During this very same era, institutional psychiatry claimed an autonomy and independence based upon specialized scientific and medical knowledge and training. The competing demands of accountability and autonomy molded in large measure the perceptions of both groups, even in the absence of compelling evidence that certain structural forms were clearly superior to others.

Curiously enough, the debate between public officials and institutional psychiatrists rarely focused on a patient population composed of individuals whose behavior was often related to an underlying somatic pathology. Efficiency, for example, was not discussed in terms of the kinds of care required for patients whose health-related problems were not amenable to any known therapy. Nor did psychiatrists ever modify their commitment to a medical model; therapy rather than care remained their central concern. Institutionalized patients remained of marginal importance, even though all claimed to be acting on their behalf.

CHAPTER NINE

The Emergence of the Mental Health Professions

AFTER 1900 American psychiatrists, reflecting a new mood of confidence, began to readjust their relationships with other branches of medicine and to transform the institutional structure within which they operated. "The rescue of our patients from jails, prisons and poorhouses, the emancipation of our institutions from the control of politics, the reform of laws based upon cruel and ignorant conceptions of the nature of mental illness, the instruction of medical students in the science of the mind, and the recognition of mental nursing . . . ," declared Thomas W. Salmon in his APA presidential address in 1924, "are today, in large measure, realized." But these significant advances had been achieved at some cost; they had been realized at the expense of a growing gap between psychiatry and medicine. Fortunately this breach was being repaired. "Our point of view," he observed, "is welcomed with a warmth that is sometimes embarassing." Mental hygiene work, the treatment of mental disorders in general hospitals, the integration of psychiatry into the medical curriculum, had all reduced "the scientific isolation of psychiatry."[1]

To the medical profession generally, Salmon's words represented more wishful thinking than reality. But to his psychiatric colleagues, Salmon's address was a harbinger of a brighter future. By the 1920s and 1930s a general consensus had developed on the need to blur the distinction between institutions—general hospitals and mental hospitals—and between fields—medicine and psychiatry. Even J. K. Hall, an optimistic skeptic who often dissented from the more exaggerated claims of his fellow practitioners, believed that the integration of medical and psychiatric practice and institutions could only redound to the advantage of the American people. "I wonder how long it may be," he wrote to a colleague and friend, "before the medical profession is able to think of a state hospital as a general hospital in which mental disease is also treated? That ought to be the ideal of every state hospital; and the ideal for every general hospital ought to be that of a hospital in which mental disease can also be treated."[2]

The effort to transcend the traditional institutional base of psychiatry was accompanied by deeds as well as words. In the decades preceding World War II, a concerted effort was made to broaden the responsibilities and functions of both psychiatry and mental hospitals. In addition to the growing emphasis on mental hygiene, psychiatrists fought for the establishment of outpatient departments in mental hospitals. They also supported the creation of psychiatric wards within general hospitals, and insisted that their specialty had a mission to safeguard and promote the mental health of the entire community.

Admittedly, the changes in the context of psychiatric practice broadened occupational choices and appeared to elevate the status of a specialty long associated with mental hospitals. Nor did psychiatrists force themselves upon an unwilling public; their assurances that they could improve the mental health of all concerned were eagerly accepted. In one important sense, psychiatry and other medical specialties assumed a role that in an earlier era had been filled by the church. There was, however, one crucial difference. Premodern religious thinkers had assumed that human beings could never achieve a state of grace by themselves because of their intrinsically sinful nature and inability to control the world which they inhabited. By way of contrast, twentieth-century prophets who elevated science and technology to the status of a religion believed that humanity had the wisdom and power to achieve perfection through institutional means.

In redefining the functions and responsibilities of their specialty, psychiatrists helped to create an environment conducive to the emergence of other mental health professions, including psychiatric social work, occupational therapy, and clinical psychology. Furthermore, their outward reach brought them into contact with a variety of social and behavioral scientists concerned with normal and abnormal behavior of both individuals and groups. Initially psychiatrists welcomed the involvement and assistance of these new occupational groups and disciplines. They looked forward to the creation of a broad coalition which, under psychiatric leadership, could assume responsibility for treatment and prevention. Such hopes, however, quickly floundered on the shoals of philosophical and ideological differences, professional rivalry, and jurisdictional disputes. By the 1920s and 1930s many of these newer occupational groups were questioning psychiatric authority, thereby fostering interprofessional friction.

In creating an environment conducive to other groups, psychiatrists inadvertently shifted the agenda pertaining to the mentally ill. Many new occupational groups were only marginally concerned with the chronic cases that constituted a large proportion of the institutionalized mentally ill. Occupational therapy, a hospital-based specialty, was for the most part not directly relevant to the needs of patients whose condition was related to an underlying somatic pathology. Psychiatric social work and clinical psychology, on the other hand, focused largely on outpatient and community work. The broadening of professional opportunities in mental health, therefore, reinforced the inclination to overlook institutionalized patients. Indeed, the rise of the mental health professions ultimately created a new and different target population generally found outside mental hospitals.

I

By the turn of the century, psychiatrists were increasingly challenging the consensus forged by the founding fathers of the specialty. During the 1850s the members of the AMSAII committed themselves to therapeutic hospitals limited to no more than 250 beds. After some conflict, the limit was raised to 600 in 1866 and reaffirmed in 1876.[3] Between 1890 and 1940, by way of contrast, little effort was made to establish maximum limits. William A. White, for example, thought that hospitals with 4,000 to 5,000 patients or more were not unreasonable. The issue, he insisted, was qualitative, not quantitative; the quality of care was far more significant than the issue of size. Adolf Meyer, on the other hand, favored smaller and decentralized hospitals within a state system. After undertaking a study of the Massachusetts system in late 1911, he opposed the suggestion that state hospitals reach a maximum capacity of 2,000 beds. Large institutions led to "excessive institutionalizing." Above all, he feared that "apparent administrative economy" would "overrule effectiveness of our work against mental disorder."[4]

Despite the differences of opinion, however, a consensus emerged on the need to define a new relationship between community and hospital—one that gave far broader responsibilities to the hospital for the maintenance of mental health in addition to their traditional therapeutic role. This consensus brought about a radical reorientation of American psychiatry. In the nineteenth century, it was an article of faith that the treatment of mental disorder required an institutional setting removed from the community. In 1851 the AMSAII took the position that every "hospital for the insane should be in the country, not within less than two miles of a large town, and easily accessible at all seasons." As late as 1880 Thomas S. Kirkbride in the revised edition of his classic work on mental hospitals suggested that ten or twelve miles would not be considered unobjectionable if there were adequate railroad facilities. The hospital and community, in other words, were two distinct and separate entities.[5]

By the early twentieth century, on the other hand, there was a clear effort to blur the traditional distinction between hospital and community. If psychiatrists had responsibility for the preservation of mental health, how could they remain confined within the walls of an isolated and self-contained community while many potential patients resided elsewhere? Equally significant, how could psychiatry become part of scientific medicine—already identified with new general hospitals located in urban areas and linked with medical schools—if its members continued to stand outside the mainstream of medical practice generally? Faced with these and similar issues, American psychiatrists began to reorient their practice in a way that they hoped would give a new sense of vitality to institutions whose only *raison d'être* seemed to be the care that they provided for large numbers of chronically ill individuals. This is not to imply that psychiatrists were no longer concerned with patients whose prospects for recovery were either remote or nonexistent, for such was not the case. But, like many other professional groups during this period, they sought a more positive role for both themselves and their institutions, and in so doing broke sharply with the legacy of their predecessors.

The earliest efforts to overcome the preoccupation of psychiatrists with traditional mental hospitals grew out of changes in medical education. During the last quarter of the nineteenth century a small group of physicians—many of whom had studied in Germany, where they were exposed to new medical and scientific currents—had begun to transform American medical education. Fearful of being left out of the mainstream of scientific medicine, some psychiatrists began to search for some way of integrating psychiatric and medical education. But so long as the practice of psychiatry was limited to mental hospitals and lacked formal or informal relationships with urban general hospitals and medical schools, it was difficult to introduce meaningful changes.[6]

In an effort to overcome some of these drawbacks, Walter Channing proposed to the managers of the Boston Dispensary in 1897 that their institution could benefit by the addition of a physician with "special knowledge in mental disease." Such an individual could familiarize medical students and young physicians with the specialty of psychiatry, and at the same time deal with incipient and unrecognized cases of mental disease on an outpatient basis. Channing's request was approved, and by the end of the year the new department had come into existence. During the first three years Channing and another physician saw about four hundred patients. Some became insane, and were either treated at the dispensary or else sent to a mental hospital. In other instances it appeared that early treatment prevented an incipient case of mental disease from becoming worse. On the basis of his experience, Channing concluded that there was a far higher incidence of insanity in the community than was generally suspected, and he pointed to the large number of "defective children" who previously had escaped notice because of their age. Indeed, he believed that children were the major target population of the dispensary. The virtue of an outpatient clinic, he wrote, was its ability to provide diagnostic and therapeutic services without resorting to institutionalization. A dispensary-based psychiatric practice could also revitalize hospital practice by diminishing the deadly influence of institutional routine as well as by exposing physicians to the actual development of mental disease from its inception.[7]

Although dispensary treatment of mental disease never became significant (partly because the dispensary was already on the road to extinction), interest in outpatient practice intensified. The founding of a few psychopathic hospitals, the beginnings of an organized mental hygiene movement, a growing concern with providing "aftercare" services for discharged patients, and a general receptivity to parole, furloughs, or trial home visits in order to ease the transition of patients from institution to community, all acted as catalysts. Support for outpatient services came from psychiatrists and social workers, for both groups perceived advantages to themselves and to the community. There was no hostility to the idea from external sources, if only because there seemed to be few valid arguments against a system that promised to enhance health by preventing disease or intervening therapeutically at a stage when the individual was still in a functional state.[8]

Within a very brief period of time outpatient practice became identified with community mental health programs and institutions. In 1916 Owen Copp gave a paper at the meetings of the AMPA entitled "The Psychiatric Needs of a Large Community," which argued that all communities should integrate institutional and outpatient facilities under qualified psychiatrists. His list of functions for such an institution was broad and sweeping; it included a plea for "close cooperative relations . . . with boards of health, organized charity, reformatory and penal agencies, educational commissions and societies for protection of child life." Copp's paper received an enthusiastic reception from his colleagues. "I am sure," noted an Indiana psychiatrist in a typical response,

> the sooner that we hospital men free ourselves from the idea that our activities should be limited to the management of the institutions themselves, the better. We must realize fully that the subject of the treatment of mental diseases is one not only of hospital care and treatment, but of community care and treatment, also; and, therefore, we must make our institutions psychiatric centers which reach out into the community and by advice and treatment prevent many mental upsets and the necessity of many commitments to the institutions. At the same time we should improve and extend the after care and social systems.[9]

Copp's paper did not represent a plan for a remote future. In 1913 New York State authorized each of its mental hospitals to establish an outpatient department. That same year the Psychopathic Department of Boston State Hospital (later the Boston Psychopathic Hospital) opened its own outpatient facility. Following the reorganization of the Massachusetts State Board of Insanity in 1914, its members immediately moved to establish similar divisions in all state hospitals and to make them "reach out into the community and be responsible for the mental health of the districts covered by each." The Board's plan envisaged geographical districts, each having comprehensive psychiatric facilities that provided outpatient services, after care, family care, and functioned as a mental hygiene unit as well. By 1920 Massachusetts had thirty-three outpatient clinics and New York twenty-five. Other states began to follow suit; Pennsylvania was third with nine clinics, Michigan had seven, and thirty other states had from one to four each.[10]

In theory the justification for outpatient clinics was that the treatment they gave to both incipient cases of mental illness and to children made subsequent institutionalization unnecessary. In practice, however, there was little evidence to support such claims. Admittedly, it was easier to deal with individuals who did not require hospitalization, but there was no way of predicting whether these persons were the ones requiring institutionalization in the future. Meyer, a staunch supporter of community psychiatry, advised a colleague in the Department of Medicine at the University of Chicago to establish a "real clinic" with its own beds. The human personality, he wrote, was "extensively influenced by its setting, and the setting is difficult to control." The patients whom psychiatrists found "most instructive and important to study" were precisely those who required round-the-clock attention and care. Out-patient work in psychiatry, on the other hand, belonged "to the most difficult and often most unsatisfactory tasks a physician can be confronted with. It is definitely not the ground on which to begin medical teaching and of which to expect a foundation for research unless one limits oneself to psychiatry on a talking level."[11]

Aside from the issue of effectiveness, outpatient clinics were largely irrelevant to the needs of hospital populations and dealt with a quite different clientele. In a five-year period from 1913 to 1918, the outpatient facility at Boston Psychopathic handled 6,532 new cases. Of these, 58 percent were adults, 16 percent adolescents, 24 percent children, and 5 percent infants. In a seven-and-a-half-year period in the 1920s nine outpatient clinics in Pennsylvania received 4,091 new cases, of which 65 percent were children of sixteen years or less. Many were referred to the hospital by a variety of organizations—including schools and social agencies—because of disorderly conduct, failure in school, delinquency, neurological symptoms, or "early signs of mental disease." Hospital populations, as already noted, included different kinds of cases. The emphasis on outpatient work, therefore, tended to deflect interest away from patients in hospitals and to stimulate interest in noninstitutional practice. Moreover, the enthusiasm for community mental health suggested a desire to escape from the seemingly insoluble and depressing problems of the traditional mental hospital. The enthusiastic rhetoric of community mental health, therefore, rested, at bottom, on a profoundly pessimistic foundation.[12]

The desire to alter the context of psychiatric practice and to provide an alternative to traditional institutional care took other forms as well. The most significant development involved an effort to establish psychiatric wards in general hospitals. Interest in treating the mentally ill in general hospitals came as a result of the failure by most states to establish psychopathic hospitals during the early decades of the twentieth century. The needs seemed as obvious as the benefits. A psychopathic ward in a general hospital, noted Dr. Albert W. Ferris (president of the New York State Commission in Lunacy) in 1910, could provide proper facilities for the reception and temporary detention of allegedly insane persons pending proper disposition of their cases. Such a facility could also receive borderline cases for observation and decision. "The psychopathic ward," he insisted, "is a most important link in the chain; a most essential agency for the early protection and conservation of the recently developed or the recently discovered case of mental impairment."[13]

Psychiatric wards in general hospitals, however, seemed to offer other benefits. Most significant, they opened up the possibility of reintegrating psychiatry and medicine. In this way psychiatry could share in the growing prestige of the field of medicine. Psychiatrists would have new alternatives to institutional employment, and links with general medicine would provide a source of patient referrals. Equally important, the specialty might attract a new and different clientele—especially children and those adults whose psychoneurotic condition did not require commitment to traditional state hospitals. As conditions of work improved, more young physicians might be attracted to a career in psychiatry, and physicians in other specialties would become sensitized to the psychological and emotional needs of their patients.[14]

Leaders recognized that offering alternative careers to psychiatrists might prove detrimental to the efforts to staff mental hospitals with qualified personnel. New recruits, observed C. Macfie Campbell, one of the rising leaders of the specialty, might be "less content than ever to accept the conditions which have been associated in the past with the state hospital service." Nevertheless, he expressed the hope that as the mental hospital approached the "medical standards" of general hospitals, its attractiveness for career possibilities would be enhanced. "The visiting physician of a general hospital makes a very valuable contribution to its work, but he lives his life apart from the hospital." As similar conditions developed in mental hospitals, positions would become more desirable. "Freedom from undue administrative cares, opportunity for work on individual patients and not merely for the superficial supervision of masses, life in the community not confined to the hospital limits," Campbell concluded, "are factors desired by the young psychiatrist and are perhaps attainable."[15]

Before World War II, however, the effort to establish psychiatric wards in general hospitals met with only limited success. In 1930 the NCMH polled all 603 general hospitals approved for intern training by the AMA Council on Medical Education and Hospitals. The survey hoped to elicit information on clinics and wards in general hospitals where "mental patients" (a term that included the mentally diseased and defective, epileptics, and alcoholics and drug addicts suffering from mental disorders) might be examined or treated. Of the 421 hospitals replying, 282 reported no facilities. Only 56 hospitals had wards and 97 clinics (31 had both), and the total bed capacity was merely 3,298. Even these figures overstated the case; many of the beds were in neurological rather than in strictly psychiatric wards, and the survey included military and veterans hospitals in its tally. Most of the general hospitals with psychiatric facilities were concentrated in a small number of states with large concentrations of psychiatrists. In 1938 the situation remained much the same; 153 (including some sanatoria, 12 Veteran Administrations, and 18 military and Public Health Service institutions) out of about 5,000 general hospitals accepted mental patients.[16]

The effort to break down the barrier between community and mental hospital, in a certain sense, reflected the needs and perceptions of psychiatrists rather than of their patients. The very establishment of psychiatric wards in general hospitals assumed that there would be clients who could function outside institutions but who were in need of some kind of medical aid or assistance. That the "isolation" of the mental hospital grew out of the characteristics of a very different kind of patient was recognized even if its significance was never central. This point was articulated in the professional journals in the field. In April, 1923, a special committee of the editorial board of *The Modern Hospital*, in cooperation with the NCMH and A. L. Bowen (the former superintendent of charities of the Illinois Department of Public Welfare), prepared a series of articles on state mental hospitals. The second article was devoted to a discussion of the state hospital's "isolation" from both the medical and social world, and identified two crucial developments that had brought about this situation. First, the article (mistakenly) argued that the state hospital had traditionally been "an asylum, with a function purely custodial," and had never reshaped itself after the example of the modern general hospital. Secondly, the "character and residence" of mental hospitals were fundamentally different: patients were "permanent residents," and "active medical service" was "very limited." Their medical staff was overworked and overwhelmed by routine tasks, thereby killing the initiative of physicians. The remedies proposed by the committee were enlightening. It urged the superintendent and staff to become involved in the area's "professional, business, social and civic world," to establish clinics for paroled patients and for others "who feel the need for advice and assistance," to foster links with the community's physicians, and to open the hospital to all. Left unanswered was the question of how these changes, assuming their implementation, would alter the lives of patients in the state hospital.[17]

II

When psychiatrists reached out to a broader constituency and defined new roles and missions for themselves and for their institutions, they inadvertently strengthened the claims of other groups to professional legitimacy in the mental health field. Initially such groups were welcomed as allies. They could aid in breaking down the isolation of institutional psychiatrists from medicine, and help to blur the sharp line that separated the hospital from the community.

By the 1920s social work and occupational therapy had acquired a distinct status within the mental health professions. Such social and behavioral sciences as psychology and sociology were also seeking to establish an identity that would enhance their own role in the field. The mental hygiene movement, in addition, brought together diverse groups that heretofore had shown little concern for the problems of institutional psychiatry. The result was the creation of a broad but amorphous coalition to promote mental health. Before 1930 the coalition functioned in a relatively harmonious manner, since the benefits to each component did not appear to involve a loss to others. Beneath the surface, however, lay elements of discord. After 1930 the coalition began to experience growing pains, and internal tensions and conflicts surfaced. Psychiatrists increasingly viewed other occupational groups as a threat to their dominance in the field. The effort to broaden the base of psychiatric practice, moreover, only enhanced the possibility that practitioners would be unable to maintain the kind of authority traditionally enjoyed in institutions. The movement of psychiatrists into the community, as a matter of fact, brought them face to face with large numbers of individuals who had claims of legitimacy of their own insofar as mental health was concerned.[18]

Before 1900 the major challenges to psychiatric authority came from neurologists and state officials, neither of whom seriously threatened the internal authority of psychiatrists. As long as the specialty was identified with institutions, its members rarely encountered conflicts arising out of their role in the community. The linkages between psychiatry and Protestant Christianity during the nineteenth century further minimized the possibility that the issue of behavior and morality would pit physicians against the community.

Nor did the creation of training schools for nurses and attendants in mental hospitals alter the structure of authority. Although female nurses (as well as their male counterparts) served as links between the medical staff and patients, they lacked formal authority or recognition. In 1920, for example, E. J. Taylor, the associate superintendent of nurses at the Johns Hopkins Hospital, complained to Meyer that nurses disliked working at the Phipps Clinic because of the failure of the medical staff to give "help, consideration and respect." "So much is this true," she added,

> that the criticism has spread beyond the School [for Nurses] and beyond the city and it has been made a matter of comment at conferences of professional people interested in the preparation of women for Public Health Nursing, Mental Hygiene and Social Work. . . .
>
> I want to tell you, however, that I made it very clear [at a recent conference] that it was not because the nurses themselves had lost their ideals but because of a failure on the part of the Medical Staff to appreciate any but their own needs and an unwillingness to co-operate in the nurses' education. Why the physicians in this department, more than in any other, should feel that the function of a nurse is that of a hand maiden to the physician and that the nursing of mental patients is embodied in custodial care is more than I can understand. . . .

It is the greatest insult to the intelligence and honor of the women, who in every way are equal and in many instances superior educationally and socially to the Medical Students, that they cannot be entrusted with the facts concerning the patient's illness and the plan of treatment the physician is following.[19]

Taylor's complaints reflected the ambiguous position of nurses generally. During the late nineteenth century such women as Isabel Hampton (who headed the pioneer Training School for Nurses at the Johns Hopkins Hospital) attempted to establish professional standards for nurses and thus to elevate their status. The absence of authority within hospitals, the female character of the specialty, the decline in the number of nurses from middle- and upper-class backgrounds, and the need for large numbers of nurses at relatively low salaries, all caused the profession to remain stationary in the twentieth century. Although women would continue their struggle to elevate professional standards, they were unable to mount a serious challenge to the superior authority of physicians.[20]

Similarly, the growing heterogeneity of psychiatry did not reshape the pattern of authority. A survey by the NCMH in 1919 of the medical staffs of state hospitals found that 141 out of 844 physicians (16.7 percent) were females, but none had attained a superintendency. The bulk of female physicians were concentrated in a relatively small number of states. Illinois, Indiana, Iowa, Massachusetts, Michigan, Minnesota, New York, Ohio, and Pennsylvania accounted for 73.8 percent of the total, and more than one-third were in New York and Massachusetts. Many Southern states, on the other hand, did not have a single female physician. The presence of female physicians—most of whom encountered considerable hostility from many of their male counterparts who believed that women in general lacked the traits necessary for the practice of psychiatry or the administration of hospitals—did not appreciably alter the internal structure of authority. Most female physicians treated only other women, and advancement for them within mental hospitals was completely closed. After delivering a paper on the status of female physicians in mental hospitals, Dr. Mary M. Wolfe of the Department for Women at the Norristown State Hospital in Pennsylvania observed that a woman had to have "a tremendous amount of native ambition before she can be ambitious for the reason that there are no material rewards for her" in terms of advancement. Like many other women, Wolfe retreated into a defensive position by denying the relevancy of sex. "The whole matter," she concluded in ambiguous words susceptible of a variety of meanings, "resolves itself into a question of individual ability, attainment and character and not into a question of sex." As a matter of fact, Louise G. Rabinovitch, the first female physician to own and publish a psychiatric periodical (the *Journal of Mental Pathology*), never even received a hearing because her militant criticisms of American psychiatry, which reflected her European training, appeared so alien.[21]

After the turn of the century, however, the structure of psychiatric authority began to change. New occupational groups came into existence following the introduction of innovations in psychiatric practice and theory. In time these groups organized themselves into professional associations which—by definition—claimed a measure of authority and autonomy within their own spheres. Initially institutional psychiatrists welcomed the newcomers, since they performed what appeared to be useful and important functions and remained distinctively subordinate. But as these new occupations gained a sense of identity and common purpose, their members sought greater recognition and independence. Ultimately this development led to friction. One case in point was the emergence of psychiatric social work.

During the last three decades of the nineteenth century American welfare practices underwent fundamental changes. Prior to that period, philanthropy reflected a religious imperative. After the 1870s, however, welfare was increasingly committed to an ideal of "scientific" charity and to the use of administrative and bureaucratic procedures. Initially the new profession of social work limited its concerns to the urban poor. The early interest of the NCCC in the social problems of insanity soon diminished, and by 1900 the organization devoted little time to the institutionalized mentally ill.[22] The introduction of the new social work to psychiatry after the turn of the century, oddly enough, followed the development of several trends: outpatient work in neurology, interest in discharged patients, and changes in psychiatric thought.

Although the bitter conflict between some neurologists and institutional psychiatrists had largely abated by the mid-1880s, underlying tensions were still present. Many neurologists in private practice continued to treat psychiatric patients on an outpatient basis and implicitly challenge their institutional colleagues. In 1889 the *Journal of Nervous and Mental Disease* included an article in which the author urged that wards in general hospitals be established for the treatment of acutely insane persons. The following year a Committee of the New York Neurological Society recommended that no state laws preclude the treatment of the mentally ill in general hospitals. Following the presentation of a paper on the management of convalescence and the aftercare of the insane at the meetings of the American Neurological Association in 1894, members voted on a motion introduced by C. L. Dana, an eminent New York neurologist, to establish a Committee on the After-Care of the Insane. The committee decided to poll hospital superintendents, neurologists, and persons prominent in state welfare on the founding of after-care associations and convalescent hospitals for the insane. The former, modeled on agencies in France, would help discharged patients to find housing and employment and supervise them in the weeks following their return to the community.[23]

The Committee received fifty replies or about 90 percent of those polled. Six were dubious about the desirability and practicability of after-care associations, to say nothing about administrative problems relating to the effort of keeping track of discharged patients. Fifty-four were strongly in favor. The Committee therefore supported the establishment of privately supported after-care organizations, and urged members to take the lead. Despite the favorable responses, nothing concrete followed. Meyer believed that the absence of movement was due to a combination of circumstances: a reluctance to emulate European charities; the desire of discharged patients to cut all ties with mental hospitals in order to avoid any possible stigma resulting from public knowledge of hospitalization; the fact that many had friends or relatives to provide support and the belief that it would be unwise to replace familial responsibility by "paternalism."[24]

Interest in the possibilities of after-care, however, persisted. The tendency to interpret mental disorder in environmenal terms provided an added stimulus to seek information about the family and community of mentally ill persons. Meyer himself sent his wife in 1904 to visit his patients on Ward's Island and their families in the city in order to obtain "a broader social understanding of our problem and a reaching out to the *sources* of sickness, the family and the community." Two years later he urged the use of "nonprofessional" visitors to gather background data. As Director of the New York Pathological Institute, he was also in a position to exert influence. At the quarterly conference of state hospital superintendents in 1906, Meyer gave a paper on after-care and prevention. The superintendents then adopted a resolution requesting the State Charities Aid Association to organize a state-wide system of after-care. The Association was favorably inclined, since it had gone on record a year before in favor of such a plan. With the support of such figures as Mary Vida Clark and Louisa Lee Schuyler, the Association moved quickly, and by the end of 1906 the proposal had been implemented. That there was a difference between Meyer's concept of visitation and that of the Association was evident from the fact that the latter's Sub-Committee on Prevention and After-Care envisaged the use of both volunteers and "professional workers." "In connection with no other disease," it noted in 1909, "is an understanding on the part of the physician of the patient's previous manner of life more essential to intelligent treatment, and in no class of homes could a social worker undertake more preventive and ameliorative work than in those homes where either an inherited family tendency or an existing mode of life has already sent at least one member of the household to an institution for the insane."[25]

The New York after-care program thereafter grew at a modest rate. During 1909 117 cases were under supervision, and the agent of the subcommittee reported making 617 visits on behalf of patients. Two years later the State Commission in Lunacy agreed to assume responsibility for the program, given the fact that the experiment had proved a success. The subcommittee conceded that it was impossible to know "how these patients would have fared without . . . advice and assistance," nor could it determine whether or not it had "prevented relapses . . . [and] deferred relapses." Nevertheless, its members were "morally convinced" that threatened relapses had been averted or postponed. The assumption by the state of the after-care program led to relatively rapid growth. In 1917 social workers made 5,731 visits to the homes of patients, found employment for 135, and arranged shelter for 51.[26]

Nor did Massachusetts lag behind New York. Boston Psychopathic Hospital had a social service department when it opened in 1913. That same year the legislature asked the State Board of Insanity to study the possibility of establishing a social service department at each hospital, and in 1914 the Board made after-care a responsibility of the outpatient department. Other states began to follow suit. The results, however, raised some questions.

Wisconsin appointed an individual to look after the interests of paroled patients from the Northern Hospital for the Insane, but he visited them only once every six months. The California State Board of Charities and Corrections, on the other hand, reported in 1916 that much after-care work "could not avoid being superficial" because of insufficient staff.[27]

After-care, however, had only limited possibilities insofar as the career expectations of social workers were concerned. Much more exciting were the opportunities growing out of the newer emphasis on the significance of the social environment in molding the personality and behavior of the individual. One manifestation of this concern was the growing psychiatric emphasis on the life history of the individual. Another was the growth of an organized mental hygiene movement, committed to the proposition that mental health and the social environment were intimately related. Nor was the preoccupation with developmental processes unique to psychiatry or to social work. In the decades following the 1880s Americans increasingly rejected the earlier emphasis upon logic and deduction and turned toward an explanation of social life in terms of process, change, history, and culture. The nineteenth century, as Morton White observed, "was the century of history, evolutionary biology, psychology and sociology, historical jurisprudence and economics; the century of Comte, Darwin, Hegel, Marx, and Spencer." The very concept of the social sciences presupposed a historical-developmental approach.[28]

Although psychiatrists conceded the significance of the social environment in molding personality, their practical work revolved around the individual patient. Consequently, social workers filled a void by defining their field in terms of the social environment. Mary Jarrett—one of the founders of psychiatric social work—noted that the psychiatrist lacked "the special knowledge of community conditions which the art of social investigation and social adjustment requires, and therefore he needs a specialist whose findings and results he can use rather than an assistant to whom he must give specific direction." Jarrett was also concerned with the need to differentiate psychiatric social work from nursing. Psychiatric nurses, she noted, were "not equipped with this special skill and knowledge to deal with community matters," and the educational standards for social workers were higher than those for nurses. Social diagnosis, wrote Mary Richmond in a classic work in 1917, "is the attempt to arrive at as exact a definition as possible of the social situation and personality of a given client." Thus the social worker acted as an indispensable partner to the psychiatrist, providing the background data on family and community environment, without which an understanding of disease processes would be incomplete. The essential contribution of the psychiatric social worker to an understanding of mental illness, therefore, was social casework. Indeed, one individual even employed the term "sociotherapy" in order to identify the contributions of the psychiatric social worker.[29]

Slowly but surely occupational opportunities developed for those seeking a career in the new and promising field of mental health. Leading psychiatrists, as well as the NCMH, offered encouragement and often emphasized the need for collaboration. In 1919 E. E. Southard identified five groups, each of which had a role to play in the care and treatment of the mentally ill: psychiatrists, psychologists, psychiatric social workers, occupational therapists, and psychiatric nurses. The readiness to accept social workers could be seen in several developments in the field: the establishment of such facilities as the Judge Baker Foundation in Boston; a concern with psychological testing as a means of predicting adaptive and learning abilities; and the sponsorship by the NCMH of a course in 1918 to train social workers for military psychiatric hospitals which led to the founding of the Smith College Training School for Social Workers. Publication of *The Kingdom of Evils* by E. E. Southard and Mary C. Jarrett was also representative of the early efforts to define in specific terms the attributes of psychiatric social work.[30]

Before 1920 psychiatric social work was based on the assumption that a knowledge of the social environment was vital to an understanding of individual behavior. The gathering of such information by means of social casework was, in theory, the primary function of the specialty. In practice, however, social casework was fluid rather than fixed. The daily activities of social workers centered on providing assistance and aid to distressed individuals and to help them take advantage of a variety of supportive services. But after 1920 psychiatric social work became concerned less with the need to mobilize community resources and to establish links between the triad of patient, psychiatrist, and community, and more immersed in the "psychological factors underlying behavior." "There is no clear-cut division within the work of the psychiatrist and the psychiatric social worker in respect to the procuring of social information for the social diagnosis—information which may also be of use in the medical diagnosis," observed Louise C. Odencrantz in 1929. Eleven years later George M. Stevenson (Medical Director of the NCMH) in his introduction to Lois M. French's exhaustive study of psychiatric social work, wrote that the profession found "its ultimate validation in the treatment and prevention of mental diseases, in the alleviation of lesser emotional ills and behavior disturbances, and in mental hygiene education, which aims to bring about a more effective and satisfying way of living." Stevenson's comments underlined the extent to which psychiatric social workers had adopted the belief that mental illness involved an inability of individuals to adjust to their environment. The new specialty, observed French, involved greater consideration of "the mental or psychological factors in social maladjustment," and its practitioners were "bound up with the client, his family and social relationships, and with community resources that may be called upon for aid." Treatment, according to a group of psychiatric social workers who prepared a statement defining their specialty in 1925, "means the supervision of the patient in the community in such a way as to bring about a better social adjustment for him."[31]

Along with attempts to blur the distinction between psychiatry and social work went an effort to establish a professional organization of psychiatric social workers. As early as 1916 Massachusetts social workers employed in mental hospitals had founded an organization to discuss common problems. Four years later a small group of social workers, most of them associated with Boston Psychopathic Hospital, began to discuss the possibility of founding a more representative organization, not limited to a specific type of institution or geographical area. By mid-1920 the Psychiatric Social Workers Club had come into existence, with the express goal of maintaining "standards of psychiatric social work."[32]

That all seventeen charter members of the new organization were women was not surprising. Social work itself had grown out of a nineteenth-century ideal of volunteer social service in which a "friendly visitor" bridged the barriers of class, religion, and nationality in an effort to uplift the poor and downtrodden. Economic changes in American society also tended to make sex roles more rigid and to make psychiatric social work a largely female specialty. In preindustrial society men and women functioned in a setting that did not distinguish sharply between home and work. During the nineteenth century, however, economic and technological changes separated home and work; increasingly women assumed primary responsibility for overseeing the welfare of the family while the husband worked elsewhere. It was understandable, therefore, that psychiatric social workers, virtually all of whom were women before 1940, tended to define their jurisdiction in terms of the family. Such a role was compatible with more general notions about a "separate sphere" for women that had developed during the nineteenth century. Middle-class women in particular were attracted to such an occupational role; their background, education, and sex provided them with the presumed attributes necessary to maintain the integrity of the family and to engage in moral uplift and regeneration. Even after social work altered its character, it continued to attract women seeking careers outside or in addition to home and marriage. Precisely because social work emphasized disinterested ideals of service and moral uplift, it remained an occupation in which a woman could pursue a career and simultaneously realize her feminine identity.

In 1922 there was an important organizational change within the profession. The Psychiatric Social Workers Club became the Section on Psychiatric Social Work of the American Association of Hospital Social Workers. In an effort to differentiate psychiatric social work from social work, the Section in 1926 decided to function as an independent national organization and became the American Association of Psychiatric Social Workers (AAPSW). Although beset by financial problems and by a relatively small membership, the AAPSW managed to create a separate identity for its members. It did so by holding annual meetings, preparing published materials and a journal, and, above all, developing a set of qualifications and educational standards required of entry into the field. In 1926 the A.B. degree was made a qualification for membership (although a grandfather clause permitted those without the degree but with experience to remain as members). The following year a separate category of junior membership was created. Eligibility for either category required a college degree, and at least nine months of training in psychiatric social work at an approved school. Active members in addition had to have one or more years of actual experience.[33]

From the very beginning, the AAPSW hoped to foster close relationships with the APA. Collaboration between psychiatrists and psychiatric social workers would presumably benefit patients, and at the same time enable the newly emerging profession to legitimize its functions by identifying with an older and far more powerful organization. Yet beneath the surface lurked different perceptions about relationships between psychiatry and psychiatric social work. Even Southard—who pioneered in establishing a social service department at Boston Psychopathic, co-authored a classic text with Mary C. Jarrett, and generally supported psychiatric social workers in their quest for a professional identity—had reservations. "I am afraid I must confess to one at least," he wrote in an unpublished paper,

> namely, that psychiatric social work must be dominated far more than certain other branches of medico-social work, and again far more than certain other branches of social service at large, by the physician and alienist. This prejudice, if it be a prejudice, does not hesitate to concede to the trained social worker every latitude in the technique of social investigation and almost every latitude in the offering of advice and in the choice of domestic and economic steps to take in the given case. But decisions concerning medico-social therapy ... are decisions which are, in my opinion, medical decisions. Decisions concerning the relative parts played by heredity and environment in a given case, whether a case is "morbid" or "vicious," how much improved family surroundings might help a case, whether syphilis is to be suspected, whether there is an element of sex-perversion in the case, whether questionable statements of patients are best regarded as truths, lies, delusions, or mixtures of these—all these decisions and a vast number of similar ones are decisions hardly to be entrusted to such social workers as the schools have yet developed.[34]

Jessie Taft, on the other hand, had quite different perceptions. A doctoral recipient from the University of Chicago, her dissertation (published in 1916) dealt with the problem facing women who were confronted with the dualism that existed between home and workplace. Between 1915 and 1918 Taft served as director of the Social Service Department of the New York State Charities Aid Association's Mental Hygiene Committee. In 1918 she published an article on "The Limitations of the Psychiatrist." That she was aware of sex roles was evident; psychiatric social workers were always identified as females and psychiatrists as males. Initially, Taft wrote, the psychiatric social worker viewed the psychiatrist as a "god, holding in his hands the knowledge of good and evil." Within a clinical setting, on the other hand, social workers recognized the "limitations" of their fellow professionals. Psychiatrists never conceived of the patient "as a living problem." Admittedly, psychiatrists were overworked and therefore could not follow up patients after their discharge from hospitals. Nor was the psychiatrist "compelled to treat his patient as he exists in real life—a member of a family, an economic factor in industry, and a citizen of the State." Given the limitations imposed upon psychiatrists by the setting in which they functioned, they had only two alternatives. The psychiatrist either simply acted as a diagnostician, or else he had to "recognize his own limitations and endeavor to make as intelligent as possible the agent through whom, whether he likes it or not, he must ultimately act."[35]

By 1928 the AAPSW's Committee on Education and Standards was in direct contact with the APA, which shortly thereafter agreed to establish a Committee on Psychiatric Social Work. The reaction of Clarence O. Cheyney, chairman of the APA Committee on Medical Services, suggested that collaboration was more difficult to achieve in practice than in theory. How could one professional organization, he asked, establish standards for another? Nor were hospital superintendents necessarily interested in higher standards for psychiatric social workers, if only because of the inability of hospitals to pay higher salaries to better-trained workers. Would highly trained workers find satisfaction in a mental hospital? Cheyney was equally dubious about the possibility of standardizing relationships between psychiatrist and psychiatric social worker. Social workers, after all, acted in a therapeutic manner when finding jobs for patients or engaged in informal discussions and in offering advice. "I realize very well," he added, "that some social workers might be inclined to take things entirely in their hands, but it seems that such a situation could be controlled by the oversight of her work that the physician would be expected to keep." The APA Committee on Psychiatric Social Work remained primarily interested in the shortage of trained workers for state hospitals. Its members even suggested that "efficient social workers can be produced by proper guidance and training without the requirement of a college education." Such a position was hardly popular with the AAPSW, which feared the adverse consequences of reducing educational standards.[36]

During the 1930s relationships between the APA and AAPSW remained outwardly cordial, but lacked any substantive foundation. By this time the APA was moving rapidly toward board certification, and devoted relatively little attention to other groups.

The overwhelmingly female composition of the AAPSW was hardly an inducement to close collaboration, since an elevation in the status of a female-dominated profession implied a less prestigious status and a diminution in the authority of psychiatrists. Nor did the fact that a substantial number of psychiatrists were females make any great difference; these women tended to identify more with their profession than with their sex. The AAPSW, on the other hand, never lost interest in developing close collaborative relationships with the APA and in defining the role and function of psychiatric social work in more precise terms. Nevertheless, the heterogeneous nature of the new specialty proved a barrier. As late as 1937 only 13.5 percent of the membership of the AAPSW were employed in mental hospitals; the remainder were divided among such institutions as child guidance clinics (14.4 percent), educational institutions (13.0 percent), and family welfare agencies (17.8 percent). In 1931 the AAPSW's Committee on Psychiatric Social Work in Mental Hospitals noted that positions in such institutions were neither desirable nor stimulating. From time to time the APA conceded the need for trained psychiatric social workers, but there is little evidence that its rank and file were concerned with the problem. In 1938 Dr. Samuel W. Hartwell, who chaired the APA committee charged with fostering closer relationships with the AAPSW, conceded that his colleagues were "not as interested in this problem as they should be." "In other words," observed Hester B. Crutcher (Director of Social Work of the New York State Department of Mental Hygiene and an advocate of hospital psychiatric social work), "I glean that few members in the APA care whether school keeps or not." The following year the AAPSW Executive Committee endorsed continuation of the effort to foster the employment of social workers in mental hospitals "to the end that psychiatrists and psychiatric social workers may be drawn closer together rather than to be drifting apart, as seems to be the tendency now."[37]

Cooperation, nevertheless, proved elusive. By 1940 the APA and AAPSW had established a joint committee to deal with questions of mutual interest. The chasm between them was evident from the composition of each delegation. All seven representatives from the AAPSW were women. With the exception of Dr. Esther L. Richards (who headed the outpatient department at the Phipps Clinic at Hopkins for many years), all of the psychiatrists were males. Beyond a vague consensus on the need for higher educational standards for psychiatric social workers, there was little evidence of significant substantive agreement.[38]

Despite its failure to achieve meaningful recognition from the APA, the AAPSW continued its quest during the 1930s to elevate psychiatric social work and to define its attributes in order to give it professional status. In 1931 it commenced a long-term trend study by Lois Meredith French to clarify "the activities and opinions of the members," which in turn would "contribute definitely to a clarification of the diverse developments in psychiatric social work and to a crystallization of certain agreements and disagreements which should result in an increase 'in the established knowledge regarding our problems and distinctive procedures.'" The Association also rejected an offer of Dr. Lawson Lowrey to designate the *American Journal of Orthopsychiatry* as its offical organ; it decided instead to convert its *Quarterly News Letter*, issued from 1926 to 1930, into a formal quarterly journal. By the mid-1930s the Association had appointed a committee to formulate a curriculum for psychiatric social work. The curriculum adopted in 1939 called for a formal course of study that included instruction in the development of personality, clinical psychiatry, problems of personal and social adjustment in children, the social implications of health and disease, clinical significance of mental measurement, as well as fieldwork in psychiatric hospitals and clinics.[39]

Psychiatric social workers between 1926 and 1940 also devoted considerable energy to trying to define in authoritative terms the nature of their specialty and thereby to achieve a measure of professional recognition. The Association *News-Letter* published a large number of articles on the significance and role of psychiatric social work. Members also sought to identify themselves with the relatively new and seemingly popular mental hygiene movement. In 1929 *Mental Hygiene* devoted an issue to the young specialty; that same year Lee R. Porter and Marion E. Kenworthy published their study on *Mental Hygiene and Social Work*. Psychiatric social work, observed Lois French eleven years later, "represents social work practiced in connection with psychiatry and mental hygiene in organizations that have for their primary purpose the study, treatment, and prevention of mental and nervous disorders."[40]

Despite the outpouring of published materials, psychiatric social work remained a marginal specialty before 1940. The doubts expressed by Abraham Flexner in a famous address before the

NCCC in 1915 ("Is Social Work a Profession?") remained as compelling as ever. Flexner had identified six criteria that characterized a profession. Professions, he noted, "involve essentially intellectual operations with large individual responsibility; they derive their raw material from science and learning; this material they work up to a practical and definite end; they possess an educationally communicable technique; they tend to self-organization; they are becoming increasingly altruistic in motivation." In his eyes medicine clearly fulfilled these requirements. The same, however, was not true of social work. The specialty was less a definite field than "an aspect of work in many fields." Indeed, social work lacked "specificity in aim" and suffered from "excessive facility in speech and in action." In practice the social worker was a "mediator" who was required to invoke the assistance of others.[41]

Although Flexner had directed his comments to social work generally, they were equally applicable to psychiatric social work. Before 1940 the specialty was unable to move beyond the generalizations about the relationship between an individual's social (and especially family) environment and the onset of mental disease. The absence of a specific occupational focus and the rejection of a service function also proved impediments to dreams of gaining professional status and recognition. In her presidential address in 1930, Mildred C. Scoville conceded "the present nebulous state of psychiatric social work," but expressed the hope that it was "only a temporary phase representing a necessary process through which the profession must evolve in order, first of all, to know itself and its potentialities and, secondly, to realize and achieve its proper adjustment within the entire field of social work." The determined effort of the specialty to identify itself with psychiatry and mental hygiene did not alter its marginal role, given the equally vague nature of mental hygiene. That psychiatric social work remained an overwhelmingly female-dominated occupation proved an additional liability, given the low status accorded such occupations.[42]

Most significant, if least recognized, was the fact that psychiatric social work, disclaimers to the contrary, all but ignored the character of the institutionalized mentally ill population or their specific needs. An emphasis on the social etiology of mental illness was attractive in theory, but had little or no relevance to those already in hospitals. There is little evidence to suggest that psychiatric social workers were even aware of the growing mass of statistical data delineating the character of the institutionalized population; the outlook of its members was conditioned by internal needs and perceptions. Although its members had achieved a small measure of recognition by 1940, as a group they remained in a distinctly subordinate position to psychiatrists.

Psychiatric social workers were not alone in their efforts to create a professional self-identity. Both within and without mental hospitals a variety of groups pursued a similar course, trying to legitimize their specific role in the rapidly burgeoning mental health field. Indeed, the very process of professionalization contained an internal stimulus. As one group developed a common identity and moved in an exclusionary direction, others in related occupations tended to examine their own roles. Common interests, in turn, helped to forge a new consciousness and promoted the creation of organizations that were perceived as vehicles for elevating standards, thereby presumably benefitting patients as well as elevating the status of practitioners. Internally, the process of differentiation and professionalization stimulated friction, if only because of the relative inequality of the various groups involved.

Psychiatric nursing, of course, was an example of a specialty that was not especially successful in creating a specific self-identity. This was so partly because of the generalized nature of the work, the inability to define a body of data whose mastery would become a precondition for a specialty, and the female nature of nursing. Occupational therapists, on the other hand, were somewhat more successful in creating an organization, partly because the lead was taken by male psychiatrists who dominated the organization, and thus conferred upon it a certain legitimacy that did not threaten the dominance of psychiatry.

Occupational therapy was by no means a new idea. Nineteenth-century hospital superintendents had always recognized that meaningful labor and recreation had a beneficial impact upon institutionalized patients. They made no effort, however, to create a new specialty; common sense and a division of labor along sex lines were deemed sufficient. Their most pressing problem was the lack of adequate opportunities and facilities. After 1900, on the other hand, there was a growing interest in what became known as "invalid therapy"—a term used by Susan E. Tracy in her *Studies in Invalid Therapy* (1910). In 1911 Tracy offered a course on the subject at the Massachusetts General Hospital; other hospitals as well as Teachers' College at Columbia University soon followed suit. Even earlier Meyer had become interested in the possibilities of occupational therapy because of his growing concern with the concept of habit formation. When the Phipps Psychiatric Clinic opened in 1913 he hired Eleanor Clarke Slagle to organize a program. Slagle had been introduced to occupational therapy by Julia Lathrop, a close friend of Meyer who played a leading role in public affairs in Illinois. On her own, Slagle took a course on "invalid occupation" in 1908 offered by the Chicago School of Civics and Philanthropy (later the school of social work at the University of Chicago). Subsequently she became a leading figure in the field, and along with George Edward Barton and Dr. William R. Dunton, Jr., of the Sheppard and Enoch Pratt Hospital in Maryland, helped to found a national organization.[43]

After 1914 Barton initiated a movement to found a national organization. He wanted to exclude individuals concerned merely with "arts and crafts" and "largely without any knowledge of medicine whatever," and urged that such terms as "occupation workers" be dropped in favor of a designation that included "therapeutics." "I shall insist always," he wrote to Dunton in 1916, "that this be the matter of prime importance, both from my interest in the development of a new line of medicine, and from my horrid vision as a sociologist of what may occur if therapeutics is forgotten." His efforts led to the founding of the National Society for the Promotion of Occupational Therapy in 1917—an organization later renamed the American Occupational Therapy Association. The experiences of World War I stimulated interest in rehabilitation generally, and by 1922 the organization had begun publication of the *Archives of Occupational Therapy*, which three years later became *Occupational Therapy and Rehabilitation*. The organization was instrumental in formulating standards for training, and eventually established a national register for qualified therapists. At the same time a number of states established departments to supervise occupational therapy, New York being the most prominent.[44]

When Dr. C. Floyd Haviland became Commissioner of the New York State Hospital Commission in 1921, one of his first acts was to establish the position of Director of Occupational Therapy and to appoint Slagle to fill the vacancy in 1922. Under her direction the percentage of patients receiving occupational treatment in the state's public hospitals rose from 4.8 percent in 1922 to 31.9 percent in 1927. Between 1923 and 1936 the number of occupational therapists employed in public hospitals rose from 54 to 357. Those associated with the state's hospitals emphasized the benefits associated with occupational therapy even in the absence of any controlled studies. Benjamin Malzberg—one of the earliest and most important students of psychiatric epidemiology—conceded in 1929 that "a better measure of the outcome" was needed, even though he believed that the "record of accomplishment is an enviable one."[45]

Like psychiatric social work, occupational therapy was an overwhelmingly female occupation. In 1932, for example, 419 persons were qualified by virtue of their education and experience to be listed in the main register of the American Occupational Therapy Association. Of these, no less than 408 were women. Nevertheless, males played a disproportionately important organizational role. The president and vice president were males; Slagle, the only female official, was secretary-treasurer. Of fifteen members on the Board of Management, six were men. The relative dominance of males thus gave to the young specialty a greater degree of legitimacy than it might have otherwise possessed. Occupational therapy also did not develop independently of psychiatry. Dr. William R. Dunton, Jr., was one of the founders of the Association, served as its president, and edited *Occupational Therapy and Rehabilitation* for many years. Occupational therapists, moreover, never attempted to define their functions in a manner that brought them into conflict with psychiatrists. Although borrowing psychiatric explanations, occupational therapy remained an applied specialty and was concerned largely with technique rather than with substantive isssues related to mental illness. Its growth and development, therefore, were relatively noncontroversial and did not pose any significant threat to psychiatric authority.[46]

Psychiatric social work and occupational therapy had at least one common denominator; both were accepted as legitimate parts of the mental health professions even though there may have been conflict over their precise roles. Other specialties had their origins outside medicine, but in a later stage of development the activities of their members began to intrude upon the mentally ill. This was particularly true of psychology, a discipline with roots in philosophy rather than in medicine. During the latter part of the nineteenth century a "new" psychology emerged that defined its character in terms of modern science. In the United States the new psychology quickly found a place in higher education—a field which increasingly organized its institutions along disciplinary lines that reflected the commitment to the scientific study of the individual and the group. Experimental psychology was followed by applied or clinical psychology, which grew out of the efforts to measure mental abilities by standardized testing.

As long as psychology remained a research-oriented academic discipline, there was little conflict with psychiatry. Such figures as Edward Cowles, August Hoch, William A. White, and Adolf Meyer were all receptive to psychological research and were themselves familiar with the leading psychologists in Europe and America. Shortly after assuming the superintendency of St. Elizabeths, White began to consider the possibility of creating a department of psychology. Meyer had close contacts with such figures as Edward B. Titchener, and had engaged in a long correspondence with him after both had attended the famous Clark University conference in 1909 that brought Freud on his only visit to the United States. When planning for the opening of the Phipps Clinic at Hopkins, Meyer expressed the hope that psychology and philosophy might be separated in order that the former could be made "part of the biological sciences and utilizable as a supplement of the courses of physiology and medicine." Meyer raised the possibility of developing a psychology department under John B. Watson that could offer "courses in psychology of a type less doctrinaire than philosophy-bred psychology has been." In 1914 Meyer collaborated with Watson and Knight Dunlap in offering a course in psychology for medical students. The venture, however, was not especially successful. The previous year Dr. E. Stanley Abbot gave a paper at the AMPA urging that courses in psychobiology be incorporated in the medical curriculum.[47]

In less than a decade, however, evidence of friction between psychiatry and psychology was visible. New occupational opportunities for psychologists in clinics and schools had been stimulated by the use of intelligence tests as screening devices for determining fitness for military service during World War I; the mental hygiene movement and the rise of industrial psychology created still other career possibilities. Such developments had the potential for conflict, even though the actual number of applied or clinical psychologists during the 1920s was small. Psychiatrists, who were also moving into positions outside mental hospitals, increasingly perceived of psychologists as rivals, especially when the latter appeared to be assuming therapeutic functions. In 1920 and 1921 Dr. Thomas H. Haines of the NCMH undercut the efforts of J.E.W. Wallin to persuade the Missouri legislature to establish a Bureau of Mental Defectives. Wallin believed that the opposition to his plan was but another manifestation of the underlying hostility of psychiatrists toward psychology. Only four years earlier Dr. Charles L. Dana told his colleagues at the New York Psychiatrical Society that it was their "function and duty to inquire whether psychology is filling a need in all these advancing lines; whether it is doing its work wisely, and whether it requires, or would be helped by, guidance and cooperation from those trained to understand and manage human bodies as well as human minds; whether, in fine, this applied and academic psychology is a good thing, or a bad thing, or being something of each is, as St. Chrysostom said of women, simply 'a desirable calamity.' " Dana's use of a sexual image was more than mere rhetoric; during the 1920s perhaps half or more of those identified as applied psychologists were female. The conflict between the two groups, therefore, transcended professional issues and involved male-female relationships as well.[48]

Growing tensions led the young but influential National Research Council to sponsor a conference in the spring of 1921 on the relations of psychiatry and psychology. Chaired by Clark Wissler, the meeting brought together prominent individuals and organizational representatives from both specialties. The very issues discussed by the participants revealed broad-ranging differences. How was it possible to differentiate medical, psychological, social, and educational problems? If psychologists dealt with the control of behavior, how could they be distinguished from physicians? Should psychologists be permitted to practice for fees, and should they be certified and licensed? What constituted adequate training? How could psychiatry and psychology cooperate? Should the term "clinical" be dropped from the language of psychology because it implied a medical problem?

In a written statement to the participants, Robert S. Woodworth, the eminent psychologist, described the natural rivalry of psychiatry and psychology, which in turn led to offensive behavior by both.

The offensive behavior of which psychologists are guilty consists in a crowding in upon the field of the psychiatrist, in aping the medical profession, and treading on the sensitive medical toes. The offense of the psychiatrist consists in staking out, on paper, an exclusive claim to a large unoccupied domain, and insisting that the psychologist shall only work there in subordination to himself.

The remainder of Woodworth's statement was conciliatory; he suggested that psychologists cease using the term "diagnosis," on the grounds that it was a medical term, and that they should not presume to trespass on medical grounds. Nor was "treatment" an appropriate term, since psychologists were dealing with people who were not ill but who had certain problems. His observation that feeblemindedness and neuroses did not constitute illnesses, however, led one physician to insist that such a statement demonstrated "peculiar ignorance and lack of grasp of the situation." David Mitchell, a psychologist, observed that the word "medical" had been used in such an "all-inclusive" manner that there was "a claim being made which is difficult to support." Subsequent discussions on certification, licensing, and training indicated that there was little common ground between psychiatry and psychology. The disagreement proved so basic that the conference was unable to agree on a set of general resolutions; the participants consented to circulate a transcript of their deliberations. Years later Carl E. Seashore, a highly regarded psychologist, recalled that the meeting had "every element of an intensive war. Both sides were contesting for 'living space.' Each considered the other an intruder."[49]

Admittedly, there were instances of collaboration. Many psychologists and psychiatrists collaborated at child guidance clinics with minimal friction. In 1927 Worcester State Hospital began a famous research project on schizophrenia under the general direction of Roy G. Hoskins (whose specialty was endocrinology) that brought together a number of medical specialties as well as experimental and clinical psychologists, including David Shakow. President Herbert Hoover's White House Conference on Child Health and Protection included a Subcommittee on Psychology and Psychiatry that sought to minimize differences. Nevertheless, long-standing hostilities persisted. Psychologists, insisted the editor of the AMA's *Archives of Neurology and Psychiatry*, were "attempting to grab the whole field." The consensus of those physicians at the fourth Conference on Psychiatric Education in 1936 was that psychologists should not deal with clinical problems unless they had been trained in medicine as well. "My personal experiences with clinical psychologists have been only pleasant, I must say," Eugen Kahn of the Yale School of Medicine observed, "but I have the feeling that there are definite tendencies, at least on the part of some clinical psychologists, toward dealing with patients. I do not like it at all. If the clinical psychologist is dealing with patients, he should do so under some control by a medical man, say the psychiatrist. I don't mean to say that the clinical psychologists couldn't do some educational work, but I do think therapy ought not to be in the domain of the clinical psychologist."[50]

As the boundaries of psychiatry breached the walls of the traditional mental hospital, the specialty also began to lose some of the unity that had characterized its early history. By the 1920s a younger group began to define what they called "social psychiatry." In doing so they posed an implicit challenge to their institutional colleagues. In 1924 the American Orthopsychiatric Association came into being. At the first meeting V. V. Anderson, chairman of the organizing committee, berated some of his more traditionally-inclined colleagues.

> To the institutional psychiatrist the field is limited to the frank pathology of the psychopathic hospital, nor do they ("the old school psychiatrists") recognize those psychiatrists who are dealing with social problems primarily, and whose work is always coordinated with psychologists and social workers. It is necessary to raise the status and secure recognition for the "social" psychiatrists.

His words were echoed by others, including Herman M. Adler, Thomas W. Salmon, Bernard Glueck, and Karl Menninger. Indeed, William Healy insisted that the importance of the sociological element required a more "varied" membership. Eight years later Dr. David M. Levy of the New York Institute for Child Guidance, in his presidential address before the Association, alluded to the "revolution" that had taken place in psychiatry and spoke approvingly of the "alliance with the clinical psychologist and the social worker." The new specialty, he added in terms that implied little regret, "will be assailed by a host of contenders from without and within the field of psychiatry. Within the field there are the traditional psychiatrists of the right wing who disown us for leaving the hospital, and others who would push us further into the left and compel us to pursue our methods only along one line." Levy concluded by calling upon his colleagues to "remain sensitive to contributions in the field from all sources."[51]

III

As American psychiatrists reshaped their specialty by cutting themselves loose from their nineteenth-century institutional origins, they helped to foster conditions that stimulated the growth and development of other occupational groups concerned with the mentally ill. Paradoxically, the result was tension and conflict rather than harmony and cooperation. By the 1920s many psychiatrists found themselves threatened as challenges to their dominance, if not to their legitimacy, mounted. The manner in which they would respond to new circumstances would play a significant role in future decades and influence nor only their own careers, but the lives of their institutionalized patients as well.

CHAPTER TEN

The Psychiatric Response

PERSUADED OF THE legitimacy of their authority but fearful of challenges both within and without medicine, psychiatrists began to ponder seriously the future of their specialty in the 1920s and 1930s. Compounding their anxieties was the fact that their medical brethren held them in low esteem and often distinguished between scientific medicine and psychiatry. Arlie W. Bock, an internist at the Harvard Medical School who was sympathetic toward psychiatry, observed in 1933 that psychiatrists had "managed so successfully to shroud their art in mystic terminology that we have often regarded them in the light of mesmerists, if not, at times, most impractical people. Just what goes on behind their closed office doors has seemed so evanescent to most practitioners as to border on the ludicrous." Similarly, the Committee on the Costs of Medical Care, which undertook a comprehensive study of American medical care between 1927 and 1932, noted that psychiatry was among the lowest paid of the specialties. In its survey in 1931, the Committee found that the average gross income of specialists was $16,304. Neuropsychiatry, on the other hand, ranked near the bottom with a figure of $10,008; the only lower paying specialties were anaesthesia and physical therapy. The highest paying specialty, pathology, had an average gross income of $26,090.[1]

Equally revealing was the attitude of officials at the Rockefeller Foundation, which played a crucial role in supporting the medical and biological sciences before World War II. When Dr. Frankwood E. Williams sent Edwin R. Embree a pamphlet, the latter (who served as director of the Division of Studies) responded that although he was "more interested . . . in psychology and psychiatry than any other subject," he was "less satisfied or less convinced by discussions of given phases of subject matter in these fields than in physics, chemistry, or other aspects of biology." By the 1920s the Foundation was seeking to reduce its financial commitment to the NCMH, through which it funneled much of its support for psychiatric activities. Indeed, Embree always drew a distinction between biological medicine and psychiatry. Alan Gregg, who became director of the newly reorganized Division of Medical Sciences in 1931, also lacked faith in psychiatry, and by 1939 succeeded in terminating Rockefeller support of the general activities of the NCMH.[2]

Threatened by the rise of new occupational groups and lacking a firm base within orthodox medicine, psychiatrists began to cast about for new policies that would preserve their authority and reverse the seeming decline in their status. In 1921 they reorganized the AMPA, which became the American Psychiatric Association. In the succeeding two decades the APA attempted to reshape psychiatric education and gain a secure position within medical schools, in the hope of placing the specialty on a more secure foundation. Ultimately its efforts led to the creation of the American Board of Psychiatry and Neurology in 1934. Taken together, these developments helped to transform the structure of psychiatry by inadvertently reducing the attractiveness and significance of institutional practice. The change influenced not only the careers of psychiatrists, but the lives of hundreds of thousands of institutionalized patients as well.

I

For most psychiatrists their seemingly marginal status within medicine stood in sharp contrast to the position of their nineteenth-century predecessors. In 1853 the relatively young AMA had attempted to induce the AMSAII to affiliate. The latter rebuffed the former, largely because its members, who enjoyed a superior status and a higher income, had little to gain from such a merger. As late as 1901 Dr. Carlos Macdonald, former president of the New York State Commission in Lunacy, could point to the financial advantages of employment in a mental hospital. In addition to a salary of $3,500 to $4,500 in New York, a superintendent received benefits equal to $10,000 or $12,000 per year— an income that only the most successful practitioners could hope to equal or exceed. Even assistant physicians did well; their salaries, in addition to maintenance for themselves and their family, exceeded the average for medicine as a whole.[3]

After 1900, however, the situation began to change. The identification of medicine with science and technology, and the reorganization of medical education, combined to elevate the status of physicians. The eventual decline in the relative number of physicians that followed the closing of many medical schools in the early years of the twentieth century only hastened the process. As the prestige of medicine rose, that of psychiatry declined. Mobility diminished as the rising number of assistant physicians exceeded the growth in the number of mental hospitals, thus making it more difficult to attain a superintendency. The seeming backwardness, if not obsolescence, of psychiatry—as compared with scientific medicine—also hastened the specialty's decline. When Richard Dewey asked White to recommend an individual for the position of first assistant in 1906, White declined. "Men who have the sort of ability that you desire either do not want to go into institution work or else are already well provided for." In 1911 the quarterly conference of state hospital superintendents and other officials in New York debated their growing inability to attract young medical graduates to a career in institutional psychiatry, despite the very real advantages of employment in New York's public hospitals as compared with those in other states. In future years such complaints became common nationally. This was particularly true when postwar inflation hurt institutional salaries. At the same time young physicians were turning away from hospital employment, where working conditions and medical practice appeared to suffer as compared with noninstitutional alternatives.[4] Moreover, the AMPA, which had been founded in 1844 and for decades remained the sole organizational representative of psychiatry, began to find its authority eroded as other organizations and journals directly or tangentially related to psychiatry began to proliferate.

Under such circumstances it was not surprising that psychiatrists were receptive to new policies. The change in the name of their professional organization was symbolic; in 1921 the American Medico-Psychological Association became the American Psychiatric Association. Similarly, the venerable *American Journal of Insanity* was renamed the *American Journal of Psychiatry*. In 1925 White, who had begun his career in a mental hospital and risen to the superintendency of St. Elizabeths Hospital, paid homage to the "old-fashioned hospital superintendent" in his presidential address. But he then went on to call for far-reaching changes that would transform the structure and functions of the APA along the lines of the now successful and powerful AMA. Seven years later William L. Russell echoed the words of his predecessor. "The Association," he concluded in his presidential address, "may, perhaps, have reached a parting of the ways. It is no longer the only national organization in the field of psychiatry. It may, therefore, decide to continue, and endeavor to develop further, its organized activities in regard to hospitals and other forms of psychiatric service, or it may decide to leave these to other organizations, and to devote itself exclusively to discussions of the problems of clinical, scientific, and educational psychiatry." Although Russell had always been identified with institutional psychiatry, his preference was clearly for change. "I am unable to believe," he added, "that the broader way will not be chosen." Russell's hopes were soon realized. The APA had already begun a sustained period of organizational growth and elaboration that would reflect the fact that a growing proportion of its members were no longer affiliated with public mental hospitals.[5]

II

Much more significant than the reorganization of the APA was the effort to enhance the training and education of psychiatrists through professional certification. Board certification, of course, was defended as a necessary step to upgrade the qualifications of psychiatrists and to protect the public against unqualified practitioners. Although both elements played a major role, the context within which the American Board of Psychiatry and Neurology came into existence in 1934 was somewhat far more complex. Indeed, an analysis of the events leading to its creation suggests that a generalized fear that other medical and nonmedical specialties were slowly intruding upon the jurisdiction of psychiatrists also played an important part. Such fears stimulated an effort to define in more precise terms the attributes of a psychiatrist and the training that was required.

Before 1900 there was virtually no effort to provide systematic instruction in psychiatry at the hundreds of medical schools then in existence. On occasion such individuals as Pliny Earle, Isaac Ray, and William A. Hammond offered a series of lectures on insanity, but these were never incorporated into existing medical curricula. That formal educational requirements were for the most part absent mattered but little. For much of the nineteenth century the M.D. degree carried little significance. More important, psychiatry was a specialty in which informal controls were effective. Physicians seeking to enter the specialty had to serve a long apprenticeship in a mental hospital. An informal network composed of superintendents and prominent lay figures such as

Dorothea L. Dix played an important role in recruitment and advancement, even though strictly political appointments were by no means absent. Consequently, the caliber of individuals who became superintendents remained above that of the medical profession generally.[6]

By the 1880s and 1890s, on the other hand, institutional psychiatry was under attack from various quarters and its status within medicine had begun to decline. Equally significant, the transformation of medical education between 1870 and 1920 for the most part excluded psychiatry. In 1913 Dr. Charles W. Burr (Professor of Mental Diseases at the University of Pennsylvania) published an article in the *Journal of the American Medical Association* highly critical of the existing state of affairs. "I wish at the outset to make several confessions," he observed.

> First, I have never personally known a genius who devoted himself to teaching psychiatry. Second, psychiatry is the most backward of all the sciences fundamental to the art of medicine. Third, the time devoted to mental diseases in medical schools is too short to teach anything beyond the alphabet. Fourth, I have not yet been convinced that the study of formal psychology throws any light on psychiatry.[7]

Burr's criticisms were by no means inaccurate. When Dr. D. W. Roberts, a physician on the staff of the State Hospital for Nervous Diseases, was elected professor of nervous and mental diseases at the University of Arkansas Medical Department in 1915, he wrote to White requesting a list of books and articles in order to help in the preparation of lectures. Several surveys confirmed the belief that psychiatric education was in a dismal state. Nor was there any evidence of improvement in subsequent years. In its final report in 1932, the influential Commission on Medical Education, organized in 1925 by the Association of American Medical Colleges to study education and licensure, noted that too many "untrained workers" dealt with nervous and mental disorders. "Probably in no field of health work is there so much dangerous faddism," added the Commission as it urged that investigative programs in psychiatry "be closely correlated with those in general medicine, pediatrics, neurology, and other departments." A comparable study by Ralph A. Noble for the NCMH was equally critical of medical schools, few of which provided their students with an adequate introduction to the specialty of psychiatry. In 80 percent of such schools psychiatric teaching amounted "to little more than a gesture"; confusion was characteristic. Noble was equally critical of postgraduate education in psychiatry, and raised the possibility of board certification under the aegis of the APA rather than of the AMA.[8]

During the 1920s interest in psychiatric education mounted. Thomas W. Salmon and the NCMH began to push for change. Between 1924 and 1931 the NCMH, with support from the Rockefeller Foundation, developed a fellowship program for individuals in psychiatry, psychiatric social work, and clinical psychology. More than 80 percent of the fellows were drawn from medicine. In 1928 Meyer, in his presidential address at the APA, endorsed more effective and formal training. The following year the APA Committee on Medical Services attempted to arrive at "a definition of the qualifications, limitations, and experience" necessary for the practice of psychiatry. Edward A. Strecker, its chairman, suggested the establishment of an independent American College of Psychiatry, which would emulate the accrediting functions of a body like the American College of Surgeons. At about the same time the APA and ANA began joint consideration of the problem of granting adequate recognition to training in both specialties. In this endeavor, the ubiquitous Meyer played a key role. Interest in the problem was evident; Louis Casamajor proposed the creation of a specialty board composed of elected or appointed members drawn from both organizations.[9]

The APA's interest in board certification was not in any sense unique, but rather followed developments in other medical specialties. By the early twentieth century the changes within medical science had given rise to novel problems. How could individuals pay for the increasingly high costs of medical care? How should medical services be organized, given the growing complexity of individual components? Was it desirable or possible to rationalize a system in which generalists and specialists were often adversaries? What were the precise functions of specialists, as compared with generalists? Who was to define the nature of such functions. Above all, how could the varied specialties be coordinated and regulated?

During the 1920s American medicine was grappling with all these puzzling problems. By this time the AMA had become a powerful political organization representing the interests of practicing physicians; its Council on Medical Education and Hospitals played a key role in defining medical curricula and approving residencies. The AMA might have been the vehicle to rationalize the competing interests of generalists and specialists and to develop a more organized and coherent system for the delivery of medical services. In practice, however, it faced existing specialty organizations and boards not eager to come under its jurisdiction. An effort to use state licensing boards to certify specialist training further complicated matters.

Within medicine there was general agreement on the need for a central (but private) organization to oversee the growth of specialty boards. In 1933 a new Advisory Board for Medical Specialties was created by existing and emerging specialty groups. The following year the new Board and the AMA's Council on Medical Education and Hospitals adopted a compromise that defined common standards for new specialty boards and gave both the AMA and the various national specialty associations a role. With the adoption of such standards the number of specialty boards proliferated rapidly. Before 1934 only six specialties had established organized certification mechanisms. In 1934 alone four new boards came into existence; in the succeeding six years seven more were founded.[10]

Given the divisions among physicians and the dispersal of authority, it was not surprising that specialty boards reflected the interests and concerns of their constituents; specialty certification was generally not considered within the larger context of the organization and delivery of medical services. The movement toward board certification in psychiatry illustrates how internal perceptions rather than patient needs shaped the structure and focus of a specialty.

That psychiatry was moving toward certification was surprising, if only because the trend toward specialization was strongest in fields with a surgical bent. Nevertheless, the transitional nature of psychiatry and its position as the oldest organized specialty made its members somewhat more sensitive to their ambiguous relationship with medicine. Board certification was given momentum when the AMA adopted several seemingly innocuous resolutions at its annual meetings in 1930 introduced by Dr. Tom B. Throckmorton, a delegate from the AMA Section on Nervous and Mental Diseases and a former member of the APA. The first alluded to the lack of involvement of the AMA in the problems arising out of mental disease; it authorized the creation of a special committee to launch an investigation and to report back to the Board of Trustees on the manner in which the organization could contribute to solutions. The second resolution was more important and authorized the AMA's Council on Medical Education and Hospitals "to make a thorough investigation of all hospitals caring for mental patients."[11]

Shortly thereafter, the AMA's Council on Medical Education and Hospitals employed John M. Grimes, a young physician with no prior training in psychiatry, to undertake a study of American mental hospitals. The Council arranged for sessions at its annual meeting in 1931 to deal with the survey of mental hospitals, mental hygiene, and the teaching of psychiatry. Following the adoption of another resolution at the AMA convention in 1931, the Council also began to consider taking a greater role in certifying physicians with bona fide training in a specialty, as compared with "self-constituted 'specialists.'" Throckmorton wanted the National Board of Medical Examiners, with the cooperation of the AMA's Section on Nervous and Mental Diseases, to consider establishing standards in neurology and psychiatry. At the same time the Medical Society of New Jersey was discussing the establishment of committees to accredit specialty practice.[12]

The initial reaction to these developments within the APA itself was relatively muted. Meyer agreed to participate in the Council's annual meeting in 1931. When Grimes visited the Phipps Clinic in January of that year, there was no evidence of friction. Indeed, some informal cooperation was evident. Following the convention in 1930, the AMA trustees appointed a special Committee on Mental Hygiene composed of a representative group of psychiatrists. The Council promptly asked the group to serve as an "Advisory Committee" to Grimes. By then Grimes was well along in his study. During 1931 he had prepared and mailed a questionnaire to 561 hospitals treating nervous and mental patients. By early 1932 about three-quarters of the questionnaires had been returned. He had, in addition, visited 353 institutions to gather further information. Grimes's preliminary report in February 1932 was illuminating. The Veterans Administration hospitals, he noted, provided "good custodial and therapeutic care." In public hospitals, on the other hand, overcrowding was the rule and personnel was "admittedly inadequate, attendants being both too few and too incapable, and the medical staff being greatly undermanned." Although Grimes denied that either he or the Council was "sitting in judgment," his report was hardly an unqualified endorsement of existing conditions.[13]

At the same time the movement within the APA to move toward board certification was gaining momentum. Following the recommendation in 1929 of the Committee on Medical Services, the APA appointed another committee composed of Meyer, George H. Kirby, and Edward A. Strecker to work out plans to define the qualifications and training necessary for psychiatric specialization. This group, in turn, requested Franklin G. Ebaugh to prepare an outline for board certification. The APA's Committee on Graduate Education in Psychiatry, chaired by Meyer, urged caution; specialty diplomas ought not to be a license or a condition of admission to the Association, but rather a recognition of work done and a standard attained. At about the same time the NCMH established a Division of Psychiatric Education for which it obtained funding from the Commonwealth Fund, the New York Foundation, and the American Foundation for Mental Hygiene. Ralph Noble was appointed director and Ebaugh associate director. In September 1931 the first meeting of the Division's Advisory Committee was held in New York. Six months earlier Ebaugh's outline had been published in the *American Journal of Psychiatry* in hopes that it might serve as the basis of discussions at the forthcoming APA meeting.

Beneath the surface, however, there was considerable unease. The responses to Ebaugh's draft proposal even before it was published revealed some deep divisions. There was, for example, no agreement on the relationship between psychiatry and neurology, even though Ebaugh preferred a board limited to psychiatry. More importantly, a number of prominent figures feared that the AMA might usurp prerogatives that rightfully belonged to the APA. "Our association," Edward N. Brush (editor of the *American Journal of Psychiatry*) wrote to Ebaugh, "is the oldest National body in the Country. It is the only one devoted to Psychiatry in all its relations, and in its hands alone, I feel, should be left the consummation and regulation of this very laudable project." Brush's comments revealed the intensity of the struggle within medicine between the generalists and specialists, a struggle which had begun in the late nineteenth century and reached a climax during the 1930s. The issues involved were both broad and complex, and included the manner in which medical care would be organized and which group would control specialization. Sentiment against specialization within the AMA remained strong. At the meeting of the AMA's Council on Medical Education and Hospitals in early 1933, Dr. Ray Lyman Wilbur—who had served as dean of the Stanford medical school, president of Stanford University, president of the AMA, and Secretary of the Interior in the Hoover administration—was the spokesman for a group that distrusted the judgment of specialty societies and desired some form of external control. "The minute we get into the hands of special societies and they tell us what to do in the medical profession," he noted, "we have lost the opportunity to grow in American Medicine." Within this framework, the APA was seeking the right to control its own destiny.[14]

During 1931 and 1932 a number of other leading figures in the APA developed misgivings about the AMA investigation. James V. May suggested that hostility toward White might have played a role. In a characteristically gentle manner, White expressed the hope that even though Grimes was not a psychiatrist, he would nevertheless "be free from prejudice and have an open-minded attitude and one capable of assimilating facts. Sometime picking a man from outside of a group produces unexpectedly good results. Let us hope for the best." One issue that was raised proved troublesome; should the APA cooperate with the AMA in board certification as well as in the latter's investigation of mental hospitals? This question was made even more irksome by the lack of clarity manifested by Dr. William B. Cutter, Secretary of the Council on Medical Education and Hospitals. Cutter endorsed close cooperation with the psychiatric Advisory Committee, but hesitated to offer the APA representation on the Council. Ultimately the APA Executive Committee decided against attending a meeting in February 1932 until it knew "more definitely just what the objectives of the AMA are in regard to hospitals."[15]

Even on the issue of cooperation with the AMA there was no clear consensus. Meyer favored such cooperation, but insisted that a "conservative and experienced" individual represent the APA. William L. Russell, however, preferred that the APA remain "the principal agency in shaping the standards and policies of the hospitals." Russell was especially critical of Grimes, who allegedly had stated that there would be "a number of empty wards in the state hospitals" following completion of his own investigation. James V. May, the new president of the APA, shared Russell's views and believed that the absence of qualified psychiatrists in the AMA posed a serious threat to the APA. H. Douglas Singer, on the other hand, preferred a cooperative stance, a view he shared with White. Distressed at the course of events, White nevertheless believed that "we now have to deal with things as they are in the best way we can." He urged his colleagues to cooperate with the AMA in order to retain some influence on the final outcome.[16]

Slowly but surely the attitude of a number of leading APA figures toward the AMA grew more hostile. There was relatively little disagreement on the proposition that the APA should play a dominant role in all matters pertaining to mental illness. The differences concerned the appropriate tactics to be employed to gain such ends. Singer, a member of the Advisory Committee and the editorial board of the AMA's *Archives of Neurology and Psychiatry*, believed that the AMA had a legitimate role to play because psychiatry was part of medicine, but he also felt that the survey should be supervised by psychiatrists. George M. Kline, Commissioner of the Massachusetts Department of Mental Diseases, was opposed to the AMA investigation and questioned the qualifications of Grimes. The most intense opposition came from May, who took every opportunity—private and public—to attack the AMA. His presidential address at the APA meetings in the spring of 1933 involved a denunciation of a variety of groups claiming jurisdiction over mental illness. "It is quite obvious," he told his colleagues in blunt language,

> that measures of some kind will eventually be adopted either by the American Medical Association, the state medical societies, the National Board of Medical Examiners, or all of these organizations, for the qualification of specialists in the various branches of medicine, including our own, unless this Association decides to qualify candidates for specialization in the field of psychiatry, and insists upon a recognition of its authority to take such action. . . .
>
> It will at least be conceded, I think, that if we are to maintain a position of supremacy in our own field we must establish standards fully equivalent to those already erected by the surgeons, internists, opthalmologists, otolaryngologists, obstetricians and gynecologists, dermatologists, and pediatrists.

White, on the other hand, did not believe that the AMA was following a course "in which they consciously intended to be vicious or destructive to the interests of the mental hospitals," and he urged a policy of cooperation in order to preserve the ability of the APA to influence events.[17]

The intense resistance of members of the APA probably induced the AMA to curtail its activities. In February, 1933, Grimes presented a preliminary report to the Council on Medical Education and Hospitals, which was to be transmitted to the delegates at the June meeting. White, who had been sent a copy, was critical of parts of it. When the report was presented to the delegates at the June meeting of the AMA, much of the information secured by personal visitations had been deleted. Grimes subsequently described this action as a "suppression of the truth." The report itself was relatively bland and more descriptive than analytic. It did not involve an appraisal of methods of diagnosis and treatment "which of necessity could be made only by experts in the field," but sought rather to "present a panorama of the provisions for the care of mental diseases." The document was largely a description of the number and distribution of hospitals, patients, medical and nonmedical personnel, and facilities, and included statistical tables and a copy of the questionnaire sent to every institution. The Committee on Medical Education and Hospitals recommended that the report be accepted and filed, pending a final report in 1934, and the delegates concurred. No action was taken in the future, and all AMA involvement in the project ceased.[18]

Grimes was furious at the actions of the AMA. In 1934 he wrote and published a book at his own expense to vindicate his report. In widely distributed letters, Grimes posed several questions. "Why was that report buried and forgotten? . . . Why were its disclosures not reported to the medical profession for whose benefit it was ordered and financed, nor even to the medical directors and superintendents through whose cooperation it was carried to a successful conclusion?" The book itself accused "a small group of men, located in the East but nationally known" of opposing the project and securing the discontinuation of Grimes's services to the AMA. "It is my deep conviction," he observed in the Preface,

> that, in suppressing this information, the secretary of the Council and the chairman of the Advisory Committee, together with any other members of the Council or the Committee who understood and agreed with the policy of suppression, were guilty of a most regrettable error. In so doing, they have placated a few disgruntled Wise Men from the East; but they ignored an opportunity to plead the case of all America's most neglected and most helpless group of hospital patients, and failed also to keep faith with those hospital superintendents and other workers who had labored with them in the collection of the data they buried and forgot.[19]

Aside from the inclusion of certain detailed statistical data, Grimes devoted much of his book to an analysis of mental hospitals. His description of institutional shortcomings was familiar, and echoed the complaints of many hospital superintendents. Mental hospitals, Grimes insisted, were not like other hospitals, given the fact that patients measured their stay in years. Moreover, the care of patients was entrusted to "attendants and industrial managers," and there was no truly meaningful doctor-patient relationship. The lowest quality of care was to be found in local and county institutions, and the highest in federal hospitals. Individuals were hospitalized "not because they are mentally ill, but because of unsocial or antisocial manifestations." Grimes condemned in particular the practice of "dumping old people into state hospitals," and insisted that responsibility for such individuals rested with their family rather than with the state. The state did "not owe each of these families a dollar a day for the next ten years or more, and the space into which these old people are crowded at state hospitals is needed for other patients." What was required was a third reform movement, Grimes concluded, one comparable in scope to the two earlier ones led by Dix and Beers—both of whom were laypersons. Nor was additional funding required; a reallocation of resources would lead to desirable results. Grimes identified five crucial steps: a policy of "de-institutionalization" based upon "paroling all parolable patients"; the development of an effective parole system under medical supervision; the expansion of the acute services at mental hospitals; reform in the care of chronic patients in order to create the hope of a more normal life; and the fostering of closer relations between mental hospitals, on the one hand, and the community and general hospitals, on the other.[20]

That Grimes's book was ignored by psychiatrists and by the general public was not because it was radical in character. As a matter of fact, Grimes did not reject the paramount roles that physicians were to play in caring for and treating the mentally ill. Nor was there any disposition on the part of psychiatrists to quarrel with many of his conclusions, including the deemphasis on custodial care, the greater reliance on parole, and the rejection of the practice of admitting aged persons. The hostility toward him was rather a function of the interprofessional rivalry between the AMA—which represented a general constituency—and the APA, a good part of whose strength still lay with hospital-affiliated members. Fearing a threat to its authority from a variety of sources, the APA was reinforced in its determination to control psychiatric practice.

As the thrust toward the establishment of a specialty board grew stronger, the APA faced still another problem related to its uneasy relationship with neurology. Although there were clear differences between psychiatric and neurological practice, there also was a large gray area where the two met. Many psychiatrists had been trained in neurology, and insisted upon the necessity of understanding the physiology and functions of the brain. Nevertheless, the two specialties had their own organizations and tended to practice in quite distinct settings. Members of the ANA and the AMA Section on Nervous and Mental Diseases (which was dominated by neurologists) were not especially sympathetic toward their psychiatric colleagues, whom they tended to regard as scientific illiterates. "If American psychiatry is to be judged by its scientific output, it has certainly made a very poor showing in the last few years," observed T. N. Weisenberg, editor of the *Archives of Neurology and Psychiatry*. "Most of it has been poor stuff." Many prominent psychiatrists, therefore, had misgivings about creating a specialty board that included psychiatry and neurology. "I am afraid," William L. Russell told Ebaugh, "that we have no reason to feel any great confidence in the American Neurological Association in psychiatric matters. The Section on Neurology and Psychiatry of the American Medical Association is also so strongly neurological that I am afraid one could not feel sure of psychiatric control of any project in which it had a part." The discussions among members of the advisory committee of the NCMH's Division of Psychiatric Education indicated that Russell's concerns were shared by others. Meyer, on the other hand, hoped to hold the two specialties together.[21]

Neurologists, who often identified themselves as neuropsychiatrists—a term that came into vogue during World War I as a result of a political accommodation*—were also fearful of the

* According to Dr. Frankwood E. Williams, the former medical director of the NCMH, the term "neuropsychiatrist" was popularized during World War I. The NCMH had established a Committee for Organizing Psychiatric Units for Base Hospitals. Neurologists, however, were reluctant to serve in such units; most preferred to retain their professional affiliation. A name change, on the other hand, ran the risk of angering psychiatrists. Hence the term "neuropsychiatry" came into existence. "In renaming the unit neuro-psychiatric unit," Williams recalled in 1935, "it was neither Dr. [Pearce] Bailey's idea, I am sure, and not mine, nor Dr. Salmon's, when he was later consulted, nor anyone else's, so far as I know, that we were naming a specialty in medicine. The name grew not out of a medical need but a political one. The term had only political significance to those of us who used it first in the war work or in connection with the war work. I do not

growth of nonmedical specialties in the mental health field. They were not averse, therefore, to some form of collaboration with psychiatrists. Weisenberg, who disliked lay psychoanalysts and clinical psychologists because their goal was "entirely commercialism," proposed in 1931 that the APA and ANA work together in establishing educational standards. The general confusion over the definition of the qualifications for specialty practice in general only spurred the drive for certification.[22]

Despite internal friction between the three organizations—APA, ANA, and AMA—as well as the hostility to some of Ebaugh's proposals, the desire to formalize educational requirements and create a specialty board grew more intense. Internal dissent and interprofessional rivalries were overshadowed by concern with the rapidly proliferating number of medical specialties that threatened to diminish medical and particularly psychiatric authority over nervous and mental diseases. It was for this very reason, perhaps, that the AMA decided to all but bury its own independent investigation. At any rate, at the APA meetings in the spring of 1932 the Committee on Revision of the Constitution introduced a series of resolutions. One in particular had major consequences, though it is not clear that the committee was aware at the time of the significance of its action. In defining membership, the proposed Article III established six categories (Fellows, Associate Members, Life Members, Honorary Members, and Corresponding Members), and provided for an Examining Board of five to report and recommend on every application for every class of membership. The Board was also required to submit to the APA Council "the procedures by which it proposes to pass upon the fitness of new applicants for membership." Although not a specialty board in the conventional sense, the proposed Examining Board could easily become the basis for the establishment of such a board.[23]

At the very same time that the APA was considering constitutional revision, the NCMH's Division on Psychiatric Education (organized in 1930) completed its study of psychiatric education.

think that any of us felt that it represented anything that existed at the time in medicine or had any idea that its use would continue after the war or that men would come to call themselves "Neuropsychiatrists" and I think that some of us were somewhat chagrined when after the war some comparatively few men did continue use of the term in reference to their practice, for it did not seem to us then and it does not seem to me now that there is any justification for the use of the term medically." Williams to Frank Norbury, Nov. 14, 1935, AFMH Papers, uncatalogued, AP.

As a result, the organization began to push for the integration of psychiatry in the general medical curriculum as well as for the establishment of separate departments of psychiatry within medical schools. In interviews with sixty medical school deans, the Division found that the most frequently expressed criticisms of psychiatry included its "lack of integration, isolation; inadequate personnel; varying terminology; inexactness; therapeutic inefficiency." Nevertheless, fifty-four out of sixty were sympathetic to suggestions to alter the medical curriculum in order to improve training in psychiatry. For psychiatrists the benefits were obvious. The specialty would cement a relationship with a powerful and more prestigous group of medical schools and thus strengthen the ability of psychiatrists to withstand jurisdictional encroachments by nonmedical personnel and at the same time enhance standards of practice. The role of the NCMH was also welcome, since the Division of Psychiatric Education reflected the dominant role of the APA. Its Advisory Committee included Meyer as chairman, as well as Albert M. Barrett (University of Michigan Psychopathic Hospital), Earl D. Bond (Pennsylvania Hospital), C. M. Campbell (Boston Psychopathic Hospital), Clarence O. Cheyney (New York Psychiatric Institute and Hospital), Arthur H. Ruggles (Butler Hospital), and William L. Russell (New York Hospital). Only Lawson G. Lowrey (New York Institute for Child Guidance) and Maurice H. Rees (dean of the University of Colorado School of Medicine) were not actively involved in the APA.[24]

In the spring of 1933 a number of events coalesced to give new vigor to the movement to create a specialty board. Just prior to the annual convention of the APA, the NCMH convened the first Conference on Psychiatric Education. At this meeting the delegates discussed a variety of options, and it became clear that the creation of a specialty board had unanimous support. It was equally evident that there was a strong desire to minimize the role of the AMA and to maximize that of the APA. The delegates to the APA meetings immediately thereafter adopted the new Constitution, which included the creation of an Examining Board composed of not less than five members. May's presidential address only added fuel to the fire, since he was highly critical of those medical and nonmedical specialties that were encroaching on psychiatric jurisdiction. "The only question at issue," he insisted, was whether psychiatric "standards are to be left to the judgment of neurologists, psychologists, internists, general practitioners, sociologists, social workers, biologists, biochemists, laymen and amateurs not occupied for the time being with other fads, or whether they are to be established and maintained by The American Psychiatric Association."[25]

The new APA Examining Board (composed of Cheyney, Campbell, Meyer, White, and Ebaugh) came into existence soon thereafter. Both the ANA and the Section on Mental and Nervous Diseases of the AMA immediately indicated their concerns and misgivings. It was evident that a specialty board simply under the aegis of the APA ran the risk of not achieving the status and recognition desired by psychiatrists. "We . . . must not get too far from the neurologists who are the chosen people for extramural psychiatry if we align ourselves too much apart from the medical profession in general," warned Meyer. "We need the medical profession on our side," he added, "and the neurologists are our closest neighbors." Meyer's comments reflected the concerns of many of his colleagues, who believed that training in neurology was essential for psychiatric practice.[26]

By the end of 1933 there was general agreement that an American Board of Psychiatry and Neurology should be established. The new organization would have four representatives each from the APA, ANA, and the Section on Mental and Nervous Diseases (of whom two would be psychiatrists and two neurologists). In the spring of 1934 there was further agreement that the new board, notwithstanding its name, would conduct separate examinations in psychiatry and neurology, and that the classification of a "neuropsychiatrist" would neither be recognized nor accepted. A political compromise, in other words, nullified the earlier agreement that had given rise to the very concept of "neuropsychiatry." The new arrangements were satisfactory to both the APA and ANA, each of which gained a measure of assurance that the definition of their specialty and control over education and certification would remain in their respective hands.[27]

Thus, in October 1934, the American Board of Psychiatry and Neurology was formally organized. It immediately affiliated with the Advisory Board for Medical Specialties, which had come into existence the previous February in order to control and to rationalize the possible proliferation of specialty boards. The creation of the new board by no means ended internal conflict. At the first meeting differences between psychiatrists and neurologists surfaced again. Louis Casamajor commented that the representatives of each specialty "got along like a couple of strange bulldogs," and that they even fought over whether psychiatry or neurology should come first in the title of the organization. Eventually they reached agreement that each specialty would conduct its own examination, although an individual could be certified in both by passing two separate examinations. Recognizing the problems that would be presented by those already in practice resulted in the adoption of a "grandfather clause."[28]

By the beginning of 1938, 421 physicians had been duly certified by the new Board (229 in both psychiatry and neurology and 192 in psychiatry alone). The APA's Committee on Psychiatric Standards and Policies expressed the hope that in the future hospital medical officers would come from the ranks of those who had been board-certified. That its members were dimly aware that the Board could aid in the effort to alter institutional psychiatry was indisputable. They noted in approving tones the development of "extra-mural psychiatry" and the "introduction of psychiatric concepts and techniques into general medicine." They also supported the idea that "community work should be a major function of the mental hospital and not merely an incidental one." Although in no way suggesting that traditional mental hospitals were obsolete, their report clearly indicated a move away from the kinds of patients found in institutions and toward a quite different clientele.[29]

III

The attempt of psychiatrists to retain a dominant position in the mental health professions took an additional form as well. During the 1930s the specialty attempted to shore up its foundations by developing closer ties with medicine, which it hoped to cement by incorporating psychiatry directly into the medical school curriculum. The lead in this effort was taken by the Division of Psychiatric Education of the NCMH, which served as the institutional vehicle to further the integration of psychiatry and medicine.

In 1933 Ralph A. Noble completed the first comprehensive analysis of psychiatry in medical education. Sponsored by the Division on Psychiatric Education, the study revealed a dismal state of affairs. Psychiatry, according to practitioners, dealt not only with mental disease, but with the study of the whole personality, and therefore should have permeated the education and practice of all physicians. The existing situation, on the other hand, was quite different. Only two percent of the time in medical school curriculums was devoted to psychiatry; many schools offered even less. Clinical facilities and personnel for instruction were inadequate to nonexistent. As a group, both medical school deans and the teaching staff were sympathetic; they were critical of the isolation of psychiatry from medicine and of the obscurantist terminology characteristic of the specialty. Noble warned his colleagues that there was a "great need for clear thinking in the psychiatric field before other groups without biological foundations became entrenched." He concluded with a series of recommendations, including the integration of psychiatry into preclinical education, the development of cooperative relations with medicine, surgery, and pediatrics during the clinical years, and substantive changes at the postgraduate level.[30]

Oddly enough, the creation of the American Board of Psychiatry and Neurology also led to friction, since there was some sentiment that the Division of Psychiatric Education was no longer needed. Ebaugh, who had by this time succeeded Noble as its director, distinguished between board certification and education, and argued that the continued existence of the Division was crucial to the integration of psychiatry into medical education. Ebaugh was successful in his efforts. During the 1930s the Division was one of the major vehicles for educational reform, and sponsored a number of national conferences on psychiatric education. Yet neither the Division of Psychiatric Education nor the specialty as a whole were especially successful in their efforts to persuade medical schools to alter their curriculum. A. Warren Stearns, Dean of Tufts Medical School and a psychiatrist, observed in 1934 that his specialty had kept pace with the advance of civilization through its "humanitarian efforts in improving the care of the insane and through contributions in the field of criminology, child guidance, industrial hygiene, [and] education." But Stearns conceded that psychiatry had been blocked in its "really legitimate field," namely, "in dealing with those forms of mental disease which are ordinarily called insanity."[31]

Stearns's perceptive comments illuminated the situational ambiguity facing his colleagues. Psychiatry had originated as one of the first of the medical specialties, and practitioners were aware of the advantages, both to themselves and to their patients, of retaining their medical affiliation. On the other hand, much of their daily work related to patient care and administration. Their institutionalized patients required care for the most part, and the absence of firm knowledge of mental diseases only magnified this need. That much of the medical profession tended to denigrate psychiatric medicine was largely the result of their unfamiliarity with the problems presented by patients in mental hospitals. The dilemma facing psychiatry, therefore, grew out of the discontinuity between the daily activities of practitioners and their idealized image of what they were doing. Many were somewhat aware of the contradictions, but were rarely able to resolve them. Meyer, for example, conceded in late 1933 that a specialty board had "a very difficult task":

> Psychiatry is the most human part of medicine and one's capacity for becoming a danger to patient, public and profession is very hard to establish and measure. What will flunk a man in psychiatry? And by what safeguards can we make sure that a man who passes will be a safe psychiatrist? What we can do is establish minimum standards and danger-lines and a demand of having at least studied some types of cases and some types of books. Which ones? What type and range of neurology? general medicine, etc.? We *can* lift the standards, but largely by stirring the interest. What should we like to be examined in to be standardized ourselves? Honestly and accurately? How can we avoid a getting-by system? . . .
>
> It is obvious that we can only make an approximation, and establish a kind of morale—having had apprenticeship, and practical and theoretical grounding, and evidence of having made something of the occasion and of the efforts of teacher and pupil to be entitled to be a doctor, or teacher, or man of authority in using poisons and dangerous methods, including love treatment (psychoanalysis) and morphine and being trusted to be either in cahoots with the patient or to be the boss empowered to send him to an asylum and place of legalized detention and "treatment."

Such questions posed tragic choices, and Meyer, like most of his colleagues, tended to push them out of sight because of the absence of any clear answers.[32]

When Ebaugh and Charles Rymer published their study of psychiatry in medical education in 1942, remarkably little had changed. "Probably no other subject is in a greater state of flux—a harsher critic may even say confusion," they admitted. Ebaugh and Rymer attributed this situation to the dominance of an organic point of view that blocked investigation of the personality aspects of mental illness and led to therapeutic nihilism, thus making psychiatry

irrelevant to most physicians. But their own commitment to a
"genetic-dynamic" psychiatry did little to clarify issues, and they
offered no evidence that their approach would transform custodial
hospitals into therapeutic institutions. Their recommendations
echoed those of Noble a decade earlier. They urged that a number
of steps be taken: that three or four percent of the total medical
curricular hours be devoted to psychiatry; that medical schools
develop working relationships with psychopathic hospitals, outpatient facilities, and child guidance clinics; that general hospitals
establish psychiatric wards; that greater attention be paid to up-
grading psychiatric teaching personnel; and, above all, that the
isolation of psychiatry from medicine be breached by integrating
the teaching of psychiatry into the medical curriculum. The call
for such changes was itself an indication that psychiatrists had
yet to achieve the secure role that they had been seeking for nearly
half a century and thought they had achieved during the first
quarter of the twentieth century.[33]

IV

Preoccupied with a vision that transcended their institutional
origins, psychiatrists welcomed the creation of a mental hygiene
movement and extended the jurisdiction of their specialty beyond
the walls of the traditional mental hospital after 1900. Like others
of their generation, they saw themselves playing a crucial role in
promoting health and preventing disease. Their efforts, however,
gave rise to unforseen consequences, not the least of which was
the rise of other groups that claimed a degree of professional
autonomy. Consequently, internal professional concerns tended
to dominate the specialty of psychiatry; its members were increasingly preoccupied with the need to justify their authority
against those who threatened their autonomy. The emphasis on
certification and education was a natural and understandable response of individuals aware of the successes of their colleagues
in a more biologically oriented medicine.

Board certification reflected a faith that the content of psychiatry had reached a level susceptible to fairly precise measurement. In a larger sense, such beliefs were characteristic of other
occupational groups that defined themselves in professional terms
and were persuaded that they possessed the ability to control
events within their respective spheres of competence. In a more
limited sense, however, the emphasis on certification and edu-

cation was, in part, an attempt to secure reenforcements from the field of medicine in general in order to support the legitimacy of the psychiatric claim to overarching competence (as contrasted with the various would be usurping professionals). The effort to shift the foundations of psychiatric practice seemed appropriate in view of the widespread (if not always accurate) belief that scientific medicine was responsible for the decline in mortality from infectious diseases and the increase in life expectancy at birth. By identifying with the field of medicine, on the other hand, psychiatric practice increasingly shifted from mental hospitals to outpatient facilities, child guidance clinics, and private practice. As the locus of practice changed, the careers of psychiatrists were less and less bound up with the hundreds of thousands of patients in mental institutions whose conditions were seemingly beyond any effective interventions. Indeed, after 1945 the role of state hospital psychiatrists in the APA was sharply reduced. By 1956 only about 17 percent of the 10,000 or so members of the APA were employed in state mental hospitals or Veterans Administration facilities; the remainder were either in private practice or employed in various government or educational institutions, including community clinics.[34] To the degree that psychiatrists succeeded in identifying themselves with the larger medical profession, they were less and less prone to act—as their nineteenth-century predecessors had acted—as the representatives of the institutionalized mentally ill.

CHAPTER ELEVEN

Mental Hospitals and Psychiatry Between the Wars

BETWEEN World Wars I and II the commitment to institutional care of the mentally ill remained unchanged. Mental hospitals during this era were among the public institutions least affected by the unprecedented economic depression of the 1930s. To be sure, many states cut appropriations for the care of the mentally ill, but a declining price level compensated in part for the drop in the level of funding. More significantly, mentally ill persons without visible means of support fared far better in material terms inside hospitals than they would have outside in communities, if only because they received minimum levels of care. Similarly, institutional employment assured psychiatrists of a stable salary at a time when the inability of Americans to pay for medical care caused severe hardships among physicians in private practice. As a matter of fact, the Great Depression may well have postponed the searching examination of the character of mental hospitals that began after World War II and that gave rise to a sustained effort to dismantle the institutional structure established more than a century before.

Curiously enough, the Great Depression had a relatively insignificant effect on the internal environment of mental hospitals. It may have hastened the commitment of more aged persons because families were unable to care for them, but it clearly was not responsible for a trend that had started decades earlier. Indeed, dismal economic conditions did not appreciably diminish the spirit of therapeutic innovation that had begun with the introduction of fever therapy in the 1920s and continued in the succeeding decade with insulin and metrazol shock therapy and prefrontal lobotomy. Many of these new approaches had been developed by European psychiatrists. Their incorporation into American medical practice was related to several variables: the migration to America of European refugee physicians after Hitler came to power in 1933; the seeming effectiveness of such novel therapies; and perhaps most important of all, the fact that these new approaches were compatible with a scientific psychiatry and were beyond the competence of the newer nonmedical occupational groups within the mental health field. Having been trained and socialized as physicians, institutional psychiatrists were receptive to somatic therapies that went beyond custodial care of patients. The autonomy and independence enjoyed by physicians also precluded any legal or informal barriers that might have been imposed against the introduction of novel therapies whose effectiveness was questionable.

I

Between the end of World War I and the beginnings of the Great Depression most states increased their spending. Education and road construction benefitted the most from the rise in state appropriations, but there was also a modest increase in expenditures for patients in mental hospitals. Between 1922 and 1929 (using the 1926 dollar as a standard), the per capita increase in state spending was about 60 percent. The per capita expenditure for maintenance at public hospitals (in dollar terms) rose in the same period from $282 to $312. The increase in expenditures, however, was not accompanied by an expansion in the revenue base. Many states enacted a tax on gasoline, which by 1929 accounted for a quarter of all receipts, but it failed to produce sufficient revenue. The difference between expenditures and revenue was reflected in the rapid rise in state indebtedness.[1]

When the Great Depression began, few states were in a position to withstand the shocks to which they were subjected. Deeply in debt from the deficit spending of the 1920s, they faced a sharp decline in revenues. At the same time, they were confronted with unprecedented demands from millions of unemployed individuals. Some attempted to increase revenue by imposing new taxes. But many simply reduced their expenditures by as much as a quarter or a third.[2]

Generally speaking, state mental hospitals suffered less than other public institutions. Between 1929 and 1930 per capita expenditures at all state hospitals fell from $312 to $302, but dollar purchasing power may have risen because of a declining price level. The low point came in 1934, when per capita costs bottomed out at $246. From that point on, however, there was a steady rise. By 1940 per capita expenditures had nearly reached pre-depression levels. A study conducted by the NCMH in 1934 concluded that

budget reductions had had little direct impact upon institutionalized patients. As in the past, most superintendents tended to
maintain existing levels of funding for food and for other basic
necessities and to reduce expenditures in personnel and physical
plant. Between 1929 and 1933 the ratio of all attendants and
nursing (excluding graduate nurses, who constituted an insignificant proportion of the total nursing staff) to patients rose from
1:12 to 1:13. The ratio may have reached 1:14 by 1934. Funding
for hospital libraries, on the other hand, fell precipitously. Some
institutions introduced such cost-saving features as cafeterias. In
a perverse sense, the high unemployment level actually benefitted
hospitals, if only because they were able to recruit and retain
higher-quality workers. High turnover rates in personnel, which
had been characteristic of hospital employment, dropped sharply
during the 1930s. On the other hand, the slightest indication of
an upturn in the economy was accompanied by increasing turnover rates. In Ohio the turnover rate rose from 13 percent in 1935
to 31 percent in 1936, when economic conditions improved somewhat.[3]

Hospital physical plants were hardest hit. A virtual halt to new
construction and a decline in normal maintenance had major
consequences. Their effect was not to be felt, however, for years
to come. Sensitive to the problem, the NCMH urged the federal
government to allocate funds for hospital construction. The Public Works Administration provided 12 million dollars, but about
90 percent of these funds went to Massachusetts, New York, New
Jersey, and Illinois—states that already provided above-average
care for their institutionalized population.[4]

Despite the fact that state mental hospitals suffered proportionately less than other public facilities, the exacerbation of
crowding, shrinking budgets, and physical plant deterioration created a renewed interest in alternatives to traditional institutional
care. Horatio M. Pollock, the Director of Mental Hygiene Statistics of the New York State Department of Mental Hygiene, raised
the possibility of extra-institutional care of the chronic mentally
ill. "I am fully convinced," he informed Hincks, "that family care
could be used to advantage in relieving overcrowding in mental
hospitals and in obviating the necessity of new hospital construction; also that family care is better than hospital care for many
types of patients."[5]

Although Pollock's proposals did not arouse opposition, they
failed to attract widespread support. A few states inaugurated

family care systems during the 1930s and early 1940s, including California, Illinois, Maryland, Michigan, Nebraska, New York, Pennsylvania, and Rhode Island. Most programs remained relatively small in scope, and in no state did the number of patients in private homes reach two percent.[6] The benefits to the state of family care, while potentially significant, were not immediately evident, since the system involved direct payment to third parties. Nor were hospital officials enthusiastic, if only because they would inherit the very real problems of supervising a highly decentralized system in order to safeguard against abuses. After World War II the system changed dramatically. The creation of new federal programs, in particular, provided states with both the opportunity and incentive to shift financial responsibility for the care of many mentally ill persons to the federal government. It was under these changed circumstances that the so-called policy of "deinstitutionalization" became attractive.

II

Economic adversity did not dampen the enthusiasm for new psychiatric therapies. The receptivity toward therapeutic innovation was understandable. In one sense it grew out of psychiatry's attempt to emulate the alleged successes of scientific medicine. Just as surgery symbolized the success of scientific medicine, so too novel psychiatric interventions would demonstrate the specialty's ability to influence the outcome of mental diseases. Moreover, there was a growing awareness that the constant increase in the number of chronic patients might well undermine the state support that was so necessary. The systematic collection of data by the United States Census Bureau on an annual basis beginning in 1926, as well as the even more detailed information collected in New York and Massachusetts, underscored the fact that mental hospitals were overwhelmingly custodial in nature. Finally, the close ties between American and European psychiatrists, which was strengthened by the exodus of German-Jewish psychiatrists and neurologists, proved significant, and often served as a conduit through which new methods and ideas developed in Europe were introduced in the United States.

The interest in therapeutic innovation, of course, was not specific to the 1930s. During the early decades of the twentieth century psychiatrists often attempted to take advantage of newly developed medical techniques. The older emphasis on "moral" treatment—one which involved the creation of a new environment in order to alter the circumstances that had given rise to mental disease and its physiological manifestations—had diminished. This change in emphasis occurred for several reasons. An ever-increasing proportion of patients in hospitals had severe somatic disorders, and a psychologically oriented therapy was of marginal importance. Environmental modifications were difficult in large and complex institutions, and often were not relevant to the kinds of patients being admitted. In addition, medical training emphasized the physiological basis of disease. Aside from their personal desire to reestablish ties with a biologically grounded medicine, psychiatrists were also concerned with the welfare of their patients, and were receptive to novel therapies that might enable individuals to leave the hospital and to resume a functional role in both a family and a societal setting.

During the 1920s psychiatrists continued to employ many of the same therapies as their predecessors. Drugs were still widely used as a substitute for physical restraint. The drugs administered to patients included paraldehyde, sulphonal, trional, veronal, chloralhydrate, the bromides, hyoscine, and morphine. Salvarsan remained one of the few specific drugs in use, and was often prescribed for the many paretics in hospitals. A renewed emphasis on occupational therapy and hydrotherapy was also evident, stimulated in part by the founding of the American Occupational Therapy Association, as well as by the efforts on the part of attendants and nurses to gain greater professional status. The focal infection theory of mental illness likewise drew some support, and many patients had allegedly infected teeth removed or underwent tonsilectomies in an effort to improve their mental condition.[7]

Much of the interest in therapy during the 1920s tended to focus on syphilis. Before 1917 a number of prominent psychiatrists, including E. E. Southard and Harry Solomon at Boston Psychopathic Hospital, devoted considerable attention to the disease. This interest persisted in the postwar period. Indeed, the 1920s saw the introduction of vigorous new interventionist therapies. In general, neurosyphilis therapy fell into two general categories. The first involved the use of specific drugs, generally in the arsphenamine family, but including mercury, bismuth, and the iodides as well. The second was a nonspecific approach directed toward the strengthening of the body's immunological sys-

tem with the hope of inhibiting or destroying invading spiro-
chetes.

The most significant therapeutic innovation of the 1920s grew
out of the work of Julius Wagner-Jauregg, an Austrian psychiatrist
who eventually received the Nobel Prize in 1927 for his work.
Trained in experimental pathology and internal medicine at the
University of Vienna, Wagner-Jauregg early in his career noted
that mental symptoms occasionally disappeared in patients ill
with typhoid fever. His observation led him to undertake a study
of the effects of fever on psychoses. Initially he attempted to
transmit erysipelas to paretic patients, but found that in some
cases there was no systemic reaction. By 1890 he had begun to
experiment with various bacterial substances, including Robert
Koch's tuberculin. The dangers inherent in this procedure led to
a temporary halt in his experiments. Wagner-Jauregg nevertheless
continued his work and found that a combination of tuberculin
and mercury gave rise to promising results. Since relapses were
common, he began to experiment with other substances, and
eventually became interested in using malaria to produce a fever
in mental patients. During World War I Wagner-Jauregg obtained
blood from a soldier infected with malaria, and innoculated a
number of paretic individuals. The results seemed more than
promising; four of eight cases achieved what appeared to be a
complete remission; two improved slightly; one relapsed into a
melancholy state; and the last case resulted in a remission more
than a year after the initial treatment.[8]

Wagner-Jauregg's work received an enthusiastic reception both
in Europe and the United States. By the early 1920s such influential institutions as St. Elizabeths Hospital and the New York
Psychiatric Institute had begun to emulate his example, and most
mental hospitals followed suit. Fever therapy, along with such
arsphenamine substances as trypasamide, became the dominant
mode of therapy in cases of paresis. Their popularity was understandable. Both were capable of being administered to large numbers of patients in institutions with a modest medical staff, and
both seemed to be based on a rational and scientific therapeutics.
In one case a specific substance killed the spirochete; in the other
a general reaction of the immunological system produced similar
results. Malaria therapy, moreover, offered hope for the future.
White began to employ the new approach at St. Elizabeths not
because of "any tremendous optimism" as to results, but rather
because he believed it "exceedingly important to prevent such

problems as that of paresis from getting into the discard because of a general feeling of hopelessness about it."[9]

Variations on malarial fever therapy followed rather quickly. If fever was the key element, perhaps the use of the malarial plasmodium was not indispensable. By 1927 the Illinois State Psychopathic Institute was inoculating patients with rat-bite fever organisms. The procedure had milder effects, but appeared less useful. At the same time some psychiatrists began to expand the use of malarial treatment to other mental diseases. In 1925 the Utica State Hospital inoculated some schizophrenics, and the New York Psychiatric Institute followed suit. The results at both institutions were not encouraging.[10]

Throughout the 1930s, however, interest in fever therapy persisted. Most institutions claimed high rates of remissions and improvement in paretic individuals treated with malaria inoculation. Their data suggested that about half of all paretics fell into these two categories. Indeed, fever therapy seemed so promising that physicians pursued a number of different approaches. Some patients were injected with typhoid vaccine, some underwent diathermy, and in some cases fever was induced by means of radiant energy in cabinets with limited air space. By 1937 the first International Conference on Fever Therapy had been called in New York City.[11]

Medical researchers were aware that fever therapy posed severe problems. Wagner-Jauregg noted in 1922 that the malarial plasmodium could not yet be cultivated or preserved for any length of time outside the human body. Thus a malarial patient had to be brought together with a paretic. Wagner-Jauregg's solution was more difficult in the United States, if only because the size of the country and the fact that malaria had largely disappeared from northern regions made it difficult to bring individuals together. One possibility was to inoculate one paretic with the blood of another paretic with malaria. The danger of such a procedure was obvious, namely, that the *treponema pallidum* might be introduced into the blood of patients without syphilis. White refused to authorize the use of syphilitic donors at St. Elizabeths, but few shared his concern. White was one of the only psychiatrists to raise an ethical issue involved in such therapeutic experimentation. Most of his colleagues assumed that responsibility for therapy—even admittedly experimental and questionable procedures—lay exclusively in their hands. The possibility of external review or accountability was never even raised within the context of psychiatric practice before World War II.[12]

Despite the optimistic claims of advocates, the evidence to support the alleged effectiveness of fever therapy was extraordinarily weak. The criteria to judge either remission or improvement was vague, and the fact that the psychiatric therapist was also the evaluator vitiated the results still further. Equally compelling was the absence of any control group or follow-up procedure. Some advocates were vaguely aware of the problems of empirical and nonspecific therapies in general, but were unable to break with the prevailing therapeutic styles. A partisan of malarial fever therapy conceded in 1930 that the procedure "has been greatly abused as a method of treatment and . . . has too easily taken this country by storm." His comments were echoed by others. In spite of the excellent reported results, A. E. Bennett insisted that his personal experiences with malarial fever therapy were "far from satisfactory." He pointed to the "inherent dangers of engrafting one serious disease on another" and concluded that the procedure was "not a permanently sound" therapeutic technique. Rather than rejecting the general principle, however, he endorsed "safer, more readily controlled and efficient forms of artificial fever therapy."[13]

The enthusiastic reception and persistence of fever therapy in the 1920s and 1930s was by no means an isolated phenomenon. The 1930s witnessed an acceleration in the introduction and acceptance of a number of therapeutic innovations that set the decade apart. In a historical sketch of somatic treatment in psychiatry published in 1939, Oskar Diethelm deplored the fact that therapeutic activities were so largely guided by a spirit of empiricism, and he called for the imposition of experimental controls. Diethelm implicitly criticized many of his colleagues by suggesting that they should inhibit their unrestrained acceptance of new approaches then current. "It is important in medicine," he wrote, "to recognize fully the responsibility with regard to those who follow voluntarily, that is physicians; to those who follow blindly, that is lay people; and to those who are forced to follow, that is patients." The pleasure of being a pathfinder was "alluring but leads to all the dangers of adventure."[14]

Diethelm's warnings were not issued in a vacuum. During the 1930s interventionist therapies of all kinds proliferated. In general, the patients least affected were those who fell into the aged category. Most psychiatrists recognized that they could not appreciably influence the condition of patients whose behavior appeared to be a function of the aging process. Therapy, therefore, was directed toward younger persons, including those diagnosed as paretics, schizophrenics, or manic depressives. For such groups psychiatrists pursued increasingly aggressive therapies. The rapid spread of novel interventions was not accidental. In the post World War I era, the efforts of psychiatrists to identify with medicine resulted in a greater receptivity toward and interest in somatic procedures. Equally significant, the existence of a mature and sophisticated communications network made up of the medical press, medical schools, and professional organizations facilitated the rapid spread of ideas and practices. A desire to overcome therapeutic pessimism and to justify the medical character of mental hospitals was also important during a decade of economic disaster.

Therapy in the 1930s tended to be highly eclectic. In addition to fever therapy, for example, psychiatrists and syphilologists administered a number of different drugs, including those in the arsphenamine family as well as in such other heavy metals as bismuth and mercury. Sedatives, including sodium bromide, sodium rhodonate, and sodium amytal were also often used. Indeed, the rationale for sedatives sometimes changed; their use was defended on therapeutic grounds rather than on grounds of convenience. In such cases reports of alleged therapeutic successes were often picked up by the popular press and given wide circulation. In 1931 the *Literary Digest* ran a piece entitled "Chemical Cure for Insanity." The article summarized the views of Wilder D. Bancroft of Cornell University. In a talk before the American Chemical Society, Bancroft, alluding to the earlier work of Claude Bernard, suggested that abnormal brain conditions caused by chemical inbalances could be corrected by the use of such substances as sodium rhodanid and sodium amytal. During the remainder of the decade investigators pursued numerous other leads in the hope of finding an effective substance that might have minimal toxic effects.[15]

The most striking therapeutic innovation of the 1930s, no doubt, was the introduction of what became popularly known as "shock" treatment. The technique was initially developed by Manfred Sakel, a Viennese physician. In 1928 Sakel observed mental changes in diabetic drug addicts whom he had treated with insulin, which was first isolated in 1922. The injection of a sufficiently large dose of insulin drastically lowered the sugar content of the blood and thus induced a hypoglycemic state. In this state of "shock," the patient went into a deep coma which could be relieved by the administration of sugar. After the process was over, the patient's mental condition appeared to improve. Sakel then conceived of the idea of deliberately using the procedure on psychotic patients, especially schizophrenics. For several years he refined the technique by experimentation, and between 1933 and 1935 reported highly encouraging results.

Sakel's work created a significant theoretical problem, for his procedure seemed at variance with many of the biological principles ordinarily involved in therapy. Fever therapy, for example, was based on the rational and accepted principle that an infectious agent could be neutralized or eliminated by activating the body's immunological system. Hypoglycemic treatment, on the other hand, had no relationship to the known biological and physiological principles of that period. Sakel himself was cognizant of this anomoly, but he insisted that his therapy was not to be measured by ordinary standards. He noted that medical knowledge of schizophrenia was virtually nonexistent; it was impossible to determine whether it was a disease entity or a symptomatic clinical picture. Nevertheless, the absence of a rational basis for the new therapy was not an argument against its use, particularly if the results were promising. Sakel provided a possible working hypothesis, though he conceded he could be wrong. The products of the adrenal system, he noted, sensitized cells excessively, and consequently normal stimulii produced pathological effects. Insulin neutralized the products of the adrenal system and kept cells quiescent, thus reducing pathological behavioral effects. But even if his explanation was in error, Sakel argued, why abandon a seemingly effective therapy?[16]

Insulin shock therapy posed another dilemma. To what degree should physicians be permitted to experiment with new therapies on patients with long-standing chronic conditions that left them totally disabled or non-functional? Should therapies whose effectiveness or consequences were unknown be used even if there seemed to be some immediate benefit, no matter how slight? It was, of course, possible to explore in abstract terms such theoretical and ethical considerations. In practice, however, the situation was far more complex. By the 1930s hospitals were filled with thousands of chronic patients who appeared to be destined to remain institutionalized until the end of their lives. If there was even a remote chance of aiding them, should the opportunity be deferred or permitted to pass until conclusive data was available? Within the context of the time, it was understandable that many psychiatrists leaped at the opportunity to act.

In late 1936 and early 1937 Sakel visited the United States. By that time a few hospitals had introduced his therapy on an experimental basis. Privately there were both doubts and reservations that mirrored the dilemma posed by any new and unverified technique. C. M. Hincks, General Director of the NCMH, wrote to a Swiss physician for an evaluation. White, a committed partisan of a more psychoanalytically oriented approach, was skeptical. "I have a suspicion," he wrote to Hincks, "that some of these schizophrenic patients get well with insulin shock treatment and other similar methods that are exceedingly painful and disagreeable in order to get out of the sanitarium where they use such methods or at least to escape their repetition." Abraham Brill (one of Freud's most important disciples in America) and Meyer, on the other hand, were more sympathetic, if only because they were willing to try anything that might aid the thousands of schizophrenics who languished for years in mental hospitals. Schizophrenia, Brill told White, "is so hopeless that anything that holds out hope should be tried." Meyer introduced hypoglycemic treatment at the Phipps Clinic. "There is no doubt about the value of the attitude of seeking help on the part of the patient that gets stimulated," he told White, "and the results reported by my Swiss friends are of a character that make it really an obligation to try out." Overholser, on the other hand, feared that a treatment which was effective in some cases, had become overly "popularized and prematurely hailed as a panacea."[17]

At about the same time that insulin shock therapy came into use, Ladislas von Meduna, a Hungarian physician, developed a kind of variation of the technique that utilized a drug to induce convulsions in schizophrenics. The origins of this approach lay in Meduna's observations that epileptics rarely were schizophrenic; that convulsive attacks in schizophrenia had beneficial therapeutic effects; and that epilepsy combined with schizophrenia seemed to have a brighter outlook for recovery than epilepsy without schizophrenia. He therefore postulated "a sort of biological antagonism" between the two diseases. "Without being able to characterize these pathological conditions," Meduna noted, "I feel justified in asserting, *a priori*, that these courses are mutually exclusive or they do, at least to a great degree, weaken each other in their mutual effects." Initially he used camphor to induce a convulsive fit, but eventually settled on metrazol—a powerful drug capable of causing convulsions. Although Meduna's work was initially overshadowed by Sakel's, both therapies came into widespread use at about the same time.[18]

Between 1937 and 1940 the use of insulin and metrazol shock therapy swept across the United States with startling rapidity. "Here everybody is going nuts on the insulin and metrazol therapy of Dementia Praecox," observed Smith Ely Jelliffe in a perhaps unconscious pun. "Something very intriguing about it all," Jelliffe added, even though he could provide no explanation.[19] The popularity of shock treatment, however, was neither a mystery nor an accident. In the first place, it was a somatic therapy, and hence overcame the long-standing hostility toward therapies that relied on verbal communication or intangible environmental modifications.[20] Secondly, psychiatrists were predisposed toward any therapy that offered some hope for schizophrenics or for other patients whose condition seemed impervious to known therapies. Third, shock therapy—unlike psychotherapies—could with some discrimination and preparation be used for substantial numbers of institutionalized patients. Fourth, as a somatic therapy, shock fitted into the medical model of disease and—by implication— lay beyond the authority of nonmedical groups then seeking recognition in the mental health field. Finally, although mental hospitals were less affected by the Great Depression than other institutions, their managers were by no means unaware of their vulnerability. Consequently, they may have been more receptive to novel interventionist therapies that demonstrated the usefulness of their institutions.

Without doubt, the rapid acceptance of shock therapy was facilitated by the vast publicity in the popular media. Magazines and newspapers, as well as the radio, disseminated information about the new therapy, suggesting it was a major breakthrough. Indeed, the APA Committee on Public Education felt constrained to issue a public statement toward the end of 1936 denying that insulin therapy was the only method available for the treatment of schizophrenia. Conceding that the new approach would find a "useful place," the Committee nevertheless warned that its exact value was as yet undetermined and that it was "not a specific, nor by any means a cure."[21]

By 1940 virtually every mental hospital had introduced insulin and metrazol therapy. Yet for many psychiatrists the new therapies posed serious theoretical as well as practical difficulties.

The technique had no theoretical basis, and any conclusive evidence regarding its effectiveness was lacking. "Shock" treatment, as a matter of fact, was an example of a therapy that was introduced in the absence of any data relating to its therapeutic qualities. To many psychiatrists the new approach created an agonizing dilemma. Should the thousands of chronic patients in institutions be deprived of a therapy that promised hope? Or should its use be postponed, perhaps for years, until conclusive data verified or disproved its therapeutic qualities? Given the extraordinarily high proportion of chronic patients, the rush to employ a new but untested therapy was understandable. The irony of the situation was not lost on some of the more prominent leaders of the specialty. "I wish I could develop some explanation satisfactory to myself about how the medication brings the improvement," J. K. Hall observed, "but we may never know in truth how treatment brings about either improvement or recovery." But did not the improvement of even a few patients justify the use of the treatment?[22]

The widespread use of insulin and metrazol therapy was accompanied by an extensive literature on the subject. Some of this literature was simply didactic in nature; it provided instructions on the use of each therapy in order to minimize the risks to the patient. The dangers inherent in both therapies were self-evident. Diabetic comas were sometimes fatal, and pulmonary edema, epileptic seizures, and respiratory distress were not uncommon. Under the best of conditions, the mortality rate from insulin therapy ranged as high as one to five percent. The risks from metrazol (a cardiac stimulant) were different; the inducement of convulsions sometimes led to various kinds of fractures or respiratory problems, but the mortality rate was considerably lower.[23]

But much more of the literature was concerned with the problem of evaluating the effectiveness of these novel techniques. Aware of the dilemmas posed by the use of an empirical therapy having few links to any known theory, a number of psychiatrists and other researchers attempted to measure results. Their findings at best proved inconclusive, if only because the results differed from state to state and institution to institution. The most extensive studies were undertaken in New York. Aggregate results of metrazol and insulin therapy were kept on standardized forms by each New York state hospital and forwarded to a central agency, where they were carefully analyzed by either Benjamin Malzberg or Horatio M. Pollock, two of the nation's most sophisticated statisticians.[24]

In 1938 Malzberg published an initial study of the effectiveness of insulin treatment. He began by noting the deficiencies in existing statistical studies. Few investigators had reported on as many as 100 cases, and in any such series the probable errors of results were high. More serious was the complete absence of an adequate control group. To overcome such methodological shortcomings, some physicians from each state hospital were initially sent to Harlem Valley State Hospital, where they received training in the new therapy from Sakel himself. A standardized statistical form for each patient was prepared. Upon completion of the treatment, each individual form was forwarded to Malzberg, who eventually gathered data on 1,039 schizophrenics. Malzberg then compared the insulin-treated patients with a corresponding control group admitted in 1935 and 1936 and followed until mid-1937. The results revealed some striking differences. Sakel's therapy raised the recovery rate from 4 percent in untreated cases to 13 percent in treated cases. The differences in the "improved" category were equally striking: 11 to 27 percent, respectively. Overall, 65 percent of the insulin-treated group manifested some degree of improvement, as compared with only 22 percent in the control group. Improvement rates among catatonics and paranoids were significantly higher than those among hebephrenics. The earlier in the course of disease that the treatment began, the greater appeared to be the prospect of recovery and rehabilitation. The results, concluded Malzberg, provided comfort and encouragement.[25]

A year later Malzberg conducted a follow-up study of patients who had been treated with insulin in order to determine whether or not the results were lasting. He found data on 1,026 of the original group of 1,039, for 13 had died during treatment. Originally about 65 percent had "improved"; a year later this number had fallen to 49 percent. Within these categories, however, there was considerable shifting. In the original group, 134 persons had "recovered"; in the follow-up study this figure had fallen to 73. The 282 individuals who had originally been placed in the "much improved" class declined to 111, but 43 had moved upward into the "recovered" category. Malzberg realized the difficulty of getting a normative base for comparative purposes. The closest was a study conducted some years before by Raymond G. Fuller and Mary Johnston, who had analyzed a group of schizophrenics discharged from New York state hospitals between 1909-1911, 1914-1916, and 1919-1921, and followed them until 1928. Fuller and Johnston found that about one-quarter of first admissions with schizophrenia were considered "recovered" or "improved," as compared with the higher figure in the post-insulin era. Malzberg noted that the insulin-treated group was not limited to first admissions (which traditionally had the highest recovery and improvement rates), thus making the differences even more significant. The results of insulin therapy, therefore, could be construed only in positive terms even if the responsible mechanisms remained unknown.[26]

Using similar data, Pollock attempted to study the effectiveness of metrazol treatment as well as to compare the relative efficacy of metrazol and insulin. Analyzing a sample of 1,140 patients treated with metrazol, he found that recovery and improvement rates at different institutions were far from uniform. The overall findings were not encouraging (Table 11-1). Pollock suggested that the data raised "grave doubts as to the wisdom of continuing this treatment." In addition, convulsive therapy had substantial injury rates, thereby adding an element of risk. The only cases in which the use of metrazol was justified, he added, were those in which insulin therapy failed to yield any favorable results.[27]

Few of the other efforts to measure therapeutic effectiveness matched the relative sophistication of the studies by Malzberg and Pollock. Many, for example, omitted the use of any control group whatsoever; others used such a small sample as to vitiate the efficacy of their findings. Much more serious, however, was the absence of any standardized criteria for the attributes of such categories as "recovered," "much improved," "improved," or "unimproved." Moreover, the judgment of the patient's condition was made by the very same physician responsible for administering the therapy, thus raising doubts about the objectivity of the eval-

TABLE 11-1

COMPARATIVE RESULTS OF METRAZOL TREATMENT, INSULIN TREATMENT, AND UNTREATED CONTROL GROUP (PERCENTAGE)

	Recovered	Much Improved	Improved	Unimproved	Still in Hospital	Died
Metrazol	1.6	9.9	24.5	63.5	0	0.5
Insulin	12.9	27.1	25.3	33.4	1.3	3.5
Control	11.2	7.4	7.5	65.8	0	4.6

uation. In a critical analysis of the literature on insulin and met-razol therapy, Solomon Katzenelbogen pointed to the flaws and weaknesses in the design of many experiments. "The enthusiasm aroused by a new, dramatic and—according to numerous reports—almost universally successful method of treatment, and the active interest of the therapist in getting results after spending so much time and effort," he observed, "are factors which may account for some unintentional leniency in the estimation of the condition of patients who had received treatment; these factors obviously would not be present in the evaluation of the control group."[28]

Despite the encouraging results of insulin therapy, a marked sense of unease persisted among most psychiatrists. The puzzle of using therapies that could not be reconciled with theory or any known physiological data remained troubling. Few psychiatrists, therefore, were willing to offer enthusiastic or unrestrained sup-port either publicly or privately. Katzenelbogen, for example, noted that even favorable outcomes could not be regarded as conclusive evidence without other kinds of data. Along with others, he was sensitive to the therapeutic benefits of any kind of activity in-volving patients and physicians. It was possible, he added, that the major merit of nonspecific treatment lay "in rendering the patient more receptive for the common hospital therapeutic tools, such as occupational therapy, socialization, and other manifold forms of psychotherapy. The ability of the physician and the med-ical personnel to establish good rapport with the patient and to act, generally speaking, as psychotherapists, plays, therefore, a large part in the outcome of the insulin treatment." Yet even Katzenelbogen was unwilling to recommend discontinuation of a therapy that might aid recovery or improvement of patients who might otherwise remain institutionalized for much of their adult lives. Since insulin therapy succeeded in certain cases where the usual hospital treatment had failed, he concluded, it would be "unwise to drop the insulin therapy altogether—even after the era of enthusiasm is over. But it is indeed unwise to use it indis-criminately, as if it were a panacea for all cases of schizophre-nia."[29]

The use of insulin and metrazol, although greeted initially with enthusiasm, created serious problems at many institutions. In-sulin therapy required an adequate number of trained physicians and nurses, and not all hospitals were able to meet this standard. The superintendent of the Huntington State Hospital in West Virginia, for example, refused to authorize insulin therapy because of the limited size of his staff. Metrazol, on the other hand, was more easily administered, but often resulted in a substantial number of injuries to patients. Some hospitals discontinued its use, or else began to experiment with curare in order to minimize the risks of fractures. After the initial enthusiasm with the new therapy had died down, the results were sufficiently minimal to discourage its continued use.[30]

As problems of insulin and metrazol therapy multiplied, some psychiatrists were attracted to alternative forms of shock therapy. In 1937 two Italian physicians passed an electric current through the head of a dog in order to induce an epileptic fit. After additional research, they applied the method to schizophrenics. By 1940 electroshock therapy had begun to replace metrazol therapy. The new procedure sharply reduced the risk of injury, though it did not eliminate it entirely. Indeed, the growing belief that various forms of shock could have therapeutic benefits led to the development of other techniques, including the inhalation of nitrogen in order to deprive the brain of oxygen and thereby decrease its activity. In this process nitrogen seemed to replicate some of the same physiological consequences of insulin and metrazol, but it did not produce the harsh side-effects nor pose the same dangers.[31]

Nowhere was the receptivity toward radical therapies better illustrated than in the introduction and acceptance of prefrontal lobotomy in the late 1930s. Interest in surgical treatment of mental illness was by no means novel. Nineteenth-century studies, including the famous case in which J. M. Harlow reported the recovery of an individual who had sustained considerable injury to the frontal lobes by a crowbar, had stimulated concern with brain structure and function. As knowledge of functional localization in the forebrain accumulated toward the turn of the century, physicians were increasingly attracted to the possibility that surgery might play a major role in the treatment of mental diseases. The rapid development of surgical technology acted as a stimulant. Even before 1900 there were occasional efforts to employ surgical procedures involving the brain to treat mental illness. The emergence of behaviorism in psychology offered a further rationale for surgical techniques, for if learning were simply a form of conditioning, structural modifications could alter behavioral patterns.[32]

The initial prefrontal lobotomy for the relief of mental disorder was performed in 1935 by Dr. Egas Moniz, a professor of neurology at the University of Lisbon. Moniz had concluded that the mental

processes of psychotic individuals might be altered by interrupt-
ing some of the connections between the prefrontal lobes and
other parts of the brain. The procedure he employed was relatively
simple, and involved the trephining of the skull with the insertion
of a leucotome to sever the connecting fibers of the prefrontal
areas from the rest of the brain. The results appeared promising,
for violent behavioral patterns diminished sharply. In 1936 Moniz
published the results of his research in book form.[33]

Walter Freeman and James W. Watts of the Department of Neurology at George Washington University Hospital in Washington,
D.C., were among the first Americans to emulate Moniz's procedure. Initially they selected six patients suffering from anxiety,
apprehension, nervous tension, and insomnia. The results were
satisfactory; symptomatic relief was almost immediate even though
patients lost "some spontaneity, some sparkle, [and] some flavor
of the personality." Freeman and Watts warned that indiscriminate use of the procedure "could result in vast harm," and they
urged that prefrontal lobotomy be used experimentally for a small
group of cases "in which conservative methods of treatment have
not yielded satisfactory results."[34]

Despite its radical and irreversible nature, interest in psycho-
surgery began to grow just prior to World War II. A simple and
apparently safe procedure, prefrontal lobotomy appeared to hold
out hope for individuals who failed to respond to any other treatment. Hostility to the idea, however, was not long in coming.
After learning of Moniz's work, for example, White sought the
advice of his friend Smith Ely Jelliffe about the possibility of
subjecting his patients at St. Elizabeths to the operation "as a
legitimate experiment in therapy." Yet White's distaste for the
procedure was clear. "I could express the whole matter in one
word," he declared, "but I do not want you to do that because it
would be unmailable. However, something that is worth while
in this situation may have escaped me, but you naturally know
my disinclination to consider the destruction of the organ in which
the difficulty lies as legitimate therapy." The more common reaction among practitioners was one of puzzlement and skepti-
cism, though not to the point where the procedure was rejected.
By 1940 some hospitals were beginning to use the operation on
a more than occasional basis. During the early months of 1940,
64 major intracranial operations were performed at State Hospital
No. 4 in Missouri, the majority of which were prefrontal lobot-
omies.[35]

What was the impact of these aggressive therapeutic techniques so characteristic of the period between the two world wars? The answer to this question must be divided into two distinct parts— the first dealing with psychiatrists and the second with patients. To psychiatrists the 1930s was a decade in which their specialty appeared to be on the threshold of the long-sought-after integration with medical science. Receptivity to therapies went hand-in-hand with the creation of a specialty board and the broad effort to elevate the status of psychiatry within medical schools. J. K. Hall spoke for many of his colleagues when he insisted that the most important task was "to awaken the interest of the members of the medical profession in general" about psychiatry. "Although our progress is slow," he added, "I do feel that we are making some progress. The psychiatrist is nowadays listened to with more attention and with more respect than he was listened to only a few years ago." When a Methodist minister inquired in 1936 about training that would enable him to deal with the mental problems of his parishioners, the response of C. M. Hincks was clear. "The practice of psychiatry is so rooted in medical science that it could not possibly be entrusted to the hands of a layman, no matter how wide his readings on the subject has been. Many mental ailments have their causes in physical conditions and only the trained psychiatrist is qualified to examine a patient and diagnose his case." Even if psychiatrists misjudged their standing among other physicians, there is little doubt that the new therapeutic innovations reflected and fostered a kind of confidence in their ability to deal with mental disease.[36]

For the institutionalized mentally ill, on the other hand, the results of such activism were somewhat more ambiguous. Psychiatrists obviously believed that the new therapies offered hope to patients who in the past had looked forward to a bleak future. There is little doubt that many of the new techniques appeared to be effective insofar as recovery and improvement rates were concerned. In 1935 Pollock wrote that the new methods used in the treatment of general paresis had given rise to remarkable results. Comparing the period from 1926 to 1931 with the preceding five years, he found that recovery and improvement trends were up and mortality down. In an analysis of the ten years between 1933 and 1942, Henry D. Sheldon of the U.S. Census Bureau noted a modest upward trend in discharge rates. In 1933 57.1 out of every 100 patients separated from state hospitals had been discharged and the remainder had died. By 1942 the number had increased to 61.0. During the same period the number discharged as "recovered" and "improved" increased from 85.2 and 88.8 (per every 100 discharges). Similarly, Malzberg observed in 1940 that the future was hopeful, given the successes in treating paresis and schizophrenia (but excluding aged patients, for whom no treatment existed). A. Warren Stearns, Dean of the Tufts College Medical School, wrote in 1939 that in the past, patients had been sent to state hospitals "solely for care," whereas now it was "possible to think in terms of treatment."[37]

Although recovery rates for conditions such as paresis and schizophrenia seemed to be rising, the causal explanation and the reliability of the data on these diseases remained obscure. In a book on psychotherapy published in 1937, Dr. Leland E. Hinsie invited Carney A. Landis, a young psychologist well versed in statistical methodology, to contribute a chapter that would provide a statistical evaluation of psychotherapy. Although Landis confined most of his comments to psychotherapy, many were applicable to the newer somatic therapies as well. Any therapeutic method—physical or psychological—had to satisfy two specific tests, Landis declared. First, was the method "self-evidently rational" in that it included a logical explanation which a qualified expert accepted as rational? Second, did the method produce the results it claimed, and was there a logical and obvious relationship between the method and the result or cure? In the case of psychiatric diseases, Landis observed, the essential nature or cause of the condition was unknown, and there was little consistency in the usage of such terms as "recovered" or "improved." An examination of the data from institutions employing extensive psychotherapy revealed that the varieties of treatment had "but little difference in their ultimate effectiveness." Indeed, Landis found comparable results for dissimilar techniques. He concluded his chapter by quoting Pierre Janet's observation that the "psychotherapist who understands his patient well and who knows how to use psychological stimulation succeeds with any method that he cares to use."[38] Landis's analysis was applicable to the newer somatic therapies as well. In many instances certain treatments had no rational basis in theory. Recovery—even assuming its reality—was not necessarily a consequence of a particular act; it may have been a response by patients to the fact that they were receiving attention from a physician already predisposed to believe in the efficacy of his treatment. In this sense the change in the recovery rates may have had no direct relationship to the specific therapy.

Much of the alleged data pertaining to results, moreover, lacked methodological sophistication. In an analysis of "recoveries" at Warren State Hospital in Pennsylvania, Morton Kramer and his associates noted that favorable statistical data, even if accurate, did not prove therapeutic effectiveness. Any explanation of the results had to account for the kind of risks arising from admission to hospitals, comparability of diagnoses, the actual (as contrasted with the perceived) condition of the patient at the time of release. Administrative and community considerations also influenced release rates. As a matter of fact, two studies of the research activities of mental hospitals conducted in 1936-1937 and 1939-1941 provided little persuasive evidence that their medical staffs had the capability to engage in research.[39] Whatever the case, the therapeutic claims of the 1930s were for the most part not based on conclusive data. These claims reflected rather the confident outlook of psychiatrists, who believed in the efficacy of their therapies and who were unwilling to accept a caretaker role for patients who had lapsed into chronic states of dependence. In the end faith in science and the scientific method shaped the activism of practitioners during the 1920s and 1930s.

III

Beneath the confidence that gave rise to therapeutic activism, there lurked an underlying sense of insecurity. The creation of the American Board of Psychiatry and Neurology in 1934 was one manifestation of the unease as psychiatrists sought to repel the encroachments of other occupational groups upon the specialty. The Great Depression only strengthened these feelings, even though mental hospitals suffered less than other public institutions. Out of the contradictory and ambiguous sentiments of this decade came the creation of the Mental Hospital Survey Committee in 1936, a body that presaged a new role for the federal government.

That yet another organization involved with mental hospitals came into existence at this time was not surprising. Beginning in 1924, as we have already seen, the APA had expressed interest in rating hospitals and, by indirection, in imposing standards. Although no formal action was taken for some years, concern with the project persisted. The Great Depression revived interest, and in the early 1930s the Association's Committee on Standards and

Policies submitted an outline for such a survey. Lack of funds at the time proved an insuperable barrier. The creation of the American Board of Psychiatry and Neurology the following year, however, strengthened the hands of those who wished to impose minimum national standards to strengthen psychiatric authority. At the same time the Committee on Standards and Policies reiterated its belief that some form of grading could be employed as a lever to define standards within the specialty. Shortly thereafter it circulated a questionnaire, which became the basis for establishing a three-part rating system for public hospitals. Institutions in part were to be evaluated according to the degree to which they were independent or dependent upon lay or political authorities. The APA then authorized its Executive Committee to proceed with the classification and grading of hospitals.[40]

At about the same time the relationship between the NCMH and the Rockefeller Foundation had reached a crisis. Alan Gregg, who headed the Division of Medical Sciences, had a low opinion of the NCMH because it lacked long-range goals. Since Gregg was unwilling to redirect the Committee's activities, he inaugurated a move to end Foundation support. Such a development threatened the very existence of the NCMH, which lacked a broad constituency and a stable source of funds. Because some Foundation officials were sympathetic with the goal of improving care within hospitals, the Committee in 1935 began to entertain the idea of a project to evaluate institutional care and treatment and to upgrade professional training in neurology and psychiatry. The latter effort in particular was compatible with the traditional concern of the Rockefeller Foundation with medical education.[41]

The idea for such a venture may have been suggested by the massive survey then underway of all hospitals in New York City under the auspices of the United Hospital Fund and under the direction of Haven Emerson, then director of Columbia University's School of Public Health and a physician with a national reputation. George E. Vincent, former president of the Rockefeller Foundation, headed the committee responsible for the survey. After the creation of the hospital survey, the NCMH raised the possibility of taking responsibility for psychiatric and mental hygiene issues. By July, 1935, the NCMH had appointed a committee to consider the possibility of participating in the venture. A meeting was arranged between a number of psychiatrists, Emerson, and three representatives from the United States Public Health Service (PHS), including Walter L. Treadway, the Assistant Surgeon General. Clarence M. Hincks, General Director of the NCMH, was enthusiastic, and subsequently suggested a cooperative relationship between his organization and the PHS. Shortly thereafter the NCMH began to consider the possibility of sponsoring a national survey of the mentally ill.[42]

Since the NCMH included the very same individuals who had played a major role in the APA, it was natural that the two organizations would act in unison. In February, 1936, the NCMH convened a meeting in New York that included representatives from the APA and ANA. Those present formulated tentative plans for a survey of mental hospitals under the general supervision of a new committee. The NCMH shortly thereafter applied for and received a grant of $16,000 per year for three years from the Rockefeller Foundation to finance the undertaking. Gregg was hopeful that the new departure might "lead to an important advance in the work of the National Committee." He also informed Hincks that the goal of the new Mental Hospital Survey Committee should not be the improvement of the best hospitals, but rather the encouragement of "the not quite good to change their status for the better."[43]

At the APA convention in May, 1936, the Survey Committee was formally organized, and included representatives from all the major medical associations and the PHS. Treadway was named chairman and Samuel W. Hamilton operational director. The APA agreed to contribute $5,000. The PHS also made a grant in services of $13,000 a year for three years, and assigned Drs. Grover A. Kempf and Joseph Zubin, as well as a clerk, to the new Committee. To the PHS such an action represented a departure from its traditional concerns. Before World War I several suggestions had been made to establish a department of mental disease or a division of mental hygiene within the PHS to stimulate research and improve treatment. None, however, had gained Congressional approval. The PHS in the meantime had been made responsible for excluding insane aliens, but its responsibility went no further. Within the PHS, Walter Treadway had carried out several studies of mental illness and mental deficiency, and the relationship between immigration and mental illness—studies which had had no effect upon the PHS whatsoever. In 1929 Congress had authorized two federal institutions to confine and treat drug addicts and also created a Narcotics Division in the PHS. Both of these moves had grown out of the involvement of the federal government with drug addiction following passage of the Harrison Act in 1914. The following year the Narcotics Division became the Division of Mental Hygiene after passage of still another law dealing with medical and psychiatric care in federal penal institutions. The new Division's activities in the 1930s, however, reflected its narrow legal mandate, and did not serve as a spearhead to expand federal responsibilities.[44]

The involvement of the PHS with the Mental Hospital Survey Committee, on the other hand, began a process that would radically alter the role of the federal government after 1945 insofar as the mentally ill were concerned. By 1939 Dr. Lawrence Kolb, who succeeded Treadway as Director of the Division of Mental Hygiene, proposed the establishment of a "National Neuropsychiatric Institute" modeled after the National Cancer Institute founded two years before. Kolb's proposal received support from psychiatrists, although the AMA was opposed. Nevertheless, the coming of World War II ended any hope of favorable action.[45]

The activities of the Survey Committee from the very beginning reflected the pressing concerns of psychiatrists. In mid-1936 the Committee decided to confine the survey to public and privately endowed mental hospitals (including the feebleminded and epileptic). The survey was to focus on state administrative structures, economic problems, public policy, the adequacy of institutional structures and equipment, the competence of professional, subprofessional, and technical personnel, research activities, and undergraduate education in psychiatry and neurology. That psychiatric perceptions dominated was evident from the agenda, which emphasized disease process and professional autonomy rather than the specific needs of the patient population. Psychiatrists, understandably, found it difficult to perceive of themselves in a caretaker role. Trained in the ethos of scientific medicine, they defined their specialty in terms of active therapeutic methods and, by indirection, rarely addressed themselves to the needs of those for whom therapies were unavailable.[46]

In 1937 J. G. Wilson, a senior surgeon employed by the PHS, conducted an extensive study of the degree to which state hospital administrations were dominated by politics. He concluded that political interference was "active" in seventeen states, "slight or infrequent" in eight, and "absent" in twenty-four. Wilson's analysis was based on the assumption that "politics" should not play a role in administration and that a high degree of professional autonomy and independence was desirable. Using much of the data gathered by Wilson, Winfred Overholser gave a paper at the

APA convention in 1939 in which he argued that states with a sufficiently large population should adopt the Massachusetts and New York model. This model called for a separate state agency whose responsibilities were limited to the mentally ill and one which was headed by a qualified psychiatrist. If structured in an appropriate manner, such an agency could sharply reduce "the intrusion of political considerations" and maximize "ideals of service, progress and square dealing," Overholser concluded.[47]

Most of the energies of the Mental Hospitals Survey Committee were focused on an extensive survey of state hospitals. Hamilton and his associates eventually visited 149 facilities. These institutions, along with 33 others, provided the detailed data for the survey. In a number of instances the staff cooperated with public authorities in preparing detailed studies of conditions within a given state as well as recommendations to remedy existing shortcomings. In North Carolina, for example, the legislature authorized an investigation in 1935, and Hamilton provided assistance to those in charge. The final report in North Carolina, which ran to nearly 400 pages, however, was disregarded and discarded. In other states—including Iowa, Virginia, Utah, and Wisconsin—the Committee, upon invitation by public officials, prepared detailed reports and offered extensive recommendations.[48]

Hamilton gave his colleagues at the convention in 1939 of the APA a preliminary report on the activities of the Committee. His paper was at once pessimistic and optimistic, and reflected the extraordinarily wide variations among mental hospitals. Medical staffs, for example, ranged from one physician to every 125 patients to a low of one to 1,011. Much of Hamilton's paper analyzed current trends, including the rapid increase in the number of patients, the growing size of hospitals, the inadequacies in training and research, and mounting staff shortages. The Great Depression, he noted, had increased levels of political interference, but at the same time certain states had adopted "better standards of administrative control."[49]

By early 1939 a new crisis was pending. The Rockefeller Foundation had decided to end all funding for administrative activities of the NCMH, and it declined to renew its grant to the Survey Committee as well. In notifying Hincks of the decision to end a relationship that dated back to 1915, Gregg resorted to some blunt language. Aside from "mental hygiene propaganda," the NCMH had done little to merit further financial support. Its activities could just as easily be absorbed by the APA, PHS, National Research Council, or other organizations. Members of the NCMH, he wrote to another foundation official, "have not had effective organization, and the rather large sums of money that they have secured in the form of small but widely scattered contributions have been mostly devoted to a letter and publicity campaign for getting more such contributions."[50]

The absence of funding led to a request by the NCMH that the PHS assume responsibility for the survey. Treadway, who had resigned some months before from the Survey Committee, agreed, and in mid-1939 it became part of the PHS. Overholser was sharply critical of the actions that the Rockefeller Foundation had taken. A voluntary and professional organization without axes to grind, he informed Gregg, inspired confidence among state officials "in a way which cannot be expected of any Federal agency acting by itself alone." There was even widespread feeling among some state officials that the federal government "is attempting to secure too much control over the states."[51]

The absorption of the Survey Committee by the PHS actually made little difference. Even before the merger, the PHS had been publishing some of the results of the survey. Moreover, the Committee lacked any permanent foundation. After the outbreak of World War II, it virtually disappeared from sight as wartime concerns became dominant. The Committee was significant, not because of its effect on public policy, but because it reflected many of the psychiatric concerns of the prewar era.

Three major studies came out of the work of the Survey Committee. The first, prepared by Grover A. Kempf and published in 1939, dealt with admission procedures. Kempf's study was predicated on the belief that qualified physicians should play the dominant role in the determination of sanity. After summarizing the diversity of state laws, he recommended an admissions procedure that required a certificate by two licensed and reputable physicians that a person required treatment in a hospital and a judge's approval of such a document. Conceding that some procedural safeguards were necessary for the protection of a patient's property and civil rights, Kempf's study was predicated on the belief that admission procedures should reflect medical and psychiatric considerations.[52]

The second study was prepared by Joseph Zubin and Grace C. Scholz. Zubin, a psychologist trained in statistics, had already published a relatively brief preliminary report in 1938, providing data on the regional distribution of the mentally ill, mentally defective, and drug addicts in institutions during 1935.[53] Two years later he and Scholz completed a more detailed and comprehensive analysis. Their data revealed wide variations between regions in terms of first-admission rates, overcrowding, numbers of physicians and staff, and maintenance expenditures. Insofar as the differences in rates of hospitalization were concerned, endemic factors did not appear to play a major role; the variables of age, availability of hospital facilities, urban-rural distribution, and other environmental factors were far more important. As far as hospital facilities were concerned, New England and the Middle Atlantic states consistently spent more than the national average, and the South Atlantic, East South Central, and West South Central regions consistently less. Nor were the variations a reflection of economic administration; regions that provided more adequate care tended to have higher per capita expenditures. The conclusions of the Zubin-Scholz report were straightforward; they urged that more facilities be constructed, and that medical and nursing staffs be brought up to APA standards.[54]

A year later the Survey Committee published its final and most comprehensive study. Prepared by Hamilton, Kempf, Scholz, and Eve G. Caswell, the report was based upon a three-year study of mental hospitals. Although the 126-page document was largely devoted to the presentation of data, it tended to reflect the assumptions of psychiatrists. Hamilton and his colleagues were aware of the split that had developed between medicine and psychiatry in the late nineteenth century—a cleavage that unfortunately had given rise to a feeling that mental hospital physicians "were somewhat out of the current of medical thought and pursuing matters that were detached, abstruse, metaphysical, and not soundly grounded in science." They noted also the historic difference between mental and general hospitals. Unlike general hospitals, mental institutions depended upon government for their funds and hence remained under lay control for the most part. The result was gross underfunding for mental as compared to general hospitals. "Medical and nursing standards," noted the study, "and standards in all types of therapy had been affected unfavorably, as is shown by any comparison of the personnel of the mental hospital with that of the general hospital."[55]

Although the study appeared to be an objective description of institutions, its authors often reached conclusions that bore little relationship to their data. "Good" institutions, they observed, were related to a variety of considerations: high standards of public service; reasonable levels of public and private financial support; hospital boards made up of disinterested individuals concerned only with the public good; general attitudes of sympathy toward persons in distress; an active medical profession; the absence of "partisan politics"; the selection of "strong" individuals as superintendents; the maintenance of good public relations; and the stimulus offered by the existence of high quality private institutions. Conversely, a variety of elements militated against "proper standards": a callous disregard for human needs; general poverty; partisan politics; an inability to distinguish between penal and custodial problems in the case of "restless, difficult citizens"; weak institutional administration; crude and ill-trained staffs; and the isolation of hospitals from scientific thought.[56]

IV

At the very moment that the Mental Hospital Survey Committee was summing up the case for psychiatric autonomy and defining the problem in largely medical terms, the basis was being laid for a significant shift in public policy away from institutional care of the mentally ill. World War II interrupted a process that in the long run was to undermine the very legitimacy of mental hospitals as institutions. Once the war ended, however, the trends already at work in the prewar era resumed their march.

On the eve of World War II—as the reports of the Survey Committee clearly demonstrated—the commitment of Americans to institutional care of the mentally ill appeared unshakeable. By 1939 there were 182 state and 122 city and county mental institutions in the United States out of a total of 557. The state facilities, however, cared for 82.7 percent of the total number of institutionalized patients, and the latter for only 8.9 percent. In absolute numbers, state hospitals had 382,964 patients and city and county institutions barely 41,185. The remainder of the patients were distributed in Veterans Administration hospitals (26,083) or private (12,799) institutions. Since the number of patients was increasing more rapidly than the number of institutions—a result of both policy decisions and demographic changes—hospitals mushroomed in size. In the 1880s the typical state hospital held about 500 patients; by 1939 only 12 state hospitals had fewer than 500 patients; 30 contained between 500 and 1,500, 62 between 1,500 and 3,000, 24 between 3,000 and 4,500, and 3 exceeded 4,500. The costs of such institutional complexes were by the standards of the era quite considerable. The Survey Committee estimated that total costs, including overhead charges and capital investment, exceeded 200 million dollars annually. Expenditures and quality of care in these facilities varied widely. Nevertheless, the prevailing attitude was that, with sufficient resources, the future would be brighter than the past. When a popular journalist attacked mental hospitals, Winfred Overholser responded with a vigorous defense. If mental hospitals "can be provided with adequate funds and can be kept free from the slimy hand of spoilsman politics," he wrote, "the psychiatrists of this country may be trusted to raise the standards of the mental hospitals even higher than they are at present."[57]

Despite Overholser's confident outlook, public faith in institutional care slowly eroded. As mental hospitals cared for more and more persons whose disabilities were in part related to the aging process, it became evident that the rise in the institutional population would be faster than that of the general population, thereby creating a clamor for more facilities. The chronic nature of the illnesses of other patients simply intensified these developments. Indeed, by the late 1930s nearly 18 percent of patients were on parole. In some states parole involved a trial period to determine whether the individual could function outside the institution. But in others—especially the South—parole was motivated mostly by crowded institutional conditions. Parole represented, in part, a movement toward deinstitutionalization.[58]

At the very same time that the mental hospital was assuming a greater custodial function, American psychiatrists were slowly cutting themselves loose from their institutional origins. This is not to imply that they were unconcerned about the fate of chronic patients, for such was not the case. It is only to note that their attention as professionals tended to be focused on those patients from whom interventionist therapies presumably would make a difference. Those psychiatrists who continued to be employed within institutions emphasized new therapies; others simply left institutional work and practiced in different settings. Whatever the case, by the time of World War II, the interests of most psychiatrists were no longer congruent with those of mental hospitals.

IN THE DECADES followed World War II a sustained attack on the legitimacy of mental hospitals gathered momentum. One manifestation of the hostility toward institutional care was the movement to "deinstitutionalize" a patient population that exceeded half a million by the mid-1950s. Reaction against mental hospitals was perhaps most graphically illustrated in the work of the prestigious Joint Commission on Mental Illness and Health, which had received a unanimous mandate from Congress in 1955 to recommend a national policy for the mentally ill. In its final report in 1961, the Commission proposed that no new mental hospitals be constructed. All existing state hospitals with more than 1,000 beds, it added, should be "gradually and progressively converted into centers for the long-term and combined care of chronic diseases, including mental illness."[1]

The members of the Joint Commission were not merely articulating a vision of things to come. Their report, in fact, reflected the movement away from mental hospital care launched during the 1950s. In 1955 the resident population of state and county mental hospitals peaked at 559,000, and then began to decline. Between 1960 and 1975 the total fell from 536,000 to 193,000. This decline was even more startling than these statistics suggest. In 1940, 434,000 Americans out of a total population of 133 million were in mental hospitals; by 1977 only 159,000 were institutionalized out of a total of 217 million.[2]

Paradoxically, much of the decline in the number of patients in mental hospitals was more apparent than real. During the 1960s the number of mental patients in chronic nursing homes rose precipitously as states attempted to reduce their expenditures by taking advantage of new federal programs. In 1963 the population of state and county mental hospitals was 504,604; six years later it had declined to 369,969. During this same period, the number of individuals with mental disorders in chronic nursing homes increased from 221,721 to 426,712 (of which 367,586 were aged sixty-five or older). The change in the source of funding, in other words, was the occasion once again for redefining aging and senility, but in nonpsychiatric terms.[3]

Those individuals and groups who contributed to the attack on the legitimacy of mental hospitals by urging deinstitutionalization argued that hospitals represented the vestigial remnants of a distant and unenlightened past. The basis of their judgments, however, often differed. Some emphasized the harmful and dehumanizing effects of prolonged institutionalization; others pointed to the availability of new psychoactive drugs and psychological therapies that presumably obviated the need for traditional mental hospitals; many were concerned with the alleged violations of the rights of the mentally ill; the politically minded hoped to shift fiscal responsibility from states to the federal government; and, finally, many individuals hoped to diminish any involvement by government in general.

All of these arguments possessed some element of truth. Yet those who led the attack on traditional hospital care failed to recognize that their existential involvement in the present precluded an appreciation of the historical context that shaped both their perceptions and behavior. They had begun with the assumption that mental hospitals served no purpose other than to perpetuate their own existence, and therefore merited extinction. In arguing for a virtual end to traditional mental hospital care, they contributed toward the creation of a history based more on myth than on reality. Myths, of course, are not without significance. In this instance myth served to justify a reversal of a policy whose origins dated from the early nineteenth century. Once viewed as the harbingers of progress, mental hospitals were now portrayed as monuments to human degradation, brutality, and indifference.

The reality represented by mental hospitals was quite different from the myth. This is not to insist that all mental hospitals were "good" institutions. Diversity, as a matter of fact, was the rule; hospitals varied in both qualitative and quantitative terms. That many hospitals had serious defects and shortcomings goes without saying: the quality of care left much to be desired; staff-patient relationships were often disruptive; internal regimes sometimes rested on coercion; and the institutional environment was in many instances anti-humanistic. Yet these shortcomings were not limited to mental hospitals; they simply mirrored the imperfections and limitations of most human institutions.

The one-sided notion that all mental hospital care was no more than abuse of patients, moreover, precluded consideration of some probable consequences of closing down all mental hospitals.[4] Critics of institutions, precisely because they discussed the issue of involuntary commitment largely in terms of abstract individual rights, often avoided the far more difficult task of evaluating the moral dilemmas that arise if certain individuals are not committed. An absolutist definition of freedom can negate other humanitarian and ethical principles. It is entirely possible to honor the absolute right to liberty of persons in an advanced state of senility by not hospitalizing them. But at the same time does this not deny them their right to care from society when they are helpless, and allow them to die from exposure, starvation, or neglect?

Equally important, few institutions—if any—are either absolutely moral or immoral; the mental hospital was no exception to this rule. With all of its shortcomings, it was among the few institutions that provided some minimal basic care for persons whose mental and physical condition—whatever the origins of this condition—rendered them dependent upon others for their very survival. This basic fact alone—to say nothing about those individuals who benefitted from their confinement and were able to return to the community—should have tempered the unyielding attack on the legitimacy of mental hospital care. To patients the choice was not between mental hospital forms of care and other alternatives; the choice at the time was between institutional care or no care at all.

The role of the mental hospital in providing care for thousands of dependent persons, curiously enough, was largely ignored. Failure to understand the historical context of traditional mental hospital care had decidedly adverse consequences. During and after the 1950s many patients were discharged into communities unwilling or unprepared to cope with them or else into nursing homes that in many respects provided less adequate care than mental hospitals. This is not to argue that the results of the attack on the legitimacy of mental hospitals were exclusively negative, for such was not the case. In many instances criticism led to needed changes within both hospitals and communities. But for a large number of chronic patients, the move away from traditional mental hospital care had disastrous results.

In a statement to a California Senate Select Committee on Proposed Phasing Out of Hospital Services in 1973, Priscilla Allen, a former patient, understood what many professional and lay groups had failed to grasp. She explicitly rejected the generalization that hospital care was always "bad" and community care "good." Many patients discharged from hospitals, sometimes against their will, led a bleak and isolated existence. "In fact," Allen observed, "there are people who will *never* be able to adjust to life within the community." For many of these individuals the community was a threat to their very existence. In a hospital setting, on the other hand, patients

> *are able* to participate in a scaled-down, less threatening semi-community. They "go to the bank" (The Trust Office); eat in a restaurant (the canteen); attend "town meetings" (at Napa, the Imola Community Council, where it is possible to exchange ideas with the administrators of the hospital, including the Medical Director); go to the post office; attend dances; attend various churches; and hold jobs which are sometimes, though certainly not always, meaningful.

Community care and treatment, she added, "may actually mean *less real participation* than a person would enjoy 'confined' within an out-of-the community state hospital."[5]

That a former patient could understand what others failed to perceive was not surprising even if it seemed paradoxical. For more than half a century the functions of mental hospitals had been ignored. For psychiatry and allied mental health occupations, a need to present their members as professionals before a willing public and an emphasis on treatment (unjustified by evidence) had taken precedence over the task of providing humane care for dependent persons. For state and local officials, the needs of the mentally ill were rarely a central concern, and a desire to shift fiscal responsibility to other levels of government sometimes played a major role in policy determination. Lost from sight were the mentally ill—a generally inarticulate group that lacked a persuasive spokesperson to voice its views. Under such circumstances the all too human proclivity to divide the world into moral absolutes operated unchecked, and mental hospitals were identified as a kind of evil to be exorcised. The mentally ill, in fact, often became victims rather than beneficiaries of policies supposedly designed for their benefit.

The debate over public policy toward the mentally ill, of course, was part of a larger debate over social policy in general. In recent decades Americans, even when unable to arrive at a consensus, have addressed a number of issues. What is the obligation of the state toward various distressed groups, including the mentally ill? Perhaps more important, if the state has an obligation, what constitutes appropriate means of care? Are formal institutions that provide total care most desirable? Is a policy based upon the integration of dependent persons into the community better suited to existing needs? Or should the state merely provide dependent persons with a minimum cash stipend, thus permitting them to decide all issues affecting their personal well-being? Beneath such questions lies an equally pressing dilemma, namely, how to reconcile the power and authority of the state with the rights of dependent populations. The failure to agree on the outlines of a comprehensive policy toward the mentally ill is perhaps only a reflection of the inability to achieve a wider consensus on the goals and implementation of social policy in general. More than a century and a half after the creation of a system of public hospitals in the early nineteenth century, American society had yet to resolve the pressing need for providing decent and humane *care* for its dependent mentally ill citizens.

ABBREVIATIONS USED IN NOTES

Journals

AJI	American Journal of Insanity (1844-1921)
AJP	American Journal of Psychiatry (1921-)
ANP	Archives of Neurology and Psychiatry
BMSJ	Boston Medical and Surgical Journal
JAMA	Journal of the American Medical Association
JNMD	Journal of Nervous and Mental Disease
MH	Mental Hygiene
PQ	Psychiatric Quarterly

Libraries

AAS	American Antiquarian Society, Worcester, Mass.
APA	American Psychiatric Association Archives, Washington, D.C.
AP	Archives of Psychiatry, New York Hospital-Cornell Medical Center, New York, N.Y.
CLMHMS	Countway Library of Medicine, Harvard Medical School, Boston, Mass.
HLHU	Houghton Library, Harvard University, Cambridge, Mass.
JHMS	Chesney Medical Archives, Johns Hopkins Medical School, Baltimore, Md.
LC	Library of Congress, Washington, D.C.
NA	Record Group 418, National Archives, Washington, D.C.
NLM	National Library of Medicine, Bethesda, Md.
RFA	Rockefeller Foundation Archive Center, Pocantico Hills, North Tarrytown, N.Y.
SWHA	Social Welfare History Archives, University of Minnesota, Minneapolis, Minn.
UNC	Southern Historical Collection, University of North Carolina, Chapel Hill, N.C.

Organizations

AAPSW	American Association of Psychiatric Social Workers
ABPN	American Board of Psychiatry and Neurology
AFMH	American Foundation for Mental Hygiene
AMA	American Medical Association
AMSAII	Association of Medical Superintendents of American Institutions for the Insane
AMPA	American Medico-Psychological Association
APA	American Psychiatric Association
ANA	American Neurological Association
MHSC	Mental Hospital Survey Committee
NAPIPI	National Association for the Protection of the Insane and the Prevention of Insanity
NCCC	National Conference of Charities and Correction
NCSW	National Conference of Social Work
NCMH	National Committee for Mental Hygiene
PHS	Public Health Service
SCAA	State Charities Aid Association

Miscellaneous

AR	Annual Report
BR	Biennial Report
Bd.	Board
CP	*The Collected Papers of Adolf Meyer* (4 vols.)
Proc.	Proceedings
Trans.	Transactions

Prologue

1. Much of the background material in this section is drawn from my two earlier books, *Mental Institutions in America: Social Policy to 1875* (New York, 1973), and *The State and the Mentally Ill: A History of Worcester State Hospital in Massachusetts, 1830-1920* (Chapel Hill, 1966). Very different points of view can be found in Michel Foucault, *Madness and Civilization: A History of Insanity in the Age of Reason*

(New York, 1965); David J. Rothman, *The Discovery of the Asylum: Social Order and Disorder in the New Republic* (Boston, 1971), and *Conscience and Convenience: The Asylum and Its Alternatives in Progressive America* (Boston, 1980); and Andrew Scull, *Museums of Madness: The Social Organization of Insanity in Nineteenth-Century England* (London, 1979).

2. Edward Jarvis, "On the Supposed Increase of Insanity," *AJI* 8 (1852): 344.

3. Although the census of 1880 listed nearly 140 public and private hospitals, the overwhelming majority of patients were found in slightly more than 50 institutions. U.S. Census Office, *Report on the Defective, Dependent, and Delinquent Classes of the Population of the United States, as Returned at the Tenth Census (June 1, 1880)* (Washington, D.C., 1888), 39-42, 166-71.

Chapter I

1. U.S. Census Office, *Report on the Defective, Dependent, and Delinquent Classes of the Population of the United States, as Returned at the Tenth Census (June 1, 1880)* (Washington, D.C., 1888), vii-xli. Census data are notoriously inaccurate and incomplete; at best they can provide only a highly imperfect approximation of reality. See Gerald N. Grob, *Edward Jarvis and the Medical World of Nineteenth-Century America* (Knoxville, 1978), chaps. 6 and 8, for a discussion of the defects of census materials. Moreover, recategorization of data from census to census compounds the problem. The census of 1880, for example, listed 9,300 insane persons confined in almshouses. A subsequent recalculation, which probably involved a reshaping of categories, placed the number of insane paupers in almshouses in 1880 at 16,078. U.S. Bureau of the Census, *Paupers in Almshouses 1910* (Washington, D.C., 1915), 43.

2. In their analysis of rates of institutionalization from 1840 to 1941 in New York and Massachusetts, Herbert Goldhamer and Andrew W. Marshall also concluded that nineteenth-century mental hospital admissions contained "a larger proportion of psychotic cases and of severe derangement than do contemporary admissions." See their *Psychosis and Civilization: Two Studies in the Frequency of Mental Disease* (Glencoe, Ill., 1953), 35-43, 91. For a verbatim transcript of conversations with patients by a Nevada newspaper reporter in 1886, see Nev. Commissioners for the Care of the Indigent Insane *Report* (1885-1886): 13-20.

3. Cited in Dale W. Robison, "Wisconsin and the Mentally Ill: A History of the 'Wisconsin Plan' of State and County Care 1860-1915," doctoral dissertation, Marquette University, 1976, 7ff. Robison's analysis of the role of the family in commitment is based upon an examination of

incoming and outgoing correspondence of the superintendent of the Wisconsin State Hospital for the Insane, State Historical Society of Wisconsin, Madison. See also NCCC *Proc.* 17 (1890): 431, and Pa. Committee on Lunacy *AR* 16 (1898): 44-45.

4. Nancy J. Tomes, "A Generous Confidence: Thomas Story Kirkbride's Philosophy of Asylum Construction and Management," in *Madhouses, Mad-Doctors, and Madmen: The Social History of Psychiatry in the Victorian Era*, ed. Andrew Scull (Philadelphia, 1981), 121-43; Ellen Dwyer, "The Asylum and the Community: Commitment Patterns to Two Nineteenth Century Lunatic Asylums," paper presented at Organization of American Historians, Detroit, Mich., April 2, 1981; Richard W. Fox, *So Far Disordered in Mind: Insanity in California 1870-1930* (Berkeley, 1978), 84 *et passim*.

My generalization about patient narratives is based on a reading of more than seventy such works. For typical late nineteenth-century examples see the following: Henry T. Helmbold, *Am I a Lunatic? or, Dr. Henry T. Helmbold's Exposure of His Personal Experience in the Lunatic Asylums of Europe and America* (New York, 1877); William L. Trull, *An Inner View of the State Lunatic Asylum at Utica* (Cohoes, N.Y., 1881); John A. Joyce, *A Checkered Life* (Chicago, 1883); A Physician, "My Asylum Life," *Lippincott's Magazine* n.s. 6 (1883): 78-88; Adriana P. Brincklé, "Life Among the Insane," *North American Review* 144 (1887): 190-99; Anna Agnew, *From Under the Cloud; Or, Personal Reminiscences of Insanity* (Cincinnati, 1887); Clarissa C. Lathrop, *A Secret Institution* (New York, 1890); Rose and Barnara Trautman, *Wisconsin's Shame. Insane Asylums or the American Bastille!* (Chicago, 1892). The most famous account is E.P.W. Packard's *Modern Persecution, or Insane Asylums Unveiled* (2 vols.: Hartford, 1873).

5. U.S. Bureau of the Census, *Paupers in Almshouses 1910*, 17, 43; Mass. State Bd. of Lunacy and Charity *AR* 15 (1893): 103; Ala. Insane Hospital *BR* (1891-1892): 56; Ariz. Bd. of Control *BR* (1899-1900): 38; Calif. State Commission in Lunacy *BR* 1 (1896-1898): 161; Kans. Bd. of Trustees of State Charitable Institutions *BR* 3 (1880-1882): 21, 61; Mass. State Bd. of Lunacy and Charity *AR* 9 (1887): 166; Wisc. State Bd. of Charities and Reform *AR* 5 (1875): 135, 150.

6. NCCC *Proc.* 19 (1892): 94-124; George L. Harrison, *Legislation on Insanity: A Collection of all the Lunacy Laws of the States and Territories of the United States to the Year 1883, Inclusive* (Philadelphia, 1884); H. A. Millis, "The Law Relating to the Relief and Care of Dependents. V.," *American Journal of Sociology* 4 (1898): 54-63.

7. Figures computed from data in Pa. Committee on Lunacy *AR* 1 (1883): 489-94.

8. Thomas S. Kirkbride, *On the Construction, Organization, and General Arrangements of Hospitals for the Insane* (2nd. ed.: Philadelphia, 1880), *passim*; *AJI* 10 (1853): 67-69; Nancy Tomes, "The Persuasive Insti-

tution: Thomas Story Kirkbride and the Art of Asylum Keeping, 1841-1883," doctoral dissertation, University of Pennsylvania, 1978.

9. "Report of the Standing Committee on the Insane," N.Y. State Bd. of Charities *AR* 18 (1884): 137-43. This lengthy document provides a detailed description of every mental hospital and other institutions caring for the mentally ill in the state.

10. Edward C. Mann, *A Manual of Psychological Medicine and Allied Nervous Diseases* (Philadelphia, 1883), chap. 12; Joseph G. Rogers, "Report on the Therapeutics of Insanity," *AJI* 40 (1884): 344-52; P. M. Wise, "Physical Health of the Insane," *Journal of Social Science* 35 (1897): 120-24; Irwin H. Neff, "Uses of Electricity in the Treatment of Insanity," *AJI* 52 (1896): 322-24; Samuel Bell, "Thyroid Extract," *JAMA* 31 (1898): 1230-32; William Mabon and Warren L. Babcock, "Thyroid Extract," *AJI* 56 (1899): 257-73.

11. "Report of the Commissioners of Lunacy, to the Commonwealth of Massachusetts. January, 1875," Mass. *House Document No. 60* (1875): 30; Rogers, "Report on the Therapeutics of Insanity," *AJI* 40 (1884): 345-52; Henry M. Wetherill, "The Modern Hypnotics," *AJI* 46 (1889): 28-47; Mann, *Manual of Psychological Medicine*, 233ff.; *JNMD* 16 (1889): 636-44; Calif. State Commission in Lunacy *BR* 1 (1896-1898): 124; W. A. McClain, "Routine Medication in Asylum Practice," *Medical Record* 48 (1895): 516; H. B. Wilbur, " 'Chemical Restraint' in the Management of the Insane," *Archives of Medicine* 6 (1881): 271-92; *Medico-Legal Journal* 9 (1891-1892): 225. Data on nineteenth-century drug addiction can be found in David T. Courtwright's insightful *Dark Paradise: Opiate Addiction in America Before 1940* (Cambridge, 1982).

12. Pa. Bd. of Commissioners of Public Charities *AR* 47 (1876): 216-18; N.Y. State Commission in Lunacy *AR* 3 (1891): 428; State Bd. of Supervision of Wisc. Charitable, Reformatory and Penal Institutions *BR* 4 (1889-1890): 60-62; J. Howe Adams, "A Systematized History of the Insane for Sixty Years," *Medical Times* 29 (1901): 326-28; P. M. Wise, "Statistical Methods; and Recoveries in the State Hospitals for the Year Ending September 30, 1895," *State Hospitals Bulletin* 1 (1896): 157-71; NCCC *Proc.* 4 (1877): 10-11.

13. See Amitai Etzioni, *A Comparative Analysis of Complex Organizations: On Power, Involvement, and Their Correlates* (rev. and enl. ed.: New York, 1975), 23-39.

14. Stephen Smith, "Care of the Filthy Classes of Insane," NCCC *Proc.* 12 (1885): 148-53.

15. U.S. Census Office, *Report on the Defective, Dependent, and Delinquent Classes . . . (June 1, 1880)*, xlii-xliii, 145-57. A study of twenty institutions in 1882 with a total patient population of 11,743, found that the daily average number of patients restrained was 178 (1.5 percent). See D. Hack Tuke, *The Insane in the United States and Canada* (London, 1885), 256-60.

16. Ala. Insane Hospital *BR* (1883-1884): 18-20 (1885-1886): 24-26 (1891-1892): 27-29; *Medico-Legal Journal* 8 (1890-1891): 311-13; Alice Bennett, "Mechanical Restraint in the Treatment of the Insane," *Medico-Legal Journal* 1 (1883-1884): 285-96; Clark Bell, "Mechanical Restraint in the Care and Treatment of the Insane," *Medico-Legal Journal* 9 (1891-1892): 203-48, 384-99, 10 (1892-1893): 3-32; Wisc. State Bd. of Charities and Reform *BR* 2 (1885-1886): 5-7; State Bd. of Supervision of Wisc. Charitable, Reformatory and Penal Institutions *BR* 2 (1885-1886): 67-69; Pa. Committee on Lunacy *AR* 7 (1889): 17-18.

17. For the background of this debate see Gerald N. Grob, *Mental Institutions in America: Social Policy to 1875* (New York, 1973), 206ff.

18. Joseph L. Bodine, "The Management of the Insane Without Mechanical Restraints," NCCC *Proc.* 3 (1876): 104-06; *Ibid.* 7 (1880): 137-42; *Medical Record* 21 (1882): 230-32; Bell, "Mechanical Restraint in the Care and Treatment of the Insane," *loc.cit.*; Bennett, "Mechanical Restraint," *loc.cit.*; Clark Bell, "Mechanical Restraint of the Insane," *Medico-Legal Journal* 13 (1895-1896): 389-94. The Bucknill controversy can be followed in Bucknill, *Notes on Asylums for the Insane in America* (London, 1876); *BMSJ* 93 (1875): 58-59, 681-86, 94 (1876): 228, 435-37, 95 (1876): 268-69; *The Lancet* (1875): 705-07 (1876): 254-55, 263-64; *Medical Record* 11 (1876): 575-76; *AJI* 32 (1876): 582-85; Eugene Grissom, "Mechanical Protection for the Violent Insane," *AJI* 34 (1877): 27-58, 217-37.

19. The range of views can be followed in Bell, "Mechanical Restraint in the Care and Treatment of the Insane," *loc.cit.* See also A. M. Shew, "Mechanical Restraint," *AJI* 35 (1879): 556-62; *idem*, "Non-Restraint in the Treatment of the Insane," *Archives of Medicine* 5 (1881): 79-85; Walter Channing, "The Use of Mechanical Restraint in Insane Hospitals," *BMSJ* 103 (1880): 173-77.

20. Bennett, "Mechanical Restraint," *loc.cit.*, 294, 296.

21. N.Y. State Commission in Lunacy *AR* 6 (1894): 321; Minn. State Bd. of Corrections and Charities *BR* 4 (1888-1890): 244-45.

22. Tenn. Bd. of State Charities *Report* (1896): 19; Pa. Committee on Lunacy *AR* 11 (1893): 28-31. In 1889 the average starting salary for male attendants in seventy-one hospitals was $21.30 per month, rising to a maximum of $27.57; the comparable statistics for females was $16.28 and $21.15. Nevada, Kansas, Texas, and Tennessee did not discriminate on the basis of sex; all other states paid women less than men for comparable work. In North Carolina black attendants received less than white males and females. Data from Minn. State Bd. of Corrections and Charities *BR* 4 (1888-1890): 246-48. By way of comparison, the average annual earnings for nonfarm employees in 1890 was $475; for manufacturing and railroads the figures were $439 and $560, respectively. U.S. Bureau of the Census, *Historical Statistics of the United*

States: Colonial Times to 1970 (Washington, D.C., 1975), Part I, 165, 168.

23. Mass. State Bd. of Lunacy and Charity *AR* 8 (1886): cxxxviii-cxxxix; Pa. Committee on Lunacy *AR* 11 (1893): 28-30; NCCC *Proc.* 21 (1894): 102-05; *JNMD* 22 (1895): 584-88.

24. Mass. State Bd. of Insanity *AR* 8 (1906): 36-38.

25. *JNMD* 11 (1884): 99-101; Ohio Bd. of State Charities *AR* 3 (1878): 92-94, 4 (1879): 27-29; Tenn. Bd. of State Charities *Report* (1896): 17-19.

26. Pa. Committee on Lunacy *AR* 9 (1891): 43-46; Mass. State Bd. of Health, Lunacy, and Charity *AR* 7 (1885): xv; Minn. State Bd. of Corrections and Charities *BR* 4 (1888-1890): 257-64.

27. Minn. State Bd. of Corrections and Charities *BR* 4 (1888-1890): 19; R.I. Bd. of State Charities and Corrections *AR* 10 (1878): 15; Kans. Bd. of Trustees of State Charitable Institutions *BR* 3 (1880-1882): 15; Ohio Bd. of State Charities *AR* 9 (1884): 41; Pa. Committee on Lunacy *AR* 8 (1890): 28-29, 19 (1901): 43.

28. See U.S. Census Office, *Report on the Defective, Dependent, and Delinquent Classes . . . (June 1, 1880)*, xxiv. For the significance of class and ethnic differences before 1875 see Grob, *Mental Institutions in America*, 221-56. Unfortunately, no surviving sources offer precise descriptions of actual ward life and staff-patient relationships. That social and class tensions existed is clear, but it is extraordinarily difficult to pinpoint their precise intensity.

29. Ark. State Lunatic Asylum *AR* 1-2 (1883-1884): 45-46 (1884). See also J. W. Babcock, "The Colored Insane," NCCC *Proc.* 22 (1895): 164-86, and J. M. Buchanan, "Insanity in the Colored Race," *New York Medical Journal* 44 (1886): 69-70.

30. E. B. and Augustin Fleming, *Three Years in a Mad-House* (Chicago, 1893), 25-27.

31. Mich. Bd. of State Commissioners for the General Supervision of Charitable, Penal, Pauper, and Reformatory Institutions *BR* 2 (1873-1874): 35-39, 3 (1875-1876): 35; Mich. State Bd. of Corrections and Charities *BR* 5 (1879-1880): 106-10; Pa. Committee on Lunacy *AR* 8 (1890): 25.

32. Pa. Committee on Lunacy *AR* 1 (1883): 482, 489-94. For typical complaints about the problems of crowding see the following: Conn. State Bd. of Charities *BR* (1890-1892): 37; *idem AR* 16-17 (1897-1898): 31-32, 57-58; Ill. Bd. of State Commissioners of Public Charities *BR* 15 (1897-1898): 32-35; Ind. Bd. of State Charities *AR* 5 (1894): 31; Kans. Bd. of Trustees of Charitable Institutions *BR* 6 (1886-1888): 48; Minn. State Bd. of Charities and Corrections *BR* 5 (1890-1892): 20-21; N.C. Bd. of Public Charities *BR* (1891-1892): 27-28 (1899-1900): 7-15; R.I. Bd. of State Charities and Corrections *AR* 29 (1897): 135-39; S.D. State Bd. of Charities and Corrections *BR* 4 (1894-1896): 11-12; Gerald N.

Grob, *The State and the Mentally Ill: A History of Worcester State Hospital in Massachusetts, 1830-1920* (Chapel Hill, 1966).

33. Horatio M. Pollock, "The Development and Extension of the Parole System of the New York State Hospitals," *PQ* 1 (1927): 53; Pa. Committee on Lunacy *AR* 9 (1891): 34-36.

34. R.I. Bd. of State Charities and Corrections *AR* 30 (1898): 16; N.C. Bd. of Public Charities *BR* (1893-1894): 143.

35. Ill. Bd. of State Commissioners of Public Charities *BR* 13 (1893-1894): 109-10.

36. Ala. Insane Hospital *BR* (1883-1884): 16; Col. State Bd. of Charities and Corrections *BR* 9 (1907-1908): 218; J. W. Babcock to Katherine Guion, Sept. 25, 1891, Babcock Papers, South Caroliniana Library, University of South Carolina, Columbia; Clark R. Cahow, *The History of the North Carolina Mental Hospitals 1848-1960* (New York, 1980), chap. 2; Howard N. Rabinowitz, *Race Relations in the Urban South 1865-1890* (New York, 1978), chap. 6.

37. Grob, *Mental Institutions in America*, 118-30.

38. N.Y. State Commissioner in Lunacy *AR* 3 (1875): 24-29, 43-45, 59-63, 6 (1878): 28-35, 7 (1879): 34-35; N.Y. State Bd. of Charities *AR* 11 (1877): 212-20, 12 (1878): 245-51, 13 (1879): 148-56, 158-59, 166-68, 14 (1880): 177-82, 186-93, 199-200, 16 (1882): 20, 149-63, 20 (1886): 262-79, 21 (1887): 43-46, 217-18, 226-29, 231-34, 236, 247-52, 255-58, 22 (1888): 81-84, 25 (1891): 203-04; *AJI* 33 (1876): 262-66, 277-93, 44 (1887): 305-06; Pa. Bd. of Commissioners of Public Charities *AR* 9 (1878): 39-41; Pa. Committee on Lunacy *AR* 3 (1885): 7-10, 13 (1895): 50-58; *Neurological Contributions* 1 (1879): 97-101; NCCC *Proc.* 11 (1884): 59-60; Charles Lawrence, *History of the Philadelphia Almshouses and Hospitals* (n.p., 1905).

39. S. V. Clevenger, "Insanity in Chicago," *Chicago Medical Journal and Examiner* 47 (1883): 449-65.

40. S. V. Clevenger, "Our Insane," *ibid.* 48 (1884): 139-65; Clevenger to Chicago Citizens' Assn., Oct. 27, 1884, A. Schmidt to Asylum Investigating Committee of the Citizens' Assn., Nov. 13, 1884; H. Pickard to Asylum Investigating Committee (AIC), Nov. 14, 1884, Harold N. Moyen to the AIC, Nov. 14, 1884, Otto L. Schmidt to the AIC, Nov. 14, 1884, Clevenger to AIC, Nov. 17, 1884, Clevenger to the Governor of Illinois, Oct. 28, 1885, Joseph H. Bauland to Clevenger, June 5, 1889, draft of letter of Clevenger to Joseph H. Bauland, June 10, 1889, Clevenger Papers, NLM; James G. Kiernan, "County Provision for the Insane," *Chicago Medical Journal and Examiner* 51 (1885): 424-38; *JNMD* 12 (1885): 475-85; Ill. Bd. of State Commissioners of Public Charities *BR* 9 (1885-1886): 118-19; *Neurological Review* 1 (1886): 44-55; *Chicago Medical Journal and Examiner* 53 (1886): 233-25; E. C. Spitzka, "Insane Hospital Supervision," *Chicago Medical Journal and Examiner* 53 (1886): 289-317; Victor Robinson, *The Don Quixote of Psychiatry* (New York, 1919), 59-99; *AJI* 52 (1895): 278-80.

Chapter II

1. For an analysis of the emergence of the modern general hospital see Charles E. Rosenberg, "Inward Vision & Outward Glance: The Shaping of the American Hospital, 1880-1914," *Bulletin of the History of Medicine* 53 (1979): 346-91, and Morris J. Vogel, *The Invention of the Modern Hospital: Boston, 1870-1930* (Chicago, 1980).
2. James M. Keniston, "Recollections of a Psychiatrist," *AJI* 72 (1916): 465-68; Richard Dewey, *Recollections of Richard Dewey: Pioneer in American Psychiatry* (Chicago, 1936), 98ff.; William A. White, *William Alanson White: The Autobiography of a Purpose* (Garden City, N.Y., 1938), 40-46. See also the biographical entries in Henry M. Hurd, ed., *The Institutional Care of the Insane in the United States and Canada* (4 vols.: Baltimore, 1916-1917), IV, 337-543.
3. John A. Pitts, "The Association of Medical Superintendents of American Institutions for the Insane, 1844-1892: A Case Study of Specialism in American Medicine," 233-34, doctoral dissertation, University of Pennsylvania, 1978.
4. Keniston, "Recollections of a Psychiatrist," *loc.cit.*, 468-69; Richard Dewey, "Present and Prospective Management of the Insane," *JNMD* 5 (1878): 92. See also Conn. State Bd. of Charities *AR* 14-15 (1895-1896): 51-52 (1896).
5. Northern (Wisc.) Hospital for the Insane *AR* 2 (1874): 23-24.
6. For Gray's thinking see the following: "Insanity, and Its Relation to Medicine," *AJI* 25 (1868): 145-72; "The Dependence of Insanity on Physical Disease, *ibid.* 27 (1871): 377-408; "Pathology of Insanity," *ibid.* 31 (1874): 1-29; "General View of Insanity," *ibid.* 31 (1875): 443-65; Utica State Lunatic Asylum *AR* 27 (1869): 17-19, 28 (1870): 21ff., 29 (1871): 62-63, 30 (1872): 24-25, 32 (1874): 23-24. See also Robert J. Waldinger, "Sleep of Reason: John P. Gray and the Challenge of Moral Insanity," *Journal of the History of Medicine and Allied Sciences* 34 (1979): 163-79, and Charles E. Rosenberg, *The Trial of the Assassin Guiteau: Psychiatry and Law in the Gilded Age* (Chicago, 1968), passim.
7. Charles F. Folsom, "Recent Progress in Mental Disease," *BMSJ* 105 (1881): 393. See also William B. Goldsmith, "Report on Progress in Mental Disease," *ibid.* 108 (1883): 345-46; Ala. Insane Hospital *AR* 18 (1878): 12-13.
8. Charles F. Folsom, "The Classification of Mental Diseases," *BMSJ* 103 (1880): 73-75; Clark Bell, "Report of the Progress of Classification of Mental Diseases," *Alienist and Neurologist* 7 (1886): 414-29, 533-34; H. M. Banister, "On the Classification of Insanity in Asylums or Hospitals for the Insane," *Neurological Review* 1 (1886): 205-12; *Journal of Social Science* 22 (1887): viii-xii; H. P. Stearns, "Classification of Mental Diseases," *AJI* 44 (1888): 350-60; Pliny Earle to Clark Bell (copy), April 16, 1886, Earle Papers, American Antiquarian Society,

Worcester, Mass. See also T. J. Mitchell, "The Nomenclature of Insanity; and Obscurity in its Diagnosis," AMPA *Proc.* 2 (1895): 232-36.

9. Mary Putnam Jacobi, "The Prophylaxis of Insanity," *Archives of Medicine* 6 (1881): 120.

10. Henry P. Stearns, *Insanity: Its Causes and Prevention* (New York, 1883), 68.

11. Walter Channing, "A Consideration of the Causes of Insanity," Mass. State Bd. of Health, Lunacy, and Charity *AR* 5 (1883): ccxxi-ccxlix, also reprinted in *Journal of Social Science* 18 (1884): 68-92; *AJI* 33 (1876): 299-307; Ala. Insane Hospital *AR* 18 (1878): 12ff.; Jennie McCowan, "The Prevention of Insanity," NCCC *Proc.* 9 (1882): 36ff., 82-93; Edward C. Mann, *A Manual of Psychological Medicine and Allied Nervous Diseases* (Philadelphia, 1883), 52-66; John T. Carpenter, "A General Practitioner's View of the Causes and Prevention of Insanity," *JAMA* 7 (1886): 225-28, also reprinted in Medical Society of the State of Pa. *Trans.* 18 (1886): 125-34; J. B. Andrews, "The Causation of Insanity: Heredity and Environment," N.Y. State Medical Assn. *Trans.* 8 (1891): 294-301; Charles E. Atwood, "Teachings of Recent Investigations into the Causation of Insanity," *AJI* 48 (1892): 331-41.

12. J. D. Roberts, "Insanity in the Colored Race," *North Carolina Medical Journal* 12 (1883): 254; J. M. Buchanan, "Insanity in the Colored Race," *New York Medical Journal* 44 (1886): 67-70; T. E. Oertel to Adolf Meyer, July 30, Sept. 17, 1896, Apr. 10, May 9, Sept. 9, Oct. 22, 29, Nov. 8, 1897, Jan. 5, 1898, Meyer Papers, Series I, JHMS. For additional references see the *Journal of Mental Science* 20 (1874): 154-56; *JNMD*, 12 (1885): 174-75, 290-93, 13 (1886): 229-44; *AJI* 43 (1886): 278-80, 49 (1892): 56-66, 251-52, 50 (1893): 257-59; Miss. State Medical Assn. *Trans.* 22 (1889): 112-20; *Alienist and Neurologist* 12 (1891): 19-30; NCCC *Proc.* 22 (1895): 164-86; *JAMA* 27 (1896): 1185-88, 28 (1897): 537-38; *Bulletin of the American Academy of Medicine* 2 (1896): 616-21; *Virginia Medical Semi-Monthly* 11 (1897): 129-33. For a general discussion see John S. Haller, Jr., "The Physician Versus the Negro: Medical and Anthropological Concepts of Race in the Late Nineteenth Century," *Bulletin of the History of Medicine* 44 (1970): 154-67.

13. Pliny Earle, *The Curability of Insanity: A Series of Studies* (Philadelphia, 1887), *passim; idem*, "A Glance at Insanity, and the Management of the Insane in the American States," NCCC *Proc.* 6 (1879): 42-59; *idem*, "The Curability of Insanity: A Statistical Study," *AJI* 42 (1885): 179-209. For a critical analysis of Earle's statistical analysis see J. Sanbourne Bockoven, "Moral Treatment in American Psychiatry," *JNMD* (1956): 296-98.

14. Charles E. Rosenberg, "The Bitter Fruit: Heredity, Disease, and Social Thought," *Perspectives in American History* 8 (1974): 189-235.

15. Stearns, *Insanity*, 66; Channing, "A Consideration of the Causes of Insanity," *loc.cit.*, 76-83.

16. John P. Gray, "Heredity," *AJI* 41 (1884): 1-21.
17. The atmosphere of the 1880s and 1890s can be followed in the papers and discussions of such organizations as the National Conference of Charities and Corrections, the Association of Medical Superintendents of American Institutions for the Insane, and others, as well as the reports of the various state boards of charity. For examples see the following: NCCC *Proc.* 14 (1887): 192-214, 18 (1891): 222-29, 385-93; N.Y. State Bd. of Charities *AR* 19 (1885): 26-28, 257-65, 20 (1886): 11-16, 24, 21 (1887): 17-19, 27 (1893): 5-7, 11-12, 14, 38-41; *AJI* 40 (1886): 149-56.
18. Mass. State Bd. of Lunacy and Charity *AR* 8 (1886): civ.
19. *BMSJ* 98 (1878): 281.
20. Richard S. Dewey, "Present and Prospective Management of the Insane," *loc.cit.*, 62-93.
21. Theodor Meynert, *Psychiatry: A Clinical Treatise on Diseases of the Fore-Brain Based Upon a Study of Its Structure, Functions, and Nutrition* (New York, 1885), vii; Erwin H. Ackerkecht, *A Short History of Psychiatry* (New York, 1959), 65-71; Barbara Sicherman, "The Quest for Mental Health in America 1880-1917," 155-61, doctoral dissertation, Columbia University, 1967.
22. Walter Channing, "The Treatment of Insanity in its Economic Aspect," *Journal of Social Science* 13 (1881): 97; Edward Cowles, "Advanced Professional Work in Hospitals for the Insane," NCCC *Proc.* 25 (1898): 285-93; Adolf Meyer to M. Volkmar, Feb. 23, 1893, Meyer to A. Forel, Jan. 3, Dec. 28, 1893, Sept. 17, 1900, Meyer to Clarke Gapen, Sept. 10, 1894, Meyer to G. Alder Blumer, Oct. 23, 1894, Meyer to Julia Lathrop, c. May 1, 1895, Meyer to H. M. Quinby, Sept. 9, 1899, July ?, 1900, Meyer to the Trustees of the Worcester Insane Hospital, c. 1900, Meyer Papers, Series I, JHMS; H. M. Hurd to Meyer, Apr. 9, 1895, Meyer Papers, Series II, JHMS.
23. Utica State Lunatic Asylum *AR* 27 (1869): 17-19, 28 (1870): 21-23, 65-69; Gerald N. Grob, *The State and the Mentally Ill: A History of Worcester State Hospital in Massachusetts, 1830-1920* (Chapel Hill, 1966), 304-08; Ill. Bd. of State Commissioners of Public Charities *BR* 6 (1879-1880): 51; Mass. State Bd. of Lunacy and Charity *AR* 8 (1886): cxxxix, 15 (1893): 74-75; N.Y. State Commissioner in Lunacy *AR* 10 (1882): 168-69.

Chapter III

1. Cf. Robert Fuller, *An Account of the Imprisonments and Sufferings of Robert Fuller, of Cambridge* (Boston, 1833), and Elizabeth T. Stone, *A Sketch of the Life of Elizabeth T. Stone, and of Her Persecutions. With an Appendix of Her Treatment and Sufferings While in the*

Charlestown McLean Asylum, Where She was Confined Under the Pretence of Insanity (n.p., 1842).

2. Material on Packard is drawn from Gerald N. Grob, *Mental Institutions in America: Social Policy to 1875* (New York, 1973), 263ff.; Richard Dewey, "The Jury Law for Commitment of the Insane in Illinois (1867-1893), and Mrs. E.P.W. Packard, Its Author, also Later Developments in Lunacy Legislation in Illinois," *Chicago Medical Recorder* 35 (1913): 72-84; Myra S. Himelhoch and Arthur H. Shaffer, "Elizabeth Packard: Nineteenth-Century Crusader for the Rights of Mental Patients," *Journal of American Studies* 13 (1979): 343-75. For examples of state legislation see *AJI* 29 (1872): 249-58, 30 (1874): 481-89; Iowa Hospital for the Insane at Mt. Pleasant *BR* 7 (1872-1873): 27-31, 38-39, 8 (1874-1875): 24-25; Mass. Bd. of State Charities *AR* 11 (1874): 98-100, 13 (1876): 125-27; Pa. Committee on Lunacy *AR* 2 (1884): 15a-16a; NCCC *Proc.* 11 (1884), 323-25; Minn. State Bd. of Corrections and Charities *BR* 3 (1886-1888): 19, 309-12.

3. Isaac Ray to John W. Sawyer, Feb. 21, 1875, Butler Hospital Manuscripts, Providence, R.I.

4. *AJI* 32 (1876): 346-55.

5. Mass. State Bd. of Charities, *AR* 11 (1874): 98-100, 13 (1876): 125-27.

6. For background material on the NCCC see Grob, *Mental Institutions in America*, chap. 7; Robert H. Bremner, *The Public Good: Philanthropy and Welfare in the Civil War Era* (New York, 1980); and James Leiby, *A History of Social Welfare and Social Work in the United States* (New York, 1978).

7. The discussions at the NCCC can be followed in their *Proc.* See especially 1 (1874): 4-7, 2 (1875): 45-49, 3 (1876): 72-106, 114-19, 4 (1877): 3-30, 134-60, 5 (1878): 10-11, 18-20, 79-101, 143-51, 6 (1879): 42-94, 7 (1880): 90-121. Between 1874 and 1879 and NCCC was known as the Conference of Charities; for the next two years it became the Conference of Charities and Correction; and in 1882 it became the NCCC. In 1917 it changed its name to the National Conference of Social Work.

8. For the origins of neurology in the 1870s see the following: Bonnie Ellen Blustein, "A New York Medical Man: William Alexander Hammond, M.D. (1828-1900), Neurologist," doctoral dissertation, University of Pennsylvania, 1979, and "New York Neurologists and the Specialization of American Medicine," *Bulletin of the History of Medicine* 53 (1979): 170-83; *Semi-Centennial Anniversary Volume of the American Neurological Association 1875-1924* (n.p., 1924), *passim*. The orientation of neurology can be followed in Hammond's "Clinical Lectures Delivered at the Bellevue Hospital Medical College, Session of 1870-'71," *Journal of Psychological Medicine* 5 (1871): 1-53, 311-46, 534-50, 6 (1872): 625-61, and his book *A Treatise on the Diseases of the Nervous System* (New York, 1871).

9. William A. Hammond, *A Treatise on Insanity and Its Medical Relations* (New York, 1883), ix.

10. *JNMD* 1 (1874): 225; *American Psychological Journal* n.s. 3 (1875): 82-83; Edward C. Spitzka, "Reform in the Scientific Study of Psychiatry," *JNMD* 5 (1878): 201-29. The unpublished title of Spitzka's address was "The Study of Insanity Considered as a Branch of Neurology, and the Relations of the General Medical Body to This Branch." The most detailed analysis of the controversy between the neurologists and psychiatrists is Bonnie Ellen Blustein's " 'A Hollow Square of Psychological Science': American Neurologists and Psychiatrists in Conflict," in *Madhouses, Mad-Doctors, and Madmen: The Social History of Psychiatry in the Victorian Era*, ed. Andrew Scull (Philadelphia, 1981), 241-70. See also Barbara Sicherman, "The Quest for Mental Health in American 1880-1917," doctoral dissertation, Columbia University, 1967, 12ff.; John A. Pitts, "The Association of Medical Superintendents of American Institutions for the Insane, 1844-1892: A Case Study of Specialism in American Medicine," doctoral dissertation, University of Pennsylvania, 1978, 150-86; Bluestein, "A New York Medical Man," 259-81.

11. *Medical Record* 13 (1878): 299-300; Eugene Grissom, "True and False Experts," *AJI* 35 (1878): 1-36; *JNMD* 5 (1878): 379-82, 760-61; Spitzka, "Merits and Motives of the Movement for Asylum Reform," *JNMD* 5 (1878): 694-714; Spitzka letter in *St. Louis Clinical Recorder* 5 (1878): 246-52; William A. Hammond, *An Open Letter to Eugene Grissom* (New York, 1878), and *A Second Open Letter to Eugene Grissom* (New York, 1878).

12. W. A. Hammond, "The Non-Asylum Treatment of the Insane," *Medical Society of the State of N.Y. Trans.* (1879): 280-97. This publication, and others, received wide circulation in pamphlet form.

13. My generalizations about this conflict are based on the following sources: *JNMD* 6 (1879): 341-47, 488-500, 7 (1880), 512-15, 9 (1882): 241-57, 401-02, 10 (1883): 618-29, 11 (1884): 277-87; *Neurological Contributions* vol. 1 no. 1 (1879): 1-22, 92ff., vol. 1 no. 2 (1880): 1-28, vol. 1, no. 3 (1881): 61-67; *BMSJ*, 101 (1879): 167-68, 319-20, 102 (1880): 257-58, 103 (1880): 574; E. C. Seguin, "Lunacy Reform," *Archives of Medicine* 2 (1879): 184-98, 310-18; *Medical Record* 16 (1879): 541-42, 565, 614, 618-19, 17 (1880): 246, 553; W. A. Hammond, "The Treatment of the Insane," *International Review* 8 (1880): 225-41; *Alienist and Neurologist* 1 (1880): 260-62; E. C. Spitzka, "What Has Been Done by the Asylum Association in the Interest of Scientific Psychiatry?" *Chicago Medical Review* 1 (1880): 273-80; *Gaillard's Medical Journal* 30 (1880): 506-19; "Report of the Select Committee Appointed by the Senate of 1880 and 1881 to Investigate the Condition of the Insane Asylums," N.Y. *Senate Document No. 68* (March 7, 1882); "Testimony Taken Before the Select Committee of the Senate Appointed May 25,

1880, to Investigate Abuses Alleged to Exist in the Management of Insane Asylums, as Well as to Inquire into the General Subject of Lunacy Administration in This State," N.Y. *Senate Document No. 96* (April 5, 1882).

14. Pitts, "The Association of Medical Superintendents of American Institutions for the Insane," 169-80.

15. Van Deusen v. Newcomer, *40 Mich. 90*, in *Albany Law Journal* 19 (1879): 407; Thomas M. Cooley, "Confinement of the Insane," *Southern Law Review* n.s. 6 (1880): 576, 584-85. Three years earlier another writer proposed that state hospitals be "depopulated" and that states "must cease making a monopoly of insanity." He suggested that public institutions accept only "indigent and pauper patients," and that private facilities care for all others. He also endorsed the establishment of.a board of commissioners of lunacy modeled after the English example to guard the personal liberties of the insane. Ely Van de Warker, "Insane Asylum Management," *Penn Monthly* 8 (1877): 618-34.

In New York the Medico-Legal Society was deeply involved in efforts to alter laws pertaining to lunacy. See "Report of the Permanent Commission to Answer the Senate Resolutions of January 4, 1882, in Reply to the Letter of the Attorney-General and State Commissioner in Lunacy of the State of New York," *Medico-Legal Journal* 1 (1883-1884): 25-43; "Report of the Select Committee on Proposed Amendments to the Lunacy Laws," *ibid.* 54-81; and Edward C. Mann, "A Plea for Lunacy Reform," *ibid.* 158-73.

16. *National Association for the Protection of the Insane and the Prevention of Insanity* [Constitution, By-Laws, Statement of the New York Committee and Papers by Doctors G. M. Beard, J. S. Shaw and E. C. Seguin] (Boston, 1880); NCCC *Proc.* 7 (1880): 90-121, 137-75. The best accounts of NAPIPI can be found in Sicherman, "Quest for Mental Health," 49-72, and Albert Deutsch, "The History of Mental Hygiene," in *One Hundred Years of American Psychiatry*, ed. J. K. Hall (New York, 1944), 339-55.

17. *NAPIPI* [Constitution, By-Laws], 3-5.

18. *Papers and Proceedings of the National Association for the Protection of the Insane and the Prevention of Insanity at the Stated Meeting Held in New York City, January 20, 1882* (New York, 1882); NCCC *Proc.* 8 (1881): 7-8, 317-21; Dorman B. Eaton, "Despotism in Lunatic Asylums," *North American Review* 132 (1881): 263-75; *JNMD* 8 (1881): 151-53, 369-71; *BMSJ* 108 (1883): 132-33; *American Psychological Journal* 1 (1883-1884): 1-23, 100-03, 306-10, 342-54, 422-28; Spitzka, *Insanity: Its Classification, Diagnosis and Treatment* (New York, 1883), 402; Sicherman, "Quest for Mental Health," 55ff.

19. Orpheus Everts, "The American System of Public Provision for the Insane, and Despotism in Lunatic Asylums," *AJI* 38 (1881): 113-39.

20. The debate at the AMSAII appears in the *AJI* 38 (1881): 186-231. Gray

never abandoned his hostility toward NAPIPI. See "The Rights of the Insane," *ibid.* 39 (1883): 411-32.

21. John B. Chapin, "Public Complaints Against Asylums for the Insane, and the Commitment of the Insane," *AJI* 40 (1883): 33-49.

22. Edward C. Mann, "On the Relation Between Law and Medicine, with Especial Reference to the Principles of the Medical Jurisprudence of Insanity," *Medico-Legal Journal* 4 (1886-1887): 105-17; Philip Zenner, "Insanity: Some Points of Medico-Legal Interest," *JAMA* 11 (1888): 769-71; John B. Chapin, "On the Preparation of Medical Certificates of Insanity and Expert Testimony," Pa. Committee on Lunacy *AR* 7 (1889): 66-77; Walter Channing, "Lunacy Legislation, as Proposed by Dr. Stephen Smith and Others," *AJI* 45 (1889): 339-50; NCCC *Proc.* 17 (1890), 430-31, 21 (1894): 294-96; Mass. State Bd. of Lunacy and Charity *AR* 12 (1890): 164-67; Albert Bach, "Lunacy, Real and Ficticious, and its Treatment," *Medico-Legal Journal* 8 (1890-1891): 314-30; Ill. Bd. of State Commissioners of Public Charities *BR* 12 (1891-1892): 62-82; Stephen Smith, "Proposed Change in the Legal Status of the Insane," *AJI* 50 (1894): 325-44; Henry P. Stearns, "Lunacy Commissions," *AJI* 51 (1894): 1-9; *BMSJ* 133 (1895): 326-28; Clark Bell, "Mechanical Restraint in the Care and Treatment of the Insane," *Medico-Legal Journal* 9 (1891-1892): 203-48, 384-99, 10 (1892-1893): 3-32.

23. S. Weir Mitchell, "Address Before the Fiftieth Annual Meeting of the American Medico-Psychological Association . . . 1894," *JNMD* 21 (1894): 413-37 (also published in the AMPA *Proc.* 1 [1894]: 101-21); "Letters from Physicians," *JNMD* 21 (1894): 443-73.

24. AMPA *Proc.* 1 (1894): 22; Walter Channing, "Some Remarks on the Address Delivered . . . by S. Weir Mitchell . . . 1894," *AJI* 51 (1894): 171-81; H. A. Tomlinson letter, in *JNMD* 21 (1894): 512-15. For other reactions to Mitchell see Mass. State Bd. of Lunacy and Charity *AR* 16 (1894): 96-107; *Medical Record* 46 (1894): 48-49; *BMSJ* 131 (1894): 66-68; *JNMD* 21 (1894): 597-604, 22 (1895): 181-83, 718-28.

25. Ill. Bd. of State Commissioners of Public Charities *BR* 4 (1875-1876): 73-76.

26. AMPA *Proc.* 1 (1894): 28-29. See also Joseph Workman, "The Public Care of the Insane and the Management of Asylums," *Alienist and Neurologist* 5 (1884): 492-501; *AJI* 47 (1890): 199ff.

27. Henry Smith Williams, "Politics and the Insane," *North American Review* 161 (1895): 394-404. State charity boards were equally opposed to political considerations in the selection of superintendents, but they were less concerned with maximizing psychiatric autonomy than they were in ensuring a climate in which their own roles would not be impaired. The Ohio board, for example, sought a nonpartisan administration of welfare institutions, a not atypical goal. See Ohio Bd. of State Charities *AR* 4 (1879): 19-20, 5 (1880): 36-43, 10 (1885): 12-13, 11 (1886): 14-16, 15 (1890): 14-21, 16 (1891): 9-13.

28. *AJI* 52 (1896): 446-52.
29. Dewey, *Recollections*, 147ff.; newspaper clipping, April 18, 1893, in Shobal Vail Clevenger Papers, NLM; Adolf Meyer to Lothar R. Frankl-Hochwart, July 10, 1893, Meyer Papers, Series I, JHMS: Meyer to G. Stanley Hall, Dec. 7, 1895, Library, Clark University, Worcester, Mass.
30. William O. Krohn to Clevenger, Mar. 7, 1893, F. P. Morris to Clevenger, Mar. 7, May 17, 1893, Clevenger to Morris, May 25, 1893, Clevenger to William Dose, Mar. 27, 1893, Dose to Clevenger, Apr. 23, June 2, 1893, Clevenger to Altgeld, May 25, 28, 1893, Clevenger to Samuel Dodds, May 28, 1893, Clevenger to C. H. Bradley, June 1, 1893, Clevenger to James Bradbury, June 1, 1893, Clevenger to G. F. Lovell, June 1, 1893, Clevenger to Thomas Riley, June 1, 1893, Chapman Dean to Dr. Effie, June 2, 1893, Clevenger to Board of Trustees of Illinois Eastern Hospital for the Insane, June 3, 4, 1893, Clevenger to Dr. Boody, June 4, 1893, Clevenger to Edmund Sill, June 30, 1893, Sill to Clevenger, June 17, 1893, Dean to Clevenger, June 25, 1893, Clevenger Papers, NLM; Meyer to Lothar R. Frankl-Hochwart, July 10, 1893, Meyer Papers, Series 1, JHMS; Victor Robinson, *The Don Quixote of Psychiatry* (New York, 1919), 106-22; Harry Barnard, *Eagle Forgotten: The Life of John Peter Altgeld* (New York, 1938): 169-70.
31. Hiram Corson, *A Brief History of Proceedings in the Medical Society of Pennsylvania . . . to Procure the Recognition of Women Physicians by the Medical Profession of the State* (2nd ed.: Norristown, 1894), 53; Calista V. Luther, "Woman's Work in the Care of the Insane," Alumnae Assn. of the Woman's Medical College of Pa. *Trans.* 25 (1900): 38; Mary Putnam Jacobi, "Shall Women Practice Medicine?" *North American Review*, 134 (1882): 52-75. For an analysis of the movement of female doctors into psychiatry see Constance M. McGovern, "Doctors or Ladies? Women Physicians in Psychiatric Institutions, 1872-1900," *Bulletin of the History of Medicine* 55 (1981): 88-107. Material on female prisons can be found in Estelle B. Freedman, *Their Sister's Keepers: Women's Prison Reform in America, 1830-1930* (Ann Arbor, 1981).
32. "Report of the Commissioners of Lunacy, to the Commonwealth of Massachusetts. January, 1875," Mass. *House Document No. 60* (1875): 79; Corson, *A Brief History, passim*; Hiram Corson et al., "Report on the Propriety of Having an Assistant Female Superintendent for the Female Department of Every Hospital for the Insane Under the Control of the State," Medical Society of the State of Pa. *Trans.* 12, Part 1 (1878): 167-79; Pa. Committee on Lunacy *AR* 6 (1888): 22-24, 10 (1892): 13-14, 11 (1893): 25-27; Margaret A. Cleaves, "The Medical and Moral Care of Female Patients in Hospitals for the Insane," NCCC *Proc.* 6 (1879): 73-83; *ibid.* 8 (1881): 8-11, 27-28; G. C. Paoli and James G. Kiernan, "Female Physicians in Insane Hospitals. Their Advantages

and Disadvantages," *Alienist and Neurologist* 8 (1887): 21-29; Edward
N. Brush, "On the Employment of Women Physicians in Hospitals for
the Insane," *AJI* 47 (1891): 323-30.
33. Alice Bennett, "Mechanical Restraint in the Treatment of the Insane," *Medico-Legal Journal* 1 (1883-1884): 285-96; Deutsch, "The History of Mental Hygiene," in *One Hundred Years of American Psychiatry*, 342 n.21; McGovern, "Doctors or Ladies?," 88-107.
34. For a defense of the original principles of the AMSAII, see the following: *AJI* 32 (1878): 153-63; John Curwen, "On the Propositions of
the Association of Superintendents of American Hospitals for the Insane," *Alienist and Neurologist* 1 (1880): 1-17, 165-78, and "The Organization of Hospitals for the Insane," *ibid.* 1 (1880): 509-17, 2 (1881):
67-79, 208-21; Thomas S. Kirkbride, *On the Construction, Organization, and General Arrangements of Hospitals for the Insane* (2nd
ed.: Philadelphia, 1880); *JNMD* 8 (1881): 336-47.
35. *AJI* 42 (1885): 60-63.
36. *Ibid.* 64-77.
37. *Ibid.* 44 (1887): 128, 45 (1888): 50-57. See *Propositions and Resolutions of the Association of Medical Superintendents of American Institutions for the Insane* (Philadelphia, 1876).
38. *AJI* 45 (1888): 127-43.
39. Edward Cowles, "The Advancement of the Work of the Association,
and the Advantages of a Better Organization," *ibid.* 48 (1891): 118-24.
The discussion of Cowles's paper appeared in *ibid.* 100-06, 110.
40. *Ibid.* 104.
41. *Ibid.* 49 (1892): 276-87.
42. Edward Cowles, "The Advancement of Psychiatry in America," *AJI*
52 (1896): 364-86, also reprinted in AMPA *Proc.* 2 (1895): 47-70.
43. *AJI* 52 (1895-1896): 129-32, 442-45; form letter written by Adolf
Meyer, Nov. 27, 1894, L. Pierce Clark to Meyer, Jan. 30, 1897 (Series
I), Irwin H. Neff to Meyer, May 23, June 9, 1896, Meyer Papers, Series
II, JHMS; William Malamud, "The History of Psychiatric Therapies,"
in *One Hundred Years of American Psychiatry*, 291ff., 320-21.
44. For the influence of German medicine on American physicians see
Thomas N. Bonner, *American Doctors and German Universities: A
Chapter in International Intellectual Relations 1870-1914* (Lincoln,
1963).

Chapter IV

1. For an analysis of public policy before 1875 see Gerald N. Grob, *Mental
Institutions in America: Social Policy to 1875* (New York, 1973), and
"Reflections on the History of Social Policy in America," *Reviews in
American History* 7 (1979): 293-306.

2. U.S. Bureau of the Census, *Insane and Feeble-Minded in Hospitals and Institutions 1904* (Washington, D.C., 1906), 5.

3. Mich. Bd. of State Commissioners for the General Supervision of Charitable, Penal, Pauper, and Reformatory Institutions *BR* 2 (1873-1874): 43-44, 70-71. See also Mich. State Bd. of Corrections and Charities *BR* 5 (1879-1880): 54-59.

4. N.J. State Charities Aid Assn. *AR* 8 (1893): 27-28, 10 (1895): 55-56; Pa. Bd. of Commissioners of Public Charities *AR* 13 (1882): 5a-6a; Mass. Bd. of State Charities *AR* 13 (1876): ix-xxiv; Mass. State Bd. of Health, Lunacy, and Charity *AR* 5 (1883): cxi-cxii, 6 (1884): xcviii-ci, 71-72, 214-23.

5. N.Y. State Bd. of Charities *AR* 12 (1878): 20-25, 50-54, 14 (1880): 16-19, 17 (1883): 187-246; William P. Letchworth and Sarah M. Carpenter, "Report on the Chronic Insane in Certain Counties, Exempted by the State Board of Charities, from the Operation of the Willard Asylum Act," *ibid.* 15 (1881): 276-77; N.Y. State Commissioner in Lunacy *AR* 5 (1877): 6-8, 11 (1884): 349-56.

6. U.S. Bureau of the Census, *Insane and Feeble-Minded in Hospitals and Institutions 1904*, 37; NCCC *Proc.* 2 (1875): 43.

7. Mass. State Bd. of Charities *AR* 14 (1877): xli-xlii; N.Y. State Bd. of Charities *AR* 15 (1881): 15-16; S.D. State Bd. of Charities and Corrections *BR* 1 (1889-1890): 30-31, 4 (1894-1896): 9; Ala. Insane Hospital *BR* (1883-1884): 13-15. See also Ohio Bd. of State Charities *AR* 3 (1878): 9, 76, 5 (1880): 9-10; Vt. Supervisors of the Insane *BR* (1883-1884): 6-7; Kans. Bd. of Trustees of State Charitable Institutions *BR* 5 (1884-1886): 19; Pa. Committee on Lunacy *AR* 6 (1888): 13-14; Ind. Bd. of State Charities *AR* 6 (1895): 19; Wyo. State Bd. of Charities and Reform *AR* 6 (1896): 22-23.

8. N.Y.S. Commission in Lunacy *AR* 2 (1890): 83-87; "Communication from the Comptroller Submitting to the Senate the Report of the Agent Appointed to Examine the Charitable Institutions of the State of New York . . . April 9, 1879," N.Y. *Senate Document No. 67* (April 9, 1879): 6 *et passim*.

9. See Pa. Bd. of Commissioners of Public Charities *AR* 8 (1877): 8-14.

10. See the statement of Frederick H. Wines in the N.J. State Charities Aid Assn. *AR* 18 (1903): 96.

11. NCCC *Proc.* 8 (1881): 67; George W. Burchard to Pliny Earle, Aug. 22, 1881, Earle Papers, AAS.

12. For sophisticated analyses of these themes see Robert H. Wiebe, *The Search for Order 1877-1920* (New York, 1967), and Samuel P. Hays, *American Political History as Social Analysis* (Knoxville, 1980).

13. My generalizations about Massachusetts are based on the following: Gerald N. Grob, *The State and the Mentally Ill: A History of Worcester State Hospital in Massachusetts, 1830-1920* (Chapel Hill, 1966); Barbara G. Rosenkrantz, *Public Health and the State: Changing Views*

in Massachusetts, 1842-1936 (Cambridge, 1972); Geoffrey Blodgett, *The Gentle Reformers: Massachusetts Democrats in the Cleveland Era* (Cambridge, 1966); Barbara M. Solomon, *Ancestors and Immigrants: A Changing New England Tradition* (Cambridge, 1956).

14. Mass. Bd. of State Charities *AR* 12 (1875): xiv-xxxii, civ, 13 (1876): xxviiff.

15. *Ibid.* 14 (1877): xxxvii; "Report of the Commissioners of Lunacy, to the Commonwealth of Massachusetts. January, 1875," Mass. *House Document No. 60* (January, 1875); Mass. *Senate Document No. 190* (May 11, 1875); "Report of the Commission Appointed to Inquire into the Expediency of Revising the System of Administration of the Public Charities of the Commonwealth, December, 1877," Mass. *Public Document No. 38* (1877).

16. Mass. *Senate Document No. 1* (1879): 14-18; Grob, *The State and the Mentally Ill*, 244-46; Rosenkrantz, *Public Health and the State*, 85-87; William D. Mallam, "Butlerism in Massachusetts," *New England Quarterly* 33 (1960): 186-206; Richard Harmond, "The 'Beast' in Boston: Benjamin F. Butler as Governor of Massachusetts," *Journal of American History* 55 (1968): 266-80.

17. Mass. State Bd. of Health, Lunacy, and Charity *AR* 2 (1880): xxxiii, 3 (1881): lxvii-lxix, 4 (1882): lxxix-lxx, lxxvi-lxcii, 6 (1884): lxxix, 7 (1885): lxxvi-lxxxi; Henry R. Stedman, "The Family System as an Accessory Provision for Our Insane Poor," *ibid.* 6 (1884): clxii-clxxxvi.

18. Mass. State Bd. of Lunacy and Charity *AR* 8 (1886): cviii-cxi; Henry R. Stedman, "The Family System in Practice," *ibid.* 10 (1888): 134-52; NCCC *Proc.* 13 (1886): 264-66. See also *BMSJ* 116 (1887): 242, 265-66.

19. Mass. State Bd. of Lunacy and Charity *AR* 13 (1891): 82-85, 18 (1896): 85-88; Mass. State Bd. of Insanity *AR* 4 (1902): 58-62; Owen Copp, "Some Results and Possibilities in Family Care of the Insane in Massachusetts," *AJI* 59 (1902): 299-313, and "Further Experience in Family Care of the Insane in Massachusetts," *AJI* 63 (1907): 361-75.

20. Copp, "Some Results and Possibilities," *loc.cit.*, 310-11, and "Further Experience," *loc.cit.*, 362-63.

21. Figures compiled from Mass. State Bd. of Insanity *AR* 4 (1902): xxv, 7 (1905): xxxvii, 16 (1914): 295. That family care was not widely adopted in the United States is evident in the discussions in *Family Care of Mental Patients: A Review of Systems of Family Care in America and Europe*, ed. Horatio M. Pollock (Utica, 1936).

22. Walter Channing, "The New Massachusetts Board of Insanity," *Charities Review* 8 (1898): 358-63; *Report of the Commission to Investigate the Public Charitable and Reformatory Interests and Institutions of the Commonwealth. February, 1897* (Boston, 1897), 18-32; Mass. State Bd. of Insanity *AR* 1 (1899): 13-21, 27-33; Grob, *The State and the Mentally Ill*, 329-32.

23. The laws defining the powers of the State Bd. of Charities and the

Commissioner in Lunacy can be found in the N.Y. State Bd. of Charities *AR* 15 (1881): 410-38. See also David M. Schneider and Albert Deutsch, *The History of Public Welfare in New York State 1867-1940* (Chicago, 1941), 18ff.

24. N.Y. State Commissioner in Lunacy *AR* 8 (1880): 9-18. See also Ordronaux's *Jurisprudence in Medicine in Relation to the Law* (Philadelphia, 1869).

25. N.Y. State Commissioner in Lunacy *AR* 10 (1882): 133-34, 12 (1884): 349-50; Stephen Smith, *Who Is Insane?* (New York, 1916), 219.

26. Smith, *Who Is Insane?* 219-22; N.Y. State Bd. of Charities *AR* 22 (1888): 114-16. See also J. N. Larned, *The Life and Work of William Pryor Letchworth: Student and Minister of Public Benevolence* (Boston, 1912), chap. 7.

27. N.Y. State Charities Aid Association *AR* (1886): 21, 15 (1887): 23-29; Smith, *Who Is Insane?* 224; Larned, *Life and Work of William Pryor Letchworth*, 294-96; N.Y.S. Commission in Lunacy *AR* 1 (1889): 25, 43-48, 66-69, 80-81.

28. N.Y.S. Commission in Lunacy *AR* 2 (1890): 22ff., 5 (1893): 6-11, 297-301, 474-84, 6 (1894): 329-59, 7 (1895): 7, 403-13, 710-30; N.Y. State Bd. of Charities *AR* 25 (1891): 69-82.

29. The similarities between the two boards can be followed in the N.Y.S. Commission in Lunacy *AR* 5 (1893): 474-84, and the Mass. State Bd. of Insanity *AR* 10 (1908): 118-41. On the other hand, the New York Board opposed the Massachusetts system of boarding out certain patients in families. See N.Y.S. Commission in Lunacy *AR* 9 (1897): 283-84, 20 (1908): 51-52.

30. John B. Chapin to G. Alder Blumer, Jan. 16, 1902, Clarence B. Farrar Papers, APA.

31. The decline in the almshouse population may be seen in three reports by the U.S. Bureau of the Census: *Paupers in Almshouses 1904* (Washington, D.C., 1906); *Paupers in Almshouses 1910* (Washington, D.C., 1915); and *Paupers in Almshouses 1923* (Washington, D.C., 1925). The changes in age-specific first admission rates are found in Herbert Goldhamer and Andrew W. Marshall, *Psychosis and Civilization: Two Studies in the Frequency of Mental Disease* (Glencoe, 1953), 54ff., and Benjamin Malzberg, "A Comparison of First Admissions to the New York State Civil Hospitals During 1919-1921 and 1949-1951," *PQ* 28 (1954): 314. Data on population growth can be found in the various federal censuses; data on New York and Massachusetts institutional populations are taken from Mass. State Bd. of Insanity *AR* 2 (1900): xii-xv, 12 (1910): 168-71; Mass. Commissioner of Mental Health *AR* 21 (1940): 288ff.; N.Y. State Bd. of Charities *AR* 24 (1890): 22; N.Y.S. Commission in Lunacy *AR* 12 (1900): 103-05; N.Y.S. Dept. of Mental Hygiene *AR* 52 (1939-1940): 208-12.

32. That Massachusetts and New York pioneered in the nineteenth century and others followed is incontrovertible. Unfortunately, scholars in neither the discipline of history nor the social and behavioral sciences have been able to account for the similarities and differences between states in any meaningful way. What, for example, was responsible for the speed of policy innovation and emulation? Was political culture, demographic, economic, and regional variations, or past tradition the key variable? In a study of the diffusion of innovation among states, Jack L. Walker developed a model that included a comparative innovation score for each state. New York led with a score of .656; Massachusetts was second with .629. If Walker's composite scores had been based on nineteenth-century innovations (the overwhelming majority of his examples were drawn from the twentieth century), Massachusetts would have moved into first place. Walker conceded that a great deal of additional investigation was required to understand the origins and diffusion of innovation. Walker, "The Diffusion of Innovations Among the American States," *American Political Science Review* 63 (1969): 880-99.

33. The laws relating to the functions and authority of the board can be found in Wisc. State Bd. of Charities and Reform *AR* 5 (1875): 4-11. See also Dale W. Robison, "Wisconsin and the Mentally Ill: A History of the 'Wisconsin Plan' of State and County Care 1860-1915," 92-98, doctoral dissertation, Marquette University, 1976.

34. Wisc. State Bd. of Charities and Reform *AR* 6 (1876): 8-12, 7 (1877): 13-20, 10 (1880): 173-85; Robison, "Wisconsin and the Mentally Ill," 111-24.

35. Wisc. State Bd. of Charities and Reform *AR* 7 (1877): 14, 16, 8 (1878): 37, 72, 9 (1879): 133, 159, 10 (1880): 21, 40, 48-50, 124, 11 (1881): xii, 270; Bernett O. Odegard and George M. Keith, *A History of the State Board of Control of Wisconsin and the State Institutions 1849-1939* (Madison, n.d.), 161-63; H. H. Giles, "County Care of Insane Paupers," NCCC *Proc.* 9 (1882): 101; Robison, "Wisconsin and the Mentally Ill," 121-36.

36. Wisc. State Bd. of Charities and Reform *BR* 3 (1887-1888): xii, 4 (1889-1890): 3-18; NCCC *Proc.* 8 (1881): 97-99.

37. NCCC *Proc.* 9 (1882): 97-119, 231-40, 259-61.

38. For the position of the AMSAII see *AJI* 22 (1865): 68-74, 23 (1866): 147-250, and Grob, *Mental Institutions in America*, 313ff.

39. For the range of attitudes toward the Wisconsin system, see NCCC *Proc.* 8 (1881): 97-99, 9 (1882): 97-119, 231-40, 10 (1883): 43-49, 12 (1885): 113-16, 13 (1886): 280-87, 18 (1891): 78-84, 320-24, 23 (1896): 9, 181-90, *AJI* 45 (1888): 154-55; C. B. Burr, "A Winter Visit to the Wisconsin County Asylums," *AJI* 55 (1898): 283-99; Robison, "Wisconsin and the Mentally Ill," 141; Richard Dewey, "County Asylums

for the Chronic Insane," Wisc. State Medical Society *Trans.* 18 (1886): 21-27; Henry M. Hurd, ed., *The Institutional Care of the Insane in the United States and Canada* (4 vols.: Baltimore, 1916-1917), I, 168-75, III, 824-49; W. B. Lyman, "The Wisconsin County Care System," AMPA *Proc.* 5 (1898): 280-87; Thomas W. Salmon to Clifford W. Beers, Sept. 26, 1913, Salmon Boxes, AFMH Papers, AP.

40. George W. Jacoby, "State Care *Versus* County Care of the Insane," *New York Medical Journal* 49 (1889): 589-91; Oscar Craig, "The New York Law for the State Care of the Insane," N.Y. State Bd. of Charities *AR* 25 (1891): 72-74; Mich. State Bd. of Charities and Corrections *BR* 14 (1897-1898): 216-17; Minn. State Bd. of Corrections and Charities *BR* 2 (1884-1886): 258-68, 3 (1886-1888): 18-19, 277-79, 7 (1894-1896): 12-14; Md. Lunacy Commission *Report* 2 (1887): 6, 25-27, 13 (1898): 11-13, 23 (1908): 19-21; Adolf Meyer to Henry A. Cotton, Mar. 12, 1910, Meyer Papers, Series I, JHMS; *JAMA* 30 (1898): 674-75; N.J. Council of State Charities and Correction *AR* 1 (1884): 3-11 (in N.J. *Legislative Documents* [1885], vol. 2, *Document No. 33*); N.J. State Charities Aid Assn. *AR* 1 (1886): 13ff., 4 (1889): 72-74, 9 (1894): 13, 19-21, 17 (1902): 7-13, 36-37; N.J. State Charities Aid and Prison Reform Assn. *AR* 26 (1911): 6-9, 27 (1912): 6, 12-13, 29 (1914): 12-13, 32 (1917): 3-5; N.J. Dept. of Charities and Corrections *AR* 8 (1912): 7-9; James Leiby, *Charity and Correction in New Jersey: A History of State Welfare Institutions* (New Brunswick, 1967), 110-19; Harold S. Hulbert, "Medieval Care of the Insane in Modern Times. 'The County Care System,' " *Journal of the Michigan State Medical Society* 16 (1917): 401-06.

41. Pa. Bd. of Commissioners of Public Charities *AR* 9 (1878): 6-9, 10 (1879): 9-12, 11 (1880): xi-xii, xxi-xxii, xxvi, 30, 14 (1883): viii-ix, 19 (1888): x-xi; Pa. Committee on Lunacy *AR* 1 (1883): 419-40, 3 (1885): 5-6, 9 (1891): 9-20, 12 (1894): 8-13.

42. Pa. Committee on Lunacy *AR* 14 (1896): 14-18, 67-76, 15 (1897): 7-15, 43-51, 16 (1898): 7-10; Pa. Bd. of Commissioners of Public Charities *AR* 27 (1896): 3-7, 28 (1897): 3-4.

43. Wisc. State Bd. of Control *BR* 20 (1928-1930): xxii, 21 (1930-1932): 90; Pa. Dept. of Welfare, Secretary of Welfare, *BR* 5 (1929-1930): 75.

44. C. Floyd Haviland, *The Treatment and Care of the Insane in Pennsylvania Being the Report of a Survey of All the Institutions in Pennsylvania Caring for the Insane Made for the Public Charities Association of Pennsylvania* (Philadelphia, 1915), 12-13, 20-21, 68-69, 80-94; Haviland to Adolf Meyer, Apr. 25, 1915 (Series I), Thomas W. Salmon to Meyer, Feb. 8, 17, 1917, Meyer to Salmon, Feb. 10, 1917 (Series II), Meyer Papers, JHMS; Pa. Committee on Lunacy *AR* 33 (1914-1915): 279-84, 34 (1915-1916): 275-322, 35 (1916-1917): 253-59; "Report of the Committee on the Survey of State Mental Hospitals of Penn-

sylvania," Pa. Dept. of Welfare, *Mental Health Bulletin* 11 (Oct. 15, 1933): 3-9, 11-19.

45. Pa. Committee on Lunacy *AR* 27 (1909): 10-21. Shortly after Wisconsin had inaugurated its county care system, Daniel Hack Tuke (the distinguished British psychiatrist) visited the state. He had a generally favorable view of the county asylums, but noted that continued success depended on two elements: continued supervision by a Board of Charities having a competent and dedicated membership; and a careful selection of patients. D. H. Tuke, *The Insane in the United States and Canada* (London, 1885), 82-89.

46. These generalizations are based on a reading of the Wisc. State Bd. of Control's *BR* 1-23 (1890/1892-1934/1936). The declining interest of the State Bd. of Control's interest in the county asylums is evident from their reports; generally speaking, they devoted only about 1 percent (or less) of their written reports to the county asylums. For a more extended analysis see Robison, "Wisconsin and the Mentally Ill," 98-102, 231-32, 240-42, 259-60, 293-96.

47. Ill. Bd. of State Commissioners of Public Charities *BR* 1 (1869-1870): 82ff.

48. *Ibid.* 4 (1875-1876): 74-77. For the position of the AMSAII see Grob, *Mental Institutions in America*, 313ff.

49. Pliny Earle, "Gheel," *AJI* 8 (1851): 67-78; John M. Galt, "The Farm of St. Anne," *ibid.* 11 (1855): 452-57; Grob, *Mental Institutions in America*, 321-26. English psychiatrists were equally fascinated with the Gheel model and its potential application to British circumstances. See William Ll. Parry-Jones, "The Model of the Gheel Lunatic Colony and its Influence on the Nineteenth-Century Asylum System in Britain," in *Madhouses, Mad-Doctors, and Madmen: The Social History of Psychiatry in the Victorian Era*, ed. Andrew Scull (Philadelphia, 1981), 201-17.

50. Ill. Bd. of State Commissioners of Public Charities *BR* 1 (1869-1870): 84-91, 7 (1881-1882): 111-12; Wines to Pliny Earle, Apr. 26, 1879, Earle Papers, AAS.

51. Ill. Bd. of State Commissioners of Public Charities *BR* 5 (1877-1878): 64-67; William W. Burke, "The Supervision of the Care of the Mentally Diseased by the Illinois State Board of Charities (1869-1909)," 35-36, doctoral dissertation, School of Social Service Administration, University of Chicago, 1934.

52. NCCC *Proc.* 5 (1878): 10-11, 143-50; Ill. Bd. of State Commissioners of Public Charities *BR* 7 (1881-1882): 112; Richard Dewey, *Recollections of Richard Dewey: Pioneer in American Psychiatry* (Chicago, 1936), 136ff.

53. Ill. Bd. of State Commissioners of Public Charities *BR* 7 (1881-1882): 116-20, 21 (1908-1909): 478; Dewey, *Recollections of Richard Dewey*, 138-39.

54. Ill. Bd. of State Commissioners of Public Charities *BR* 7 (1881-1882): 120, 8 (1883-1884): 88-92; Richard S. Dewey, "Differentiation in Institutions for the Insane," *AJI* 39 (1882): 1-21 (the discussion on Dewey's paper appears in *ibid.*, 159-67); Dewey, "Congregate and Segregate Buildings for the Insane," NCCC *Proc.* 10 (1883): 441-56. See also the debate at the meetings of the NCCC in 1882 in *ibid.* 9 (1882): 268-80.

55. Tuke, *Insane in the United States and Canada*, 79, 174, 260.

56. Ill. Bd. of State Commissioners of Public Charities *BR* 15 (1897-1898): 45-46; Ill. Bd. of Administration *AR* 2-3 (1911-1912): 491.

57. This paragraph is based on a reading of the S. V. Clevenger Papers, NLM. See also James W. Walker to Adolf Meyer, Apr. 29, 1897, Meyer Papers, Series I, JHMS.

58. *Report to the Governor of Illinois Concerning the Treatment of the Insane, August 2, 1894* (Springfield, 1894), in *The Collected Papers of Adolf Meyer*, ed. Eunice Winters (Baltimore, 1950-1952), II, 39; Meyer to Clarke Gapen, Sept. 10, 1894, Meyer to G. Alder Blumer, Oct. 23, 1894, Meyer to Julia Lathrop, c. May 1, 1895, Meyer Papers, Series I, JHMS; Meyer to G. Stanley Hall, Dec. 7, 1895, Library, Clark University, Worcester, Mass.; Meyer, "The Problem of the Public Care of the Insane," *Illinois Medical Journal* 14 (1908), in *Collected Papers of Adolf Meyer*, IV, 24-29. For an uncritical account see Eunice E. Winters, "Adolf Meyer's Two and a Half Years at Kankakee May 1, 1893-November 1, 1895," *Bulletin of the History of Medicine* 40 (1966): 441-58.

59. Ill. Bd. of State Commissioners of Public Charities *BR* 15 (1897-1898): 45. For a detailed analysis of Kankakee see Mildred E. Buck, "The Illinois Eastern Hospital for the Insane (Kankakee State Hospital) 1877-1909—With Special Reference to Standards of Architectural Construction," M.A. thesis, Graduate School of Social Service Administration, University of Chicago, 1926.

60. N.C. Bd. of Public Charities *AR* 9 (1877): 1-5 (1890): 33 (1896): 43-45, *BR* (1901-1902): 173; Clark R. Cahow, *People, Patients and Politics: The History of the North Carolina Mental Hospitals 1848-1960* (New York, 1980), chaps. 1-3; Tenn. Bd. of State Charities *Reports* (1896-1898): no pagination (first two pages). See also Michael Heymann, "Condition and Needs of the South," NCCC *Proc.* 30 (1903): 370-72, and T. O. Powell, "A Sketch of Psychiatry in the Southern States," *AJI* 54 (1897): 21-36.

61. *First Biennial Report of the Secretary of State in Relation to the Indigent Insane* (Carson City, 1869), 3-4; Nev. Commissioners for the Care of the Indigent Insane *Report* (1873-1874): 3-5 (1879-1880): 18-19 (1881-1882): 3-9; Mont. State Bd. of Commissioners for the Insane *AR* 1 (1892): 3-5, 3 (1894): 20-21; *Report of Drs. Mitchell & Mussigbrod Contractors for Care and Keeping of the Insane. State of Montana* (n.p., 1895), 3-12.

62. Wyo. State Bd. of Charities and Reform *AR* 1 (1891): 4-8, 10-11; Col. State Bd. of Charities and Corrections *BR* 1 (1892): 7-9, 24-26, 2 (1893-1894): 45-46, 4 (1897-1898): 108-10.

63. N.J. Council of State Charities and Correction *AR* 1 (1884): 3-5 (in N.J. *Legislative Documents*, 1885, vol. 2, *Document No. 33*); N.J. State Charities Aid Assn. *AR* 1 (1886): 13-17, 38-48, 4 (1889): xi-xix, 9 (1894): 19-21, 16 (1901): 11, 17 (1902): 7-13, 18 (1903): 99, 19 (1904): 13; N.J. Dept. of Charities and Corrections *AR* 1 (1905): 3-9, 3 (1907): 32-37; Leiby, *Charity and Correction in New Jersey*, chaps. 9-10.

64. Conn. State Bd. of Charities *AR* 1 (1881-1882): 6, 3 (1883): 3-4, 5 (1885): 3-6, 16-17 (1897-1898): 11-15; N.H. Bd. of Commissioners of Lunacy *AR* 1 (1890): 7-10, 2 (1891): 7-9, 4 (1893): 7, 152-57; N.H. State Bd. of Charities and Corrections *BR* 3 (1898-1900): 28-32, 4 (1901-1902): 10-11, 19-21.

Chapter V

1. Edward Cowles, "The Relation of Mental Diseases to General Medicine," *BMSJ* 137 (1897): 277-82.

2. Adolf Meyer to Andrew MacFarlane, Oct. 30, 1907, Meyer Papers, Series I, JHMS.

3. See John Burnham, "Psychiatry, Psychology and the Progressive Movement," *American Quarterly* 12 (1960): 457-65. The distinction between coercive and environmental reform has been made by Paul Boyer, *Urban Masses and Moral Order in America, 1820-1920* (Cambridge, 1978), 175ff.

4. Bernard Sachs, "Advances in Neurology and Their Relation to Psychiatry," *AJI* 54 (1897): 17; Charles G. Wagner, "Recent Trends in Psychiatry," *ibid.* 74 (1917): 1-14.

5. Meyer rejected paresis as a paradigm of mental disease, but he was not typical. See his "A Review of the Recent Problems of Psychiatry," in *Nervous and Mental Diseases*, ed. A. Church and F. Peterson (4th ed., 1904), reprinted in *The Collected Papers of Adolf Meyer*, ed. Eunice Winters (4 vols.: Baltimore, 1950-1952), II, 353ff. (hereinafter cited as *CP*).

6. Biographical data on Meyer can be found in Alfred Lief, ed., *The Commonsense Psychiatry of Dr. Adolf Meyer: Fifty-Two Selected Papers, Edited, With Biographical Narrative* (New York, 1948); Gerald N. Grob, *The State and the Mentally Ill: A History of Worcester State Hospital in Massachusetts, 1830-1920* (Chapel Hill, 1966), chap. 8; Theodore Lidz, "Adolf Meyer and the Development of American Psychiatry," *AJP* 123 (1966): 320-32.

7. Meyer, "British Influences in Psychiatry and Mental Hygiene," *Journal of Mental Science* 79 (1933): in *CP*, III, 403-05.

8. Meyer in *Contributions Dedicated to Dr. Adolf Meyer by His Col-

leagues, Friends and Pupils, ed. S. Katzenelbogen (Baltimore, 1938), in *CP,* II, 228; Meyer, "Genetic-Dynamic Psychology Versus Nosology," *Zeitschrift für die gesamte Neurologie und Psychiatrie* 101 (1926): in *CP,* III, 65.

9. Meyer, "A Short Sketch of the Problems of Psychiatry," *AJI* 53 (1896-1897): in *CP,* II, 273-82. See also Meyer's "A Review of the Signs of Degeneration and of Methods of Registration," *AJI* 52 (1895-1896): in *CP,* II, 256-72.

10. Meyer's review of Kraepelin appeared in the *AJI* 53 (1896-1897): in *CP,* II, 413-17. See also John C. Burnham's *Psychoanalysis and American Medicine: 1894-1918; Medicine, Science, and Culture* (New York, 1967), *passim,* and Karl Menninger, Martin Mayman, and Paul Pruyser, *The Vital Balance: The Life Process in Mental Health and Illness* (New York, 1963), 457ff.

11. Meyer, "Objective Psychology or Psychobiology with Subordination of the Medically Useless Contrast of Mental and Physical," *JAMA* 65 (1915): 860-63. Meyer's later hostility to Kraepelinian classification can be seen in H. M. Pollock to Meyer, June 25, 27, Sept. 25, 1918, Meyer to Pollock, June 26, 28, Sept. 21, 1918, E. E. Southard to Meyer, July 18, 25, Dec. 11, 1918, Jan. 6, 1919, Meyer to Southard, July 22, 26 (?), Dec. 16, 1918, Feb. 4, 1919, Samuel T. Orton to Meyer, Apr. 15, 19, 1919, Meyer to Orton, Apr. 17, 25, 1919, Meyer Papers, Series II, JHMS. See also Meyer's "Emil Kraepelin, M.D., 1856-1926," *AJP* 73 (1926-1927): in *CP,* III, 522-23, and "Genetic-Dynamic Psychology Versus Nosology," *loc.cit.,* 61-63.

12. Grob, *The State and the Mentally Ill,* 294ff. A reading of *The Collected Papers of Adolf Meyer* reveals his emphasis on the importance of patient records.

13. See Meyer, "An Attempt at Analysis of the Neurotic Constitution," *American Journal of Psychology,* 14 (1903): in *CP,* II, 322; *idem,* "Remarks on Habit Disorganizations" (1903) in *CP,* II, 421-31; Burnham, *Psychoanalysis and American Medicine,* 160. For Meyer's hostility toward psychoanalysis by the 1920s and after see Meyer to William L. Russell, Dec. 13, 1928, Meyer to Clara Thompson, Dec. 10, 1929, Meyer to Abraham Myerson, Nov. 26, 1937 (Series I), Meyer to M. J. Exner, Mar. 26, 1931, Meyer Papers, Series II, JHMS. Ruth Leys discusses the problem in her article "Meyer's Dealing with Jones: A Chapter in the History of the American Response to Psychoanalysis," *Journal of the History of the Behavioral Sciences* 17 (1981): 445-65.

14. Meyer to William Healy, Oct. 29, 1917, Meyer Papers, Series I, JHMS: Smith Ely Jelliffe to Harry Stack Sullivan, June 1, 1937, Jelliffe Papers, LC. Meyer's Salmon lectures were finally edited by Eunice Winters and Anna M. Bowers and published seven years after his death under the title *Psychobiology: A Science of Man* (Springfield, 1957).

15. Arthur O. Lovejoy to Meyer, Feb. 25, 1916, Meyer to Lovejoy, May

22, 1916, Meyer Papers, Series I, JHMS (Lovejoy was critiquing Meyer's article "Objective Psychology or Psychobiology with Subordination of the Medically Useless Contrast of Mental and Physical," *JAMA* 65 [1915]: 860-63, in *CP*, III, 38-43); Meyer to E. B. Titchener, Sept. 18, 23, 28, Oct. 23, 30, 1909, Titchener to Meyer, Sept. 19, 20, 25, Oct. 26, 1909, Meyer Papers, Series I, JHMS; Edward J. Kempf to Meyer, Dec. 21, 27, 1918, Jan. 2, 12, 21, 1919, Meyer to Kempf, Dec. 24, 1918, Jan. 8, 16, 1919, Series I, *ibid.*; Meyer to Walter B. Cannon, May 7, 16 (not sent), 21, 1931, Cannon to Meyer, May 13, 1931, Series I, *ibid.* See also Fielding H. Garrison to Meyer, Sept. 20, Nov. 2, 19, 1927, Meyer to Garrison, Nov. 1, 5, 1927, Ives Hendrick to Meyer, Apr. 16, May 2, 1940, Meyer to Hendrick, Apr. 25, 1940, Series I, *ibid.*

Although Meyer was trained in neurology, his efforts to create a psychobiology were not especially informed by work in neurophysiology or endocrinology. He was aware of behaviorism, but never accepted its basic tenets. (See Meyer to Ira Remsen, Oct. 8, 1909, Meyer Papers, Series III, JHMS; John B. Watson, "Content of a Course in Psychology for Medical Students," c. 1912, Meyer to Watson, Jan. 11, 1912, May 29, June 2, 3, 1916, Watson to Meyer, Jan. 16, 1912, June 1, 1916, Series I, *ibid.*) The early twentieth-century debate over the mind-body problem is illuminated in John C. Burnham's "The Mind-Body Problem in the Early Twentieth Century," *Perspectives in Biology and Medicine* 20 (1977): 271-84.

16. Stewart Paton, *Psychiatry: A Text-Book for Students and Physicians* (Philadelphia, 1905), 225-27; Charles G. Hill, "Presidential Address," *AJI* 64 (1907): 1. Cf. Henry J. Berkley, *A Treatise on Mental Diseases* (New York, 1900), 97ff.

17. N.Y.S. Commission in Lunacy *AR* 17 (1905): 175-76; AMPA *Proc.* 13 (1906): 301-09, 15 (1908): 82; *AJI* 74 (1917), 255-60, 285-87, 320, 75 (1918): 287-88; *Statistical Manual for the Use of Institutions for the Insane, Prepared by the Committee on Statistics of the American Medico-Psychological Association in Collaboration with the Bureau of Statistics of the National Committee for Mental Hygiene* (New York, 1918); "The Value of the Uniform System of Records and Statistics of the American Psychiatric Assocation," mss. attached to letter from Albert M. Barrett to Meyer, Nov. 4, 1921, Meyer Papers, Series II, JHMS; E. E. Southard, "Recent American Classifications of Mental Diseases," *AJI* 75 (1919): 331-49, and "The Genera in Certain Great Groups or Orders of Mental Diseases," *ANP* 1 (1919): 95-112; Samuel T. Orton, "On the Classification of Nervous and Mental Diseases," *AJI* 76 (1919): 131-44, 204-05; Meyer to E. E. Southard, Dec. 16, 1918, Meyer to Samuel M. Orton, Apr. 17, 25, 1919, Orton to Meyer, Apr. 15, 19, 1919, Meyer Papers, Series II, JHMS.

18. Paton, *Psychiatry*, 16-25.

19. E. Stanley Abbot, "The Criteria of Insanity and the Problems of

Psychiatry," AMPA *Proc.* 9 (1902): 106-22 (also published in the *AJI* 59 [1902]: 1-16); H. A. Tomlinson, "The Unity of Insanity," AMPA *Proc.* 13 (1906): 137-51.

20. My generalizations in this paragraph are based upon a wide reading of psychiatric and neurological journals and a sampling of the medical press during this era. Specific examples include the following: E. E. Southard, "A Series of Normal Looking Brains in Psychopathic Subjects," *AJI* 69 (1913): 689-704; Phoebus A. Levene, "Some General Considerations on the Methods of Investigating Auto-Toxic Diseases," *State Hospitals Bulletin* 2 (1897): 344-56; L. Vernon Briggs, "Autointoxication as a Cause of Mental Disease," *Alienist and Neurologist* 33 (1912): 281-306; Francis M. Barnes, Jr., "Chemistry of Nervous and Mental Diseases," *AJI* 68 (1912): 431-72; Paul G. Weston, "Analysis of Blood of Insane Patients," *ANP* 3 (1920): 147-50; Henry A. Cotton, "The Role of Focal Infections in the Psychoses," *JNMD* 49 (1919): 177-207, and *The Defective Delinquent and Insane: The Relation of Focal Infections to Their Causation, Treatment and Prevention* (Princeton, 1921); John G. Fitzgerald, "Immunity in Relation to Psychiatry," *AJI* 67 (1911): 687-703; Milton A. Harrington, "The Endocrine Glands in Dementia Praecox," *State Hospital Quarterly* 4 (1919): 183-89; E. M. Green to Meyer, Oct. 5, 13, 1911, Meyer to Green, Oct. 9, 1911, Meyer Papers, Series I, JHMS; NCCC *Proc.* 35 (1908): 286-303; A. J. Rosanoff, "Heredity in Relation to Insanity and Eugenics," *Proceedings of the Mental Hygiene Conference and Exhibit . . . November 8th to 15th, 1912* (New York, 1912), 71-84.

21. See Meyer's "A Discussion of Some Fundamental Issues in Freud's Psycho-Analysis," *State Hospitals Bulletin* 2 (1910): 827-48; William A. White, "The New Functional Psychiatry," *Archives of Diagnosis* 3 (1910): 323-39; *idem, Outlines of Psychiatry* (New York, 1913); *idem,* "Psychoanalytic Tendencies," AMPA *Proc.* 23 (1916): 275-83; *idem,* "Psychoanalysis and the Practice of Medicine," *JAMA* 68 (1917): 1591-96; White to Andre Tridon, July 18, 1919, White Papers, RG 418, NA; *idem, Foundations of Psychiatry* (New York, 1921). For the reception of Freud in the United States I have relied on John C. Burnham, *Psychoanalysis and American Medicine: 1894-1918: Medicine, Science, and Culture* (New York, 1967); Nathan G. Hale, Jr., *Freud and the Americans: The Beginnings of Psychoanalysis in the United States, 1876-1917* (New York, 1971); Jacques M. Quen and Eric T. Carlson, eds., *American Psychoanalysis: Origins and Development* (New York, 1978).

22. Edward J. Kempf, "Autobiographical Notes," 1-2, in Kempf Papers, Sterling Library, Yale University, New Haven, Conn.; *Edward J. Kempf: Selected Papers*, ed. Dorothy C. Kempf and John C. Burnham (Bloomington, 1974), 6-7. W. A. Robinson to William A. White, Feb. 24, 1917, White to Robinson, Mar. 6, 1917, T. P. Scott to White, Jan. 11, 1911,

White to Scott, Jan. 16, 1911, White Papers, RG 418, NA; Smith Ely
Jelliffe to L. Kerschbaumer, Apr. 18, 1940, Jelliffe Papers, LC.
23. Charles G. Hill, "Presidential Address," *AJI* 64 (1907): 6; Donald
Gregg, "A Comparison of the Drugs Used in General and Mental Hospitals," *BMSJ* 171 (1917): 476-77. For a sampling of the varieties of
psychiatric therapies, see the following: Emory Lanphear, "Lectures
on Intracranial Surgery," *JAMA* 24 (1895): 883-86; J. Percy Wade, "On
the Use of a New, Safe, and Efficient Hypnotic in the Treatment of
the Insane: Chloretone," *JNMD* 27 (1900): 447-52; Richard Dewey,
"Mental Therapeutics in Nervous and Mental Diseases," *AJI* 57 (1901):
661-76; Joseph M. Buckley, "The Possible Influence of Rational Con-
versation on the Insane," *ibid.* 59 (1902): 117-27; Orpheus Everts,
"Therapeutics of Insanity," *JAMA* 42 (1904): 1008-11; N.Y.S. Commission in Lunacy *AR* 17 (1905): 208-16; Arthur W. Rogers, "Some
Remarks on the Use of Opium in Mental Diseases," *Wisconsin Medical
Journal* 3 (1905): 554-59; F. X. Dercum, "The Tools of Our Trade,"
JAMA 64 (1915): 878-83; John L. Van De Mark, "Medical Treatment
of Disturbed Patients," *State Hospital Quarterly* 7 (1922): 304-10.
24. See Lawrence D. Longo, "The Rise and Fall of Battey's Operation: A
Fashion in Surgery," *Bulletin of the History of Medicine* 53 (1979):
244-67, and Carroll Smith-Rosenberg and Charles Rosenberg, "The
Female Animal: Medical and Biological Views of Woman and Her Role
in Nineteenth-Century America," *Journal of American History* 60 (1973):
332-56.
25. W. B. Goldsmith, "A Case of Moral Insanity," *AJI* 40 (1883): 162-77;
Robert A. Kitto, "Ovariotomy as a Prophylaxis and Cure for Insanity,"
JAMA 16 (1891): 516-17; I. S. Stone, "Can the Gynecologist Aid the
Alienist in Institutions for the Insane?" *JAMA* 16 (1891): 870-73; C. B.
Burr, "The Relation of Gynecology to Psychiatry," W. P. Manton,
"Gynecology Among the Insane, From the Gynecologist's Point of
View," David Inglis, "The Limitations of Surgery in the Treatment of
the Neuroses," all in Mich. State Medical Society *Trans.* 18 (1894):
458-87; C. C. Hersman, "The Relation Between Uterine Disturbances
and Some of the Insanities," *American Gynecological Journal* 3 (1893):
29-35.
26. "Removal of the Ovaries as a Therapeutic Measure in Public Institutions for the Insane," *JAMA* 20 (1893): 135-37. See also *ibid.* 20
(1893): 182-83, 258; Joseph Price, "Operative Interference for the Relief
of the Insane," *Columbus Medical Journal* 16 (1896): 435-38; Francis
M. Barnes, "Psychiatry and Gynecology," *Surgery, Gynecology and
Obstetrics* 22 (1916): 579-91. See also Constance M. McGovern, "Doctors or Ladies? Women Physicians in Psychiatric Institutions, 1872-
1900," *Bulletin of the History of Medicine* 55 (1981): 99-101.
27. Henry A. Cotton, "The Role of Focal Infections in the Psychoses,"
JNMD 49 (1919): 177-207; *idem, The Defective, Delinquent and In-*

sane, passim; idem, "The Etiology and Treatment of the So-Called Functional Psychoses. Summary of Results Based Upon the Experience of Four Years," *AJP* (1922): 157-94.

28. L. M. Jones to William A. White, Sept. 24, 1919, White to Jones, Sept. 26, 1919, J. G. Whiteside to White, Nov. 13, 1922, White to Whiteside, Nov. 14, 1922, White to A. T. Hobbs, Mar. 7, 1924, White Papers, RG 418, NA; J. K. Hall to Albert Anderson, July 27, 1922, Hall Papers, UNC; Meyer to Cotton, Mar. 26, 1921, Meyer Papers, Series I, JHMS; Meyer's Introduction to Cotton's *The Defective, Delinquent and Insane; AJP* 79 (1922): 195-210. Edward N. Brush wrote a hostile review of Cotton's book in the *AJP* 79 (1922): 124-25.

29. Augustus S. Knight to Meyer, Jan. 4, 1923, Meyer to Knight, Jan. 10, 1923, Dec. 5, 1925, Meyer Papers, Series I, JHMS. The original copy of Greenacre's report was either lost or misplaced during the 1960s when the N.J. Dept. of Human Services made several moves. The original was consulted by Professor James Leiby. Professor Leiby graciously gave me a copy of his notes on the Greenacre report, taken from "Trenton State Hospital Survey—1924-1926 Made by Dr. Phylis [*sic*] Greenacre with the Cooperation of Dr. Adolf Meyer The Johns Hopkins Hospital Baltimore Md." See also Leiby's *Charity and Correction in New Jersey: A History of State Welfare Institutions* (New Brunswick, 1967), 119-22, 220-24, and Phyllis Greenacre to Gerald N. Grob, personal communication, Nov. 16, 1978.

30. Meyer to L. Hektoen, Dec. 5, 1924, May 20, 1925, Joseph E. Raycroft to Meyer, June 6, Sept. 12, 16, 25, 1925, Jan. 25, 28, 1926, May 17, June 3, 1927, Meyer to Raycroft, Jan. 18, 27, Feb. 1, 1926, May 19, June 4, 1927, Augustus S. Knight to Meyer, Jan. 26, 1926, Meyer to Knight, Jan. 27, 1926, Meyer to Henry A. Cotton, Sept. 15, Oct. 14, 1925, Nov. 8, 1926, Meyer to Mrs. Henry A. Cotton, Jan. 18, 1926, Cotton to Meyer, May 28, June 10, 1927, Meyer Papers, Series I, JHMS; "Summary of Investigation Made by Board of Managers of Trenton State Hospital With Regard to Testimony Concerning the Work of This Hospital to the Joint Legislative Investigating Committee," n.d., copy in *ibid.,* Series I.

31. S. Katzenelbogen, "The Trenton State Hospital," c. late 1930, copy in Meyer Papers, Series I, JHMS.

32. Leiby, *Charity and Correction,* 223-24; Cotton to Meyer, May 8, 1933, Meyer Papers, Series I, JHMS; Cotton, "The Physical Causes of Mental Disorders," *American Mercury* 29 (1933): 221-25.

33. C. R. Bardeen, "Scientific Work in Public Institutions for the Care of the Insane," *AJI* 55 (1899): 465-79.

34. N.Y.S. Commission in Lunacy *AR* 7 (1895): 104-07, 8 (1896): 75-79, 9 (1897): 75-236; Ira T. Van Gieson, "Remarks on the Scope and Organization of the Pathological Institute of the New York State Hospitals," *State Hospitals Bulletin* 1 (1896): 255-74, 407-88.

35. N.Y.S. Commission in Lunacy *AR* 11 (1899): 21-54; G. Alder Blumer to Meyer, Jan. 31, Feb. 6, 1900, Meyer to Blumer (draft), Jan. 31, 1900, Meyer Papers, Series I, JHMS; *AJI* 56 (1900): 724-25.
36. N.Y.S. Commission in Lunacy *AR* 12 (1900): 40-46; Van Gieson to Meyer, Apr. 26, 1900, Meyer to Van Gieson, Apr. 27, 1900, Meyer Papers, Series I, JHMS.
37. N.Y.S. Commission in Lunacy *AR* 12 (1900): 39-40; Meyer to Peter M. Wise, June 14, 1900, with enclosed memo, Meyer Papers, Series I, JHMS. Meyer's growing unhappiness at Worcester is evident in the following: Meyer to August Forel, c. summer, 1899, Meyer to H. M. Quinby, Sept. 9, 1899, July ?, 1900, Meyer Papers, Series I, JHMS. See also Grob, *The State and the Mentally Ill*, 309ff.
38. N.Y.S. Commission in Lunacy *AR* 13 (1901): 18-22; P. M. Wise to Meyer, June 27, 30, 1900, Meyer to Wise, June 29, 1900, Meyer to Van Gieson, June 29, 1900, Frederick Peterson and William L. Parkhurst to Meyer, Oct. 14, 1901, Meyer Papers, Series III, JHMS; Meyer to Henry M. Hurd, June 18, 1901, Hurd to Meyer, July 17, 1900, Meyer to William H. Welch, n.d., Meyer to August Forel, August 13, 1900, Meyer Papers, Series I, JHMS.
39. N.Y.S. Commission in Lunacy *AR* 14 (1902): 33-39, 15 (1903): 31-38, 40-48, 16 (1904): 32-48, 17 (1905): 62-81, 21 (1909): 96-106. For a description of a visit to a state hospital, see Meyer, "Review of the Work at Utica—July 5-12, 1903," mss. copy in George Henry Torney Papers, CLMHMS.
40. H. L. Palmer to Meyer, Nov. 13, 1903, Series III, Robert M. Schley to Meyer, Dec. 23, 1908, Meyer Papers, Series I, JHMS; C. P. Oberndorf, *A History of Psychoanalysis in America* (New York, 1953), 84.
41. William L. Russell to Meyer, Oct. 2, 1905, Meyer to William C. Sanger, Oct., 10, 1911, Series III, Alice E. Schley to Meyer, Dec. 19, 1906, Robert M. Schley to Meyer, n.d., c. 1906, Meyer to Robert M. Schley, Jan. 20, 1907, Meyer to Frederick Peterson, June 30, July 5, 28, Dec. 5, 1906, Peterson to Meyer, July 4, Sept. 29, Dec. 25, 1906, Homer Folks to Peterson, Oct. 17, 1906, Peterson to Folks, Nov. 19, Dec. 25, 1906, Meyer, "Report to Miss Schuyler, Mr. Folks and Dr. Mabon Concerning the Reconsideration of the Plans for the Psychopathic Hospital" (June 7, 1907), Henry Phipps to William H. Welch, June 12, 1908, Meyer to Welch, undated, c. 1908, June 30, 1908, Welch to Meyer, June 15, 19, July 15, 1908, Meyer Papers, Series I, JHMS; N.Y.S. Commission in Lunacy *AR* 18 (1906): 59-62, 1232-35.
42. The history of the Psychiatric Institute under Hoch and Kirby can be followed in N.Y.S. Commission in Lunacy *AR* 22 (1910): 45-46, 23 (1911): 96-103; N.Y.S. Hospital Commission *AR* 26 (1914): 295-312, 28 (1916): 158-70, 30 (1917-1918): 2-3, 139-40, 34 (1921-1922): 58-61, 27 (1924-1925): 17-20, 38 (1925-1926): 89-90; N.Y.S. Dept. of Mental Hygiene *AR* 42 (1929-1930): 125-26, 128, 134-37. Hoch's movement

away from his early somaticism and his interest in psychological factors is especially evident in his important but neglected *Benign Stupors* (New York, 1921).

43. Mass. State Bd. of Insanity *AR* 11 (1909): 39. Biographical data on Southard are found in Frederick P. Gay, *The Open Mind: Elmer Ernest Southard 1876-1920* (n.p., 1938), and Mass. Dept. of Mental Diseases *Bulletin* 4 (1920).

44. Smith Ely Jelliffe to Karl Menninger, May 29, 1939, Jelliffe Papers, LC; E. E. Southard, "The Psychopathic Hospital Idea," *JAMA* 61 (1913): 1973; Mass. State Bd. of Insanity *AR* 11 (1909): 46, 12 (1910): 77-78, 85, 13 (1911): 35-36, 15 (1913): 43-47, 17 (1915): 50; Mass. Commission on Mental Diseases *AR* 2 (1917): 41-42; Southard, "A Study of the Dementia Praecox Group in the Light of Certain Cases Showing Anomalies or Sclerosis in Particular Brain Regions," *AJI* 67 (1910): 119-76; Gay, *Open Mind*, 100-01.

45. Mass. State Bd. of Insanity *AR* 12 (1910): 81, 15 (1913): 27-28, 17 (1915): 52-54, 71-73; Mass. Commission on Mental Diseases *AR* 1 (1916): 40-42, 2 (1917): 40; E. E. Southard and Harry C. Solomon, *Neurosyphilis: Modern Systematic Diagnosis and Treatment Presented in One Hundred and Thirty-Seven Case Histories* (Boston, 1917); Southard to Thomas W. Salmon, July 24, 1919, Salmon Boxes in AFMH Papers, AP.

46. Ill. Bd. of State Commissioners of Public Charities *BR* 19 (1905-1906): 551, 20 (1907-1908): 95-98; Ill. Bd. of Administration *AR* 2-3 (1911-1912): 29-31, 607-15, 624-26, 4-5 (1913-1914): vol. 2, 149, 6-7 (1915-1916): vol. 2, 164-67; Ill. State Charities Commission *AR* 6 (1915): 18-19; Ill. Dept. of Public Welfare *AR* 4 (1920-1921): 56-57.

47. Ill. Dept. of Public Welfare *AR* 6 (1922-1923): 62.

48. Wisc. State Bd. of Control *BR* 13 (1914-1916): 106-16, 14 (1916-1918): 96-98, 15 (1918-1920): 140-41, 17 (1922-1924): 152-54, 18 (1924-1926): 282. There were earlier attempts to create close relationships between mental hospitals and universities, but few succeeded. In Michigan the state hospitals were unwilling to commit their own funds to university-based research; they wanted additional funds from the state for the establishment of such laboratories or institutes. Moreover, hospital trustees were disinterested in research; among superintendents, as the medical director of the Eastern Michigan Asylum noted, "there is no unanimity of opinion as to how the work should be conducted." E. H. Christian to Meyer, Nov. 21, 1903, Irwin H. Neff to Meyer, Nov. 21, 1903, Meyer Papers, Series I, JHMS.

49. E. E. Southard to Thomas W. Salmon, July 24, 1919, Salmon to Southard, July 21, 1919, Salmon Boxes in AFMH Papers, AP.

50. Minn. State Bd. of Corrections and Charities *BR* 2 (1884-1886): 106-07; Matthew D. Field, "Detention Hospitals for the Insane," *JNMD* 20 (1893): 599-608, also reprinted in ANA *Trans.* 19 (1893): 7-17.

51. J. Montgomery Mosher, "Pavilion F, A Department for Mental Diseases of the Albany Hospital," NCCC *Proc.* 34 (1907): 423.

52. *Ibid.*, 422-31.

53. Albert M. Barrett, "Hospitals for the Acute and Recoverable Insane," NCCC *Proc.* 34 (1907): 397-411; Mich. State Bd. of Corrections and Charities *BR* 18 (1905-1906): 151-52.

54. Meyer, "Reception Hospitals, Psychopathic Wards, and Psychopathic Hospitals," AMPA *Proc.* 14 (1907): 191. For evidence of widespread interest in such institutions, see Mass. State Bd. of Insanity *AR* 4 (1902): 13-15; Md. Lunacy Commission *Report* 17 (1902): 20-23, 20 (1905): 7-11; N.Y.S. Commission in Lunacy *AR* 14 (1902): 7-8, 18 (1906): 1232-35; Ind. Bd. of State Charities *AR* 14 (1903): 31; William J. Herdman, "Reception Hospitals for the Insane," NCCC *Proc.* 30 (1903): 434-38; R.I. Bd. of State Charities and Corrections *AR* 36 (1904): 20-21; Minn. State Bd. of Control *BR* 3 (1904-1906): 60-61; *JAMA* 44 (1905): 218-19; C. P. Bancroft, "Reception Hospitals and Psychopathic Wards in State Hospitals for the Insane," *AJI* 65 (1908): 57-62; M. S. Gregory, "Reception Hospitals, Psychopathic Wards and Psychopathic Hospitals," *AJI* 65 (1908): 63-76.

55. Adolf Meyer and C. Macfie Campbell, "The Henry Phipps Psychiatric Clinic: Its Relation to Medical Education and Research and to the Mental Hygiene of the Community," c. 1920, typed mss. in Meyer Papers, Series I, JHMS.

56. Meyer to Harvey Cushing, Apr. 26, 1919, Meyer to David T. Layman, Jr., June 21, 1922, *ibid.*; Alan M. Chesney, *The Johns Hopkins Hospital and the Johns Hopkins University School of Medicine* (3 vols.: Baltimore, 1943-1963), III, 90-94, 188-92, 233-42.

57. Meyer to Harvey Cushing, Apr. 26, 1919, Richard S. Lyman, "Dr. Lyman's Impressions of the HPPC at the Start, about 1925 & to-day," Mar. 23, 1939, Meyer Papers, Series I, JHMS. For some of the troubled relationships between psychology and psychiatry see John B. Watson, "Content of a Course in Psychology for Medical Students," c. 1912, Meyer to Watson, Jan. 11, 1912, May 29, June 2, 3, 1916, Watson to Meyer, Jan. 16, 1912, June 1, 1916; A. H. Sutherland to Meyer, Feb. 22, Mar. 9, 23, 1914, Meyer to Sutherland, Mar. 5, 20, 25, 1914, Madison Bentley to Meyer, Feb. 22, 1914, *ibid.*

58. The events leading to the establishment of the Psychopathic Hospital are detailed in L. Vernon Briggs and collaborators, *History of the Psychopathic Hospital, Boston, Massachusetts* (Boston, 1922). In this volume Briggs reprinted a large number of manuscript and published material, making it an indispensable source book.

59. The conflict can be followed in Briggs, *History of the Psychopathic Hospital*; idem, *A Victory for Progress in Mental Medicine: Defeat of Reactionaries, the History of an Intrigue* (Boston, 1924); idem, *Occupation as a Substitute for Restraint in the Treatment of the Mentally*

Ill: A History of the Passage of Two Bills Through the Massachusetts Legislature (Boston, 1923); Meyer, *CP*, IV, 43-69; Southard to Meyer, June 15, 1911, Meyer to Southard, June 18, 1911, Meyer to L. Vernon Briggs, June 18, July 21, Oct. 2, 1911, Meyer to H. B. Howard, June 29, 1911, Owen Copp to Meyer, July 15, 1911, Meyer to Copp, July 21, 1911, Meyer Papers, Series III, JHMS; Henry R. Stedman to William A. White, Apr. 26, 30, 1911, White to Stedman, Apr. 30, 1911, White Papers, RG 418, NA.

60. Southard, "The Psychopathic Hospital Idea," *JAMA* 61 (1913): 1974.
61. Mass. Commission of Mental Diseases *AR* 2 (1917): 154-55.
62. "Report of Director of Psychopathic Hospital to the Trustees of the Boston State Hospital, February, 1915," in "Report of the Director of the Psychopathic Department of the Boston State Hospital 1915," and "Report of the Director of the Psychopathic Department of Boston State Hospital for the Month of May, 1916," in "Notes to Trustees 1916," mss. vols., CLMHMS; Briggs, *History of the Psychopathic Hospital*, 158.
63. Donald Gregg, "A Comparison of the Drugs Used in General and Mental Hospitals," *BMSJ* 171 (1917): 476-77; Milton Greenblatt et al., *From Custodial to Therapeutic Care in Mental Hospitals* (New York, 1955), 40-41.
64. C. Macfie Campbell to Meyer, Jan. 20, 1921, Meyer Papers, Series I, JHMS; Campbell, "The Work of the Psychopathic Hospital," *MH* 14 (1930): 887-88.
65. Mass. Commissioner of Mental Diseases *AR* 2 (1921): 216-20.
66. For a slightly different interpretation, see Jacques M. Quen, "Asylum Psychiatry, Neurology, Social Work, and Mental Hygiene: An Exploratory Study in Interprofessional History," *Journal of the History of the Behavioral Sciences* 13 (1977): 3-11.

Chapter VI

1. Thomas W. Salmon, "Some New Fields in Neurology and Psychiatry," *JNMD* 46 (1917): 90-99.
2. Mental hygiene encompassed a variety of concerns and activities. This chapter, however, will focus only on those aspects of the movement that were related to the mentally ill.
3. Henry P. Stearns, *Insanity: Its Causes and Prevention* (New York, 1883), 238. Similar statements appear in the following: *AJI* 33 (1876): 299-307; Nathan Allen, "The Prevention of Disease and Insanity," NCCC *Proc.* 5 (1878): 79-90; Ala. Insane Hospital *AR* 18 (1878): 13-44; Mary Putnam Jacobi, "The Prophylaxis of Insanity," *Archives of Medicine* 6 (1881): 12-35; Charles F. Folsom, "The Prevention of Insanity," American Public Health Assn. *Public Health Reports and Papers* 7 (1881): 83-90; Walter Channing, "A Consideration of the

Causes of Insanity," *Journal of Social Science* 18 (1884): 68-92; Jennie McCowen, "The Prevention of Insanity," NCCC *Proc.* 9 (1882): 36ff.; Edward C. Mann, *A Manual of Psychological Medicine and Allied Nervous Diseases* (Philadelphia, 1883), chap. 3; John T. Carpenter, "A General Practitioner's View of the Causes and Prevention of Insanity," *JAMA* 7 (1886): 225-28.

4. Charles P. Bancroft, "Hopeful and Discouraging Aspects of the Psychiatric Outlook," AMPA *Proc.* 15 (1908): 110.

5. For information on Beers I have drawn extensively from Norman Dain's authoritative *Clifford W. Beers: Advocate for the Insane* (Pittsburgh, 1980).

6. Beers, "To Whom It May Concern," Jan. 1, 1905, AFMH Papers, AP; Dain, *Beers*, 53-56.

7. Beers to Victor M. Tyler, Jan. 2, 1905, Beers to George M. Beers, Jan. 3, 1905, G. M. Beers to Beers, Mar. 15, 1905, Beers to Robert Beers, Jan. 5, 1905, Beers to William James, June 9 (two letters), July 10, Aug. 12, 1906, Mar. 24, 1907, Beers to Longmans, Green and Co., Mar. 12, 1907, Beers to Herbert Fisher, Mar. 15, 1907, AFMH Papers, AP; William James to Beers, July 1, 1906, Mar. 17, 1907, James Papers, HLHU; Dain, *Beers*, 56-67.

8. William M. McDonald, Jr., to Beers, June 7, Sept. 6, 1907, Beers to McDonald, June 10, Sept. 13, 1907, Charles W. Page to Beers, Mar. 8, June 28, 1906, Mar. 22, May 14, 1907, Beers to Page, May 22, Sept. 18, 1906, Mar. 31, Apr. 12, 23, 1907, August Hoch to Beers, Jan. 4, 1907, Whitefield N. Thompson to Beers, Mar. 7, 1907, W. E. Fisher to Beers, June 18, 1907, Beers to Fisher, June 21, 1907, AFMH Papers, AP.

9. Beers to Meyer, Sept. 24, 30, Oct. 7, 14, 16, 24, 25, 26, 29, Nov. 7, 1907, Meyer to Beers, undated letter, Meyer to Henry S. Noble, Feb. 28, 1908, Meyer Papers, Series II, JHMS; Stewart Paton to Beers, May 30, 1907, Meyer to Beers, Oct. 10, 26, 1907, Beers to Meyer, Oct. 29, 1907, Meyer "To Whom It May Concern," Oct. 27, 1907, Meyer to the Editor of the N.Y. *Sun*, Apr. 1, 1908, Beers to Herbert W. Fisher, Oct. 23, 1907, AFMH Papers, AP; Meyer review in *North American Review* 187 (1908): 611-14. The various drafts of *A Mind That Found Itself* are found in boxes 1-6 of the Beers Papers in Sterling Library, Yale University, New Haven, Conn. The most accurate treatment of the relationship between Beers and Meyer can be found in Dain's *Clifford W. Beers*; Eunice E. Winters's "Adolf Meyer and Clifford Beers, 1907-1910," *Bulletin of the History of Medicine*, 43 (1969): 414-43, is fatally marred by the author's close association with Meyer and her uncritical analysis.

10. Dain, *Clifford W. Beers*, 89; Beers, *A Mind That Found Itself* (New York, 1908).

11. Beers "To Whom It May Concern," Jan. 1, 1905, Beers to Charles W. Page, May 22, 1906, Beers to Herbert W. Fisher, June 15, 1906, Beers

to William James, Apr. 16, 1907, Beers to Stewart Paton, July 22, 1907, Beers to Anson Phelps Stokes, Aug. 9, 1907, AFMH Papers, AP; William James to Beers, Apr. 21, 1907, James Papers, HLHU. My discussion of Beers and Meyer and the formation and early history of the NCMH to 1911 is based on a careful reading of the voluminous manuscript material in the AFMH Papers (AP), the William James Papers (HLHU), and the Meyer Papers (JHMS). Because of the limitations of space, I have cited only a relatively small number of letters; fuller substantiation of my generalizations can be found in these collections. The most detailed and reliable study is Dain's *Clifford W. Beers*, chaps. 7-12.

12. Beers to Meyer, Oct. 26, 1907, Meyer Papers, Series II, JHMS; Meyer "To Whom It May Concern," Oct. 27, 1907, Beers to Meyer, Nov. 13, 1907, Beers to Herbert W. Fisher, Nov. 6, 1907, Meyer to Henry S. Noble, Feb. 13, 1908, AFMH Papers, AP.

13. Beers to Herbert W. Fisher, Nov. 6, 1907, Beers to Joseph H. Choate, Jan. 10, 1908, Beers to Theodore Roosevelt, Mar. 4, 1908, William Loeb to Beers, Mar. 9, 1908, Beers to Frederick T. Gates, Mar. 9, 1908, AFMH Papers, AP.

14. "Preliminary Prospectus or Scope of the Planned Work of the Connecticut Society for Mental Hygiene" (New Haven, 1908), printed copy in AFMH Papers, AP.

15. Meyer to Beers, Apr. 6, 23, 29, July 18, 29, 1908, Beers to Meyer, July 21, Aug. 11, 1908, Beers to William James, Apr. 8, June 16, July 31, Aug. 12, 1908, "Minutes of the First Meeting of the Connecticut Society for Mental Hygiene (May 6, 1908)," AFMH Papers, AP; *The Connecticut Society for Mental Hygiene* (n.p., c. 1908), copy in *ibid*.

16. Beers to Meyer, Oct. 27, Dec. 22, 23, 31, 1908, Meyer to Beers, Dec. 19, 22, 1908, undated letter, c. late 1908 or early 1909, AFMH Papers, AP.

17. "Minutes for the Founding of a National Committee of Mental Hygiene. February 19, 1909," Beers to Meyer, Dec. 23, 31, 1908, Feb. 15, 1909, AFMH Papers, AP.

18. William James to Beers, Feb. 21, 26, 1909, Beers to James, Feb. 22, 25, 1909, Beers to Meyer, Feb. 26, Mar. 1, Apr. 5, 1909, Meyer to Beers, Feb. 27, Apr. 3, 1909, AFMH Papers, AP; Dain, *Clifford W. Beers*, 132-33.

19. Meyer to Beers, Mar. 2, Oct. 25, Nov. 13, 29, 1909, Meyer to George Blumer, Feb. 19, 1910, Beers to James, Feb. 22, 1909, Jan. 11, 1910, Beers to Anson Phelps Stokes, Oct. 8, 1909, Stewart Paton to Beers, Oct. 25, 1909, AFMH Papers, AP; Meyer to Stewart Paton, Dec. 11, 1909, Meyer Papers, Series II, JHMS. For a detailed account of the Beers-Meyer relationship, see Dain, *Clifford W. Beers*, chap. 10.

20. Meyer to Beers, Nov. 30, 1909, Meyer to Anson Phelps Stokes, Feb. 25, 1910, Meyer to James, Feb. 28, 1910, Beers to James, Mar. 10, 16,

1910, AFMH Papers, AP; James to Beers, Mar. 3, 5, 1910, James Papers, HLHU.

21. Beers to Meyer, Jan. 27, 28, 31, Feb. 1, Sept. 6, Dec. 19, 1910, Meyer to Beers, July 22, 1910, Russell H. Chittenden to Meyer, Feb. 25, Mar. 2, 4, Apr. 18, 1910, Meyer to Chittenden, Feb. 26, Mar. 3, Apr. 2, 1910, Meyer to George Blumer, Feb. 26, Dec. 2, 10, 1910, Blumer to Meyer, Dec. 1, 9, 12, 1910, Anson Phelps Stokes to Meyer, Mar. 9, 1910, Meyer to Stokes, Mar. 12, 1910, Meyer Papers, Series II, JHMS; George Blumer to Charles P. Emerson, c. Apr., 1910, Meyer to Henry B. Favill, May 8, 1910, Beers to James, July 22, 1910, Meyer to Beers, Aug. 14, Dec. 10, 1910, AFMH Papers, AP.

22. Summary of the proceedings of the third annual meeting of the NCMH, p. 2, mss. copy in AFMH Papers, AP; William H. Welch to Beers, Nov. 4, 1911, "Conclusion," undated item by Beers, Beers to George M. Beers, Dec. 25, 1911, "Income of the National Committee for Mental Hygiene, Inc. From 1909 to and including 1934," *ibid.*

23. Biographical data culled from Earl D. Bond, *Thomas W. Salmon, Psychiatrist* (New York, 1950). For Salmon's views on immigration, see his "The Relationship of Immigration to the Prevalence of Insanity," *AJI* 64 (1907): 53-71; "Insanity and the Immigration Law," *State Hospitals Bulletin* 4 (1911): 379-98; "Immigration and the Prevention of Insanity," *BMSJ* 169 (1913): 297-301; "Immigration and the Mixture of Races in Relation to the Mental Health of the Nation," in *The Modern Treatment of Nervous and Mental Diseases*, ed. William A. White and Smith Ely Jelliffe (2 vols.: Philadelphia, 1913), I, 241-86; "Minutes of the 4th Annual Meeting of the Committee for Mental Hygiene . . . Feb. 17, 1912," 26-30, mimeographed copy in AFMH Papers, AP; Salmon to Homer Folks, July 11, 1913 (with enclosure "Memorandum for Mr. Folks"), Salmon to Stewart Paton, Jan. 16, 1915, Arthur P. Kellys (?) to Salmon, Feb. 26, 1915, Salmon Boxes in AFMH Papers, AP.

24. For the vagueness of etiological thinking, see Meyer to Salmon, Nov. 23, 1911, Meyer Papers, Series I, JHMS. The antiprostitution movement can be followed in Mark T. Connelly, *The Response to Prostitution in the Progressive Era* (Chapel Hill, 1980).

25. Beers to Jane Addams, Feb. 27, 1911, William L. Russell to Beers, May 24, 1911, "Minutes of the 4th Annual Meeting of the National Committee for Mental Hygiene . . . Feb. 17, 1912," 13-15, AFMH Papers, AP.

26. "A Summary of Crises in the Financial History of the National Committee for Mental Hygiene, showing that it was rescued by substantial gifts from a few individuals of wealth who had the vision to see the needs and meet them" (June 10, 1929), AFMH Papers, Uncatalogued, AP.

27. Beers to Samuel S. Marquis, Dec. 22, 1913, AFMH Papers, AP; Meyer

to Stewart Paton, May 19, 1913 (Series I), Jerome D. Greene to Meyer, Sept. 14, 1914, Meyer to Greene, Sept. 17, 1914, Meyer Papers, Series III, JHMS; Beers to William A. White, Apr. 11, 1918, with enclosed "Report of the Activities of the Rockefeller Foundation in Mental Hygiene 1915-1918," 1-2, 19-22, White Papers, RG 418, NA; William H. Welch to John D. Rockefeller, June 29, 1913, "Memorandum by Mr. Greene on National Committee for Mental Hygiene," Dec. 4, 1913, "Memorandum on National Committee for Mental Hygiene," Dec. 16, 1913, Welch to Greene, Dec. 22, 1914, Memorandum by Greene on NCMH, Dec. 29, 30, 1914, Salmon to Greene, Sept. 10, 16, Oct. 29, 1915, June 5, Nov. 3, 1916, Record Group 1.1, Series 200 (NCMH), RFA.

There is no adequate study of the activities of the Rockfeller Foundation. E. Richard Brown's *Rockefeller Medicine Men: Medicine and Capitalism in America* (Berkeley, 1979), and Christine Mary Shea's "The Ideology of Mental Health and the Emergence of the Therapeutic Liberal State: The American Mental Hygiene Movement, 1900-1930" (doctoral dissertation, University of Illinois, 1980), are both long on argument and short on evidence.

28. Cole Blease to J. W. Babcock, Jan. 16, Mar. 12, 13, 1914, Babcock to Blease, Mar. 12, 1914, Benjamin R. Tillman to Babcock, June 17, 1918, Babcock Papers, South Caroliniana Library, University of South Carolina, Columbia, S.C.; Arthur P. Herring, *Report to Hon. Richard I. Manning Governor of South Carolina on the State Hospital for the Insane at Columbia, South Carolina with Recommendations* (Columbia, 1915); Richard Manning to William A. White, Mar. 27, 1915, White Papers, RG 418, NA; S.C. State Bd. of Charities and Corrections, *AR* 1 (1915): 49, 2 (1916): 56-62; *AJI* 71 (1915): 800-01; *The Survey* 34 (1915): 13-14; NCSW *Proc.* 44 (1917): 348-50.

29. "Report of the Activities of the Rockefeller Foundation in Mental Hygiene 1915-1918," included with letter from Beers to William A. White, Apr. 11, 1918, White Papers, RG 418, NA; C. S. Yoakum, "Care of the Feeble-minded and Insane in Texas," *Bulletin of the University of Texas, Humanistic Series* No. 16 (1914); Tenn. Bd. of Control *BR* 1 (1915-1916): 19-27; C. Floyd Haviland, *The Treatment and Care of the Insane in Pennsylvania Being the Report of a Survey of All the Institutions in Pennsylvania Caring for the Insane* (Philadelphia, 1915); Salmon, "Report on work carried on by the National Committee for Mental Hygiene with appropriations made by the Rockefeller Foundation, January 1, 1915 to December 31, 1916," typescript copy in AFMH Papers, AP.

30. "Proceedings of the 9th Annual Meeting of the National Committee for Mental Hygiene . . . February 7, 1917," 14-15, AFMH Papers, AP. See also Salmon's "Mental Hygiene," *The American Year Book . . . 1916* (New York, 1917), 395-98.

31. Walter L. Treadway, *Care of Mental Defectives, the Insane, and Alcoholics in Springfield, Illinois: A Study by the National Committee for Mental Hygiene* (New York, 1914); Aaron J. Rosanoff, *Survey of Mental Disorders in Nassau County, New York July-October, 1916* (Utica, 1917), 11-15, 124 (Rosanoff's study was first printed in the *Psychiatric Bulletin of the New York State Hospitals* 10 [1917]); Rosanoff, "Psychiatric Problems at Large," AMPA *Proc.* 24 (1917): 257-61.

32. Herman M. Adler, *Cook County and the Mentally Handicapped: A Study of the Provisions for Dealing with Mental Problems in Cook County, Illinois: Report of Survey 1916-1917* (Utica, 1918), 4, 140.

33. John Koren, *Summaries of State Laws Relating to the Commitment and Care of the Insane in the United States* (New York, 1912), reissued as *Summaries of State Laws Relating to the Insane* (New York, 1917); *AJI* 75 (1918): 287-88; *Statistical Manual for the Use of Institutions for the Insane Prepared by the Committee on Statistics of the American Medico-Psychological Association in Collaboration with the Bureau of Statistics of the National Committee for Mental Hygiene* (New York, 1918). A detailed list of the surveys may be found in "Report of the Activities of the Rockefeller Foundation in Mental Hygiene 1915-1918," enclosed with letter of Beers to William A. White, Apr. 11, 1918, White Papers, RG 418, NA. Most of the surveys remained in manuscript form. For a typical example see Samuel W. Hamilton, "The Care and Treatment of the Insane in Colorado: A Report, submitted January 1917, to the National Committee for Mental Hygiene," typescript copy in Salmon, "Report on Work Carried on by the National Committee for Mental Hygiene with Appropriations made by the Rockefeller Foundation, January 1, 1915 to December 31, 1916," typescript copy, AFMH Papers, AP.

34. George Blumer to Beers, Mar. 2, 1915, Beers to Russell H. Chittenden, Sept. 5, 1915 (letter never sent, but Beers presented his arguments orally at a meeting with Chittenden), AFMH Papers, AP; *MH* 1 (1917): 3.

35. Salmon to Edwin R. Embree, Apr. 16, 1921, Embree to Salmon, Apr. 29, 1921, Salmon to Paton, June 6, 1922, Paton to Salmon, Aug. 12, 1922, AFMH Papers, AP.

36. Embree to Salmon, Apr. 29, 1921, AFMH Papers, AP; Embree to Walter B. James, Dec. 1, 1921, Dec. 7, 1922, Embree to Frankwood E. Williams, Nov. 12, 1924, Arthur H. Ruggles to Embree, Oct. 11, 1924, Frankwood E. Williams to Richard M. Pearce, Oct. 22, 1929, Record Group 1.1, Series 200 (NCMH), RFA; George K. Pratt, "Twenty Years of the National Committee for Mental Hygiene," *MH* 14 (1930): 399-428; *Twenty Years of Mental Hygiene 1909-1929* (New York, 1929), *passim*.

37. Frankwood E. Williams to Embree, May 1, 1925, together with "Statement in Reference to a Proposal for a Study of the Psychopathology of

Dependency," Embree to Williams, May 28, 1925, Record Group 1.1, Series 200 (NCMH), RFA.

38. Samuel W. Hamilton, "The Care and Treatment of the Insane in Missouri: The Report of a Survey of All the Institutions in Missouri Caring for the Insane with Recommendations," Mo. State Bd. of Charities and Corrections *Monthly Bulletin* 20 (1920); N.C. State Bd. of Charities and Public Welfare *BR* (1919-1920): 8, 28-32; NCMH, *A Report of the Wisconsin Mental Deficiency Survey with Recommendations* (Madison, 1921); NCMH, *Report of the Maryland Mental Hygiene Survey with Recommendations* (Baltimore, 1921); NCMH, *Report of the Mental Hygiene Survey of Cincinnati* (Cincinnati, 1922); NCMH, "A Report of the South Carolina Mental Hygiene Survey with Recommendations," *Quarterly Bulletin of the State Board of Public Welfare* 3 (1922); NCMH, *Report of the Arizona Mental Hygiene Survey with Recommendations* (n.p., 1922); NCMH, *Report of the Mental Hygiene Survey of Kentucky with Recommendations* (Frankfort, 1923); NCMH, *Report of the North Dakota Mental Hygiene Survey with Recommendations* (n.p., 1923); NCMH, *Report of a Mental Health Survey of Staten Island (The Borough of Richmond) New York City* (Utica, 1925); *Report of the Texas Eleemosynary Commission to the Governor and the Members of the Thirty-Ninth Legislature of Texas* (Austin, 1925); NCMH, *Report of the Rhode Island Mental Hygiene Survey* (New York, 1924); NCMH, *Report of a Survey of Mental Hygiene Facilities and Resources in New York City Utilized by Out-Patient Departments of Hospitals and Dispensaries, Public Schools, Social Agencies and by Courts and Protective Agencies* (New York, 1929).

39. For Beers's later career see Dain, *Clifford W. Beers*, chaps. 14-20.

40. Henry B. Elkind, "Survey of the Illinois Society for Mental Hygiene," 1936, typescript copy in AFMH Papers, AP; Meyer to William Gerry Morgan, July 2, 1930, Meyer Papers, Series I, JHMS. Meyer's public statements, on the other hand, express an almost contrary view. See *The Collected Papers of Adolf Meyer* (4 vols.: Baltimore, 1950-1952), II, 266-87.

41. Earle Saxe to Maxwell Gitelson, Dec. 16, 1939, Jan. 20, 1940, Gitelson to Saxe, Dec. 19, 1939, Gitelson Papers, LC.

42. Frankwood E. Williams, "Is There a Mental Hygiene?" *Psychoanalytic Quarterly* 1 (1932): 113-20; V. V. Anderson, *Psychiatry in Industry* (New York, 1929), and *Psychiatry in Education* (New York, 1932); Kenneth E. Appel, "Psychiatry in Industry," *Occupational Therapy and Rehabilitation* 10 (1931): 207-16; "News Letter of the Association for the Psychiatric Study of Social Issues" (1939), with form letter to John C. Whitehorn, Sept. 7, 1939, Whitehorn Papers, APA.

43. Charles E. Rosenberg, "The Bitter Fruit: Heredity, Disease, and Social

Thought in Nineteenth-Century America," *Perspectives in American History* 8 (1974): 189-235.

44. See NCCC *Proc.* 2 (1875): 96-98, 3 (1876): 16ff., 8 (1881): 217-19, 9 (1882): xxviii-xxix, 14 (1887): 192-214, 18 (1891): 222-29, 385-93, 24 (1897): 83-86, 25 (1898): 268-75.

In 1883 Foster Pratt gave a much publicized and widely circulated paper at the meetings of the American Public Health Association that purported to demonstrate that the increase of insanity in the United States since 1850 was almost exclusively attributable to foreign-born residents. The following year the AMSAII endorsed the policy of excluding the "defective classes." See Pratt, "The Increase of Insanity in the United States—Its Causes and Sources," *JAMA* 1 (1883): 668-75, also printed in American Public Health Assn. *Public Health Reports and Papers* 9 (1883): 321-46, and *AJI* 41 (1884): 63-77. The most authoritative analysis of federal legislation is E. P. Hutchinson's *Legislative History of American Immigration Policy 1798-1965* (Philadelphia, 1981).

45. The best discussions of eugenics and immigration restriction are Mark H. Haller's *Eugenics: Hereditarian Attitudes in American Thought* (New Brunswick, 1963), John Higham's *Strangers in the Land: Patterns of American Nativism 1860-1925* (New Brunswick, 1955), and Barbara M. Solomon's *Ancestors and Immigrants: A Changing New England Tradition* (Cambridge, 1956).

46. Mass. Bd. of State Charities *AR* 13 (1876): xxxvi-xlviii; N.Y. State Bd. of Charities *AR* 13 (1879): 36-43, 19 (1885): 27-28, 257-65, 20 (1886): 11-16, 24 (1890): 237-39, 258-60, 27 (1893): xxvii-xxix, 5-7, 11-12, 14, 38-41; Spencer L. Dawes, *Report on the Alien Insane in the Civil Hospitals of New York State . . . January 23, 1914* (Albany, 1914), also reprinted as N.Y. *Senate Document No. 29* (February, 1914).

47. Edward C. Spitzka, "Race and Insanity," *JNMD* 7 (1880): 613-30; James G. Kiernan, "Paranoia. Its Influence in Increasing the Number of the Insane," *Neurological Review* 1 (1886): 5-19; C. L. Dana, "Immigration and Nervous Diseases," *Journal of Social Science* 24 (1888): 43-56; H. M. Banister and Ludwig Hektoen, "Race and Insanity," *AJI* 44 (1888): 455-70; H. E. Allison in *AJI* 58 (1902): 705-08; Thomas W. Salmon, "The Relation of Immigration to the Prevalence of Insanity," *AJI* 64 (1907): 71; Albert W. Ferris, "Italian Immigration and Insanity," *State Hospitals Bulletin* 1 (1908): 279-92; George H. Kirby, "A Study in Race Psychopathology," *State Hospitals Bulletin* 1 (1909) : 663-70; Sidney D. Wilgus, "The Problem of Immigration," *State Hospitals Bulletin* 3 (1910): 117-25, 125-37 (discussion); H. M. Swift, "Insanity and Race," *AJI* 70 (1913): 143-54; Charles W. Burr, "The Foreign-Born Insane: A Racial Study of the Patients Admitted to the Insane Department of the Philadelphia General Hospital in Ten Years (1903-1912)," *JAMA* 62 (1914): 25-27.

48. U.S. Bureau of the Census, *Insane and Feeble-Minded in Institutions 1910* (Washington, D.C., 1914), 26-27; Minn. State Bd. of Control *BR* 5 (1908-1910): 191, 6 (1910-1912): 183; Morris D. Waldman, "The Alien as a Public Charge, with Particular Reference to the Insane," N.Y.S. Conference of Charities and Correction *Proc.* 13 (1912), 82ff., in N.Y. State Bd. of Charities *AR* 46 (1912): vol. I; Prescott F. Hall. "The Recent History of Immigration and Immigration Restriction," *Journal of Political Economy* 21 (1913): 735-51, and the response by H. L. Reed, "Immigration and Insanity," *ibid.* 21 (1913): 954-56; A. J. Rosanoff, "Some Neglected Phases of Immigration in Relation to Insanity," *AJI* 72 (1915): 45-58.

49. AMPA *Proc.* 16 (1909): 80-81, 17 (1910): 78-81, 19 (1912): 105-12, 181-96, 20 (1913): 26-34; *AJI* 71 (1914): 206-08; Meyer to Henry Cabot Lodge, Jan. 14, 1913, Meyer Papers, Series II, JHMS.

50. Spencer L. Dawes, "The New Immigration Law," *State Hospital Quarterly* 2 (1917): 366-70; 67th Cong. 4th sess., *Hearings Before the Committee on Immigration and Naturalization House of Representatives . . . on H.R. 14273 . . . January 30 and February 6, 1923* (Washington, D.C., 1923), 608-19; Dawes, "Immigration and the Problem of the Alien Insane," *AJP* 81 (1925): 449-62, 462-70 (discussion); "Interstate Conference on Immigration," *State Hospital Quarterly* 9 (1923): 88-103; "Meeting of Special Committee on Immigration Legislation and the Alien Insane March 21, 1924," and "Proposed Report of the Sub-Committee on Alien Insane Presented to the Committee on Mental Hygiene April 11th, 1924," Salmon Boxes in AFMH Papers, AP; Irving Fisher to Meyer, Nov. 19, 24, 1923, with "Report of the Committee on Selective Immigration of the Eugenics Committee of the United States of America," Meyer to Fisher, Nov. 22, 1923, Meyer Papers, Series II, JHMS. See also Kenneth M. Ludmerer, "Genetics, Eugenics, and the Immigration Restrictionist Act of 1924," *Bulletin of the History of Medicine* 46 (1972): 59-81.

51. Haller, *Eugenics*, chaps. 2-3.

52. See Rudolph J. Vecoli, "Sterlization: A Progressive Measure?" *Wisconsin Magazine of History* 43 (1960): 190-202; Haller, *Eugenics*, passim; and Donald K. Pickins, *Eugenics and the Progressives* (Nashville, 1968).

53. Haller, *Eugenics*, 50, 133; "Table of Sterilization . . . 1940," mimeographed copy in Assn. for Voluntary Sterilization Papers (Box 6, Folder 56), SHWA.

54. Haller, *Eugenics*, 50, 133; George K. Pratt to C. F. Williams, Jan. 5, 1932, AFMH Papers, Uncatalogued, AP.

55. Statistics from mimeographed "Table of Sterilization . . . 1940," Assn. for Voluntary Sterilization Papers (Box 6, Folder 56), SHWA.

56. Hubert Work, "The Sociologic Aspect of Insanity and Allied Defects," AMPA *Proc.* 19 (1912): 127-41, and "Legislation in Reference to Ster-

ilization," *ibid.* 21 (1914): 501-03; AMPA *Proc.* 19 (1912): 121, 20 (1913): 26-34. See also Clarence P. Oberndorf, "The Sterilization of Defectives," *State Hospitals Bulletin* 5 (1912): 106-12; Henry R. Stedman, "Report on Mental Diseases," *BMSJ* 168 (1913): 310-14; *State Hospitals Bulletin* 6 (1913): 250.

57. William D. Partlow, "Degeneracy," *Alabama Medical Journal* 19 (1907): 397-407; Partlow to E. S. Gosney, Mar. 26, 1934 (Box 5, Folder 48), K. B. Curtis to Gosney, Jan. 5, 1933 (Box 5, Folder 46), Assn. for Voluntary Sterilization Papers, SHWA; E. S. Gosney and Paul Popenoe, *Sterilization for Human Betterment: A Summary of Results of 6000 Operations in California, 1909-1929* (New York, 1930); "Appendix to Memorandum Presented at Meeting of Board of Scientific Directors of the Eugenics Record Office. Concerning the Study of Eugenics in Massachusetts. E. E. Southard," E. E. Southard Papers, CLMHMS; Eugenics Record Office *Bulletin* No. 10A (1914): 25ff., 10B (1914): *passim*. For attitudes of state agencies and hospital superintendents in various states, see the following: Calif. State Bd. of Charities and Corrections *BR* 6 (1912-1914): 37, 8 (1916-1918): 59-65; Calif. Dept. of Institutions *BR* 1 (1920-1922): 88, 2 (1922-1924): 89-90, 100-03, 3 (1924-1926): 92-97, 5 (1928-1930): 43; Del. State Bd. of Charities *Report* (1926): 9-18 (1927-1928): 10-17 (1935-1936): 42-47; *Indiana Bulletin of Charities and Correction* No. 121 (1936): 10; Iowa Bd. of Control of State Institutions *BR* 9 (1912-1914): 32, 10 (1914-1916): 39-40; Topeka State Hospital *BR* 24 (1922-1924): 4, 28 (1930-1932): 8, 31 (1936-1938): 11-12 (all in Kans. Bd. of Administration *BR*); Ky. State Bd. of Control for Charitable Institutions *BR* 5 (1911-1913): 15-16, 8 (1917-1919): 7-8 (1925-1927): 48-52 (1927-1929): 95-96; Ky. Dept. of Public Welfare *BR* (1931-1933): 74-75 (1933-1935): 72-73; Minn. State Bd. of Control *BR* 14 (1926-1928): 79, 18 (1934-1936): 176; Mont. State Bd. of Charities and Reform *AR* (1924): 6-7; Mont. State Hospital *BR* 24 (1923-1924): 23-28; Neb. Bd. of Commissioners of State Institutions *BR* 2 (1915-1916): 35-37; Neb. Bd. of Control *BR* 5 (1921-1923): 63-64, 6 (1923-1925): 44-47, 8 (1927-1929): 102-05, 11 (1933-1935): 125-26; N.C. Bd. of Charities and Public Welfare *BR* (1928-1930): 84-85; N.D. Bd. of Control of State Institutions *BR* 2 (1912-1914): 73, 126; N.D. Bd. of Administration *AR* 13-14 (1930-1932): 439; Ore. State Bd. of Control *BR* 5 (1921-1922): 61, 9 (1929-1930): 81; Tenn. Bd. of State Charities *Report* (1903): 106-08; Tex. State Bd. of Control *BR* 7 (1933-1934): 49-51, 8 (1935-1936): 62-63; Wash. (State) Dept. of Business Control *BR* 4 (1927-1928): 6; W. Va. State Bd. of Control *BR* 2 (1911-1912): 44-45, 56, 3 (1913-1914): 104-05, 138; Vt. Supervisors of the Insane *BR* (1928-1930): 5-7; Vt. Dept of Public Welfare *BR* (1936-1938): 7.

58. William A. White, "Eugenics and Heredity in Nervous and Mental Diseases," in *The Modern Treatment of Nervous and Mental Diseases*, ed. White and Smith Ely Jelliffe (Philadelphia, 1913), 17-55; White to

Dr. ? Fisher, c. 1919, White to Arthur P. Herring, Nov. 3, 1916, White Papers, RG 418, NA.

59. Ill. State Charities Commission *AR* 4 (1913): 9-10; Abraham Myerson, *The Inheritance of Mental Diseases* (Baltimore, 1925); *idem*, "Some Objections to Sterilization," *Birth Control Review* 12 (1928): 81; *idem*, "A Critique of Proposed 'Ideal' Sterilization Legislation," *ANP* 33 (1935): 453-66; Meyer, review of Emil Oberholzer's "Kastration und Sterilization von Geisteskranken in der Schweiz," in *Journal of the American Institute of Criminal Law and Criminology* 2 (1911-1912), in *CP*, IV, 316-18; Meyer, "Sterilization," undated mss., Meyer Papers, Series II, JHMS; Victor Robinson to Smith Ely Jelliffe, Oct. 3, 1935, Jelliffe to Robinson, Oct. 12, 1935, Jelliffe Papers, LC; Jacques Loeb to Simon Flexner, Aug. 4, 1923, Loeb Papers, LC; J. K. Hall, "Sterilization?" *Southern Medicine and Surgery* 99 (1937): 514. See Frederick W. Brown, "Eugenic Sterilization in the United States: Its Present Status," American Academy of Political and Social Science *Annals* 149, part III (1930): 22-35 (this issue was edited by Frankwood E. Williams, and was entitled "Some Social Aspects of Mental Hygiene").

60. Committee of the American Neurological Association for the Investigation of Eugenical Sterilization (Abraham Myerson et al.), *Eugenical Sterilization: A Reorientation of the Problem* (New York, 1936).

61. Myerson, "A Critique of Proposed 'Ideal' Sterilization Legislation," *ANP* 33 (1935): 453-66.

62. Committee of the ANA, *Eugenical Sterilization, passim*.

63. James E. Hughes, *Eugenic Sterilization in the United States: A Comparative Summary of Statutes and Review of Court Decisions* (Supplement No. 162 to the Public Health Reports: Washington, D.C., 1940). In the Introduction Hughes noted that his legislative and judicial review was prepared "because of the bearing it may have on the problem of the causes, prevalence, and means for the prevention and treatment of nervous and mental diseases." It was not intended "as an expression of the attitude of the Service nor of the views of its personnel on the wisdom of sterilization as a State policy" (p. v). In their classic work on mental diseases in 1938, Carney Landis and James D. Page concluded that sterilization would have little impact on incidence, but raised no ethical concerns and even hinted that if the efficacy of the procedure could be demonstrated, it would be a useful practice. *Modern Society and Mental Disease* (New York, 1938), 80-90, 155-57.

Chapter VII

1. I. S. Wechsler, "The Legend of the Prevention of Mental Disease," *JAMA* 95 (1930): 24-26.

2. U.S. Bureau of the Census, *Insane and Feeble-Minded in Hospitals*

and Institutions 1904 (Washington, D.C., 1906), 7; *idem, Patients in Mental Institutions 1940* (Washington, D.C., 1943), 6.

3. U.S. Bureau of the Census, *Historical Statistics of the United States: Colonial Times to 1970* (2 vols.: Washington, D.C., 1975), I, 15.

4. U.S. Bureau of the Census, *Paupers in Almshouses 1904* (Washington, D.C., 1906), 182, 184; *idem, Paupers in Almshouses 1910* (Washington, D.C., 1915), 42-43; *idem, Paupers in Almshouses 1923* (Washington, D.C., 1925), 5, 8, 33; *idem, Insane and Feeble-Minded in Hospitals and Institutions 1904* (Washington, D.C., 1906), 29; *idem, Patients in Hospitals for Mental Diseases 1923* (Washington, D.C., 1926), 27. The data in Table 7-1 are drawn from above sources.

5. Ala. Insane Hospital *BR* (1891-1892): 56; Trustees of the Ala. Insane Hospital *Report* (1925): 34 (1926): 73 (1940): 52, 97; Calif. State Commission in Lunacy *BR* 1 (1896-1898): 161, 3 (1900-1902): 85; Calif. Dept. of Institutions *BR* 6 (1930-1932): 174; Calif. Dept. of Institutions *Statistical Report* (1939-1940): 50; Iowa Bd. of Control of State Institutions *BR* 2 (1898-1899): 338, 9 (1912-1914): 268-69; Kans. Bd. of Trustees of State Charitable Institutions *BR* 3 (1880-1882): 61, 13 (1900-1902): 84; Topeka State Hospital *BR* 23 (1920-1922): 17, 31 (1936-1938): 22; Mass. State Bd. of Lunacy and Charity *AR* 9 (1887): 166; Mass. Commission on Mental Diseases *AR* 1 (1920): 218-19; Mass. Commissioner of Mental Health *AR* 21 (1940): 307-08; Ore. State Bd. of Control *BR* 4 (1919-1920): 56, 14 (1938-1940): 47; Wash. State Bd. of Audit and Control *BR* 2 (1899-1900): 54, 86; Wash. State Bd. of Control *BR* 10 (1919-1920): 152-53, 208-09; Wash. Dept. of Finance, Budget and Business *BR* 3 (1939-1940): 72, 113.

6. N.Y.S. Dept. of Mental Hygiene *AR* 52 (1939-1940): 174-75; Benjamin Malzberg, "A Statistical Analysis of the Ages of First Admissions to Hospitals for Mental Disease in New York State," *PQ* 23 (1949): 346. The data in Table 7-2 are drawn from the following sources: Malzberg, "A Comparison of First Admissions to the New York Civil State Hospitals During 1919-1921 and 1949-1951," *PQ* 28 (1954): 314; U.S. Bureau of the Census, *Fourteenth Census of the United States*, vol. II, *Population 1920* (Washington, D.C., 1922), 248; *idem, Census of Population: 1950*, vol. II, *Characteristics of the Population*, Part 32 (Washington, D.C., 1952), 58.

7. Morton Kramer et al., *A Historical Study of the Disposition of First Admissions to a State Mental Hospital: Experiences of the Warren State Hospital During the Period 1916-50* (U.S. Public Health Service Publication No. 445: Washington, D.C., 1955), 10; Carney Landis and Jane E. Farwell, "A Trend Analysis of Age at First-Admission, Age at Death, and Years of Residence for State Mental Hospitals: 1913-1941," *Journal of Abnormal and Social Psychology* 39 (1944): 3-23.

8. Mass. State Bd. of Insanity *AR* 2 (1900): 32.

9. Wisc. State Bd. of Charities and Reform *AR* 5 (1875): 135, 150; Wisc.

State Bd. of Control *BR* 15 (1918-1920): 106-07, 160; Neil A. Dayton, "A New Statistical System for the Study of Mental Diseases and Some of the Attained Results," *Bulletin of the Massachusetts Department of Mental Diseases* 18 (1934): 179-80.

10. Herbert Goldhamer and Andrew W. Marshall, *Psychosis and Civilization: Two Studies in the Frequency of Mental Disease* (Glencoe, Ill., 1953), 54, 91. Data in Table 7-3 are drawn from this source.

11. Data in Table 7-4 from Kramer et al., *Historical Study . . . of the Warren State Hospital During the Period 1916-50*, 10.

12. Ohio Dept. of Public Welfare *AR* 15 (1936): 303-04.

13. N.Y. State Commission in Lunacy *AR* 12 (1900): 26-29.

14. "The Care of the Mentally Disordered in Illinois: The State Hospitals," 7-8 (c. 1931), typescript copy in AFMH Papers, AP. For examples of other discussions by state officials see Minn. State Bd. of Control *BR* 5 (1908-1910): 8-9; Ky. Dept. of Public Welfare *BR* (1931-1933): 36; Texas State Bd. of Control *BR* 8 (1935-1936): 59.

15. William L. Russell, "Senility and Senile Dementia," *AJI* 58 (1902): 625-33; E. E. Southard and H. W. Mitchell, "Clinical and Anatomical Analysis of Insanity Arising in the Sixth and Seventh Decades," AMPA *Proc.* 15 (1908): 179-222; *Statistical Manual for the Use of Institutions for the Insane Prepared by the Committee on Statistics of the American Medico-Psychological Association in Collaboration with the Bureau of Statistics of the National Committee for Mental Hygiene* (New York, 1918), 12; Benjamin Malzberg, *Social and Biological Aspects of Mental Disease* (Utica, 1940), 52-81; Neil A. Dayton, *New Facts on Mental Disorders: Study of 89,190 Cases* (Springfield, Ill., 1940), 41-79; Horatio M. Pollock, *Mental Disease and Social Welfare* (Utica, 1941), *passim*; William F. Ogburn and Ellen Winston, "The Frequency and Probability of Insanity," *American Journal of Sociology* 34 (1929): 822-31; Ellen Winston, "Age, A Factor in the Increase of Mental Disease," *MH* 16 (1932): 650-52; Carney Landis and James D. Page, *Modern Society and Mental Disease* (New York, 1938), 27-43; *Mental Health in Later Maturity: Papers Presented at a Conference Held in Washington, D.C. May 23-24, 1941 (Supplement No. 168* to the Public Health Reports: Washington, D.C., 1942); Aubrey Lewis, "Ageing and Senility: A Major Problem of Psychiatry," *Journal of Mental Science* 92 (1946): 150-70.

16. For a sampling of psychiatric opinion, see William House, "Some Socio-Economic Problems in Neuropsychiatry," AMA Section on Nervous and Mental Diseases *Trans.* (1927): 25-26; William A. White to Louis I. Dublin, Jan. 13, 1930, White Papers, RG 418, NA; Lawrence Kolb, "The Psychiatric Significance of Aging as a Public Health Problem," in *Mental Health in Later Maturity*, 17; Winfred Overholser, "Some Mental Problems of Aging and Their Management," *Medical Annals of the District of Columbia* 10 (1941): 212-17; Trustees of the

Ala. Insane Hospitals *Report* (1925): 8 (1936): 8; Idaho Dept. of Public Welfare *Report* (1925-1926); 65; Ky. State Bd. of Control for Charitable Institutions *BR* 4 (1909-1911); 175-76; Md. Bd. of Welfare *AR* 4 (1926): 62-63; Mich. State Bd. of Corrections and Charities *BR* (1899-1900): 210; Mo. Bd. of Managers of the State Eleemosynary Institutions *BR* 6 (1931-1932): 229-30; Mont. State Hospital *BR* 24 (1923-1924): 85; Neb. Bd. of Commissioners of State Institutions *BR* 3 (1917-1918): 271-72; Nev. Hospital for Mental Diseases *BR* 15 (1911-1912): 8, 13-14; Charles G. Wagner, in N.Y.S. Commission in Lunacy *AR* 12 (1900): 22-36; Robert M. Elliott, "Dotards in State Hospitals," N.Y.S. Commission in Lunacy *AR* 19 (1907): 161-68; Ohio Dept. of Public Welfare *AR* 9 (1930): 296-97, 15 (1936): 303-04; Ore. State Bd. of Control *BR* 8 (1927-1928): 73; N.D. Bd. of Administration *AR* 15-16 (1932-1934): 106; Tenn. State Bd. of Administration *BR* (1918-1920): 247-48; Wash. State Bd. of Control *BR* 4 (1907-1908): 36; Wisc. State Bd. of Control *BR* 6 (1900-1902): 96; W. Va. State Bd. of Control *BR* 2 (1911-1912): 86.

17. The history of syphilis remains to be written. For introductions see George Rosen, "Patterns of Discovery and Control in Mental Illness," *American Journal of Public Health* 50 (1960): 855-66; Alfred W. Crosby, Jr., *The Columbian Exchange: Biological and Cultural Consequences of 1492* (Westport, Conn., 1972), chap. 4; Irwin C. Sutton, "A Concise History of Syphilis," *American Journal of Syphilis* 8 (1924): 155-61.

18. A. E. Macdonald, "General Paresis," *AJI* 33 (1877): 465. The late nineteenth-century view of syphilis and paresis can be followed in Edward C. Mann, "The Psychological and Pathological Nature of General Paralysis and its Treatment," *BMSJ* 101 (1879): 11-16; E. L. Keyes, *The Venereal Diseases Including Stricture of the Male Urethra* (New York, 1880), chap. 12; Henry M. Hurd, "A Plea for Systematic Therapeutical, Clinical and Statistical Study," *AJI* 38 (1881): 16-31; Hurd, "The Relation of General Paresis and Syphilitic Insanity," *AJI* 43 (1886): 1-18; Charles F. Folsom, "Some Points Regarding General Paralysis," *AJI* 48 (1891): 17-36; Syndey Kuh, "Syphilis of the Central Nervous System," *Alienist and Neurologist* 18 (1897): 510-37. See also William J. Mickle's classic *General Paralysis of the Insane* (2nd ed.: London, 1886).

19. N.Y.S. Dept. of Mental Hygiene *AR* 52 (1939-1940): 176; Horatio M. Pollock, "Trends in the Outcome of General Paresis," *PQ* 9 (1935): 194-211, also reprinted in Pollock's *Mental Disease and Social Welfare*, chap. 6; Malzberg, *Social and Biological Aspects of Mental Disease*, 30-32; American Psychopathological Assn., *Trends of Mental Disease* (New York, 1945), 31. For comparable data in other states see Elise Donaldson, "Syphilis as a Cause of Insanity," *Public Health Reports* 36 (1921): 67-72; Edith M. Furbush, "General Paralysis in State Hospitals for Mental Disease," *MH* 7 (1923): 565-78; Irving M. Derby, "Life

Expectancy in General Paresis," *PQ* 9 (1935): 458-85; Dayton, *New Facts on Mental Disorders, passim*; Washington State Dept. of Business Control *BR* 7 (1933-1934): 27; Ohio Dept. of Public Welfare *AR* 11-12 (1932-1933): 349, 358-60, 15 (1936): 304; Ore. State Bd. of Control *BR* 4 (1919-1920): 47; Ill. Dept. of Public Welfare *AR* 12 (1928-1929): 310; N.C. Charitable, Penal, and Correctional Institutions *BR* (1930-1932): 48; Mass. Commissioner of Mental Health *AR* 21 (1940): 161.

20. For changing views after 1900 see Charles G. Wagner, "The Comparative Frequency of General Paresis," *AJI* 58 (1902): 587-95; F. X. Dercum, "The Early Diagnosis of Paresis," *ibid.*, 575-86; Edward Cowles, "Treatment of Paresis: Its Limitations and Expectations," *ibid.*, 597-605; and James V. May, "A Review of the Recent Studies of General Paresis," *ibid.* 66 (1910): 543-49.

21. Pollock, *Mental Disease and Social Welfare*, 98-109.

22. The data for this paragraph as well as the data found in Table 7-5 are from the U.S. Bureau of the Census annual compilations of hospital statistics. The first volume, *Patients in Hospitals for Mental Disease 1923*, was published in 1926; from 1926 to 1940 comparable volumes, sometimes with slightly different titles, were issued, some covering more than one year. For an exact listing of these titles, see the bibliography at the end of this volume.

23. U.S. Bureau of the Census, *Patients in Hospitals for Mental Disease 1923* (Washington, D.C., 1926), 156; N.C. Charitable, Penal, and Correctional Institutions *BR* (1930-1932): 48.

24. Landis and Page, *Modern Society and Mental Disease*, 34-36.

25. Data from the U.S. Census Bureau annual compilations of hospital statistics. See note 22 *supra*.

26. The most significant analyses of this kind of data include Malzberg, *Social and Biological Aspects of Mental Disease*; Malzberg and Everett S. Lee, *Migration and Mental Disease: A Study of First Admissions to Hospitals for Mental Disease, New York, 1939-1941* (New York, 1956); Malzberg, "Are Immigrants Psychologically Disturbed?" in *Changing Perspectives in Mental Illness*, ed. Stanley C. Plog and Robert B. Edgerton (New York, 1969), 395-421; Dayton, *New Facts on Mental Disorders*; Horatio M. Pollock, *Mental Disease and Social Welfare*; Landis and Page, *Modern Society and Mental Disease*.

27. Raymond G. Fuller and Mary Johnston, "The Duration of Hospital Life for Mental Patients," *PQ* 5 (1931): 341-52, 552-82.

28. *Ibid.*, 552-53.

29. Benjamin Malzberg, *Mortality Among Patients with Mental Disease* (Utica, 1934). Data for this paragraph and Table 7-7 are drawn from 29, 84, 119, 143, 166, 179, 191 *et passim*.

30. *Ibid.*, 15-16; U.S. Bureau of the Census, *Patients in Hospitals for Mental Disease 1923*, 81; *idem*, *Patients in Mental Institutions 1940* (Washington, D.C., 1943), 52; Howard G. Borden, "Death Rates of the

New Jersey State Hospital at Marlboro . . . 1933," *Journal of the Medical Society of New Jersey* 30 (1933): 861-62.

31. Worcester State Lunatic Hospital *AR* 10 (1842): 17-27, 38 (1870): 38-60; Virginia Western Lunatic Asylum *AR* 23 (1850): 14-23; Calif. Insane Asylum *AR* 8 (1860): 16-32; Northampton State Lunatic Hospital *AR* 25 (1880): 56-57. See also S.C. Lunatic Asylum *AR* (1870): 14-31, and Iowa Hospital for the Insane at Mt. Pleasant *BR* 11 (1880-1881): 80.

32. U.S. Bureau of the Census, *Insane and Feeble-Minded in Hospitals and Institutions 1904*, 37, *Insane and Feeble-Minded in Institutions 1910*, 59, and *Patients in Hospitals for Mental Disease 1923*, 36.

33. Dayton, *New Facts on Mental Disorders*, 414-29.

34. *Ibid.*, 438.

35. Frank L. Wright, Jr., *Out of Sight Out of Mind* (Philadelphia, 1947), 123.

36. Even when the character of the mental hospital population was understood, it did not follow that the role of the institution would be recast. In 1939, for example, Winfred Overholser prepared an article for *Scientific Monthly* that demonstrated a familiarity with the nature of patients. Yet Overholser's conclusions differed but little from the majority of his psychiatric colleagues. See Overholser, "Mental Disease—A Challenge," *Scientific Monthly* 48 (1939): 203-09, and Edith M. Stern, "Our Ailing Mental Hospitals," *Survey Graphic* 30 (1941): 429-32.

37. Albert Deutsch's *The Mentally Ill in America: A History of Their Care and Treatment From Colonial Times*, was first published in 1937 and was prepared as a result of a subvention from the American Foundation for Mental Hygiene. Deutsch's articles appeared initially in 1945 in *PM*; they were collected in book form as *The Shame of the States* (New York, 1948).

Chapter VIII

1. The most convenient compilation of state laws dealing with the financing of institutional care is John Koren, *Summaries of State Laws Relating to the Insane* (rev. ed.: New York, 1917). See also Kans. Bd. of Control of the State Charitable Institutions *BR* 2 (1906-1908): 168-86, and N.Y.S. Dept. of Mental Hygiene *AR* 52 (1939-1940): 117.

2. For discussions of this theme see Samuel P. Hays, *American Political History as Social Analysis* (Knoxville, 1980), and *Conservation and the Gospel of Efficiency: The Progressive Conservation Movement* (Cambridge, 1959); Samuel Haber, *Efficiency and Uplift: Scientific Management in the Progressive Era 1890-1920* (Chicago, 1964); and Raymond E. Callahan, *Education and the Cult of Efficiency* (Chicago, 1962).

3. Wisc. State Bd. of Control *BR* 1 (1890-1892): 1-3, 10 (1908-1910): 4-6; N.J. State Charities Aid Assn. *AR* 18 (1903): 90; Dale W. Robison,

"Wisconsin and the Mentally Ill: A History of the 'Wisconsin Plan' of State and County Care 1860-1915," 231ff., doctoral dissertation, Marquette University, 1976; Bernett O. Odegard and George M. Keith, *A History of the State Board of Control of Wisconsin and the State Institutions 1849-1939* (Madison, n.d.), 2ff.

4. N.J. State Charities Aid Assn., *AR* 18 (1903): 86ff.

5. Henry C. Wright, *Report of an Investigation of the Methods of Fiscal Control of State Institutions* (New York, 1911), 9-13.

6. R.I. Bd. of Control and Supply *AR* 1 (1912): 5-14, 2 (1913): 6; R.I. Bd. of State Charities and Corrections *AR* 47 (1915): 10-12; R.I. Penal and Charitable Commission *AR* 1 (1917): 5.

7. Minn. Bd. of Control of State Institutions *BR* 1 (1900-1902): vii-xxiii, 1-3. See also Iowa Bd. of Control of State Institutions *BR* 1 (1898-1899): 1-17; Wash. State Bd. of Control *BR* 1 (1901-1902): 64-70; N.D. Bd. of Control of State Institutions *BR* 1 (1910-1912): 7, 2 (1912-1914): 5-7; Ore. State Bd. of Control *BR* 1 (1913-1914): 5-15.

8. Ariz. Bd. of Control *BR* 2 (1897-1898): 4-5, 3 (1899-1900): 4; Kans. Bd. of Control of the State Charitable Institutions *AR & BR* 1 (1904-1906): 344.

9. N.D. Bd. of Control of State Institutions *BR* 3 (1914-1916): 192-93; Wisc. State Bd. of Control *BR* 17 (1922-1924): 16.

10. Ill. Bd. of State Commissioners of Public Charities *BR* 20 (1907-1908): 202-05.

11. U.S. Bureau of the Census, *Summary of State Laws Relating to the Dependent Classes 1913* (Washington, D.C., 1914), 312-21 *et passim*.

12. Ill. Bd. of State Commissioners of Public Charities *BR* 20 (1907-1908): 15-36, 43-54, 185-210, 21 (1908-1909): 14-28; Ill. Bd. of Administration *AR* 1 (1910): 5-12; Ill. State Charities Commission *AR* 1 (1910): 7-31; William C. Graves "The Problem of State Supervision in Illinois," NCCC *Proc.* 36 (1909): 430-39; Graves to William A. White, Mar. 17, May 8, June 3, 1908, White to Graves, Mar. 23, 1908, White Papers, RG 418, NA.

13. This and the preceding paragraph are based on the following: Sophonisba P. Breckinridge, *Public Welfare Administration in the United States: Select Documents* (Chicago, 1927), 559-82; Ernest L. Bogart and John M. Mathews, *The Modern Commonwealth 1893-1918* (Springfield, Ill., 1920), 251-58; William T. Hutchinson, *Lowden of Illinois: The Life of Frank O. Lowden* (2 vols.: Chicago, 1957), I, 292-302; *The Institution Quarterly* (Illinois) 8 (June 30, 1917): 7-8.

14. Ohio Bd. of State Charities *AR* 28 (1903): 5-6, 33 (1910-1911): 18-19; Ohio Bd. of Administration *AR* 1 (1912): pt. 2, 5; Ohio Dept. of Public Welfare *AR* 4 (1924-1925): 10ff.

15. N.D. Bd. of Administration *AR* 1 (1919): 17-20; Mo. Bd. of Managers of the State Eleemosynary Institutions *BR* 1 (1921-1922): 8-9; Calif. Dept. of Institutions *BR* 1 (1920-1922): 3-4; *Recent Social Trends in*

the United States: Report of the President's Research Committee on Social Trends (New York, 1933), 1230.

16. Mont. State Bd. of Charities and Reform *AR* (1924): 7-8; Col. State Bd. of Charities and Corrections *BR* 14 (1917-1918): 75-76; Col. State Dept. of Charities and Corrections *BR* 1 (1923-1924): 7-12; Ga. State Bd. of Public Welfare *AR* 1 (1920): 3-8, 2 (1921-1922): 3-6, 31; La. State Bd. of Charities and Corrections *AR* 1 (1905): 4-5, *Report* 4 (1918-1920): 3-6, *BR* (1920-1922): unpaginated, *AR* (1938) (typescript copy, Tulane University Library, New Orleans, La.); N.C. State Bd. of Charities and Public Welfare *BR* (1917-1918): 5-6 (1919-1920): 5-6; Clark R. Cahow, *People, Patients and Politics: The History of the North Carolina Mental Hospitals 1848-1960* (New York, 1980), 43-44; James Leiby, *Charity and Correction in New Jersey: A History of State Welfare Institutions* (New Brunswick, 1967), chaps. 10-11.

17. Mass. State Bd. of Insanity *AR* 1 (1899): 13-21; Walter Channing, "The New Massachusetts Board of Insanity," *Charities Review* 8 (1898): 358-63; Gerald N. Grob, *The State and the Mentally Ill: A History of Worcester State Hospital in Massachusetts, 1830-1920* (Chapel Hill, 1966), 243-47, 329-32.

18. Mass. State Bd. of Insanity *AR* 1 (1899): 13-21, 16 (1914): 9-14.

19. Mass. Commission on Mental Diseases *AR* 1 (1916): 9-11, 4 (1919): 9-10, 19 (1938): 9-13.

20. N.Y. State Bd. of Charities *AR* 24 (1890): 26-30; N.Y.S. Commission in Lunacy *AR* 1 (1889): 7ff., 8 (1896): 68-74, 12 (1900): 1047-48, 16 (1904): 965.

21. N.Y.S. Commission in Lunacy *AR* 14 (1902): 5-6, 1005-18, 16 (1904): 961-68, 17 (1905): 28, 1080-88; *AJI* 61 (1905): 522-25; N.Y.S. Hospital Commission *AR* 24 (1912): 232-33. See also Koren, *Summaries of State Laws Relating to the Insane*, 164-68.

22. Ohio Dept. of Public Welfare *AR* 2 (1922-1923): 9-15, 4 (1924-1925): 10-18.

23. Pa. Committee on Lunacy *AR* 1 (1883): 419-40, 5 (1887): 22-23; Koren, *Summaries of State Laws Relating to the Insane*, 208-15.

24. Pa. Dept. of Public Welfare, Commissioner of Public Welfare *BR* 1 (1921-1922): 5-6, 23-30, Secretary of Welfare *BR* 2 (1922-1924): 3, 44-46, 5 (1929-1930): 48-52, 6 (1930-1932): 34ff. (in Pa. Dept. of Welfare *Bulletin No. 54*), 10 (1938-1940): 7-22 (in Pa. Dept. of Welfare *Bulletin No. 82*); "Report of the Committee on the Survey of State Mental Hospitals of Pennsylvania," in Pa. Dept. of Welfare *Mental Health Bulletin* 11 (Oct. 15, 1933): 5-6.

25. N.C. State Bd. of Charities and Public Welfare *BR* (1921-1922): 40, 46-47 (1924-1926): 89-91, 136-37; Cahow, *People, Patients and Politics*, 44; Va. State Bd. of Public Welfare *BR* 1 (1922-1923): 5-6, *AR* 20 (1928-1929): 9-10, 23-24 (1931-1933): 10-11, *BR* (1937-1939): 92-95; J. K. Hall to Dr. Wright Clarkson, Aug. 16, 1934, Hall to Dr. G. H. Preston, Jan.

25, 1935, Hall to H. Minor Davis, Feb. 23, 1935, Hall to Douglas S. Freeman, Jan. 15, 1936, Hall to Hunsden Cary, Dec. 16, 1936, Hall to Morton G. Goode, Dec. 16, 1936, Hugh C. Henry to Hall, Feb. 20, 1939, Hall to Henry, Feb. 24, 1939, Hall to Dr. James W. Vernon, Sept. 5, 1939, Hall to Dr. Wyndham B. Blanton, Jan. 10, 1940, Hall Papers, UNC.

26. Ill. Dept. of Public Welfare *AR* 23 (1939-1940): 410-14. See also Ky. Dept. of Welfare *BR* (1937-1939): 19-20.

27. Gerald N. Grob, *Mental Institutions in America: Social Policy to 1875* (New York, 1973), 271ff.; *idem, The State and the Mentally Ill*, 176ff. See also NCCC *Proc.* 25 (1898): 223-36.

28. N.Y. State Bd. of Charities *AR* 14 (1880): 35-37, 15 (1881): 27-28, 29 (1895): lxiii; N.Y.S. Commission in Lunacy *AR* 11 (1899): 585, 24 (1912): 232-35; N.Y.S. Hospital Commission *AR* 28 (1916): 67-70; N.Y. Dept. of Mental Hygiene *AR* 52 (1939-1940): 68; Mass. State Bd. of Lunacy and Charity *AR* 20 (1898): 16; Mass. State Bd. of Insanity *AR* 10 (1908): 153.

29. For some illustrative practices see Calif. Dept. of Institutions *BR* 1 (1920-1922): 26-29; N.H. State Bd. of Public Welfare *BR* 20 (1932-1934): 55-57; Idaho Dept. of Public Welfare *Report* (1923-1924): 67-68; Ill. Bd. of Administration *AR* 4-5 (1913-1914): vol. 1, 197-99; Ill. Dept of Public Welfare *AR* 10 (1926-1927): 142-43; Ind. Bd. of State Charities *AR* 28 (1917): 16-17; Minn. Bd. of State Institutions *BR* 2 (1902-1904): 466-67, 10 (1918-1920): 29-30; Ore. State Bd. of Control *BR* 9 (1929-1930): 13-14; N.J. Dept. of Charities and Corrections *AR* 11 (1915): 18-20; Vt. Dept. of Public Welfare *BR* (1936-1938): 39; Wash. State Bd. of Control *BR* 9 (1917-1918): 37; Wash. Dept. of Business Control *BR* 1 (1921-1922): 12-13; Wisc. State Bd. of Control *BR* 19 (1926-1928): 71. See also *State Hospital Quarterly* 2 (1917): 309-10.

30. NCCC *Proc.* 25 (1898): 281, 39 (1912): 71-76, 41 (1914): 416-27; Ohio Dept. of Public Welfare *Statistical Report State Institutions and Divisions* (1940): 24-26; Calif. Dept. of Institutions *Statistical Report* (1938-1939): 28-29, 38-39.

31. U.S. Bureau of the Census, *Mental Patients in State Hospitals 1931 and 1932* (Washington, D.C., 1934), 62, and *Patients in Mental Institutions 1940* (Washington, D.C., 1943), 63.

32. Data in Table 8-1 gathered from *ibid.*; data in Table 8-2 compiled by Dr. Grover Kempf for the Mental Hospital Survey Committee and printed in Winfred Overholser, "The Desiderata of Central Administrative Control of State Mental Hospitals," *AJP* 96 (1939): 519-21; J. K. Hall to Haskins Hobson, Jan. 31, 1936, Hall to Douglas S. Freeman, May 18, 1936, Hall to Hugh C. Henry, Feb. 24, 1939, Hall Papers, UNC.

33. For the background of Wisconsin Progressivism see David P. Thelen, *The New Citizenship: Origins of Progressivism in Wisconsin, 1885-1900* (Columbia, Mo., 1972).

34. My generalizations about segregation both within and between mental hospitals are based on a comprehensive examination of virtually all states that alluded to the issue. For examples see Alan P. Smith, "The Availability of Facilities for Negroes Suffering from Mental and Nervous Diseases," *Journal of Negro Education* 6 (1937): 450-54; Ky. State Bd. of Charities and Corrections *BR* (1929-1931): 131, 134; Md. Lunacy Commission *Report* 23 (1908): 22, 32; St. Elizabeths Hospital, "Report of Formal Inspection . . . 1924," 2, in St. Elizabeths Hospital, Administrative Files, Box 19, RG 418, NA; S.C. State Bd. of Public Welfare *AR* 1 (1920): 61, 4 (1923): 71 (these *AR* can be found in the *Quarterly Bulletin of the State Board of Public Welfare*); Tenn. Bd. of Control *BR* 2 (1917-1918): 28; Tenn. Bd. of Administration *BR* (1920-1922): 237-38; Tenn. Dept. of Institutions *BR* (1928-1930): 92-93; W. Va. State Bd. of Control *BR* 6 (1918-1920): 52-53.

The incorporation of racial concepts in psychiatric and medical thought is illustrated in the following: *Medical Record* 62 (1902): 701; *American Journal of Anatomy* 5 (1906): 353-432; *AJI* 71 (1914): 309-37, 73 (1917): 619-26; *Louisville Monthly Journal of Medicine and Surgery* 22 (1916): 259-65; *International Clinics* 26th series 3 (1916): 205-17; *AJP* 78 (1921): 69-78.

In the years preceding World War II racial attitudes began to soften. Dr. E. Y. Williams of Howard University's School of Medicine was critical of the prevailing racism of his medical colleagues. See his article "The Incidence of Mental Disease in the Negro," *Journal of Negro Education* 6 (1937): 377-92. See also *AJP* 95 (1938): 167-83; *Social Forces* 17 (1938): 201-11; and *Human Biology* 11 (1939): 514-28.

35. Joseph Zubin and Grace C. Scholz, *Regional Differences in the Hospitalization and Care of Patients with Mental Disease* (Public Health Reports *Supplement No. 159*: Washington, D.C., 1940), 74.

36. AMPA *Proc.* 2 (1895), and *List of Fellows and Members of the American Psychiatric Association 1940/1941* (n.p., n.d.). The number of institutional psychiatrists at the end of the nineteenth and in the early twentieth century was always larger than the membership of the AMPA; the gap narrowed by 1940.

37. Membership data (excluding foreign members) taken from AMPA *Proc.* 2 (1895), 17 (1910); *List of Fellows and Members of the American Psychiatric Association* (n.p., 1923); and *List of Fellows and Members of the American Psychiatric Association 1940/1941*.

38. *AJP* 79 (1922): 330, 81 (1924): 385ff.

39. *Ibid.* 81 (1924): 385ff., 82 (1925): 300-06, 83 (1926): 362, 84 (1927): 328-29, 86 (1929): 409-10; Clarence B. Farrar to Arthur P. Noyes, July 13, 1936, Farrar Papers, APA.

40. *AJP* 84 (1927): 328-29, 86 (1929): 409-10, 90 (1933): 421-27, 91 (1934): 414-20; Arthur P. Noyes to Clarence B. Farrar, Jan. 9, 1934, Farrar to Noyes, Jan. 15, 1934, Farrar Papers, APA.

41. *AJP* 92 (1935): 480-82; Noyes to Farrar, Mar. 11, 1935, Apr. 20, July 10, 1936, Farrar to Noyes, July 13, 1936, Farrar Papers, APA.

42. "Summary of Reports From Various States," mss. copy in Farrar Papers, APA.

43. "Serious Political Situation in Massachusetts," *AJP* 93 (1937): 969-74; Boston *Transcript*, July 11, 28, 1936, Boston *Herald*, July 11, 25, 29, Nov. 6, 1936, Boston *Globe*, July 11, 19, 1936, Boston *Traveller*, July 11, 23, 25, 1936, clippings in Winfred Overholser Scrapbooks. No. 1, in Overholser Papers, LC; Arthur H. Ruggles to H. Edmund Bullis, July 28, 1936, AFMH Papers, uncatalogued, AP.

44. *AJP* 93 (1937): 972-73.

45. "Further Developments in Massachusetts," *AJP* 93 (1937): 1452-55; Roy G. Hoskins to Clarence M. Hincks, Feb. 9, 1937, AFMH Papers, AP; Arthur H. Ruggles to H. Edmund Bullis, Dec. 11, 1936, AFMH Papers, uncatalogued, AP; Winfred Overholser to Clarence B. Farrar, Feb. 10, 19, 1937, Farrar to Overholser, Feb. 12, 1937, Farrar Papers, APA.

46. *AJP* 93 (1937): 969; "Report of the Special Commission Established to Study the Whole Matter of the Mentally Diseased in Their Relation to the Commonwealth, Including All Phases of Work of the Department of Mental Diseases . . . December, 1937," Mass. *House Document No. 320* (Jan. 1938): 5-8.

47. "Report of the Special Commission . . . 1937," 6-27; *AJP* 93 (1937): 1455.

48. *AJP* 94 (1938): 985-87; Overholser to Farrar, Jan. 13, 31, 1938, Ross M. Chapman to Farrar, Mar. 1, 1938, with copy of letter of Chapman to Henry R. Atkinson, Feb. 7, 1938, G. Alder Blumer to Farrar, Feb. 27, 1938, Farrar to Blumer, Mar. 1, 1938, "Time for Governor to Act," Boston *Transcript*, Jan. 29, 1938 (typed copy), Farrar Papers, APA.

49. Overholser to Farrar, Feb. 3, 20, Mar. 13, Apr. 12, June 23, July 21, Oct. 31, 1938, Farrar Papers, APA; Gregory Zilboorg to Smith Ely Jelliffe, Oct. 24, 1938, Jelliffe to Zilboorg, Nov. 4, 1938, Jelliffe Papers, LC; *New England Journal of Medicine* 218 (1938): 940; "Report of the Special Commission Established to Study the Whole Matter of the Mentally Diseased in Their Relation to the Commonwealth, Including All Phases of Work of the Department of Mental Diseases . . . March 1, 1939," Mass. *House Document No. 2400* (1939): *passim*.

50. Untitled and undated typed memo ("The Truth of the Following Statements Can Be Readily Substantiated"), c. 1913, undated letter "To the Editor of the Times," c. 1913, probably written by William L. Russell, Salmon Boxes, in AFMH Papers, AP; *AJI* 71 (1914): 225-27. For examples of comparable problems in other states, see the following: NCCC *Proc.* 29 (1902): 328-38, 37 (1910): 308-15; Charles H. Clark to William A. White, Feb. 23, 1909, White Papers, RG 418, NA; Stewart Paton to Meyer, Dec. 10, 1901 (Series I), Frank P. Norbury to Meyer,

Sept. 28, 1908, Meyer Papers, Series II, JHMS; *AJI* 71 (1915): 792-95, 72 (1915): 186-87. During his more than three decades as superintendent of St. Elizabeths Hospital—the largest and one of the most important hospitals in the United States—William A. White experienced a number of Congressional investigations. This was so for two reasons: because the hospital was located in the District of Columbia and the fact that it was a federal institution. See *Report of the Special Committee on Investigation of the Government Hospital for the Insane with Hearings May 4-December 13, 1906 and Digest of Testimony* (2 vols.: Washington, D.C., 1907) (59th Cong., 2d sess., *House Report No. 7644*); *Investigation of St. Elizabeth's Hospital . . . 1926* (Washington, D.C., 1927) (69th Cong., 2d sess., *House Document No. 605*), as well as the White Papers, RG 418, NA, for the years of 1906, 1926, 1927, and 1928.

51. The Anderson case can be followed in J. K. Hall to Albert Anderson, Oct. 25, 31, 1928, Hall to William A. White, Oct. 25, 1928, Anderson to Hall, Dec. 13, 1928, Anderson to the Board of Directors of the State Hospital at Raleigh, Dec. 4, 1928, together with statement of Board of Directors of the State Hospital for the Insane at Raleigh, Hall to Charles O'H. Laughinghouse, Dec. 19, 29, 1928, Laughinghouse to Hall, Dec. 27, 1928, Feb. 6, Apr. 24, 1929, Hall to Angus W. McLean, Feb. 1, 1929, McLean to Hall, Feb. 15, 1929, "Supreme Court of North Carolina. Spring Term 1929. State v. Albert Anderson," J. K. Hall Papers, UNC; *Southern Medicine and Surgery* 90 (1928): 830-32, 91 (1929): 46-47, 112-13, 171-72, 264, 490.

52. J. G. Wilson, "Political Interference in State Hospital Administration: A Discussion of Policies," a report made for the Mental Hospital Survey Committee and the NCMH, 1937, 1-49, typed copy in AFMH Papers, uncatalogued, AP. For background material on the Mental Hospital Survey Committee, see Walter L. Treadway, *An Organization for Promoting Mental Hospital Services in the United States and Canada* (Public Health *Reports* 51 [December 25, 1936]: Washington, D.C., 1936), 1783-91, and the *AJP* 93 (1936): 470-76, 974-81.

53. Winfred Overholser to Samuel W. Hamilton, Sept. 13, 1937, Louis Casamajor to Hamilton, Oct. 15, 1937, AFMH Papers, uncatalogued, AP.

54. C. A. Thigpen to William D. Partlow, Sept. 20, 1932, Partlow to Thigpen, Sept. 23, 1932, Partlow to Lister Hill, Sept. 4, 1937, E. W. Rucker, Jr., to Partlow, Sept. 8, 1937, Partlow to Rucker, Sept. 11, 1937, Partlow to Thomas S. Lawson, Aug. 25, 1942, William D. Partlow Papers, Special Collections, Library, University of Alabama. See also Richard Gordon, "The Development of Louisiana's Public Mental Institutions, 1735-1940," chap. 5, doctoral dissertation, Louisiana State University, 1978.

55. Overholser, "The Desiderata of Central Administrative Control of

State Mental Hospitals," *AJP* 96 (1939): 517-34. The discussion of Overholser's paper appeared in *ibid.*, 563-74.

56. L. Cody Marsh to Beers, Aug. 8, 1931, William A. Bryan to William Frazier, AFMH Papers, uncatalogued, AP.

57. Beers to Marsh, Dec. 16, 1931, *ibid.*; Smith Ely Jelliffe to C. Macfie Campbell, May 29, 1933, Harry C. Solomon to Jelliffe, June 7, 1933, Jelliffe Papers, LC; Jacob H. Friedman, "An Organization of Ex-Patients of a Psychiatric Hospital," *MH* 23 (1939): 414-20; *AJP* 95 (1938): 752-53; Ill. Dept. of Public Welfare *AR* 22 (1938-1939): 78-79; A. A. Low, "The Recovered Patients Organize for Self-Help," *Lost and Found* vol. 2 no. 1, 7-9, copy in AFMH Papers, uncatalogued, AP; A. A. Low to Clarence M. Hicks, Jan. 17, 1939, AFMH Papers, uncatalogued, AP.

Chapter IX

1. Thomas W. Salmon, "Presidential Address," *AJP* 81 (1924): 1-11.

2. J. K. Hall to Hubert A. Royster, July 3, 1933, Royster Papers, UNC. See also Hall to C. Lydon Harrell, Feb. 11, 1937, Hall to John Mc-Campbell, May 30, 1938, Hall to Winfred Overholser, Sept. 7, 1938, Hall Papers, UNC.

3. See the *Propositions and Resolutions of the Association of Medical Superintendents of American Institutions for the Insane* (Philadelphia, 1876).

4. William A. White to R. G. Ferguson, Feb. 21, 1927, White Papers, RG 418, NA; Meyer to Albert G. Getchel, Jan. 13, 1912, Meyer to [Samuel B. ?] Woodward, Nov. 21, 1911, Meyer Papers, Series I, JHMS. Meyer's analysis of conditions in Massachusetts ("The Status of the Medical and Scientific Work in the Massachusetts Hospitals for the Insane") is reprinted in Meyer, *CP*, IV, 43-69. The original drafts of this document can be found in the Meyer Papers, Series III, JHMS. For the diversity of opinion see Charles W. Pilgrim, "The Proper Size of Hospitals for the Insane," *AJI* 65 (1908): 337-45; *State Hospitals Bulletin* 1 (1908): 92ff.; Walter Channing, "The Argument for the Large Insane Hospital," *BMSJ* 167 (1912): 156-58; Mass. State Bd. of Insanity *AR* 14 (1912): 159ff. During the 1920s and 1930s psychiatrists evinced neither interest nor concern with size of hospitals.

5. *Propositions and Resolutions*, 10; Thomas S. Kirkbride, *On the Construction, Organization, and General Arrangements of Hospitals for the Insane* (2nd ed.: Philadelphia, 1880), 37.

6. For late nineteenth-century medical education see Robert P. Hudson, "Abraham Flexner in Perspective: American Medical Education 1865-1910," *Bulletin of the History of Medicine* 56 (1972): 545-61; Donald Fleming, *William H. Welch and the Rise of Modern Medicine* (Boston, 1954); and Thomas N. Bonner, *American Doctors and German Uni-*

versities: A Chapter in International Intellectual Relations, 1870-1914 (Lincoln, Neb., 1963).

7. Walter Channing, "Dispensary Treatment of Mental Diseases," *AJI* 58 (1901): 110-19.

8. For a perceptive analysis of the dispensary see Charles E. Rosenberg, "Social Class and Medical Care in 19th-Century America: The Rise and Fall of the Dispensary," *Journal of the History of Medicine and Allied Sciences* 29 (1974): 32-54.

9. Owen Copp, "The Psychiatric Needs of a Large Community," *AJI* 73 (1916): 79-88.

10. Thomas W. Salmon, "A State Treating Mental Diseases at Home," *The Survey* 31 (1914): 468-70; L. Vernon Briggs and A. Warren Stearns, "Recent Extension of Out-Patient Work in Massachusetts State Hospitals for the Insane and Feeble-Minded," *AJI* 72 (1915): 35-43; Mass. State Bd. of Insanity *AR* 16 (1914): 16-19, 17 (1915): 67-68; E. Stanley Abbot, "Out-Patient or Dispensary Clinics for Mental Cases," *AJI* 77 (1920): 217-25.

11. Meyer to Franklin C. McLean, Apr. 30, 1929, Meyer Papers, Series I, JHMS. For examples of the emphasis placed on the importance of outpatient work see the following: George K. Pratt, "Community Aspects of Psychiatry," *BMSJ* 192 (1925): 204-09; J. Allen Jackson and Horace V. Pike, "Eight Years of Clinical and Educational Work in the Community," *AJP* 86 (1929): 231-57; William C. Sandy, "Extra-Institutional Activities of Mental Hospitals," American Academy of Political and Social Science *Annals* 149, Part III (1930): 190-94; Calif. State Bd. of Charities and Corrections *BR* 10 (1920-1922): table between 50-51; Mo. Bd. of Managers of the State Eleemosynary Institutions *BR* 1 (1921-1922): 15-16, 9 (1937-1938): 29-30; Md. Bd. of Welfare *AR* 4 (1926): 26; Mass. Commissioner of Mental Diseases *AR* 10 (1929): 47-50, 11 (1930): 41-44.

12. L. Vernon Briggs, *History of the Psychopathic Hospital Boston, Massachusetts* (Boston, 1922), 158; Jackson and Pike, "Eight Years of Clinical and Educational Work in the Community," *loc.cit.*, 244-45.

13. Albert W. Ferris, "Psychopathic Wards in General Hospitals," NCCC *Proc.* 37 (1910): 264-69.

14. For discussions of these points see C. M. Campbell's comments in the *AJP* 79 (1922): 105-08; Irving J. Sands, "The Psychiatric Clinic in the General Hospital," *JAMA* 85 (1925): 723-29; George K. Pratt, "Psychiatric Departments in General Hospitals," *AJP* 82 (1926): 403-10; Thomas J. Heldt, "The Functioning of a Division of Neuropsychiatry in a General Hospital," *AJP* 84 (1927): 459-81; Groves B. Smith, "The Psychoneurosis: Their Problems in the General Hospital," *JAMA* 89 (1927): 1949-56; George W. Henry, "Some Modern Aspects of Psychiatry in General Hospital Practice," *AJP* 86 (1929): 481-99; Thomas

J. Heldt, "The Treatment of Mental Diseases in a General Hospital," *New York State Journal of Medicine* 30 (1930): 63-71.

15. *AJP* 79 (1922): 106-08.

16. Frederick W. Brown, "General Hospital Facilities for Mental Patients," *MH* 15 (1931): 378-84; Thomas J. Heldt, "Psychiatric Services in General Hospitals," *AJP* 95 (1939): 865-71.

17. "The State Hospital's Isolation," *Modern Hospital* 20 (1923): 329-31. See also Winfred Overholser, "The Interrelation of the Community and the State Insane Hospital," *Alienist and Neurologist* 39 (1918): 197-200.

18. For a perceptive discussion see John C. Burnham, "The Struggle Between Physicians and Paramedical Personnel in American Psychiatry, 1917-41," *Journal of the History of Medicine and Allied Sciences* 29 (1974): 93-106.

19. E. J. Taylor to Meyer, Apr. 19, 1920, Meyer Papers, Series I, JHMS. See also Meyer to Taylor, Apr. 21, May 7, 1920, Taylor to Meyer, May 5, 1920, *ibid.*

20. The best discussion of nursing can be found in Janet W. James, "Isabel Hampton and the Professionalization of Nursing in the 1890s," in *The Therapeutic Revolution: Essays in the Social History of American Medicine*, ed. Morris J. Vogel and Charles E. Rosenberg (Philadelphia, 1979), 201-44.

21. Samuel W. Hamilton to Meyer, Apr. 15, 1920, with "Medical Staff of State Hospitals," Meyer Papers, Series I, JHMS; Mary M. Wolfe, "The Present Status of Women Physicians in Hospitals for the Insane," AMPA *Proc.* 16 (1909): 349-56. See also William Healy to Meyer, Nov. 6, 1919, Meyer to Healy, Nov. 8, 1919, Meyer Papers, Series I, JHMS; *State Hospital Quarterly* 5 (1920): 313-16.

Rabinovitch's criticisms of American mental hospitals reflected her training in and commitment to European scientific medicine. Less controversial was her insistence that female attendants be employed in male wards to order to reduce the level of masculine brutality. Nevertheless, the last article of the *Journal of Mental Pathology* in 1909 did not contain a single article by an American psychiatrist. See *Journal of Mental Pathology* 1 (1901): 45-48, 2 (1902): 39-41, 3 (1902): 12-31, 32-34, 87-90, 4 (1903): 73-76, 5 (1903): 37-39. That Rabinovitch's position on female nurses in male wards was not unusual, see Charles R. Bancroft, "Women Nurses on Wards for Men in Hospitals for the Insane," *AJI* 63 (1906): 177-89; George T. Tuttle, "The Male Nurse," *ibid.*, 191-204; and Wash. State Bd. of Control *BR* 4 (1907-1908): 37.

22. This change can be followed in the *Proc.* of the NCCC from 1880 to 1910.

23. *JNMD* 16 (1889): 598-99, 17 (1890): 278-80; Henry R. Stedman, "The Management of Convalescence and the After-Care of the Insane," *ibid.* 21 (1894): 786-99, 814-15. For the uneasy relationship between neu-

rologists and institutional psychiatrists see F. X. Dercum, "Address in Mental Disorders," *Medical Society of the State of Pa. Trans.* 26 (1895): 115-24; Richard Dewey, "Our Association and Our Associates," AMPA *Proc.* 3 (1896): 65-86; Bernard Sachs, "Advances in Neurology and Their Relation to Psychiatry," *AJI* 54 (1897): 1-19; J. T. Eskridge, "The Mutual Relations of the Alienist and Neurologist in the Study of Psychiatry and Neurology," *AJI* 55 (1898): 195-217; Frederick Peterson, "New Paths in Psychiatry," *JNMD* 25 (1898): 44-49.

24. ANA *Trans.* 23 (1897): 129-33, and Appendix, i-xxxi; Meyer, "The Problem of 'After-Care' and the Organization of Societies for the Prophylaxis of Mental Disorders," N.Y.S. Commission in Lunacy *AR* 18 (1906): 161.

25. Meyer, "Historical Sketch and Outlook of Psychiatric Social Work," *Hospital Social Service* 5 (1922): 222-23; N.Y.S. Commission in Lunacy *AR* 17 (1905): 1094-96, 18 (1906): 119-21, 160-88, 1235-40; N.Y. State Charities Aid Assn., Committee on the Insane, Sub-Committee on Prevention and Aftercare *AR* 4 (1909): 14. See also Richard Dewey, "After-Care of the Insane," NCCC *Proc.* 24 (1897): 76-83, and "The Assistance of Destitute Convalescent and Recovered Patients, Discharged from Hospitals for the Insane," NCCC *Proc.* 32 (1905): 339-43.

26. N.Y. State Charities Aid Assn., Committee on the Insane, Sub-Committee on Prevention and Aftercare *AR* 4 (1909): 11; Homer Folks to the N.Y. State Commission in Lunacy, June 6, 1911, T. E. McGarr to Mary Vida Clark, Oct. 3, 1911, copies in Meyer Papers, Series II, JHMS; N.Y.S. Hospital Commission *AR* 29 (1916-1917): 122. See also M. Elizabeth Dunn, "History of Social Service Work in the New York State Hospitals," *State Hospital Quarterly* 9 (1924): 386-97, and Homer Folks, *Public Health and Welfare: The Citizens' Responsibility* (New York, 1958), 138-45.

27. Briggs, *History of the Psychopathic Hospital*, Chap. XI; Mass. State Bd. of Insanity *AR* 15 (1913): 139-41, 16 (1914): 16-19; Wisc. State Bd. of Control *BR* 11 (1910-1912): 152. Calif. State Bd. of Charities and Corrections *BR* 7 (1914-1916): 39.

28. Morton White, *Social Thought in America: The Revolt Against Formalism* (New York, 1952), 11 *et passim*.

29. Mary Jarrett to G. O. Ireland, May 1, 1922, U.S. Veterans Administration, Social Work Service Papers, SWHA; Mary Richmond, *Social Diagnosis* (New York, 1917), 62; M. Ryther, "Place and Scope of Psychiatric Social Work in Mental Hygiene," NCCC *Proc.* 46 (1919): 578. See also Meyer to Mary E. Richmond, Jan. 7, 1912, Meyer Papers, Series III, JHMS; Mary Jarrett, "Possibilities in Social Service for Psychopathic Patients," *BMSJ* 176 (1917): 201-04; Abraham Myerson, "The Psychiatric Social Worker," *Journal of Abnormal Psychology* 13 (1918): 168-71; NCCC *Proc.* 46 (1919): 583-99, 48 (1921): 381-85. The best general

account of the origins of social work is Roy Lubove's *The Professional Altruist: The Emergence of Social Work as a Career 1880-1930* (Cambridge, 1965).

30. E. E. Southard and Mary C. Jarrett, *The Kingdom of Evils: Psychiatric Social Work Presented in One Hundred Case Histories Together with a Classification of Social Divisions of Evil* (New York, 1922). See also Lubove, *Professional Altruist*, chaps. 3-4, and James Leiby, *A History of Social Welfare and Social Work in the United States* (New York, 1978), chap. 9-10.

31. American Assn. of Social Workers and American Assn. of Psychiatric Social Workers, *Vocational Aspects of Psychiatric Social Work* (2nd ed.: New York, 1926), 16-17; Louise C. Odencrantz, *The Social Worker in Family, Medical and Psychiatric Social Work* (New York, 1929), 273; Lois M. French, *Psychiatric Social Work* (New York, 1940), x, 199.

32. French, *Psychiatric Social Work*, 295-98; *American Association of Psychiatric Social Workers* (n.p., n.d., c. 1928), copy in AAPSW Papers (Ephemeral), SHWA.

33. Maida H. Solomon to Mildred D. Scoville, Mar. 18, 1926; AAPSW, Ways and Means Committee, 1926-1929, typed minutes; remarks by Cornelia H. Allen, President, in "Annual Report of the American Association of Psychiatric Social Workers 1933-34"; AAPSW, "Excerpts from Meetings and Minutes—1927 and 1928 of Sub-Committee on Interpretation of By-Laws"; AAPSW, Executive Committee Minutes, Mar. 21, 1936; Memorandum I-III (Feb. 1938) to the Members of the AAPSW; Summary of Material Regarding Membership from Chicago Meeting Feb. 25, 1938; "Interpretation by By-Laws Relating to Membership as Used by the Membership Committee 1937-1939"; AAPSW, Minutes of Executive Committe Meeting Apr. 23, 1940, all in AAPSW Papers, SHWA; French, *Psychiatric Social Work*, 305.

34. Southard's unpublished paper was printed in Briggs, *History of the Psychopathic Hospital*, 173.

35. Jessie Taft, "The Limitations of the Psychiatrist," *Medicine and Surgery* 2 (1918): 365-69. See also Taft's *The Woman Movement from the Point of View of Social Consciousness* (Chicago, 1916).

36. "Minutes of the Meeting of the Executive Committee of the American Association of Psychiatric Social Workers at the Commonwealth Fund . . . October 18, 1929," 10-11, AAPSW Papers, SHWA; Clarence O. Cheyney to Karl M. Bowman, May 17, 1928, copy in Meyer Papers, Series II, JHMS. See also Sybil Foster to Meyer, Dec. 13, 1929, Esther L. Richards to Meyer, Jan. 16, 1930, and Meyer to Foster (with enclosed notes), Jan. 17, 1930, Meyer Papers, Series II, JHMS.

37. *AJP* 89 (1932): 622-25, 91 (1934): 427-33; French, *Psychiatric Social Work*, 80; "Report of the Secretary of the American Association of Psychiatric Social Workers 1930-1931," 11, Hester B. Crutcher to Mildred

C. Scoville, Jan. 21, 1938, AAPSW, Executive Committee Meeting, Feb. 13, 1939, AAPSW Papers, SHWA.

38. "Notes on Roundtable Discussion: Cooperation Between Psychiatry and Psychiatric Social Work in the Social Problems of Today" (May 7, 1941), together with "Summary of Results Obtained from Questionnaire Sent Out by the Joint Committee of American Psychiatric Association and American Association of Psychiatric Social Workers," AAPSW Papers, SHWA. See also Hester B. Crutcher, *A Guide for Developing Psychiatric Social Work in State Hospitals* (Utica, 1933).

39. "The Trend Study." *News-Letter of the American Association of Psychiatric Social Workers* 1 (1932): 5-8; French, *Psychiatric Social Work, passim;* AAPSW, Executive Committee Meeting, Feb. 19, 1931, 5-6, Mar. 27, 1931, unpaginated (material from p. 7), AAPSW, "A Suggested Curriculum for Psychiatric Social Work" (c. 1935), AAPSW, "Curriculum for Professional Education in Psychiatric Social Work: Introductory Statement" (c. June, 1939), AAPSW Papers, SHWA.

40. For typical examples see the *News-Letter of the American Association of Psychiatric Social Workers* 1 (1931): 1-6, 3 (1934): 1-2, 7 (1937): 1-6, 9 (1939): 3-10; *MH* 13 (1929): 108-31; *Occupational Therapy and Rehabilitation* 7 (1928): 407-12; Lee R. Porter and Marion E. Kenworthy, *Mental Hygiene and Social Work* (New York, 1929), *passim;* Odencrantz, *The Social Worker in Family, Medical and Psychiatric Social Work, passim;* French, *Psychiatric Social Work*, 3. The entries under "Psychiatric Social Work" and "Mental Hygiene" in the various editions of the *Social Work Year Book*, 1-5 (1927-1939) are also illuminating.

41. Abraham Flexner, "Is Social Work a Profession?," NCCC *Proc.* 42 (1915): 576-90.

42. Mildred C. Scoville, "An Inquiry Into the Status of Psychiatric Social Work" (Presidential address, 1930), mimeographed copy in AAPSW Papers, SHWA.

43. W. R. Dunton, Jr., "An Historical Note," *Occupational Therapy and Rehabilitation* 5 (1926): 427-39; *idem,* "History and Development of Occupational Therapy," in *Principles of Occupational Therapy*, ed. Helen S. Willard and Clare S. Spackman (Philadelphia, 1947), 1-9; Meyer, "The Philosophy of Occupation Therapy," *Archives of Occupational Therapy* 1 (1922): 1-10; Eleanor Clarke Slagle, "Training Aids for Mental Patients," *ibid.* 1 (1922): 11-17; "History," *Occupational Therapy and Rehabilitation* 19 (1940): 27-34. For Slagle's career and bibliography of her writings see the entry in *Notable American Women 1607-1950* (Cambridge, 1971), III, 296-98.

44. Dunton, "An Historical Note," *loc.cit.,* 432, 435; "History," *loc.cit.,* 27-34.

45. C. Floyd Haviland, "Occupational Therapy from the Viewpoint of the Superintendent of a State Mental Hospital," *Occupational Therapy*

and Rehabilitation 6 (1927): 431-38; Haviland, "Presidential Address," *ibid.* 8 (1929): 231-41; Horatio M. Pollock, "Development of Occupational Therapy in the New York State Hospitals," *ibid.*, 439-44; Benjamin Malzberg, "A Statistical Review of Occupational Therapy in the New York Civil State Hospitals," *PQ* 3 (1929): 413-25; N.Y.S. Hospital Commission *AR* 35 (1922-1923): 71-77, 41 (1928-1929): 113-21; Horatio M. Pollock, "Trends in Occupational Therapy in New York State," *Occupational Therapy and Rehabilitation* 16 (1937): 267-70.

46. American Occupational Therapy Association, *1933 Directory of Qualified Occupational Therapists Enrolled During 1932 in the National Register* (New York, n.d.), 13-21. For the relatively uncontroversial acceptance of occupational therapy by psychiatrists see the "Report of Committee on Occupational Therapy," *AJP* 80 (1923): 343-48. For a sampling of the somewhat amorphous nature of the specialty, see Anna L. Tompkins, "The Organization of an Occupational Therapy Department at the Marcy Division of the Utica State Hospital," *Occupational Therapy and Rehabilitation* 5 (1926): 419-26; Marion R. Spear, "The Value and Limitations of Attendants in Occupational Therapy Departments in Mental Hospitals," *ibid.* 6 (1927): 225-27; Helen Theis, "Waste Material Available in a Large Mental Hospital," *ibid.* 6 (1927): 161-65; John E. Davis, "Psychological Objectives in the Physical Program for the Mentally Ill," *ibid.* 9 (1930): 77-82; Mary E. Black, "Therapeutic Placement of Mental Patients in State Hospital Industries," *ibid.* 15 (1936): 301-14.

47. William A. White to I. M. Bentley, Feb. 9, 1906, White Papers, RG 418, NA; Meyer to Ira Remsen, Oct. 8, 1909, Meyer Papers, Series III, JHMS; John B. Watson, "Content of a Course in Psychology for Medical Students," Meyer to Watson, Jan. 11, 1912, Watson to Meyer, Jan. 16, 1912, Series I, *ibid.*; Alfred Lief, *The Commonsense Psychiatry of Dr. Adolf Meyer: Fifty-Two Selected Papers Edited, with Biographical Narrative* (New York, 1948), 369-71; E. Stanley Abbot, "Psychology and the Medical School," *AJI* 70 (1913): 447-57. See also the Meyer-Titchener correspondence between 1909 and 1918 in the Meyer Papers, Series I, JHMS.

48. J.E.W. Wallin, *The Odyssey of a Psychologist* (Wilmington, Del., 1955), 69-82; Charles L. Dana, "Psychiatry and Psychology," *Medical Record* 91 (1917), 265-67. See also Peter Bassoe, "Problems Confronting the Section on Nervous and Mental Diseases," *JAMA* 78 (1922): 1857-58.

49. National Research Council (Division of Medical Sciences and Division of Anthropology and Psychology), "Conference on Relations of Psychiatry to Psychology" (April 30, 1921), 1-43, mimeographed copy in White Papers, RG 418, NA; Carl E. Seashore, *Pioneering in Psychology* (Iowa City, 1942), 126-33. See also C. M. Campbell to Meyer, May 4, 1921, Meyer Papers, Series I, JHMS; White to R. E. Dooley,

Dec. 10, 1921, White Papers, RG 418, NA; F. L. Wells, "The Status of 'Clinical Psychology,' " *MH* 6 (1922): 11-22; Winifred Richmond, "The Psychologist in the Psychopathic Hospital," *Journal of Abnormal and Social Psychology* 18 (1924): 299-310.

50. David Shakow, "The Worcester State Hospital Research on Schizophrenia (1927-1946)," *Journal of Abnormal Psychology* 80 (1972): 67-110; White House Conference on Child Health and Protection, *Psychology and Psychiatry in Pediatrics: The Problem: Report of the Subcommittee on Psychology and Psychiatry* (New York, 1932), 24-25; T. H. Weisenberg to Meyer, Sept. 19, 1932, Meyer Papers, Series II, JHMS; *Proceedings of the Fourth Conference on Psychiatric Education. . . . 1936* (New York, 1938), 199-203. See also the symposium, "The Relation Between Psychiatry and Psychology," *Psychological Exchange* 2 (1933): 56-64, 149-61. For a general, but somewhat inadequate, discussion of the troubled relations between psychology and psychiatry see Thomas V. Moore, "A Century of Psychology in Its Relationship to American Psychiatry," in *One Hundred Years of American Psychiatry*, ed. J. K. Hall (New York, 1944), 443-77. A more recent discussion appears in Donald S. Napoli, *Architects of Adjustment: The History of the Psychological Profession in the United States* (Port Washington, N.Y., 1981).

Elements of conflict were also present between psychiatry and other social science disciplines. Between 1927 and 1929 the APA became involved with the newly organized Social Science Research Council, leading to the convening of one Colloquium on Personality Investigation in 1927 and a second in 1929. The different focus of psychiatrists and social scientists, however, militated against sustained collaboration. At the first Colloquium, according to Harry Stack Sullivan, "the discussion proceeded after the fashion of one of the famous Irish horses, in all directions." See *AJP* 84 (1928): 729-47, 85 (1928): 378-80, 86 (1929): 426-29. A verbatim transcript of the two colloquia appeared in the *AJP*, and were also issued separately under the title: APA, Committee on Relations with the Social Sciences, *Proceedings . . . Colloquium on Personality Investigation* 1-2 (1928-1929).

51. Form letter of Karl A. Menninger, May 1, 1924, together with enclosed comments and copy of the Constitution of the American Orthopsychiatric Association, Meyer Papers, Series II, JHMS; David M. Levy, "Psychiatry and Orthopsychiatry," *American Journal of Orthopsychiatry* 1 (1931): 239-44. The latter journal began publication in 1930.

Chapter X

1. Arlie W. Bock, "Psychiatry in Private Practice," *New England Journal of Medicine* 208 (1933): 1092; Maurice Leven, *The Income of Physi-*

cians: An Economic and Statistical Analysis (Committee on the Costs of Medical Care, *Publication No. 24*: Chicago, 1932), 116.

2. Edwin R. Embree to Frankwood E. Williams, Dec. 12, 1927, Williams to Embree, May 1, 1925, with "Statement in Reference to a Proposal for a study of the Psychopathology of Dependency," Embree to Williams, May 28, 1925, Alan Gregg, written note on excerpt from MM (Max Mason) Diary, Jan. 30, 1931, excerpts from Gregg Diary, May 29, 1933, Oct. 31, 1934, Memorandum of interview with Dr. Arthur H. Ruggles, July 10, 1935, Gregg to Clarence M. Hincks, Jan. 6, 1939, Record Group 1.1, Series 200 (NCMH), RFA.

3. Gerald N. Grob, *Mental Institutions in America: Social Policy to 1875* (New York, 1973), 148-49; Carlos F. Macdonald, "The Outlook for the Young Physician in State Hospital and Sanitarium Work," *Medical News* 78 (1901): 659-62.

4. Richard Dewey to William A. White, Jan. 4, 1906, White to Dewey, n.d. (c. Jan. 1906), White Papers, RG 418, NA; "Minutes of Quarterly Conference, April, 1911," in *State Hospitals Bulletin* 4 (1911): 322ff.; *State Hospital Quarterly* 10 (1924): 1-49; Ill. Dept. of Public Welfare *AR* 4 (1920-1921): 103, 5 (1921-1922): 31, 70-71, 6 (1922-1923): 50-51, 10 (1926-1927): 146-47, 13 (1929-1930): 165; Kans. Bd. of Administration, Charitable Institutions Section *BR* 1 (1916-1918): 9 (Osawatomie State Hospital); Henry A. Cotton to White, May 31, 1916, White to Cotton, June 2, 1916, White Papers, RG 418, NA; Neb. Bd. of Control *BR* 11 (1933-1935): 73-75; Ohio Dept. of Public Welfare *AR* 18 (1939): 148. See also James V. May to White, Apr. 26, May 10, 1910, White to May, May 3, 1910, White Papers, RG 418, NA.

5. *AJI* 76 (1919): 213-14, 77 (1920): 280-85; *AJP* 78 (1921): 247, 261; William A. White, "Presidential Address," *ibid.* 82 (1925): 1-20; William L. Russell, "Presidential Address: The Place of the American Psychiatric Association in Modern Psychiatric Organization and Progress," *ibid.* 89 (1932): 1-18; *ibid.* 84 (1927): 285-86, 288-89, 89 (1932): 574-76.

6. See Grob, *Mental Institutions in America*, for a discussion of the nature of nineteenth-century psychiatry.

7. Charles W. Burr, "The Teaching of Psychiatry," *JAMA* 60 (1913): 1054-57. See also N. Emmons Paine, "Instruction in Psychiatry in American Medical Colleges," *AJI* 50 (1894): 372-80; Henry M. Hurd, "Presidential Address—The Teaching of Psychiatry," *ibid.* 56 (1899): 217-30; NCCC *Proc.* 32 (1905): 429ff.; F. X. Dercum, "The Teaching of Insanity," *JAMA* 60 (1913): 1057-58; H. Douglas Singer, "The Teaching of Psychiatry: A Reply to Drs. Burr and Dercum," *ibid.*, 1874-76; "The Present Teaching of Psychiatry in American Medical Schools," AMA Section on Nervous and Mental Diseases *Trans.* (1914): 224-25, also reprinted in *JAMA* 63 (1914): 1643-49; William W. Graves, "Some Factors

Tending Toward Adequate Instruction in Nervous and Mental Disease," *JAMA* 63 (1914): 1707-13.

8. D. W. Roberts to White, Jan. 22, 1915, White to Roberts, Jan. 26, 1915, White Papers, RG 418, NA; *Final Report of the Commission on Medical Education* (New York, 1932), 214-16; Ralph A. Noble, *Psychiatry in Medical Education: An Abridgement of a Report Submitted to the Advisory Committee of Psychiatric Education of the National Committee for Mental Hygiene* (New York, 1933), 80 *et passim*.

9. "Minutes and Proceedings of the 11th Annual Meeting of the National Committee for Mental Hygiene February 4th, 1920," 34-35, mimeographed copy in AFMH Papers, AP; Samuel Orton to Meyer, Dec. 14, 1920, with enclosed mss. "Graduate Training in Neuropsychiatry," Meyer Papers, Series I, JHMS; Frankwood E. Williams to Edwin R. Embree, Nov. 3, 1926, Embree to Williams, Nov. 8, 1926, Williams to Richard M. Pearce, Oct. 22, 1929, "National Committee for Mental Hygiene . . . 1915-1939," mimeographed document, 6, Record Group 1.1, Series 200 (NCMH), RFA; *AJP* 82 (1925): 323-25; Meyer, "Thirty-Five Years of Psychiatry in the United States and our Present Outlook," *AJP* 85 (1928): 1-31; "Report of the Committee on Medical Services," *AJP* 86 (1929): 417-22; Meyer to Edward A. Strecker, May 1, 1929, Strecker to Meyer, May 3, 1929, Meyer Papers, Series II, JHMS; Meyer to Louis Casamajor, June 10, 1929, Meyer to Strecker, June 10, 1929, Meyer to George H. Kirby, June 10, 1929, Casamajor to Meyer, Sept. 9, 1929, Meyer Papers, Series III, JHMS.

10. The discussion of the organization of medical services and board certification is based on Rosemary Stevens's important *American Medicine and the Public Interest* (New Haven, 1971).

11. AMA House of Delegates *Minutes* (June 27-30, 1930): 42.

12. E. A. Rygh to Meyer, Nov, 18, 1930, Meyer Papers, Series II, JHMS; *JAMA* 96 (1931): 2125-26, 99 (1932): 397; James V. May, "The Establishment of Psychiatric Standards by the Association," *AJP* 90 (1933): 6-8.

13. Meyer to E. A. Rygh, Nov. 24, 1930, Grimes to Meyer, Feb. 6, 1931, with report of visit of Jan. 28, 1931, Meyer to Grimes, Feb. 10, 1931, Meyer Papers, Series II, JHMS; Grimes, "Preliminary Report of Survey of Hospitals for Nervous and Mental Patients in the United States," *JAMA* 98 (1932): 839-40.

14. This and the preceding paragraph are based on Franklin G. Ebaugh, "The Proposed American Board of Psychiatry," draft copy in Meyer Papers, Series II, JHMS; *AJP* 87 (1930): 327-28, 87 (1931): 873-76; "Minutes of the First Meeting of the Advisory Committee of the Division of Psychiatric Education Held ... September 19, 1931," copy in Meyer Papers, Series II, JHMS; Lawson G. Lowrey to Ebaugh, Feb. 4, 1931, Clarence O. Cheyney to Ebaugh, Feb. 5, 1931, William L. Russell to Ebaugh, Feb. 5, 1931, George S. Stevenson to Ebaugh, Feb. 6, 1931,

Edward N. Brush to Ebaugh, Mar. 3, 1931, *ibid.; Basis of Conference on Psychiatric Education. Hotel Statler, Boston, May 28-29, 1933* (New York, 1933), mimeographed copy in NLM.

15. James V. May to White, Jan. 3, 1931, with copy of letter from May to George M. Kline, Dec. 30, 1930, White to May, Jan. 5, 27, 1931, White Papers, RG 418, NA; William L. Russell to Meyer, Feb. 5, 1932, Meyer Papers, Series II, JHMS.

16. Meyer to Russell, Dec. 17, 1931, Russell to Meyer, Dec. 21, 31, 1931, Jan. 8, 23, 27, Feb. 5, 1932, H. Douglas Singer to Russell (copy), Jan. 4, 1932, Russell to Singer (copy), Jan. 7, 16, 1932, Russell to White (copy), Jan. 27, 1932, Meyer Papers, Series II, JHMS; James V. May to White, Jan. 19, 1932, White to May, Jan. 23, Nov. 21, 1932, White Papers, RG 418, NA.

17. H. Douglas Singer to William L. Russell, Jan. 4, 1932, George M. Kline to White, Jan. 20, 1932, White to Kline, Jan. 23, 1932, James V. May to White, Jan. 25, Nov. 16, 19, 23, 1932, Russell to May, Nov. 14, 1932, May to Russell, Nov. 16, 1932, White to May, Nov. 17, 21, 1932, White Papers, RG 418, NA; White to Clarence M. Hincks, Nov. 17, 1932, May to Clarence O. Cheyney, Nov. 16, 1932, AFMH Papers, AP; James V. May, "The Establishment of Psychiatric Standards by the Association," *loc.cit.*, 8, 14.

18. AMA House of Delegates *Minutes* (June 12-16, 1933): 59ff., 87; John M. Grimes, *Institutional Care of Mental Patients in the United States* (Chicago, 1934), xii. Between January and March, 1933, White corresponded with Grimes (see Esther C. Kolbe to White, Jan. 10, 1933, White Papers, RG 418, NA). In the White Papers there is a notation that White's criticisms of the Preliminary Report, Mar. 22, 1933, was filed under AMA. A search of the AMA file in the White Papers failed to uncover the correspondence.

19. John M. Grimes to Meyer, Oct. 10, 1934, Meyer Papers, Series II, JHMS; Grimes, *Institutional Care of Mental Patients*, viii, xiv. For a slightly different version of Grimes's letter, see Grimes to John C. Whitehorn, Nov. 24, 1934, Whitehorn Papers, APA.

20. Grimes, *Institutional Care of Mental Patients*, 8, 17, 95, 97-98, 102, 113-16 *et passim*.

21. Meyer to T. N. Weisenberg, May 11, 1931, Weisenberg to Meyer, May 12, 1931, Clarence O. Cheyney to Ebaugh, Feb. 5, 1931, William L. Russell to Ebaugh, Feb. 5, 1931, Edward N. Brush to Ebaugh, Mar. 3, 1931, Russell to Meyer, July 28, 1931, "Minutes of the First Meeting of the Advisory Committee of the Division of Psychiatric Education Held . . . September 19, 1931," 20-21 *et passim*, Meyer Papers, Series II, JHMS.

22. Weisenberg to Meyer, May 12, 1931, Meyer Papers, Series II, JHMS. See also Walter Freeman, Franklin G. Ebaugh, and David A. Boyd, Jr., "The Founding of the American Board of Psychiatry and Neurology,

Inc.," *AJP* 115 (1959): 770-71. The latter account simply suggests that the drive for board certification represented an effort to uplift the standards of psychiatric practice.

23. *AJP* 89 (1932): 389-91.

24. Franklin G. Ebaugh, "The Crisis in Psychiatric Education," *JAMA* 99 (1932): 705; "Report of the Division of Psychiatric Education of the National Committee for Mental Hygiene for the Year 1931-1932," mimeographed copy in Meyer Papers, Series II, JHMS; Noble, *Psychiatry in Medical Education, passim.*

25. *Basis of Conference on Psychiatric Education. Hotel Statler, Boston, May 28-29, 1933; AJP* 90 (1933): 394-95; May, "The Establishment of Psychiatric Standards by the Association," *loc.cit.,* 9.

26. "Outline of Activities of the Division of Psychiatric Education Including a Statement Regarding the Activities of the American Board of Psychiatry and Neurology from June 1933 to June 1934," copy in Meyer Papers, Series II, JHMS; Meyer to Cheyney, Oct. 2, 1933, Cheyney to Meyer, Oct. 4, 6, 1933, C. M. Campbell to Cheyney (copy), Oct. 25, 1933, *ibid.*

27. Clarence O. Cheyney to Meyer, July 22, 1933, "Outline of Activities of the Division of Psychiatric Education . . . from June 1933 to June 1934," *ibid.*

28. Second Conference on Psychiatric Education *Proc.* (1934): 116-25; *AJP* 91 (1934): 713, 92 (1935): 226-29, 426-30, 475-77; Freeman, Ebaugh, and Boyd, "The Founding of the American Board of Psychiatry and Neurology," *loc.cit.,* 775.

29. *AJP* 95 (1938): 477-79.

30. Noble, *Psychiatry in Medical Education,* 56 *et passim;* Franklin G. Ebaugh and Charles A. Rymer, *Psychiatry in Medical Education* (New York, 1942), 108-26.

31. Ebaugh to Meyer, Apr. 12, 13, 1935, enclosed with Ebaugh to Barry C. Smith, Jan. 2, 1935, Ebaugh to Smith, Apr. 13, 1935, Meyer to Clarence M. Hincks, Apr. 15, 1935, Meyer to H. Douglas Singer, Apr. 15, 1935, H. Edmund Bullis to Meyer, Apr. 17, 1935, Singer to Hincks, n.d. (c. Apr. 1935), Meyer to Ebaugh, Apr. 18, 1935, Meyer Papers, Series II, JHMS; A. Warren Stearns, "The Future of Psychiatry in Medical Schools," Second Conference on Medical Education *Proc.* (1934): 107.

32. Meyer to Clarence O. Cheyney, Oct. 2, 1933, Meyer Papers, Series II, JHMS.

33. Ebaugh and Rymer, *Psychiatry in Medical Education,* 485ff. *et passim.*

34. I have sampled 10 percent (n = 943) of the total APA membership of 10,000. See the *Biographical Directory of Fellows & Members of the American Psychiatric Association as of October 1, 1957* (New York, 1958).

Chapter XI

1. James. T. Patterson, *The New Deal and the States: Federalism in Transition* (Princeton, 1969), 7-15; U.S. Bureau of the Census, *Patients in Hospitals for Mental Disease 1923* (Washington, D.C., 1926), 252, and *Mental Patients in State Hospitals 1929 and 1930* (Washington, D.C., 1933), 126.
2. Patterson, *New Deal and the States*, 26-49.
3. National Committee for Mental Hygiene, *State Hospitals in the Depression: A Survey of the Effects of the Economic Crisis on the Operation of Institutions for the Mentally Ill in the United States* (New York, 1934), *passim*; U.S. Bureau of the Census, *Mental Patients in State Hospitals 1929 and 1930*, 126, 132; *idem, Patients in Hospitals for Mental Disease 1934* (Washington, D.C., 1936), 37; *idem, Patients in Mental Institutions 1940* (Washington, D.C., 1943), 63; Ohio Dept. of Public Welfare *AR* 15 (1936): 308.
4. Clarence M. Hincks to Edgar Sydenstricker, Nov. 26, 1934, AFMH Papers, AP.
5. Horatio M. Pollock, "Family Care and the Institution Problem," *PQ* 7 (1933): 28-36; *idem*, "Family Care of Mental Patients," *AJP* 91 (1934): 331-36; *idem*, "Practical Considerations Relating to Family Care of Mental Patients," *AJP* 92 (1935): 559-64; *idem*, ed., *Family Care of Mental Patients: A Review of Systems of Family Care in America and Europe* (Utica, 1936), *passim*; Pollock to C. M. Hincks, Jan. 27, 1937, Pollock to H. Edmund Bullis, Jan. 29, 1937, AFMH Papers, AP.
6. Hester B. Crutcher, *Foster Home Care for Mental Patients* (New York, 1944), 181-96.
7. Cf. John L. Van de Mark, "Medical Treatment of Disturbed Patients," *State Hospital Quarterly* 7 (1922): 304-10; Rebekah Wright, *Hydrotherapy in Hospitals for Mental Diseases* (Boston, 1932); Ariz. Bd. of Directors of State Institutions *AR* 4-5 (1922-1923 and 1923-1924): 15-17; Mo. Bd. of Managers of the State Eleemosynary Institutions *BR* 2 (1923-1924): 162-63.
8. For Julius Wagner-Jauregg's career see the brief obituary in the *ANP* 44 (1940): 1319-22. A far more detailed account can be found in Joseph Gerstmann's *Die Malariabehandlung der Progressiven Paralyse* (Vienna, 1925). An English summary of the latter was published by Charles O. Fiertz, "The Malarial Treatment of General Paralysis," *State Hospital Quarterly* 11 (1926): 626-43. See also Wagner-Jauregg's "The Treatment of General Paresis by Inoculation of Malaria," *JNMD* 55 (1922): 369-75.
9. White's comment appeared in his letter to H. W. Mitchell, Apr. 25, 1923, White Papers, RG 418, NA. For the reception of malarial therapy in the 1920s see *AJP* 79 (1923): 721-23, 81 (1924): 175-225, 83 (1926): 205-06, 84 (1928): 715-27; *ANP* 17 (1926): 182-212; *State Hospital Quarterly* 11 (1926): 559-643; *Nature* 114 (1924): 164-65, 615-16; *JAMA* 87 (1926): 1821-27. For practices in various states see N.Y.S. Hospital

Commission *AR* 36 (1923-1924): 99-100, 37 (1924-1925): 110-11, 38 (1925-1926): 91-94; Minn. State Bd. of Control *BR* 13 (1924-1926): 85-87, 14 (1926-1928): 85-86; Mo. Bd. of Managers of the State Eleemosynary Institutions *BR* 3 (1925-1926): 83; Ohio Dept. of Public Welfare *AR* 5 (1925-1926): 148, 252.

10. Ill. Dept of Public Welfare *AR* 11 (1927-1928): 23, 12 (1928-1929): 23; *PQ* 1 (1927): 210-14, 2 (1928): 494-505.

11. The literature on the results of malarial fever therapy is extensive. For some typical examples see *PQ* 5 (1931): 733-39; *AJP* 88 (1931): 541-57, 93 (1936): 517-32; R. A. Vonderlehr, *Malaria Treatment of Parenchymatous Syphilis of the Central Nervous System* (Supplement No. 107 to the Public Health Reports: Washington, D.C., 1933). The discussions at the First International Conference on Fever Therapy can be found in *AJP* 94 (1937): 213-21.

12. Wagner-Jauregg, "The Treatment of General Paresis by Inoculation of Malaria," *JNMD* 55 (1922): 369-75; Watson W. Eldridge to White, June 21, 27, 1930, White to Eldridge, June 24, 28, 1930, White Papers, RG 418, NA.

13. John H. Stokes, "Critical Treatment Problems in Today's Syphilology," *JAMA* 94 (1930): 1033; A. E. Bennett, "Evaluation of Artificial Fever Therapy for Neuropsychiatric Disorders," *ANP* 40 (1938): 1141-55.

14. Oskar Diethelm, "An Historical View of Somatic Treatment in Psychiatry," *AJP* 95 (1939): 1165-79. See also Diethelm's *Treatment in Psychiatry* (New York, 1936). Diethelm's views, of course, reflected his own commitment to a form of Meyer's psychobiology, which emphasized patient treatment rather than the treatment of a disease entity.

15. *Literary Digest* 111 (1931): 16. For examples of drug therapy see *PQ* 6 (1932): 273-300, 657-64, 691-96; *JNMD* 79 (1934): 59-62; *JAMA* 109 (1937): 1786-88.

16. Manfred Sakel, "A New Treatment for Schizophrenia," *AJP* 93 (1937): 829-41; *idem*, "The Origin and Nature of the Hypoglycemic Therapy of the Psychoses," *Bulletin of the New York Academy of Medicine* 13 (1937): 97-109; *idem*, "The Methodical Use of Hypoglycemia in the Treatment of the Psychoses," *AJP* 94 (1937): 111-29; *idem, The Pharmacological Shock Treatment of Schizophrenia*, transl. by Joseph Wortis (an enlarged edition of Sakel's original articles from the *Wiener Medizinische Wochenschrift* in 1933 and 1934) (New York, 1938). See also Joseph Wortis, "Sakel's Hypoglycemic Insulin Treatment of Psychoses: History and Present Status," *JNMD* 85 (1937): 581-95.

17. C. M. Hincks to Hans Maier, Sept. 28, 1936, Maier to Hincks, Oct. 7, 1936, Winfred Overholser to Hincks, Oct. 27, 1936, White to Hincks, Oct. 27, 1936, AFMH Papers, AP; A. A. Brill to White, Oct. 31, 1936, White Papers, RG 418, NA; Meyer to White, Dec. 17, 1936, Meyer Papers, Series I, JHMS.

18. Meduna presented his ideas in a brief monograph, *Die Konvulsion-therapie der Schizophrenia* (Halle, 1937). See also Solomon Katzenel-bogen, "Critical Appraisal of the 'Shock Therapies' in the Major Psychoses and Psychoneuroses, III—Convulsive Therapy," *Psychiatry* 3 (1940): 409-20, and Meduna's brief piece in the *ANP* 35 (1936): 361-63.
19. Smith Ely Jelliffe to Tom A. Williams, Mar. 23, 1938, Jelliffe Papers, LC.
20. In 1937 and 1938 Abraham Myerson conducted a study of the attitudes of neurologists, psychiatrists, and psychologists toward psychoanalysis. The results were inconclusive, but indicated the presence of considerable opposition. More revealing were the narratives of individual letters, which are less susceptible to any facile generalization. See Myerson to Meyer, Nov. 23, 30, 1937, Meyer to Myerson, Nov. 26, Dec. 2, 1937, Meyer Papers, Series I, JHMS; Myerson to John C. Whitehorn, Jan. 24, 1938, Whitehorn to Myerson, Jan. 27, June 2, 1938, Whitehorn Papers, APA; Myerson to Hall, Jan. 25, 1938, Hall to Myerson, June 1, 1938, Hall to Karl A. Menninger, Sept. 22, 1938, J. K. Hall Papers, UNC; Myerson, "The Attitude of Neurologists, Psychiatrists and Psychologists Towards Psychoanalysis," *AJP* 96 (1939): 623-41. Throughout the 1930s there remained considerable tension between psychiatry and psychoanalaysis.
21. *AJP* 93 (1937): 985-86. For some examples of the attention given to insulin and metrazol therapy, see the following: *Time* 29 (Jan. 25, 1937): 26, 28, 34 (Nov. 20, 1939): 39-40; *New Republic* 91 (1937): 183; *Scientific American* 157 (1937): 247, 158 (1938): 176-77, 278-79; *Science News Letter* 31 (1937): 323-24, 347-48, 33 (1938): 334-37, 34 (1938): 294, 35 (1939): 212-13, 36 (1939): 339; *Forum and Century* 99 (1938): 98-102; *Newsweek* 12 (1938): 23-24; *Reader's Digest* 35 (1939): 73-75; *Hygeia* 18 (1940): 627, 668; *Science Digest* 8 (1940): 50-51.
22. J. K. Hall to D. H. Duncan, Mar. 2, 1940, Hall Papers, UNC.
23. J. P. Frostig, "Sakel's Pharmacologic Shock Treatment for Schizophrenia: Tentative Directions and System of Recording," *ANP* 39 (1938): 219-31; Joseph Wortis, "The Management of Shock Treatment of Psychoses," *Medical Clinics of North America* 23 (1939): 797-809; Calif. Dept. of Institutions and Agencies, *Statistical Report* (1938-1939): 2-8; Simon Kwalwasser, "Report on 441 Cases Treated With Metrazol," *PQ* 14 (1940): 527-46. See also *PQ* 12 (1938), and the *AJP* 94-97 (1937-1941), which included many articles on the subject.
24. For brief sketches of Benjamin Malzberg and Horatio M. Pollack see the *National Cyclopedia of American Biography*, Current Volume E. 1937-1938 (New York, 1938), 54-55, and *Who Was Who in America*, VI (Chicago, 1976), 261.
25. Benjamin Malzberg, "Outcome of Insulin Treatment of One Thousand Patients with Dementia Praecox," *PQ* 12 (1938): 528-53.

26. Malzberg, "A Follow-Up Study of Patients with Dementia Praecox Treated with Insulin in the New York Civil State Hospitals," *MH* 23 (1939): 641-51. The studies used by Malzberg for comparative purposes included Raymond G. Fuller and Mary Johnston, "The Duration of Hospital Life for Mental Patients," *PQ* 5 (1931): 341-52, 552-82, and Fuller, "What Happens to Mental Patients After Discharge from Hospital?," *ibid.* 9 (1935): 95-104.

27. Horatio M. Pollock, "A Statistical Study of 1,140 Dementia Praecox Patients Treated with Metrazol," *PQ* 13 (1939): 558-68. The data presented in Table 11-1 is drawn from p. 560. Pollock's findings were confirmed in a parallel study of John R. Ross and Benjamin Malzberg, "A Review of the Results of the Pharmacological Shock Therapy and the Metrazol Convulsive Therapy in New York State," *AJP* 96 (1939): 297-316.

28. Solomon Katzenelbogen, "A Critical Appraisal of the 'Shock Therapies' in the Major Psychoses, I—Insulin," *Psychiatry* 2 (1939): 504. My generalized comments about the nature of the studies on insulin and metrazol are based on a careful reading of such publications as the *AJP, JAMA, ANP*, and the *PQ*, to cite only a few.

29. Katzenelbogen, "A Critical Appraisal," *loc.cit.*, 502, 505. Katzenelbogen's study was the most exhaustive review of the literature, and appeared in three parts, two of which dealt with insulin therapy and one with convulsive (metrazol) therapy. They appeared in *Psychiatry* 2 (1939): 493-505, and 3 (1940): 211-28, 409-20. Katzenelbogen was on the staff of St. Elizabeths Hospital, which in 1937 and 1938 experimented with insulin coma and metrazol but found "that the results obtained did not justify the amount of personnel required to carry on this form of treatment." Memo from E. B. Reichenbach to Jay L. Hoffman, Apr. 13, 1954, in St. Elizabeths Hospital, Administrative Files, Box 9, folder "Insulin and Metrazol," RG 418, NA.

30. W. Va. State Bd. of Control *Report* 13 (1939-1943): 45; Report of State Hospital No. 1, in Mo. Bd. of Managers of the State Eleemosynary Institutions *BR* 10 (1939-1940): 6; Neb. State Bd. of Control *BR* 14 (1939-1941): 195; Simon Kwalwasser, "Report on 441 Cases Treated with Metrazol," *PQ* 14 (1940): 527-46; Leon Reznikoff, "Evolution of Metrazol Shock in the Treatment of Schizophrenia," *ANP* 43 (1940): 318-25.

31. *JAMA* 115 (1940): 462-63; F.A.D. Alexander and H. E. Himwich, "Nitrogen Inhalation Therapy for Schizophrenia: Preliminary Report on Technique," *AJP* 96 (1939): 643-55. For the rapidity with which new therapies were popularized, see *Science News Letter* 35 (1939): 275, 37 (1940): 298, and George W. Gray, "The Attack on Brainstorms," *Harpers Magazine* 183 (1941): 366-76.

32. J. M. Harlow, "Recovery after Severe Injury to the Head," Mass. Medical Society *Publications* 2 (1868): 329ff.; Emory Lanphear, "Lec-

tures on Intracranial Surgery. XI—The Surgical Treatment of Insanity,"
JAMA 24 (1895): 883-86. There is a brief historical background in John
F. Fulton's *Frontal Lobotomy and Affective Behavior: A Neurophys-
iological Analysis* (New York, 1951), Chap. 1.

33. Egas Moniz, *Tentatives Operatoires dans le Traitment de Certaines
Psychoses* (Paris, 1936), and "Prefrontal Leucotomy in the Treatment
of Mental Disorders," *AJP* 93 (1937): 1379-85.

34. Walter Freeman and James W. Watts, "Prefrontal Lobotomy in the
Treatment of Mental Disorders," *Southern Medical Journal* 30 (1937):
23-31.

35. White to Smith Ely Jelliffe, Aug. 7, 1936, Jelliffe Papers, LC; Ira C.
Nichols and J. McVicker Hunt, "A Case of Partial Bilateral Frontal
Lobotomy," *AJP* 96 (1940): 1063-83 (discussion, 1083-87); Report of
State Hospital No. 4, in Mo. Bd. of Managers of the State Eleemosynary
Institutions *BR* 10 (1939-1940): 6-7.

36. J. K. Hall to Winfred Overholser, Sept. 7, 1938, Hall Papers, UNC;
F. H. Busher to C. M. Hincks, Feb. 15, 1936, Hincks to Busher, Feb.
21, 1936, AFMH Papers, AP.

37. Horatio M. Pollock, "Trends in the Outcome of General Paresis,"
PQ 9 (1935): 194-211; Henry D. Sheldon, "Certain Trends Reflected
in Census Statistics on Patients in Hospitals for Mental Disease 1933
to 1942," in *Trends of Mental Disease* (papers presented at a symposium arranged by the American Psychopathological Association) (New
York, 1945), 34ff.; Malzberg, *Social and Biological Aspects of Mental
Disease* (Utica, 1940), 353; A. Warren Stearns, "Report on Medical
Progress: Psychiatry," *New England Journal of Medicine* 220 (1939):
709.

38. Carney Landis, "A Statistical Evaluation of Psychotherapeutic Methods," in *Concepts and Problems of Psychotherapy*, by Leland E. Hinsie
(New York, 1937), 155-69.

39. Morton Kramer et al., *A Historical Study of the Disposition of First
Admissions to a State Mental Hospital: Experience of the Warren State
Hospital During the Period 1916-1950* (U.S.P.H.S. Monograph No. 32:
Washington, D.C., 1955), 22; NCMH, *Research in Mental Hospitals
. . . 1936-1937* (New York, 1938), and *Research in Mental Hospitals:
Study Number Two . . . 1939-1941* (New York, 1942).

40. *AJP* 91 (1934): 414-20, 92 (1935): 480-82, 93 (1936): 449-51.

41. Excerpts from Alan Gregg Diary, Jan. 9, June 11, 1935, Memorandum
of Interview with Arthur Ruggles, July 10, 1935, Interoffice Memo by
Alan Gregg, c. Oct. 1935, Record Group 1.1, Series 200 (NCMH), RFA.

42. NCMH, "Committee to Consider the Possibility of Participation in
the Hospital Survey of the Metropolitan Area," copy in AFMH Papers,
AP; Clarence M. Hincks to Walter L. Treadway, Sept. 11, 1935, Treadway to Hincks, Nov. 19, 1935, *ibid.* See also United Hospital Fund,
The Hospital Survey for New York (3 vols.: New York, 1937).

43. *AJP* 93 (1936): 470-76; Alan Gregg to C. M. Hincks, Mar. 10, Apr.

20, 1936, Alan Gregg Diary, Apr. 23, 1936, Record Group 1.1, Series 200 (NCMH), RFA.

44. NCMH, "News Letter, No. 11, September, 1936," copy in AFMH Papers, AP; *AJP* 93 (1936-1937): 470-76, 974-81; Walter L. Treadway, "An Organization for Promoting Mental Hospital Services in the United States and Canada," *Public Health Reports* 51 (1936): 1783-91; Arthur P. Noyes to Clarence B. Farrar, July 10, 1936, Farrar Papers, APA; William L. Russell to White, Dec. 4, 1908, White to Russell, Dec. 7, 1908, White Papers, RG 418, NA; Thomas W. Salmon to Frederick Peterson, June 5, 1914, Salmon to William H. Welch, June 8, 1914, with enclosed memorandum, Salmon Boxes, AFMH Papers, AP; *AJI* 71 (1914): 198-200; *Division of Mental Hygiene. United States Public Health Service: Laws Establishing the Division and Authorizing Its Functions* (Public Health Reports *Supplement No. 97*: Washington, D.C., 1931); Jeanne L. Brand, "The National Mental Health Act of 1946: A Retrospect," *Bulletin of the History of Medicine* 39 (1965): 231-35.

45. Brand, "The National Mental Health Act of 1946," *loc.cit.*, 235-36.

46. *AJP* 93 (1937): 979; Samuel W. Hamilton, Grover A. Kempf, Grace C. Scholz, and Eve G. Caswell, *A Study of the Public Mental Hospitals of the United States 1937-39* (Public Health Reports *Supplement No. 164*: Washington, D.C., 1941), 3.

47. J. G. Wilson, "Political Interference in State Hospital Administration: A Discussion of Policies" (report made for the MHSC and NCMH), 1937, typed copy in AFMH Papers, uncatalogued, AP; Winfred Overholser, "The Desiderata of Central Administrative Control of State Mental Hospitals," *AJP* 96 (1939): 522-23.

48. *A Study of Mental Health in North Carolina: Report to the North Carolina Legislature of the Governor's Commission, Appointed to Study the Care of the Insane and Mental Defectives* (Ann Arbor, 1937); Clark R. Cahow, *People, Patients and Politics: The History of the North Carolina Mental Hospitals 1848-1960* (New York, 1980), 47-61; MHSC, *A Survey of the State Hospitals of Iowa* (mimeographed copy: New York, 1937), copy in University of Iowa Health Services Library, Iowa City, Iowa; MHSC, *A Survey of the Virginia Mental Hospitals* (mimeographed copy: Richmond, 1938), copy in NLM; MHSC, *A Survey of the Utah State Hospital* (mimeographed copy: n.p., 1937), copy in NLM; MHSC, *A Survey of the Care and Treatment of the Mentally Ill in Wisconsin* (mimeographed copy: New York, 1938), copy in Wisconsin State Historical Society Library, Madison, Wisc.

49. Samuel W. Hamilton and Grover A. Kempf, "Trends in the Activities of Mental Hospitals," *AJP* 96 (1939): 551-62.

50. Alan Gregg to Clarence M. Hincks, Jan. 6, 1939, excerpts of letter from Gregg to Max Mason, Mar. 23, 1939, "National Committee for Mental Hygiene . . . 1915-1939," 1-3, Record Group 1.1, Series 200 (NCMH), RFA.

51. Winfred Overholser to Gregg, Feb. 8, 1939, *ibid.*; Arthur P. Noyes to the Surgeon General, United States Public Health Service, Jan. 25, 1939, AFMH Papers, uncatalogued, AP; *AJP* 96 (1939-1940): 484-87, 1471-72.
52. Grover A. Kempf, *Laws Pertaining to the Admission of Patients to Mental Hospitals Throughout the United States* (Public Health Reports *Supplement No. 157*: Washington, D.C., 1939).
53. Joseph Zubin, *The Mentally Ill and Mentally Handicapped in Institutions* (Public Health Reports *Supplement No. 146*: Washington, D.C., 1938).
54. Joseph Zubin and Grace C. Scholz, *Regional Differences in the Hospitalization and Care of Patients with Mental Diseases* (Public Health Reports *Supplement No. 159*: Washington, D.C., 1940), 74-75 *et passim*.
55. Samuel W. Hamilton, Grover A. Kempf, Grace C. Scholz, and Eve G. Caswell, *A Study of the Public Mental Hospitals of the United States 1937-39* (Public Health Reports *Supplement No. 164*: Washington, D.C., 1941), 13.
56. *Ibid.*, 89-90.
57. *Ibid.*, 15-16, 81; Winfred Overholser, "Facts and Fiction About Our State Hospitals," *Ohio State Medical Journal* 36 (1940): 1167.
58. Hamilton et al., *A Study of Public Mental Hospitals*, 33.

Epilogue

1. *Action for Mental Health: Final Report of the Joint Commission on Mental Illness and Health 1961* (New York, 1961), xvi, 190.
2. Statistical data on mental hospital populations can be found in the following: National Institute for Mental Health, *Trends in Resident Patients, State and County Mental Hospitals 1950-1968*, N.I.M.H. *Statistical Note No. 114* (1975); U.S. Bureau of the Census, *Historical Statistics of the United States: Colonial Times to 1970* (Washington, D.C., 1975), Pt. I, 84; U.S. Bureau of the Census, *Statistical Abstract of the United States 1980* (Washington, D.C., 1980), 122.
3. Richard W. Reddick, *Patterns in Use of Nursing Homes by the Aged Mentally Ill*, N.I.M.H. *Statistical Note No. 107* (1974), 14.
4. For a graphic description of the plight of discharged mental hospital patients in New York City, see the *New York Times*, November 18, 19, 20, 1979.
5. Priscilla Allen, "A Consumer's View of California's Mental Health Care System," *PQ* 48 (1974): 2-4.
The literature on deinstitutionalization is enormous. A convenient summary and analysis can be found in Leona L. Bachrach, *Deinstitutionalization: An Analytical Review and Sociological Perspective* (DHEW Publications No. [ADM] 76-351: Washington, D.C., 1976).

THE LIMITATIONS of space make it impossible to include a complete bibliography of all relevant books and articles. The footnotes, which represent only a small proportion of the total material examined, should serve as a partial guide to surviving sources. The purpose of this section is simply to call attention to other less familiar materials, especially manuscript collections, government documents, and serial publications, and to clarify the research strategies employed in the preparation of this work.

I. PRIMARY SOURCES

A. Manuscripts

Manuscript collections of both individuals and organizations constitute an indispensable source for an understanding of the development of psychiatry and public policy. Many prominent and influential figures were frank and open in their private correspondence about issues they were more reluctant to discuss in public. This is not in any sense to suggest that public statements were falsified, for such was not the case. It is only to suggest that individuals felt less constrained in private to express their views without fear that their words would be distorted. Manuscript collections also shed a great deal of light on professional issues and on the role of both private and public organizations. Although the size of some of these collections are immense (the Adolf Meyer Papers, for example, run to about 500 lineal feet of shelf space), the ends of scholarship are ill-served by historians who ignore them. What follows in a listing of manuscript collections used in writing this book, and, where justified, a brief evaluation.

American Association of Psychiatric Social Workers Papers (1921-1958), Social Welfare History Archives, University of Minnesota, Minneapolis, Minn. A rich collection on the origins and development of psychiatric social work.
American Foundation for Mental Hygiene Collection, Archives of Psychiatry, New York Hospital-Cornell Medical Center, New York, N.Y. This collection is divided into several parts. The catalogued part includes the Clifford W. Beers papers and materials on the history of the National Committee for Mental Hygiene. A larger but equally

valuable part of the collection is not catalogued. Finally, there are four boxes containing some Thomas W. Salmon Papers.

Association for Voluntary Sterilization Records (1929-1964), Social Welfare History Archives, University of Minnesota, Minneapolis, Minn.

James W. Babcock Papers, South Caroliniana Library, University of South Carolina, Columbia, S.C. A small collection with only a few interesting items.

Clifford W. Beers Papers, Sterling Library, Yale University, New Haven, Conn. Contains the various drafts of *A Mind That Found Itself*, plus some miscellaneous items.

Boston Health League Papers, Countway Library of Medicine, Harvard Medical School, Boston, Mass.

Boston Psychopathic Hospital, manuscript volumes containing reports to trustees for the period 1912-1931 (5 vols.), Countway Library of Medicine, Harvard Medical School, Boston, Mass.

Butler Hospital Manuscripts, Butler Hospital, Providence, R.I. Contains some important letters of Isaac Ray.

Shobal Vail Clevenger Papers, National Library of Medicine, Bethesda, Md. A small collection containing useful materials on Clevenger's career in Chicago and Kankakee and the Illinois political scene in the 1880s and 1890s.

Pliny Earle Papers, American Antiquarian Society, Worcester, Mass. A rich collection covering the 1840s to 1880s.

Clarence B. Farrar Papers, American Psychiatric Association Archives, Washington, D.C.

Maxwell Gitelson Papers, Manuscripts Division, Library of Congress, Washington, D.C. Although the bulk of this collection covers the period after 1945, there are some useful materials on Gitelson's early career.

Manfred S. Guttmacher Papers, Countway Library of Medicine, Harvard Medical School, Boston, Mass.

James King Hall Papers, Southern Historical Collection, University of North Carolina, Chapel Hill, N.C. A large collection of major importance for the history of psychiatry in the South (and especially Virginia and the Carolinas).

William James Papers, Houghton Library, Harvard University, Cambridge, Massachusetts. Important for an understanding of James's relationship with Clifford W. Beers and the founding of the National Committee for Mental Hygiene.

Smith Ely Jelliffe Papers, Manuscripts Division, Library of Congress, Washington, D.C. A major collection on American psychiatry and psychoanalysis between World Wars I and II. Jelliffe served as a clearing house for a variety of intellectual debates; his correspondence was also international in scope.

Edward J. Kempf Papers, Sterling Library, Yale University, New Haven, Conn.

Thomas S. Kirkbride Papers, Institute of the Pennsylvania Hospital, Philadelphia, Pa. A major collection on mid-nineteenth century psychiatry.

Lawrence Kolb Papers, National Library of Medicine, Bethesda, Md.

Adolf Meyer miscellaneous items, Library, Clark University, Worcester, Mass.

Adolf Meyer Papers, Alan Mason Chesney Medical Archives, Johns Hopkins Medical Institutions, Baltimore, Md. This is by far the largest and most important collection on the history of American psychiatry from the 1890s to the 1940s. Meyer saved virtually every piece of paper from his early childhood to his death in 1950; he even had a stenographer prepare a verbatim transcript of his rounds in the wards and staff conferences. His correspondence was massive and the patient records extraordinarily full. Fortunately, the Chesney Medical Archives has catalogued part of the collection. Three Series have been used extensively for this book: I (correspondence with individuals), II (correspondence with societies and other organizations), and III (corporate correspondence). The collection is so extensive that there is a real danger of overestimating Meyer's influence and significance.

Charles Torrence Nesbitt Papers, Manuscripts Division, Perkins Library, Duke University, Durham, N.C. Contains a manuscript autobiography.

Winfred Overholser Papers, Manuscripts Division, Library of Congress, Washington, D.C. A somewhat thin and disappointing collection containing some correspondence and printed materials (including scrapbooks).

William D. Partlow Papers, Special Collections, University of Alabama Library, University, Ala.

Charles W. Pilgrim Papers, American Psychiatric Association Archives, Washington, D.C. Includes some APA records and correspondence for 1906-1909.

Rockefeller Foundation Papers, Rockefeller Archive Center, Pocantico Hills, North Tarrytown, N.Y. A monumental collection dealing with one of the most important national foundations. Especially useful were materials pertaining to the National Committee for Mental Hygiene (Record Group 1.1, Series 200, Boxes 32-35), the Bureau of Social Hygiene Papers (Series 3, Box 8), and Johns Hopkins University, Psychiatry, 1943-1944 (Record Group 1.1, Series 200A, Box 95).

Hubert A. Royster Papers, Southern Historical Collection, University of North Carolina, Chapel Hill, N.C.

Saint Elizabeths Hospital, Administrative Files (c. 1921-1964, with some items dated as early as 1905), Record Group 418, National Archives, Washington, D.C.

Elmer E. Southard Papers, Countway Library of Medicine, Harvard Medical School, Boston, Mass. Contains a few interesting items.

A. Warren Stearns Papers, Countway Library of Medicine, Harvard Medical School, Boston, Mass.

George Henry Torney Papers, Countway Library of Medicine, Harvard Medical School, Boston, Mass.

United States Veterans Administration, Social Work Service Papers (1921-1963), Social Welfare History Archives, University of Minnesota, Minneapolis, Minn.

William Alanson White, Personal Correspondence, in Records of Saint Elizabeths Hospital, Record Group 418, National Archives, Washington, D.C. A major collection of White's correspondence covering 1906-1937. Indispensable for the history of American psychiatry and psychoanalysis.

John Clare Whitehorn Papers, American Psychiatric Association Archives, Washington, D.C.

B. Government Documents

1. Federal Documents

The federal government did not become deeply involved with the problem of mental illness until after World War II. Nevertheless, various agencies—notably the Bureau of the Census and the Public Health Service—gathered a significant amount of data on the patient population and conditions in mental hospitals.

A. BUREAU OF THE CENSUS PUBLICATIONS

Report on the Defective, Dependent, and Delinquent Classes of the Population of the United States, as Returned at the Tenth Census (June 1, 1880) (Washington, D.C., 1888).

Report on the Insane, Feeble-Minded, Deaf and Dumb, and Blind in the United States at the Eleventh Census: 1890 (Washington, D.C., 1895).

Insane and Feeble-Minded in Hospitals and Institutions 1904 (Washington, D.C., 1906).

Paupers in Almshouses 1904 (Washington, D.C., 1906).

Insane and Feeble-Minded in Institutions 1910 (Washington, D.C., 1914).

Paupers in Almshouses 1910 (Washington, D.C., 1915).

Summary of State Laws Relating to the Dependent Classes (Washington, D.C., 1914).

Negro Population 1790-1915 (Washington, D.C., 1918).

Paupers in Almshouses 1923 (Washington, D.C., 1925).

Patients in Hospitals for Mental Disease 1923 (Washington, D.C., 1926).

Mental Patients in State Hospitals 1926 and 1927 (Washington, D.C., 1930).

Mental Patients in State Hospitals 1928 (Washington, D.C., 1931).

Mental Patients in State Hospitals 1929 and 1930 (Washington, D.C., 1933).

Mental Patients in State Hospitals 1931 and 1932 (Washington, D.C., 1934).

Patients in Hospitals for Mental Disease, 1933-1940 (an annual publication: 8 vols.: Washington, D.C., 1935-1943).

Sixteenth Census of the United States: 1940: Population: Special Report on Institutional Population 14 years Old and Over (Washington, D.C., 1943).

B. MISCELLANEOUS FEDERAL PUBLICATIONS

U.S. Congress, *Report of the Special Committee on Investigation of the Government Hospital for the Insane with Hearings May 4-December 13, 1906 and Digest of Testimony* (2 vols.: Washington, D.C., 1907: 59th Cong., 2d session, *House Report No. 7644* [February 18, 1907]).

U.S. Congress, *Investigation of St. Elizabeth's Hospital . . . 1926* (Washington, D.C., 1927: 69th Cong., 2d session, *House Document No. 605* [December 16, 1926]).

The Medical Department of the United States Army in the World War, vol. X, *Neuropsychiatry* (Washington, D.C., 1929).

Division of Mental Hygiene: United States Public Health Service: Laws Establishing the Division and Authorizing Its Functions (Washington, D.C., 1931: *Public Health Reports*, Supplement No. 97).

Elliott H. Pennell, Joseph W. Mountin, and Kay Pearson, *Business Census of Hospitals, 1935: General Report* (Washington, D.C., 1939: *Public Health Reports*, Supplement No. 154).

Walter L. Treadway, "An Organization for Promoting Mental Hospital Services in the United States and Canada," *Public Health Reports* 51 (1936): 1783-91.

Harold F. Dorn, "The Incidence and Future Expectancy of Mental Disease," *Public Health Reports* 53 (1938): 1991-2004.

Joseph Zubin, *The Mentally Ill and Mentally Handicapped in Institutions* (Washington, D.C., 1938: *Public Health Reports*, Supplement No. 146).

Grover A. Kempf, *Laws Pertaining to the Admission of Patients to Mental Hospitals Throughout the United States* (Washington, D.C., 1939: *Public Health Reports*, Supplement No. 157).

James E. Hughes, *Eugenic Sterilization in the United States: A Comparative Summary of Statutes and Review of Court Decisions* (Washington, D.C., 1940: *Public Health Reports*, Supplement No. 162).

Joseph Zubin and Grace C. Scholz, *Regional Differences in the Hospi-*

talization and Care of Patients with Mental Diseases (Washington, D.C., 1940: *Public Health Reports*, Supplement No. 159).

Samuel W. Hamilton, Grover A. Kempf, Grace C. Scholz, and Eve G. Caswell, *A Study of the Public Mental Hospitals of the United States 1937-39* (Washington, D.C., 1941: *Public Health Reports*, Supplement No. 164).

Mental Health in Later Maturity: Papers Presented at a Conference Held in Washington, D.C. May 23-24, 1941 (Washington, D.C., 1941: *Public Health Reports*, Supplement No. 168).

2. State Documents

Since the care of the mentally ill was overwhelmingly a state function before World War II, state documents constitute an indispensable source. They provide information on a variety of subjects, including mental hospital populations, conditions within institutions, and financial and administrative systems. Taken as a whole, state documents are the best source for an understanding of the evolution of public policy toward the mentally ill. Unfortunately, states never adopted a uniform and rational system of publishing or reporting their documents. Consequently, historians have tended to overlook this superlative source because of the obvious difficulties in dealing with 48 states before 1941. Furthermore, none of the nation's major research libraries have a comprehensive collection of these materials; in most cases it is necessary to use individual State Libraries or state university libraries for each state. What follows is a state by state listing of some of the major documents used in the preparation of this book. Unpublished documents that are occasionally cited are generally found in the State Library of each state.

ALABAMA

Alabama Insane Hospital, *AR*, 15-18 (1875-1878: 1877 not published), *BR* 1881/1882-1887/1888, 1891/1892-1893/1894.

Trustees of the Alabama Insane Hospitals, *Quadrennial Report*, 1919/1922, *Report*, 1923-1929, 1931-1934, 1936, 1939-1940.

Board of Control and Economy, *Quadrennial Report*, Convict Department, 1919/1922.

State Board of Administration, *Quadrennial Report*, 1922/1926, 1926/1930, *AR*, 1932-1938.

State Department of Public Welfare, *AR*, 1935/1936-1939/1940.

ARIZONA

Board of Control, *Report*, 1895/1896, *BR*, 2-5, 7 (1897/1898-1902/1904, 1906/1908), *AR*, 1908/1909-1910/1911 (typescript), 1911/1912-1915/1916.

Commission of State Institutions, *AR*, 1-2 (1917/1918-1918/1919).

Board of Directors of State Institutions, *AR*, 1-6 (1919/1920-1924/1925),

1933/1934-1934/1935 (typescript), 1937/1938, 1939/1940 (mimeographed).

ARKANSAS

Arkansas State Lunatic Asylum, *AR*, 1-2 (1883-1884).
Board of Trustees of the State Charitable Institutions, *BR*, 21, 23 (1910/1911, 1913/1915).
Board of Control for State Charitable Institutions, *BR*, 1-4 (1915/1916-1921/1922).
Department of Public Welfare, *AR*, 1937/1938-1939/1940.

CALIFORNIA

State Commission in Lunacy, *BR*, 1-3 (1896/1898-1900/1902).
State Board of Charities and Corrections, *BR*, 1-10 (1903/1904-1920/1922).
Department of Institutions, *BR*, 1-6 (1920/1922-1930/1932), *Statistical Report*, 1932/1934-1939/1940.

COLORADO

State Board of Charities and Corrections, *BR*, 1-14 (1891/1892-1917/1918).
State Department of Charities and Corrections, *BR*, 1 (1923/1924).

CONNECTICUT

State Board of Charities, *AR*, 1-24/25 (1881/1882-1905/1906), *BR*, 1907/1908-1919/1920.
Department of Public Welfare, *BR*, 1921/1922-1935/1936.
Office of the Commission of Welfare . . . and the Public Welfare Council, *BR*, 1936/1937-1939/1941.

DELAWARE

State Board of Charities, *AR*, 1920, *Report*, 1926-1927/1928, *BR*, 1929/1930, 1932/1934, *AR*, 1934/1935, *BR*, 1935/1936, *AR*, 1937/1938-1939/1940.

FLORIDA

State Welfare Board, *AR*, 1-3 (1937/1938-1939/1940).

GEORGIA

State Board (Department) of Public Welfare, *AR*, 1-5 (1920-1924/1925), *BR*, 1925/1927-1927/1928, *Report*, 1929/1931-1939/1940.
Board of Control of Eleemosynary Institutions, *Report*, 1936.
Ivan Allen, Jr., compiler, *The First Year of the State Hospital Authority February 1939-February 1940: A Report to the People of Georgia* (n.p., n.d.).
J. E. Greene and J. S. Jacob, *Conditions in the Milledgeville State Hospital: A Study of Mental Disorders as a Public Health Problem in Georgia, Bulletin of the University of Georgia* 29 (1939).

IDAHO

Department of Public Welfare, *Report*, 1919/1920-1933/1934, BR, 1935/1936.
Department of Public Welfare, Division of Charitable Institutions, BR, 1937/1938.
Department of Public Welfare, BR, 1939/1940.

ILLINOIS

Board of State Commissioners of Public Charities, BR, 4-21 (1875/1876-1908/1909).
Board of Administration, AR, 1-6/7 (1910-1915/1916).
State Charities Commission, AR, 1-7 (1910-1916).
Department of Public Welfare, AR, 1-23 (1917/1918-1939/1940).

INDIANA

Board of State Charities, AR, 1-43 (1890-1932).
Department of Public Welfare, AR, 44-45 (1933/1934-1934/1935), 1935/1936-1939/1940.

IOWA

Board of Control of State Institutions, BR, 1-22 (1898/1899-1938/1940).
State Department of Social Welfare, AR, 1937/1938-1939/1940.

KANSAS

Kansas State Insane Asylum at Osawatomie and Board of Commissioners of the Topeka Insane Asylum, BR, 1 (1876/1878).
Kansas State Insane Asylums at Osawatomie and Topeka, BR, 2 (1878/1880).
Board of Trustees of State Charitable Institutions, AR and BR, 1 (1904/1906), 2-6 (1906/1908-1914/1916).
Board of Administration, Charitable Institutions Section, BR, 1-8 (1916/1918-1930/1932).
Board of Administration, BR, 9-11 (1932/1934-1936/1938).
Semiannual Bulletin of the Kansas State Charitable Institutions Under the Board of Control, 1-9 (April, 1908-October, 1912).

KENTUCKY

State Board of Control for Charitable Institutions, AR, 1-2 (1906-1907), BR, 3-7 (1907/1909-1915/1917).
State Board of Control for Charitable and Penal Institutions, BR, 8 (1917/1919).
State Board of Charities and Corrections, BR, 1919/1921-1929/1931.
Department of Public Welfare, BR, 1931/1933-1933/1935.
Department of Welfare, BR, 1935-1937 (mimeographed), 1937/1939.

LOUISIANA

State Board of Charities and Corrections, *AR*, 1 (1905), 2-3 (1906/1907-1908/1909), *Report*, 4 (1918/1920), *BR*, 1920/1922, *AR*, 1922/1923-1926/1927, *BR*, 1928/1929-1936/1937, *AR*, 1938.

Department of Public Welfare, *AR*, 1-3 (1937-1939/1940).

MAINE

State Board of Charities and Corrections, *AR*, 1-4 (1913-1916), *BR*, 5-9 (1916/1918-1924/1926).

Department of Public Welfare, *BR*, 10-11 (1926/1928-1928/1930).

MARYLAND

Lunacy Commission, *Report*, 2-28 (1887-1913), *BR*, 1-4 (1914/1915-1920/1921).

Board of Mental Hygiene, *BR*, 1922/1923.

Board of Welfare, *AR*, 1-16 (1923-1938). The reports of the Board of Mental Hygiene are included in this publication.

Board of Mental Hygiene, *BR*, 1938/1940.

MASSACHUSETTS

Board of State Charitites, *AR*, 12-15 (1875-1878).

State Board of Health, Lunacy, and Charity, *AR*, 1-7 (1879-1885).

State Board of Lunacy and Charity, *AR*, 8-20 (1886-1898).

State Board of Insanity, *AR*, 1-17 (1899-1915).

Commission on Mental Diseases, *AR*, 1-4 (1916-1919).

Commissioner of Mental Diseases, *AR*, 1-18 (1920-1937).

Commissioner of Mental Health, *AR*, 19-21 (1938-1940).

Report of the Commissioners of Lunacy, to the Commonwealth of Massachusetts. January, 1875, Mass. *House Document No. 60* (1875).

Report of the Commission Appointed to Inquire into the Expediency of Revising the System of Administration of the Public Charities of the Commonwealth, December, 1877, Mass. *Public Document No. 38* (1878).

"Relation of the Liquor Traffic to Pauperism, Crime, and Insanity," in Mass. Bureau of Statistics of Labor *AR* 26 (1896): 3-416.

Report of the Commission to Investigate the Public Charitable and Reformatory Institutions of the Commonwealth. February, 1897 (Boston, 1897).

Report of the Special Commission Established to Study the Whole Matter of the Mentally Diseased in Their Relation to the Commonwealth, Including All Phases of Work of the Department of Mental Diseases, Mass. *House Document No. 320* (1938).

Report of the Special Commission Established to Study the Whole Matter of the Mentally Diseased in Their Relation to the Common-

wealth, Including All Phases of Work of the Department of Mental Diseases, Mass. House Document No. 2400 (1939).

MICHIGAN

Board of State Commissioners for the General Supervision of Charitable, Penal, Pauper, and Reformatory Institutions, BR, 2-4 (1873/1874-1877/1878).
State Board of Corrections and Charities, BR, 5-25 (1879/1880-1919/1920).
State Welfare Commission, BR, 26-29 (1921/1922-1927/1928).
Annual Abstract of Statistical Information Relative to the Insane, Deaf and Dumb, Blind, Idiotic, Feeble Minded, Epileptic and Either Deaf or Dumb in the State of Michigan, 3-46 (1875-1918).

MINNESOTA

Board of Control of State Institutions, BR, 1-2 (1900/1902-1902/1904).
State Board of Control, BR, 3-19 (1904/1906-1936/1938).
Division of Public Institutions, BR, 1938/1940.

MISSOURI

State Board of Charities and Corrections, BR, 1-18 (1897/1898-1931/1932).
Board of Managers of the State Eleemosynary Institutions, BR, 1-10 (1921/1922-1939/1940).

MONTANA

State Board of Commissioners for the Insane, AR, 1-6 (1892-1897), 8/9-14/15 (1899/1900-1905/1906).
State Board of Charities and Reform, AR, 2 (1894), Report, 1899/1900, BR, 1901/1902, AR, 1904, 1906, 1910, 1924, BR, 1925/1926.
Department of Public Welfare, Report, 1937-1938/1940.
State Hospital for the Insane, Report, 1913/1914-1919/1920, BR, 23 (1921/1922).
Montana State Hospital, BR, 24-28 (1923/1924-1930/1932).
Report of Drs. Mitchell & Mussigbrod Contractors for Care and Keeping of the Insane (n.p., 1895).

NEBRASKA

Board of Commissioners of State Institutions, BR, 1-3 (1913/1914-1917/1918).
Board of Control, Condensed Report, July 1, 1921, BR, 5-14 (1921/1923-1939/1941).

NEVADA

Commissioners for the Care and the Indigent Insane, Report, 1871/1872-1895/1896.
Nevada Hospital for Mental Diseases, BR, 8-19 (1897/1898-1919/1920), BR, 1921/1922-1938/1940.

First Biennial Report of the Secretary of State in Relation to the Indigent Insane (Carson City, 1869).

NEW HAMPSHIRE

Board of Commissioners of Lunacy, *AR*, 1-5 (1890-1894), *Report*, 6-16 [*BR*, 1-10] (1895/1896-1915/1916).
State Board of Charities and Correction, *BR*, 1-17 (1895/1896-1926/1928).
State Board of Public Welfare, *BR*, 18-21 (1928/1930-1934/1936).
Division of Welfare, State Board of Welfare and Relief, *BR*, 22-23 (1936/1938-1938/1940).

NEW JERSEY

Council of State Charities and Correction, *AR*, 1-3 (1884-1886).
State Charities Aid Association, *AR*, 1-32 (1886-1917).
Department of Charities and Corrections, *AR*, 1-13 (1905-1917).
Report of the New Jersey Commission on the Care of Mental Defectives (Trenton, 1914).
Report of the Commission to Investigate State Institutions Other Than Penal, Reformatory or Correctional (typescript: Trenton, 1918).
Department of Institutions and Agencies (Research Division), *The Wards of the State of New Jersey 1919-1931: A Statistical Review* (Trenton, 1931).
Summary Report of the Department of Institutions and Agencies 1923-1933 (Trenton, 1934).
Department of Institutions and Agencies (Division of Statistics and Research), *The Wards of the State of New Jersey 1929-1939: A Statistical and Pictorial Review* (Trenton, 1940).

NEW YORK

State Commissioner in Lunacy, *AR*, 3-16 (1875-1888).
State Board of Charities, *AR*, 9-26 (1875-1895).
State Commission in Lunacy, *AR*, 1-23 (1889-1911).
State Hospital Commission, *AR*, 24-38 (1912-1925/1926).
Department of Mental Hygiene, *AR*, 39-52 (1926/1927-1939/1940).
Communication from the Comptroller Submitting to the Senate the Report of the Agent Appointed to Examine the Charitable Institutions of the State of New York, N.Y. *Senate Document No. 67* (1879).
Testimony Taken Before the Select Committee of the Senate Appointed May 25, 1880, to Investigate Abuses Alleged to Exist in the Management of Insane Asylums, as Well as to Inquire into the General Subject of Lunacy Administration in this State, N.Y. *Senate Document No. 96* (1882).
Spencer L. Dawes, *Report on the Alien Insane . . . 1914*, N.Y. *Senate Document No. 29* (1914).

NORTH CAROLINA

Board of Public Charities, *AR*, 9 (1877), 1890, *BR*, 1891/1892-1893/1894, *AR* 1895/1896, *BR*, 1897/1898-1903/1904, *AR*, 1905-1916 (1906 not issued).
State Board of Charities and Public Welfare, *BR*, 1917/1918-1921/1922, 1922/1924-1938/1940.
N.C. Charitable, Penal, and Correctional Institutions, *BR*, 1930/1932-1938/1940.
A Study of Mental Health in North Carolina: Report to the North Carolina Legislature of the Governor's Commission, Appointed to Study the Care of the Insane and Mental Defectives (Ann Arbor, 1937).

NORTH DAKOTA

Board of Control of State Institutions, *BR*, 1-4 (1910/1912-1916/1918).
Board of Administration, *AR*, 1-4 (1919-1922), 5/6-21/22 (1922/1924-1938/1940).

OHIO

Board of State Charities, *AR*, 1-30 (1876-1905), *BR*, 31-34 (1906/1907-1912/1913).
Board of Administration, *AR*, 1-10 (1912-1920/1921).
Department of Public Welfare, *AR*, 1-19 (1921/1922-1940).

OKLAHOMA

Department of Charities and Corrections, *AR*, 1 (1908).
Commissioner of Charities and Corrections, *AR*, 2-4 (1910-1912), *BR*, 5-8 (1915/1916-1920/1922), *AR*, 1923-1930.
Department of Public Welfare, *AR*, 1937/1938-1939/1940.

OREGON

State Board of Charities and Corrections, *BR*, 1 (1891/1892).
State Board of Control, *BR*, 1-14 (1913/1914-1938/1940).

PENNSYLVANIA

Board of Commissioners of Public Charities, *AR*, 6-48 (1875-1917). Included in this series are the Committee on Lunacy, *AR*, 1-35 (1883-1916/1917).
Department of Welfare, Commissioner of Public Welfare, *BR*, 1 (1921/1922).
Department of Welfare, Secretary of Welfare, *BR*, 2-10 (1922/1924-1938/1940).
John D. Pennington, *A Ten Year Program for the Department of Welfare*, in Department of Public Welfare, *Bulletin No. 66* (1936).

RHODE ISLAND

Board of State Charities and Corrections, *AR*, 7-47 (1875-1915).
Board of Control and Supply, *AR*, 1-5 (1912-1916).
Penal and Charitable Commission, *AR*, 1-4 (1917-1920).
State Public Welfare Commission, *AR*, 1-12 (1923-1933/1934).
State Department of Public Welfare, *AR*, 1-4 (1934/1935-1937/1938).
State Department of Social Welfare, *AR*, 1-2 (1938/1939-1939/1940).

SOUTH CAROLINA

State Board of Charities and Corrections, *AR*, 1-5 (1915-1919).
State Board of Public Welfare, *AR*, 1-7 (1920-1926).
State Department of Public Welfare, *AR*, 1 (1937/1938).

SOUTH DAKOTA

State Board of Charities and Corrections, *BR*, 1-26 (1889/1890-1938/1940).

TENNESSEE

Board of State Charities, *Reports*, 1896/1898, *Report*, 1903, 1911, 1915, 1917, 1923.
Board of Control, *BR*, 1-2 (1915/1916-1917/1918).
State Board of Administration, *BR*, 1918/1920-1920/1922.
Department of Institutions, *BR*, 1922/1924-1934/1936.
Department of Institutions and Public Welfare, *AR*, 1937/1938.
Department of Public Welfare, *AR*, 1-2 (1938/1939-1939/1940).

TEXAS

State Board of Control, *AR*, 1 (1920), *Report*, 2 (1920/1924), *BR*, 3, 6-10 (1925/1926, 1931/1932-1939/1940). The fourth and fifth *BR* were not published.
C. S. Yoakum, *Care of the Feeble-minded and Insane in Texas*, in *Bulletin of the University of Texas*, Humanistic Series, No. 16 (1914).

UTAH

Department of Public Welfare, *BR*, 1-2 (1936/1938-1938/1940).

VERMONT

Director of State Institutions, *BR*, 1916/1918-1920/1922.
Department of Public Welfare, *BR*, 1922/1924-1938/1940.
Commissioners of the Insane, *BR*, 1875/1876-1876/1878.
Supervisors of the Insane, *BR*, 1879/1880-1938/1940.

VIRGINIA

State Board of Charities and Corrections, *AR*, 1-13 (1909-1921).
State Board of Public Welfare, *AR*, 14/15-17 (1922/1923-1925/1926).

State Department of Public Welfare, *AR*, 18-27/28 (1926/1927-1935/1937), *BR*, 1937/1939, *AR*, 1939/1940.

WASHINGTON (STATE)

State Board of Audit and Control, *BR*, 1-2 (1896/1898-1899/1900).
State Board of Control, *BR*, 1-10 (1901/1902-1919/1920).
Department of Business Control, *BR*, 1-7 (1921/1922-1933/1934).
Department of Finance, Budget and Business, *BR*, 1-3 (1935/1936-1939/1940).

WEST VIRGINIA

State Board of Control, *BR*, 1-11 (1909/1910-1933/1936), *Report*, 12-13 (1936/1939-1939/1943).

WISCONSIN

State Board of Charities and Reform, *AR*, 5-12 (1875-1882).
State Board of Supervision of Wisconsin Charitable, Reformatory and Penal Institutions, *BR*, 1-4 (1882/1884-1889/1890).
State Board of Charities and Reform, *BR*, 1-4 (1883/1884-1889/1890).
State Board of Control, *BR*, 1-23 (1890/1892-1934/1936).

WYOMING

State Board of Charities and Reform, *AR*, 1-8 (1891-1898), 9-12 (1899-1902, typescript), *BR*, 1903/1904-1930/1932.
State Department of Public Welfare, *BR*, 1936/1938-1938/1940.

C. Serials

1. Periodicals and Year Books

Two strategies were employed in researching the vast periodical literature of the period from 1875 to 1940. Those journals that dealt directly or indirectly with mental illness or else represented important national organizations such as the AMA were examined in their entirety. Since many articles also appeared in the medical and general press as well as in scholarly journals, periodical indexes were consulted. It is of course impossible to list all the individual items used, but the following publications served as important guides: *Index-Catalogue of the Library of the Surgeon-General's Office, U.S. Army*, Series I-V; *Quarterly Cumulative Index to Current Medical Literature*, 1916-1919; *Quarterly Cumulative Index Medicus*, 1927-1940; *Poole's Index to Periodical Literature*, 1802-1906; *Readers' Guide to Periodical Literature*, 1900-1940; *International Index to Periodicals*, 1907-1940; and the *Bulletin of the Public Affairs Information Service*, 1915-1940.

The following journals and year books have been examined in their entirety:

Alienist and Neurologist, 1-41 (1880-1920).

American Association of Psychiatric Social Workers, *Quarterly News Letter,* 1-16 (1926-1930). This mimeographed serial can be found in the Papers of the AAPSW, Social Welfare History Archives, University of Minnesota, Minneapolis, Minn.

American Journal of Insanity, 32-77 (1875/1876-1920/1921). Becomes the *American Journal of Psychiatry.*

American Journal of Neurology and Psychiatry, 1-3 (1882-1884/1885).

American Journal of Orthopsychiatry, 1-10 (1930/1931-1940).

American Journal of Psychiatry, 78-97 (1921/1922-1940/1941).

American Journal of Syphilis, 1-17 (1917-1933).

American Journal of Syphilis and Neurology, 18-19 (1934-1935).

American Journal of Syphilis, Gonorrhea and Venereal Diseases, 20-24 (1936-1940).

American Psychological Journal, 1-2 (1883/1884-1884).

Archives of Neurology and Psychiatry, 1-44 (1919-1940).

Archives of Neurology and Psychopathology, 1-3 (1898-1900). A continuation of *State Hospital Bulletin.*

Archives of Occupational Therapy, 1-3 (1922-1924). Becomes *Occupational Therapy and Rehabilitation.*

Boston Medical and Surgical Journal, 92-197 (1875-1927). Becomes *New England Journal of Medicine.*

Eugenical News, 1-25 (1916-1940).

Hospital Social Service, 1-28 (1919-1933).

Journal of Abnormal Psychology, 1-15 (1906/1907-1920/1921).

Journal of Abnormal and Social Psychology, 16-35 (1921/1922-1940).

Journal of the American Medical Association, 1-115 (1883-1940).

Journal of Mental Pathology, 1-8 (1901/1902-1906/1909).

Journal of Nervous and Mental Disease, 1-92 (1874-1940).

Journal of Social Science, 8-46 (1876-1909).

Mental Hygiene, 1-24 (1917-1940).

Mental Hygiene Bulletin, 1-10 (1923-1932).

Neurological Contributions, volume 1, Nos. 1-3 (1879-1881).

Neurological Review, 1 (1886).

New England Journal of Medicine, 198-223 (1928-1940).

News-Letter of the American Association of Psychiatric Social Workers, 1-10 (1931-1941).

Occupational Therapy and Rehabilitation, 4-19 (1925-1940).

Psychiatric Bulletin of the New York State Hospitals, 9-10 [1-2] (1916-1917). A continuation of *State Hospital[s] Bulletin.*

Psychiatric Quarterly, 1-14 (1927-1940).

Psychiatry, 1-3 (1938-1940).

Psychoanalytic Quarterly, 1-9 (1932-1940).

Psychoanalytic Review, 1-27 (1913/1914-1940).

Psychobiology, 1-2 (1917/1918, 1920).

Psychosomatic Medicine, 1-2 (1939-1940).
Review of Insanity and Nervous Disease, 1-5 (1890/1891-1894).
Social Work Year Book, 1-6 (1929-1941).
Southern Medicine and Surgery, 83-102 (1921-1940).
State Hospitals Bulletin, 1-2 (1896-1897).
State Hospital[s] Bulletin, New Series, 1-8 (1908/1909-1915).
State Hospital Quarterly, 1-12 (1915/1916-1926).
Year Book of Neurology and Psychiatry, 1933-1940.

2. Proceedings and Transactions

American Medical Association, *Transactions*, 26-33 (1875-1882).
American Medical Association, Section on Nervous and Mental Diseases, *Transactions*, 1906-1927.
American Medico-Psychological Association, *Proceedings*, 1-27 (1894-1920).
American Neurological Association, *Transactions*, 1-14 (1875-1888), 16-66 (1890-1940). Number 15 (1889) was never published.
Conference on Psychiatric Education, *Proceedings*, 1-4 (1933-1936). The *Proceedings* of the first conference appeared in mimeographed form under the title *Basis of Conference on Psychiatric Education. Hotel Statler, Boston, May 28-29, 1933* (New York, 1933); a copy is in the NLM.
National Conference of Charities and Corrections, *Proceedings,* 1-43 (1874-1916). Between 1874 and 1879 the title of the organization was the Conference of Charities; in 1880 and 1881 it became known as the Conference of Charities and Correction; and in 1917 it became the National Conference of Social Work.
National Conference of Social Work, *Proceedings*, 44-67 (1917-1940).
Proceedings of the First International Congress on Mental Hygiene Held at Washington, D.C., U.S.A. May 5th to 10th, 1930 (2 vols.: New York, 1932).
Proceedings of the Mental Hygiene Conference and Exhibit . . . November 8th to 15th, 1912 (New York, 1912).

II. Secondary Sources

Before 1960 the history of psychiatry and the mentally ill was a relatively uncontroversial subject. After that date the topic became the center of a heated debate. Some historians who were influenced by Michel Foucault interpreted mental hospitals as institutions for the control of deviancy or as agents of a capitalist society that valued productivity and order. Others rejected a quasi-Marxian approach without becoming apologists for psychiatrists or mental hospitals. The historical debates can be followed in Peter L. Tyor and Jamil S. Zainaldin, "Asylum and Society: An Approach to Institutional Change," *Journal of Social History* 13 (1979):

23-48, Andrew Scull, "Humanitarianism or Control: Observations on the Historiography of Anglo-American Psychiatry," *Rice University Studies* 67 (1981): 21-41, and Gerald N. Grob, "Rediscovering Asylums: The Unhistorical History of the Mental Hospital," in *The Therapeutic Revolution: Essays in the Social History of American Medicine*, ed. Morris J. Vogel and Charles E. Rosenberg (Philadelphia, 1979), 135-57. Listed below are a selection of some of the important recent contributions to the historical debate about the social context of mental illness and the role of psychiatry. Several older works have been included, if only because time has not vitiated some of their basic insights.

Burnham, John C., *Psychoanalysis and American Medicine: 1894-1918; Medicine, Science, and Culture* (New York, 1967).

Dain, Norman, *Clifford W. Beers: Advocate for the Insane* (Pittsburgh, 1980).

———, *Concepts of Insanity in the United States, 1789-1865* (New Brunswick, 1964).

Deutsch, Albert, *The Mentally Ill in America: A History of Their Care and Treatment from Colonial Times* (Garden City, N.Y., 1937; 2nd ed.: New York, 1949).

Foucault, Michel, *Discipline and Punish: The Birth of the Prison* (New York, 1977).

———, *Madness and Civilization: A History of Insanity in the Age of Reason* (New York, 1965).

Fox, Richard T., *So Far Disordered in Mind: Insanity in California, 1870-1930* (Berkeley, 1978).

Grob, Gerald N., *Mental Institutions in America: Social Policy to 1875* (New York, 1973).

———, *The State and the Mentally Ill: A History of Worcester State Hospital in Massachusetts, 1830-1920* (Chapel Hill, 1966).

Hale, Nathan G., *Freud and the Americans: The Beginnings of Psychoanalysis in the United States, 1876-1917* (New York, 1971).

Hall, J. K., ed., *One Hundred Years of American Psychiatry* (New York, 1944).

Katz, Michael B., "Origins of the Institutional State," *Marxist Perspectives* 1 (1979): 6-22.

Lasch, Christopher, "The Origins of the Asylum," in *The World of Nations: Reflections on American History, Politics, and Culture* (New York, 1974), 3-17.

Quen, Jacques M., and Carlson, Eric T., eds., *American Psychoanalysis: Origins and Development* (New York, 1978).

Rosen, George, *Madness in Society: Chapters in the Historical Sociology of Mental Illness* (Chicago, 1968).

Rothman, David J., *Conscience and Convenience: The Asylum and Its Alternatives in Progressive America* (Boston, 1980).

Rothman, David J., *The Discovery of the Asylum: Social Order and Disorder in the New Republic* (Boston, 1971).

Russell, William L., *The New York Hospital: A History of the Psychiatric Service 1771-1936* (New York, 1945).

Scull, Andrew, *Decarceration: Community Treatment and the Deviant: A Radical View* (Englewood Cliffs, N.J., 1977).

———, ed., *Madhouses, Mad-Doctors, and Madmen: The Social History of Psychiatry in the Victorian Era* (Philadelphia, 1981).

———, *Museums of Madness: The Social Organization of Insanity in Nineteenth-Century England* (London, 1979).

Sicherman, Barbara, *The Quest for Mental Health in America 1880-1917* (Ph.D. dissertation, Columbia University, 1967; reprinted New York, 1980).

moral philosophy, 34, 144
Morris County Charities Aid Association (New Jersey), 106
morphine, 13, 292
Mosher, J. Montgomery, 137
Myerson, Abraham, 140, 176-77, 392 n. 20

National Association for the Protection of the Insane and the Prevention of Insanity, 55-58, 93-94, 147
National Board of Medical Examiners, 273, 276
National Cancer Institute (Public Health Service), 311
National Committee for Mental Hygiene, 145, 147, 178, 242, 250, 289-90, 313; after World War I, 162-64; classification system of mental diseases, 118-19; Committee for Organizing Psychiatric Units for Base Hospitals, 279n.; Conference on Psychiatric Education, 281; Division on the Prevention of Delinquency, 163; Division of Psychiatric Education, 274, 279, 280-81, 283; fellowship program, 163; founding of, 153; history of, 153-63; and psychiatric education, 271; and Rockefeller Foundation, 266-67, 309, 312-13; and sterilization, 173
National Conference of Charities and Corrections, 50, 57, 75, 77, 79, 95, 101, 168, 217, 246
National Research Council, 262
National Society for the Promotion of Occupational Therapy, 259
nativism, 82
Nebraska, 174, 219-20, 291
neurasthenia, 57
neurology: origins of, 50-51; and psychiatry, 50-62, 246-47, 279-80, 282
neuropsychiatry, 279-80
Nevada, 105, 187, 207, 219-20, 328 n. 22
New Hampshire, 106, 174, 219-20; Board of Commissioners of Lunacy, 106; State Board of Charities and Correction, 106
New Jersey, 76, 96, 104-06, 124-26,

195, 209, 219-20, 290; Council of Charities and Corrections, 104-05; Department of Charities and Corrections, 106; Department of Institutions and Agencies, 210; local care of insane, 96; Medical Society, 273; State Charities Aid Association, 106; State Hospital (Marlboro), 195
New Mexico, 207, 219-20
New York City: mental hospitals, 90; Metropolitan Board of Health, 87
New York Foundation, 274
New York Neurological Society, 52-53, 89, 247
New York Pathological Institute. See New York Psychiatric Institute
New York Psychiatric Institute, 112, 127-31, 135, 138, 218, 293-94
New York State, 9, 11-12, 16, 19-20, 25-27, 33, 49, 53-54, 76-79, 82, 86-92, 95-96, 104, 127-31, 136-37, 161, 164, 168-69, 174, 182, 184-89, 191, 193-95, 202, 204-05, 207, 209-12, 215-20, 222-24, 228, 230, 239, 245, 247-48, 253, 259-60, 267-68, 290-91, 293-94, 300-02, 325 n. 2, 343 n. 32; development of state welfare administration, 210-12; Exempted Counties Act, 76-77, 86, 88-89; innovation in, 343 n. 32; outpatient clinics in mental hospitals, 239; public policy toward mentally ill, 86-90; State Board of Alienists, 216; State Board of Charities, 76-77, 86-89, 211-12, 216; State Board of Commissioners of Emigration, 216; State Care Act (1890), 89-90, 92, 96, 185, 211; State Charities Aid Association, 87-89, 205, 211-12, 248; State Commission in Lunacy, 89-91, 128, 184, 211-12, 216; State Commissioner in Lunacy, 87, 211; State Department of Mental Hygiene, 212; State Hospital Commission, 212; State Inebriate Asylum, 77; Utica State Lunatic Asylum, 9, 12, 34, 53, 89, 130, 294
New York State Medical Society, 53, 89

Noble, Ralph A., 270, 274, 283-84, 286
Noguchi, Hideyo, 132, 189
Norristown State Hospital (Pennsylvania), 66
North American Review, 58
North Carolina, 26, 38, 53, 104, 164, 174, 190-91, 209, 213-14, 218-20, 228-29, 312, 328 n. 22; Board of Public Charities, 104; Bureau of Mental Health and Hygiene, 213; investigation of mentally ill, 312; politics and mental hospital, 228-29; State Board of Charities and Public Welfare, 210, 213
North Dakota, 164, 174, 206, 209, 219-20; Board of Administration, 209; Board of Control, 206
Northampton State Lunatic Hospital, 92, 196
Norton, Harold F., 225-26
Norway, rates of hospitalization, 191
nosology. *See* classification of mental illness
Noyes, Arthur P., 140
nurses, psychiatric: compensation of, 328 n. 22; conflict with psychiatrists, 244-45; in mental hospitals, 20-21, 290
nursing, psychiatric, 258

Oberndorf, C. P., 130
occupational therapists, relationship with psychiatrists, 260
occupational therapy, 23-24, 236, 258-60
Occupational Therapy and Rehabilitation, 259
Odenkrantz, Louise C., 250-51
Ohio, 11, 25, 164, 209, 212-13, 217, 219-20, 245, 290, 337 n. 27; Board of Administration, 209, 213; Board of State Charities, 209; Department of Public Welfare, 209; Department of Public Works, 212-13
Oklahoma, 174, 219-20
opium, 13
Ordronaux, John, 87
Oregon, 174, 218-20
outpatient practice in psychiatry, 238-43

ovariectomy, bilateral, 122-23
Overholser, Winfred, 224-27, 229-31, 298, 311-13, 316, 371 n. 36

Packard, E.P.W., 47
Page, James D., 366 n. 63
paraldehyde, 13, 292
paresis, 112, 120, 132, 188-90, 192n., 296; fever therapy, 293-94; malaria therapy, 293-95
parole of mentally ill, 24-25, 86, 238, 316
Partlow, William D., 175, 230
Pathological Institute (New York State). *See* New York Psychiatric Institute
patient records, change in nature of, 115
Paton, Stewart, 118-19, 149, 163
Pavilion F of the Albany Hospital, 136-37
Peirce, Charles S., 113
pellagra, 120, 190-91
Pennsylvania, 17-20, 24-25, 48-50, 64, 66, 76, 79, 96-98, 104, 123, 159-60, 182-84, 213, 219-20, 239, 245, 291, 308; Board of Public Charities, 96-97, 213; Bureau of Mental Health, 213; Committee on Lunacy, 24, 96-98, 213; county care of the insane, 96-98; Department of Public Welfare, 213; Hospital for the Insane (Norristown), 17-18
Philadelphia Hospital, 27
Philadelphia Hospital, Insane Department, 64
Phipps, Henry, 112, 131, 137-38, 152, 156
Phipps Psychiatric Clinic (Johns Hopkins), 137-39
politics, and mental hospitals, 63-65, 222-31, 311-12
Pollock, Horatio M., 217, 290, 301-02, 306-07
poorhouses. *See* almshouses
Porter, Lee R., 256
Pratt, Foster, 363 n. 44
prevention of mental illness, 144-47. *See also* mental hygiene movement
Price, Joseph, 123
Prince, Morton, 141

Library of Congress Cataloging in Publication Data

Grob, Gerald N., 1931-
  Mental illness and American society, 1875-1940.
  Bibliography: p.   Includes index.
  1. Mental illness—Treatment—United States—
History.   2. Psychiatry—United States—History.
3. Mental health policy—United States—History.
4. Psychiatric hospital care—United States—History.
I. Title. [DNLM: 1. Mental disorders—History—United
States. 2. Hospitals, Psychiatric—History—United
States. WM 11 AA1 G8m]
RC443.G75 1983   362.2′0973   83-3047
ISBN 0-691-08332-0